The

Land

Called

Holy

The Land Called Holy

Robert L. Wilken

Palestine in Christian History and Thought

Yale University Press

New Haven and London

Published with the support of a grant from the National Endowment for the Humanities, an independent federal agency, and with assistance from the foundation established in memory of William McKean Brown.

Designed by Sonia L. Scanlon
Set in Century Schoolbook type by
The Composing Room of Michigan, Inc.
Grand Rapids, Michigan.
Printed in the United States of America by
Vail Ballou, Binghamton, New York.

Library of Congress Cataloging-in-Publication Data
Wilken, Robert Louis, 1936–
The land called holy : Palestine in Christian history and thought / Robert L. Wilken.
p. cm.
Includes bibliographical references and index.
ISBN 0-300-05491-2 (cloth)
0-300-06083-1 (pbk.)
1. Palestine in Christianity. 2. Palestine—Church history. I. Title.
BT93.8.W55 1992
263′.0425694—dc20 92-15258
CIP

A catalogue record for this book is available from the British Library.

The paper in this book meets the guidelines for permanence and durability of the Committee on Production Guidelines for Book Longevity of the Council on Library Resources. ∞

10 9 8 7 6 5 4 3 2

To Gregory and Jonathan
Fellow pilgrims to the Holy Land

And anyone who wants to take his brush and try
To paint the Earth must not look straight up at the Sun
Or he will lose the memory of all he's ever seen,
With only a burning tear to fill his eye.

Let him kneel down and press his cheek in grass and then
Look till he sees the beam the Earth reflects back upwards.
There he will find all of our lost, forgotten treasures;
Stars and Roses, the setting and the rising Sun.

—Czeslaw Milosz

Contents

Acknowledgments

I began this book while at the University of Notre Dame, and I am grateful to David Burrell, my chairman, who made it possible for me to visit the Holy Land. During my first visit there I began to conceive of a book on Palestine as a Christian holy land. I wish also to thank Nathan A. Scott, Jr., my chairman at the University of Virginia, for his support during my initial years in Charlottesville, and to the Center of Advanced Studies at the university. Part of the research for this book was made possible by fellowships from the National Endowment for the Humanities and the Lady Davis Fund of Hebrew University, for which I am grateful.

When I began work on this book, many of my ideas were unformed, and numerous points large and small were first suggested by friends and scholars and students in this country, in Israel, in Syria, Jordan, and in Europe. The list of those who have been of assistance is long, and I hope that I have not overlooked anyone: Gary Anderson, Harold Attridge, Joseph Blenkinsopp, Peter Brown, James Campbell, David Cassel, James Childress, Elizabeth Clark, John J. Collins, George Crafts, Byron Earhart, John H. Elliott, David Fekete, Tracy Fessenden, Pau Figueras, Georgia Frank, Harry Gamble, Norman Girardot, Sidney Griffith, Dennis Groh, Walter Harrelson, Moshe Herr, Yizhar Hirschfeld, Charles Kannengiesser, David Levenson, Robert Markus, Bernard McGinn, Paul Mendes-Flohr, Jerome Murphy-O'Connor, Richard John Neuhaus, Donald Nicholl, George Nickelsburg, David Novak, Rodger Payne, Louis Pedraja, Michele Piccirillo, Harold Remus, Shmuel Safrai, Khalil Samir, E. P. Sanders, David Satran, Mohammad Sawaie, Menachem Stern (may he rest in peace), Gedalia Stroumsa, Michael Swartz, Maureen A. Tilley, Yoram Tsafrir, John Wilkinson, David Winston, Franklin W. Young, Humphrey Mar, who made the drawings for the book, Lawrence Kenney, who was the manuscript editor, and finally my editor, Charles Grench, for his patience, unfailing confidence, and good taste in food.

Introduction

During the past hundred years, especially since the founding of the state of Israel, the land of the Bible and the Jewish people have been almost inseparable in the consciousness of the West. From the nineteenth-century Love of Zion societies in eastern Europe to the young Americans who move to new settlements on the West Bank today, the idea of settling the land, of living in the land, of cultivating the land has stirred the minds and hearts of Jews deeply. The charter of a society in Vilna in 1881–82 read, "The aims of the *Ohavei Zion* [Lovers of Zion] society are to spread the idea of the settlement of Eretz Israel for purposes of working its land among the sons of the diaspora and . . . to put the idea of resettlement of *Eretz Israel* into practice, to remove it from the realm of ideas into that of reality."[1]

The idea of repossessing the land excited gentiles as well as Jews. George Eliot, who was not a Jew, wrote her most mature novel, *Daniel Deronda,* about a young English orphan, Daniel, who discovered that his natural mother was a Jew. Daniel falls in love with a Jewish woman, Mirah, and under the tutelage of her wise and learned brother, Mordecai Ezra Cohen, gradually identifies with his people and their hopes. Daniel learns of the ancient dream, revived in the nineteenth century, that one day Jews would return to the land of their fathers and mothers. "Looking towards a land and a polity, our dispersed people in all the ends of the earth may share the dignity of a national life which has a voice among the peoples of East and West."[2] The young couple marries, and as the book ends they are planning to settle in Palestine. For George Eliot and the Jews whose dreams she describes so empathetically the Land of Israel was a spiritual and religious ideal, but its attainment required a political and historical outcome.

Christians have no abiding city. Their hope is set on a heavenly country, on the Jerusalem above, a city not made with human hands. In the words of the hymn "Jerusalem the Golden,"

> O sweet and blessed country,
> the home of God's elect!
> O sweet and blessed country,
> that eager hearts expect!
> In mercy, Jesus, bring us
> to that dear land of rest![3]

Yet it is evident to any visitor to the Middle East that Christianity has a peculiar relation to the lands embraced by the State of Israel, the West Bank, and Jordan. Christian pilgrims and tourists, as many as five hundred thousand a year, borne aloft on the broad wings of Swissair, El Al, and TWA, come from all parts of the world to visit the "holy places" associated with the life of Jesus: Bethlehem, Nazareth, the Church of the Resurrection, the Mount of Olives, the Sea of Galilee and the towns surrounding it. Though in other ways they may be well informed about the Middle East, few realize that Christianity's role in the land of the Bible is not restricted to the time of Jesus and Christian origins. The Christian religion has a long history in Palestine, the history of indigenous communities whose fortunes have been linked to the many conquerors—Romans, Arabs, crusaders, Turks, and Jews—and of national communities from other parts of the world, Copts from Egypt, Armenians, Syrians, Ethiopians, Russians, some of which have uninterrupted histories from antiquity to the present.

At the end of the fourteenth century a pilgrim from France reported that on his way from Jerusalem to visit the monastery of St. Catherine in the Sinai he stayed the night in a village called Beit Jala (two miles from Bethlehem). In this village, he wrote, "we laid in a supply of wine, which was delivered by the consul at Jerusalem. Because the Saracens [Muslims] themselves drink no wine, the pilgrims can get it only at very great danger and at a high price. . . . Beit Jala is populated more by Christians than by Saracens. The Christians work the vineyards where these good wines grow and you may be sure that one can properly call them good wines."[4] To this day Beit Jala remains a Christian village, and its inhabitants continue to grow grapes and produce wine.

Palestine was a Christian country for over three centuries, that is, from the late fourth century through the Arab conquest in the seventh century and beyond. Even after the Muslim conquest Christians remained the majority in the land for several centuries. Later, crusaders from the West established a Latin Kingdom in Jerusalem. Though the idea of a crusade as well as the savagery of the Christian knights may be distasteful to us today, it is well to remember that the Christian kingdom lasted nearly two hundred years, hardly an ephemeral period even in the history of this ancient land. The crusaders' presence is still visible in the medieval castles and churches and in the religious orders from the West. The brown habits of the Franciscans, who were given the title custodians of the Holy Land, can be seen in the streets of the old city. Through all this the office of patriarch (bishop) of Jerusalem has been occupied continuously for more than fifteen hundred years.

For many Christians the term *Holy Land* conjures up images of shepherds and olive trees, of dusty hills and donkeys, of Jerusalem as it existed in the age of King David or Bethlehem at the time of Jesus. It is a land without history, its people and places frozen in a biblical time frame. As Edward Robinson, professor at Union Theological Seminary in the nineteenth century, wrote during his visit to Jerusalem at Easter in 1838, "We counted it no loss [missing the events of Holy Week] . . . for the object of our visit was the city itself, in relation to its ancient renown and religious associations, not as seen in its present state of decay and superstitious and fraudful degradation."[5]

The very notion of the Holy Land as a historical land, not a mawkish apparition of the past, a land whose history is continuous with the biblical story yet not limited to it, a country whose people have displayed Christian wisdom, piety, and architecture in distinctive ways—this idea of the Holy Land is foreign to Christians, particularly those in the West. Even today few Christian pilgrims to the Holy Land venture beyond the familiar holy places associated with the Bible, returning to their homes unaware that Christian history in the land did not end with the age of the apostles.

This book is an account of how the land of the Bible, the land of Israel, the land of Canaan, if you will, became a Holy Land to Christians. There are many studies of the place of the land in the Scriptures and in Jewish history and thought, as well as studies of pilgrimage to the Holy Land, of the holy places, and of the architecture of the Church of the Holy Sepulchre and other Christian monuments in the land. But none has been devoted to the idea of a Christian Holy Land. Though Christian attitudes toward the land are related to the practice of pilgrimage and devotion to the holy places, they are not identical. When I wrote an article on the entry "Holy Land" for an encyclopedia several years ago I discovered that there were articles and books aplenty on pilgrimage and holy places but none on the Christian Holy Land.

Although I devote considerable space to the history of Christianity in Palestine, this is chiefly a book on the *idea* of the Holy Land. I have focused my attention on the spiritual and religious aspects of Christian history in the Holy Land and on the piety that came to center on the land. I have been interested in the way Christian ideas and feelings toward the land emerged and changed as Christians lived in the land and made it their own.

Only gradually, after a period when the idea was shunned, did Christians begin to view the land of the Bible as a Christian Holy Land. Land, like many other things human beings hold dear, is not a simple gift of nature; it is made, invented by those who live in and on it. As the generations passed and Palestine became a Christian country—indeed, the Christian country par excellence—a slow turning took place in Christian attitudes toward the land. What transpired in Jerusalem and Judea has no parallel elsewhere in Christian memory or experience. No other city, not even Rome, has the same place in Christian affection and imagination.

What happened to Christians during the fourth to seventh centuries has parallels to the experiences of the Israelites centuries earlier. Christians began to think of Jerusalem as their city, indeed as *the* Christian city, and Palestine as a place set apart. Monks who had practiced the solitary life in other provinces of the Roman Empire, in Armenia or Cappadocia, for example, left their native countries to live, as one of them put it, "in this desert," the desert surrounding Jerusalem. Some came with the ancient words to Abraham ringing in their ears: "Go up to the land that I will show you" (Gen 12:1). They spoke of themselves as "inhabitants of this Holy Land" and were the first to use the term *Holy*

Land in a distinctively Christian way. In the story that follows they play a key role.

Although Christians constituted the majority in Palestine in the sixth and seventh centuries and for several centuries after the Muslim conquest in 640 C.E., they were not the only inhabitants of the region. Not everyone adopted the Christian way of life. Adherents to the rites of Greece and Rome continued to live in the cities, for example, in Gaza and Scythopolis, as did Samaritans in the central hill country. And of course there were many Jews, concentrated chiefly in Galilee but not limited to that region. The imposing Christian presence in Eretz Israel did not escape the Jews who dwelled in the land during the Christian era. Jews sensed that the Christian Romans (Byzantines) had more than political and economic interests in the land. Jerusalem was not a foreign capital set on the periphery of the empire, it was a holy city, the place where Christ the Lord had lived, died, risen from the dead, and ascended into heaven.

The future, however, lay with Islam, and I have brought the story to an end with the Muslim conquest in the seventh century. Because I end my account at that point, I say little about the next stage of Christian history in the Holy Land, that is, the first centuries of Muslim rule, and nothing about the age of the crusaders. Yet it will be apparent to the reader that the crusaders were heirs of ideas and beliefs that were forged during the Byzantine period. During the rule of the western knights in the twelfth century the term *terra sancta* gained general currency in the West. With the establishment of a Christian kingdom in Jerusalem people began to speak about the Holy Land in a distinctive territorial sense, a land with fixed boundaries that could be defended by a Christian king against hostile invaders. To have pursued that story would have required a second volume.

In a small way I have tried to look beyond the Byzantine period to the beginning of Arabic-speaking Christianity in Palestine. Although Muslim occupation laid to rest political and territorial ideas among Christians, the Christian communities survived the victory of Islam. Most were natives and had no other country to go to, and many, at least initially, did not convert to the faith of their new masters. In time they learned to pray in Arabic, translated the Scriptures into Arabic, and produced devotional and theological literature in the language of their conquerors. The Arabic-speaking Christians who live today in Israel, the West Bank, and Jordan are their descendants and hence the descendants of the first Christians. They are, as it were, the only indigenous Christian community in the world.

In writing the history of Christian devotion to the Holy Land and in pointing to the later history of Christianity in the land, my intentions are historical and spiritual, not political. Whatever proprietary claims Christians once made on the land they have long been abandoned, and I do not wish to revive them. Nevertheless Christianity has a stake in the political future of the Holy Land, and the perseverance of Christians living there merits respect and admiration. They are an irreplaceable sign of continuity with the first Christian community and with Christ. Christianity, like Judaism and Islam, is not a European religion; its homeland is the Middle East.

Finally, a word on the outline of the book. Although this is a book about the Christian Holy Land, I do not get to the subject proper until the fourth chapter. Originally I had planned a brief introductory chapter, but as I read more deeply in the sources I realized that the emergence of Christian devotion to Jerusalem had to be seen not only in the context of the discovery of the tomb of Christ, the rise of pilgrimage, and so on, but also with reference to Jews who were living in the land and to Jewish attitudes toward the land. The rise of the Christian Holy Land is a neglected chapter in the history of relations between Christians and Jews. This theme led me more fully into the biblical sources than I had originally planned as well as into Jewish history and thought during the period of the second temple and the Roman and Byzantine epochs.

The first few chapters of the book may appear to be an unduly long introduction, and the reader may wonder, especially in chapter 2, why I give so much space to Jewish hopes for the restoration of Jerusalem. In part I wish to show the roots of early Christian ideas that an earthly kingdom would be established in Jerusalem (millenarianism) and their importance in shaping initial Christian views of the Holy Land. But it is not backgrounds that I am after. Ideas about the land that were formed during the centuries after exile in Babylonia became part of a vital tradition that remained very much alive among Jews long after the rise of Christianity. As Christians were developing their own ideas about the land they were very conscious of these Jewish attitudes. Without a presentation of the early history of these beliefs and of their roots in the Scriptures, a large part of the story I have to tell would be unintelligible. If I seem at times to dawdle, let the reader be assured: by the final chapter everything will find its place.

The

Land

Called

Holy

1 To Possess the Land

The Christian holy land was the work of Christians living in Palestine in the centuries before the country was conquered by the Muslims. Its architects were the holy men and women who came to live in Jerusalem and in the desert east of the city, the bishops who led the faithful in prayer and the patrons who gave of their wealth, the craftsmen who cut stones for the churches and the artists who set mosaics in the floors, the builders who raised roof beams on public buildings and homes in the cities and villages, the farmers who tilled the fields and planted orchards, and the merchants who grew rich on the mighty wave of pilgrims. The idea of a holy land, however, has its beginnings more than a thousand years earlier; to trace its origins we must travel back across the centuries to the dawn of Jewish history and the formation of the Hebrew Bible.

The first Christians, let it be remembered, were Jews, and the history of the Jewish people, as recorded in the Hebrew Bible, begins with the call of Abraham to leave his people and his land in Ur of the Chaldees (Mesopotamia) to serve the one God in a new land, the land of Canaan, west of the Jordan River. "Now the Lord said to Abram, 'Go from your country and your kindred and your father's house to the land that I will show you'" (Gen 12:1). In the view of the biblical writer, Abraham's migration from Mesopotamia to Canaan was not simply a journey of several hundred miles to a new pasture: it was the beginning of biblical history in the proper sense of the term.

In the Scriptures everything that takes place before the appearance of Abraham belongs to a primeval age. The account of creation, the story of Adam and Eve in the garden of Eden, the first murder, the great flood that covered the earth, the confusion of languages at the tower of Babel—these are all preliminary to the main event, the call of Abraham. The Hebrew Bible is a book about Abraham's descendants and the land given to them by God. Even the Christian Scriptures portray the promise of the land as the beginning of Israel's history. An early Christian sermon attributed to Stephen before he was martyred in Jerusalem begins the account of biblical history with God's words to Abraham, "Depart from your land and from your kindred and go into the land which I will show you" (Acts 7:3).

Abraham stands at the beginning of a long historical epic whose ending is incomplete. The Hebrew Bible carries the story from the call of Abraham to the return from exile in Babylonia in the fifth century B.C.E.. At that time, a company of Judeans under the leadership of the enigmatic Zerubbabel settled in Jerusalem, rebuilt the city, restored the ruined temple, and established Israelite institutions in Judea. For those who depend solely on the Hebrew Bible for instruction in Israelite history, the story of Abraham's descendants ends with the efforts of zealous Ezra and industrious Nehemiah to restore the Israelite way of life in the land promised to Abraham. Yet the ending is chimerical, only a closure, no real termination. The final sentence in the Book of Chronicles, the last book in the Jewish Bible, ends with the words "Let him go up [to Jerusalem]." The Bible is as much a book of hope as it is of history.

The Hebrew Bible leaves the reader with a sense of incompleteness, as though the curtain was rung down before the final act, and this feeling is confirmed by the message of the prophetic books. They speak of a more perfect, a more splendid, a more enduring restoration and redemption.

Indeed biblical history ends on a solemn and cheerless note. When the last historical books of the Bible were compiled, Judah was not an independent nation, and large numbers of Jews lived outside of the Land of Israel. What had been announced with bright hope in the saga of Abraham had come only to partial fulfillment.

In a prayer at the end of the book of Nehemiah, the Levites recall with gratitude the people's good fortune since ancient times, but their prayer ends in a lament over their present bondage: "Behold we are slaves this day; in the land that you gave to our father to enjoy its fruit and its good gifts, behold, we are slaves. And its rich yield goes to the kings whom you have set over us because of our sins; they have power also over our bodies and over our cattle at their pleasure, and we are in great distress" (Neh 9:36–37). Even though they were living in the land promised to Abraham's descendants, the Jews were not their own masters.

As one looks down the entire span of Jewish history, the exile in Babylonia towers above all other events save the Exodus from Egypt. Between the two events, however, there is a notable difference. The Exodus ended in triumph.[1] It is the great epic of deliverance, and it became the paradigmatic redemptive event in Jewish piety and worship. At the celebration of Passover the youngest child in the family asks, "Why is this night of Passover so different from all other nights of the year?" To which the answer is given: "On this night we celebrate the going forth in triumph from slavery to freedom." In every generation the Exodus has been celebrated as a sign of hope and deliverance, whether that redemption be from the occupation of Eretz Israel by the Romans or from cruel and arbitrary mistreatment at the hands of Soviet apparatchiks. Christians, too, from Oliver Cromwell in seventeenth-century England to Martin Luther King in the twentieth century, have invoked the Exodus as the paradigmatic story of redemption.

Only the Jews, however, have made exile (*galuth*) a central metaphor in their lives. In the words of the medieval poet Judah Halevi, the Jews are "captive[s] of desire."[2] This yearning to return has been nourished over the centuries by men and women who never saw the land or nurtured any realistic hope they would see it in their lifetimes. In poetry and works of devotion, in drawings on marriage contracts, in the bunting to festoon houses and booths during the celebration of Sukkoth, in paintings on the Torah shrine and carvings on copper plates used for Passover, Jews have displayed their longing. A marriage contract from eighteenth-century Italy, for example, used the traditional benediction "May the voice of the bridegroom and bride be heard in the cities of Judah and in the streets of Jerusalem" (*b. Ketuboth* 8a) as well as the Psalm "If I forget you O Jerusalem, let my right hand wither" (Ps 137). Marriage contracts were illustrated with a picture of the holy city, Jerusalem.[3]

For the Jew, exile became a symbol of servitude and bondage, an inescapable reminder that the promise to Abraham had not reached fulfillment. In Jewish memory, the return from exile, unlike the Exodus from Egypt, was as much marked by disappointment and disillusionment as it was by rejoicing. Even those who returned were able to do so only because of the beneficence of Israel's new masters, the Persians. Ezra was an official of the Persian court and Judea a province of the Persian empire. Full restoration, what Jewish tradition calls redemption, lay in the future.

The Promise of the Land

In the Hebrew Scriptures the promise of the land recurs as a primal motif uniting the entire biblical narrative. The promise to Abraham and his descendants appears early in Genesis, punctuating the stories of the patriarchs; it gives energy and purpose to Exodus, a book about the formation of a people in quest of their land, and is the foundation of the covenant as set forth in Deuteronomy. It is the raison d'être of the book of Joshua, which recounts the conquest of the land of Canaan and its ancient cities, Jericho, Ai, Lachish, Hazor.[4] In the last chapter Joshua gathers the tribes of Israel to address them in the name of God: "I took your father Abraham from beyond the River and led him through all the land of Canaan, and made his offspring many. . . . I brought your fathers out of Egypt. . . . Then I brought you to the land of the Amorites, who lived on the other side of the Jordan . . . and you took possession of their land" (Josh 24:3–8).

Unlike the Egyptians, who had inhabited the Nile valley for millennia, the Jews had not lived in their land "from time immemorial."[5] Long before the Israelites came to dwell in the hill country west of the Jordan River, the region had been the home of other peoples and cultures. An Egyptian courtier who had married the daughter of a local Egyptian chieftain and lived in Canaan in the twentieth century B.C.E. describes it this way: "It was a good land, called Yaa. Figs were in it and grapes. It had more wine than water. Abundant was its honey, plentiful its oil. All kinds of fruit were on its trees. Barley was there and emmer, and no end of cattle of all kinds."[6]

Even though at least half of the country is uninhabitable desert and a rugged spine of hills runs down its center, it had been inhabited for thousands of years before the Israelites. Archaeologists have found stone masks from the seventh millennium B.C.E., tiny pottery figurines from the sixth millennium, statues from the fourth millennium, cultic objects, ossuaries, an exquisitely crafted copper crown, and a scepter, all before the Canaanites. But the most imposing and intriguing cultural remains prior to the Israelite conquest were found at Canaanite sites. The Canaanites, Israel's predecessors and fellow inhabitants in the land, play a large role in the biblical story, but only as an idolatrous enemy and rival claimant to the land. Reviled and vilified by the biblical writers, they became an object of loathing to readers of the Bible and were cast on the scrap heap of Western civilization. If, however, one looks at their achievements in writing and sea-faring or examines the artistic remains of their civilization, for example, an anthropomorphic vase from Jericho or hammered gold figurines of Canaanite goddesses, it is apparent that the earlier inhabitants of Palestine were not only truculent foes and intractable combatants for control of a good and fruitful land, but also possessed a mature culture.[7]

The biblical account begins with the promise of a gift, but paradoxically God's largesse could be acquired only through military conquest.[8] The defeat and displacement of the inhabitants of the land, the Canaanites, Hittites, Amorites, Perizites, Jebusites, is an integral part of the biblical narrative. The land of Canaan had to be "dispossessed" before it could be "possessed" (Judg 11:24), and this could be accomplished only by driving out the other peoples (Deut 9:4) and blotting out all signs of their presence (Deut 25:19). A verse in Numbers reads, "If you do not drive out the inhabitants of the land before you, then those of them whom you let remain shall be as pricks in your eyes and thorns in your sides, and they shall trouble you in the land where you dwell" (Num 33:55).[9] After the Israelites conquered the land they lived in the cities built by their enemies and enjoyed the fruits of the labor of others: "I gave you a land on which you had not labored, and cities which you had not built, and you dwell therein; you eat the fruit of vineyards and olive yards which you did not plant" (Josh 24:13).

The oldest designation for the territory in the Hebrew Bible is land of Canaan, and it is remarkable that the phrase remains embedded in the text of the Scriptures even after the region came to be called the land of Israel by the Israelites. The Bible does not disguise the embarrassing historical fact that the land of Israel once belonged to other peoples and had to be taken by conquest. Even later writings within the Bible make no effort to conceal the earlier history of the land: "It was [the Lord] who smote many nations . . . and all the kingdoms of Canaan, and gave *their* land as a heritage, a heritage to his people Israel" (Ps 135:12). An analogy to biblical usage might be for Yitzhak Shamir, the prime minister of Israel, to call the land of Israel by the Arabic name Filastin (Palestine). Haunted by the memory of the Canaanites centuries later, Jewish apologists and biblical scholars will take great pains to explain how the Land of Israel came to be called the Land of Canaan.[10]

During the period of the exile, in the sixth century B.C.E., the land tradition of ancient Israel took the form in which it would be transmitted to later generations in the Scriptures.[11] The displacement from Judea and the exile in Babylonia left an enduring stamp on Israel's account of its origins. The exile in Babylonia was the culmination of a series of convulsions that shook the kingdoms of Judah and Israel and thrust the tiny nation into the vortex of historical forces that were to bruise the Israelites for centuries. The first tremors came from the movements of a new aggressive and militant empire in the East, Assyria, whose expansion threatened the stability of the entire area from Mesopotamia to Egypt. With the accession of Tiglath-Pileser II (745–727) to the throne, the Assyrians invaded the land north and west of the Sea of Galilee and "carried off the people captive to Assyria" (2 Kings 15:29). A decade later (in 722–21 B.C.E) Sargon II laid siege to Samaria and deported thousands of its inhabitants to Syria. In their place he settled immigrants from Babylonia, Elam, and Syria. This enforced migration of select members of the population, for example, craftsmen and soldiers and skilled workers and their families, uprooted people from their towns and villages and destroyed the fabric of society. Exile, a more profound and far-reaching punishment to a conquered people than occupation, deprived the people of their cultural, political, and religious institutions, perforce tied to territory, and crippled the continuity of "national" existence. On the heels of the Assyrians came the Babylonians, a rival empire that had arisen along the lower Euphrates River. In 612 B.C.E. the Babylonians, with the help of the Medes, invaded Assyria and turned its proud and famous city Nineveh "into mounds and heaps of ruins," as a Babylonian chronicle put it. With the swift rise to power of the new empire, it was only little more than a decade before Palestine fell under its sway. Jerusalem was first captured in 597 B.C.E., and in 586 King Nebuchadnezzar's armies laid siege to the city a second time and deported large numbers of the population of Judea to the territory of Nippur on the river Chebar, the grand canal of the Euphrates.

The deportation of Israelites established a permanent community of Jews in exile from their native land, and even when the opportunity to return to Judea came, some preferred to remain in their adopted countries, "unwilling to give up their possessions," in the words of Josephus

(*Ant.* 11.8), a Jewish historian writing centuries later. This disturbing fact was still recalled much later, in the Talmud.[12] In the sixth century Jews also began to settle in other countries bordering the Mediterranean, for example, Asia Minor and Egypt. As early as the sixth century there were Jews in Sardis (Sepharad) in western Asia Minor, some of whom had apparently come to stay. What began as temporary and provisional for the original deportees became for their descendants a permanent way of life that offered new opportunities as well as temptations. In the towns and cities of the diaspora the exiles from Judea built houses, planted gardens, and raised families. Some forgot their native language and the God of their ancestors.

Territorial Realism

The catastrophic events in Judea and the quiet movement of Jews out of Palestine to other lands inaugurated a new epoch in Jewish history. Although the Israelites continued to survive as an autonomous people, the days of Jewish hegemony in Palestine were over. Except for a brief period during the rule of the Hasmoneans in the second and first centuries B.C.E., the Jews would never again exist as an independent people in the region until modern times. As this political and social fact worked its way into Jewish consciousness the Jews came to think of themselves as a people displaced from their land. For this reason the hope of political restoration is a central theme in Jewish history.

In this setting the ancient promise to Abraham acquired unforeseen utility. What had been a charter of entitlement to a land that belonged to others became a hope of repossessing the land that had been taken from them. Some passages in the book of Deuteronomy reflect this form of the promise: "The Lord God will *restore* your fortunes, and have compassion upon you, and he will *gather you again* from all the peoples where the Lord your God has scattered you. If your outcasts are in the uttermost parts of heaven, from there the Lord your God will gather you, and from there he will fetch you; and the Lord your God will bring you into the land which your *ancestors possessed, that you may possess it*; and he will make you more prosperous and numerous than your ancestors" (Deut 30:3–5).[13]

The phrase used in this passage, "possess the land" or "inherit the land" (either is a legitimate translation of the Hebrew), became the standard formula to express the promise of the land to Abraham and his descendants. Indeed so deeply did it become rooted in Jewish life that centuries later Christian writers single it out as a symbol of Jewish hope to return to the land and reestablish a Jewish kingdom in Jerusalem.[14] Within the Scriptures "possess the land" acquired a wide range of specific connotations, but it always had reference to Jewish life within a specific territory.[15]

For the ancient Israelites *land* always referred to an actual land. Eretz Israel was not a symbol of a higher reality. It was a distinct geographical entity, a territory with assumed if not always precise boundaries.[16] In the Bible, ideal descriptions of the land can of course be found. The best known is the famous phrase "a land flowing with milk and honey" (Exod 3:8), but there are others: "The Lord God is bringing you into a good land, a land of brooks of water, of foundations and springs, flowing forth in valleys and hills, a land of wheat and barley, of vines and fig trees and pomegranates, a land of olive trees and honey, a land in which you will eat bread without scarcity, in which you will lack nothing, a land whose stones are iron, and out of whose hills you can mine copper" (Deut 8:7–10).

In these passages the language of the Bible evokes the Arcadian portrait of a golden age or the description of the charmed islands of the Blessed, the Elysian fields:

> As to your own destiny, prince Menelaos,
> you shall not die in the bluegrass land of Argos;
> rather the gods intend you for Elysion
> with golden Rhadamanthos at the world's end,
> where all existence is a dream of ease.
> Snowfall is never known there, neither long
> frost of winter, nor torrential rain,
> but only mild and lulling airs from Ocean
> bearing refreshment for the souls of men—
> the West Wind always blowing. (*Od.* 4.563–65)

The Greek islands of the blessed, however, were always located somewhere beyond Greece, in a lotus land far removed from the experience of ordinary mortals. The Elysian fields were home only to the dead, not to the living. They had no history.

For the ancient Hebrews, idyllic descriptions of the land are always subservient to a territorial realism.[17] The land is a geographical region that can be marked on a map, a place with *memories* as well as hopes, with a *past* as well as a future. It was the land in which the descendants of Abraham had lived and hoped to live again, a place in which to plant vineyards and build houses. The blessings associated with the land are this-worldly, for example, the fruit of one's body, the fruit of the ground, the increase of cattle, the blessing of "basket and breading-trough," of grain and wine and oil (Deut 28:4–5; 7:13).[18] No matter how utopian the language, the promised land was always a real, not an ideal, country. Hence there could be no genuine fulfillment of the promise that was not historical, which is to say, political.

Yet, the land was never simply territory, a piece of real estate, as some vulgarly refer to it today. The land needed a people, indeed a specific people, and the same texts that speak about the gift of the land also speak about the unique vocation of the descendants of Abraham, the people of Israel, within the land: "The Lord will establish you as a people holy to himself, as he has sworn to you, if you keep the commandments of the Lord your God, and walk in his ways" (Deut 28:9). The land is not inert; it offers an opportunity and a challenge. As often as the Scriptures speak of "possessing the land," they speak of "walking in the ways of the Lord" (Deut 8:6), of "hearkening to God's voice," and of "keeping all the words of the law" (Deut 17:19). Land, people, and Law are inextricably woven together.[19]

The Land Promise and the City of Jerusalem

In the original promise of the land, the city of Jerusalem played no part. The first time Jerusalem is mentioned in the Bible it is an enemy town belonging to a group of city-states in Canaan.[20] Like the land itself, Jerusalem had to be conquered and subdued, and only after its capture by the youthful David in the tenth century did it become an Israelite city. At the time the city belonged to the Jebusites, the inhabitants of the land, as they are called in 2 Samuel (5:6), descendants of the Canaanites. A town of little importance with a population of not more than a thousand, Canaanite Jerusalem (the name was carried over from earlier times) gave no sign of its future glory and grandeur. The majestic and sacred city of the Bible was a creation of the Israelites.

In the account in 2 Samuel one of David's first actions after subjugating the city was to bring the ark of the covenant to Jerusalem. The ark, a sacred chest containing the tablets of the Law, was a portable shrine that had been housed at Shiloh in the hill country north of Jerusalem, the central sanctuary of the twelve tribes. With the capture of Jerusalem the ark was brought to the city, and on its arrival David "leaped and danced" before the Lord, that is, before the ark.[21] The ark was the symbol of God's presence in the midst of Israel, and with its removal to Jerusalem God's presence was no longer portable; holiness was now bound to place.

In the ancient world a temple was not primarily a gathering place for worship like a synagogue or church or mosque. It was a dwelling place of the deity, the house of God, and the chief business of a temple was to offer sacrifices and offerings to God. David may have begun preparations to build a permanent house for the God of Israel, but according to 2 Samuel he was dissuaded from doing so by the prophet Nathan. Nathan told him that God desired that he establish a kingdom that would last forever (2 Sam 7:13). However, his successor, King Solomon, took up the task, and during his reign a temple was built on a high outcropping of rock above the city, on the threshing floor of Araunah, a Jebusite whose quarry had been purchased by David. When the building was completed, it was dedicated in a solemn ceremony, and the ark of the covenant was deposited "in the inner sanctuary of the house." As the priests came out of this "holy place, a cloud filled the house of the Lord, so that the priests could not stand to minister because of the cloud; for the glory of the Lord filled the house of the Lord" (1 Kings 8:10–11). God's majestic and mysterious presence now dwelled in Jerusalem.

Under the rule of Israel's kings Jerusalem had risen to prominence as the political and administrative hub of the kingdom; but with the building of the temple it became the cultic center as well, the dwelling place of God as well as the home of the king. Jerusalem came to be known as the city of David and the city of God. Not all holy cities combine these two functions. Banaras, the holy city in India, for example, gained its fame not from its political history, but from its religious character. It had no political importance, and its sanctity as a holy place has little to do with the rise and fall of kings and princes.[22] Not so Israelite Jerusalem; it combined piety and statecraft. Although Nebuchadnezzar's soldiers destroyed the city in 587 C.E. and burned the temple, Jerusalem lived on in the memory of the captives in Babylonia. Banished to a foreign land far from the city they had loved and cherished, their collective dreams created a new and more splendid image of the city, transforming the torn and tattered recollections of past glory into a vision of future majesty. Their imagination took wing, envisioning a Jerusalem that surpassed anything that had existed in the past. Indeed their image of the new Jerusalem may have been formed as much by the magnificence of the city of Babylon, newly rebuilt and adorned by Nebuchadnezzar II, as by their recollection of the city in Judea.

The exaltation of Jerusalem in the exilic prophets is a quantum leap beyond anything said of the city in earlier tradition. Other biblical writers praise and glorify Jerusalem, but none approaches the extravagant and unrestrained homage of Ezekiel and Isaiah. Israel's hopes now came to be focused on the rebuilding of a city, and as Jerusalem came to symbolize the hope of redemption, the traditions about the land were reoriented and reinterpreted to conform to these new images. Jerusalem had become the "type and figure of all Israel,"[23] and the slogan "possess the land" was now taken to refer to the restoration of Jerusalem.

Ezekiel's Vision of the Land

The book of Ezekiel is our most valuable testimony to the impact of the exile on the traditions about the land. Ezekiel, a priest in Jerusalem, the son of Buzi (1:3), was one of the original group of exiles whom King Nebuchadnezzar settled at a place on the river Chebar, a tributary of the Euphrates River not far from the Babylonian city of Nippur. Shortly after the arrival of the exiles, perhaps in 593 B.C.E., Ezekiel's prophecies commenced.[24] For our theme, the most important sections of the book are the oracles on restoration and the final chapters on the city and temple. The name of the city, says Ezekiel in the final sentence of the book, will be "The Lord is there." When God's glory returns "from the east" it will reside in the temple on Mount Zion, and the temple will be the axis to which everything in the land is oriented.

In his words of assurance and hope to the returning exiles Ezekiel employs a new sacral language to speak about Jerusalem. He depicts an "ideal cultic place,"[25] a sacred precinct with concentric circles of holiness that extend outward from the holy of holies. In doing so he plants the seed that will give birth to the expression "holy land." For Ezekiel's prophecy is not only a book about the temple; as the oracles in chapters 33–39 make clear, it is also a book about the land promised to the descendants of Abraham. More than any of the earlier prophets, Ezekiel is suffused with traditions about gathering the dispersed people in the land, dwelling safely in the land, inhabiting its cities and restoring its waste places, of building houses and planting vineyards, of serving God and observing his statutes in the land. Yet, as traditional as much of his language is, there is something new: the land has a center, and God's glory radiates out from its axis to envelop and sanctify everything that surrounds it.

For Ezekiel Jerusalem has become a mythical place that sits at the center of the world in the "most glorious of all lands" (20:7). "Thus says the Lord God: This is Jerusalem: I have set her in the center of the nations, with countries round about her" (5:5). Ezekiel portrays Jerusalem as a cosmic mountain, a meeting place of heaven and earth, a focal point around which all other things are located and from which they take their bearing.[26] It is a place of plentitude and perfection, a wellspring of fecundity and life. Mount Zion will be pure and untarnished and out of its temple will flow a sacred and lifegiving river brimming with abundance.

Wherever it flows there will be "very many fish," and on its banks "there will grow all kinds of trees for food. Their leaves will not wither nor their fruit fail, but they will bear fruit every month, because the water for them flows from the sanctuary. Their fruit will be for good and their leaves for healing" (Ezek 47). In his hands, Jerusalem became an exuberant source of life, a pure and perfect paradise, a place of solemn sanctity.

Ezekiel's Jerusalem is constructed on two axes, the one vertical—it sits on a "very high mountain" (40:2)—the other horizontal—it is set apart from everything that surrounds it. "This is the law of the temple; the whole territory round about upon the top of the mountain shall be most holy" (43:12). In this grid, all space is divided into sacred and profane, and everything that lies outside of the mountain belongs to profane space. But Ezekiel offers a second map, one in which the line of demarcation between the sacred and profane is not absolute.[27] Like Ecbatana, the sacred city in Persia with its series of concentric walls, each higher than the one below, Mount Zion is pictured as a series of concentric zones of holiness gradually swelling as they expand out from the center, "the most holy place" (41:4) where God's glory resides, the "place of [his] throne and the place of the soles of [his] feet" (43:7). Here the term "place" has acquired religious connotations. Reaching out from this axis there are several gradations of sanctity, each one more profane in relation to that which lies closer to the center and more sacred in relation to that which lies on the periphery. "When you allot the land as a possession, you shall set apart for the Lord a portion of the land as a *holy* district. . . . It shall be *holy* throughout its whole extent. . . . And in the *holy* district you shall measure off a section twenty-five thousand cubits long and ten thousand broad, in which shall be the sanctuary, the *most holy* place. It shall be the *holy* portion of the land; it shall be for the priests, who minister in the sanctuary and approach the Lord to minister to him; and it shall be a place for their houses and a *holy* place for the sanctuary."[28]

It is evident, however, that Ezekiel has more in mind than the temple and its territory. As he says at the beginning of chapter 45, he is speaking not simply of the temple or of the holy mountain, but of the "allotment of the land as a possession." Hence he does not limit his description of the holy territory to the city; he extends the perimeter out to include a district which shall "belong to the whole house of Israel." Chapter 45, his most explicit description of the sacred territory, foreshadows chapter 48, in which he gives a full account of the distribution of the land to the twelve tribes. There the land is much more than the vicinity around Jerusalem. Its borders extend from Syria in the north to Palmyra in the east to the brook of Egypt in the south and the Mediterranean Sea to the west.[29]

Everything that Ezekiel says about the temple and the city is inseparable from his final section on the "allotment of the land." Indeed he portrays the return and restoration as a new Exodus; just as the land was apportioned to the tribes when the land was first conquered, so in the return from exile there will be a new appropriation of the land patterned on the allotment of the land at the time of Joshua.[30] As God brought the people of Israel out of Egypt into the wilderness, so he will bring them into a "wilderness of nations" (20:35) from which he will lead them again to the "mountain height of Israel" (20:40). As the new exodus will be more glorious than the first, so will the allocation of the land take place in a new and more wonderful fashion. The chief difference, however, is that the new allotment will be "structured around the new sanctuary as its central point," as Zimmerli observes.[31]

The hope of repossessing the land, however, rests on the same foundation as the original blessing: the promise to Abraham and to his descendants. A fascinating historical detail can illustrate the point. When the exiles began to return, the natives, those who had remained behind after 587, challenged the returning exiles with the words, "Abraham was only one man, yet he got possession of the land; but we are many; *the land is surely given us to possess*" (Ezek 33:24). In other words, when you left you abandoned the land, and now it belongs to us, who have remained in the land. This passage gives an insight into the mood of those people who had survived the ravishing of the city by the Babylonians. Their "pious security" had a foundation in the knowledge that God had promised the land to the descendants of Abraham, Isaac, and Jacob.[32]

When Ezekiel describes the actual distribution of the land at the end of his book he again mentions the promise to the patriarchs: "I swore to give it to your fathers, and this land shall fall to you as your *inheritance*" (47:14). Then he proceeds to designate the specific territory that will be allotted to each tribe, beginning with Dan in the north and ending with Gad in the south. The land is divided into three segments, a northern segment that includes seven tribes, a southern segment that includes five tribes, and a central section for the tribe of Levi. The arrangement of the tribes is hierarchical, at least to a degree. The most important, Judah and Benjamin, are located contiguous to the center, Judah being moved to the north to make this possible, and the least important, Gad and Dan, placed on the northern and southern extremities. The Zadokites, a family of priests whose business was God's "service" (48:11), that is, attending to the rites in the temple, are assigned the center, a "holy portion of the land, a most holy place" (48:12).

In other ways Ezekiel's presentation of the new appropriation of the land conforms to the contours of an ideal map, disregarding the historical location of the tribal territories. The two tribes of Zebulon and Issachar, traditionally located in the north, are transferred to the south. This was Ezekiel's way of giving prominence to the temple. Everything is now oriented to the center, and when the exiles returned it was no longer possible to conceive of the land without including the city and temple, a view that would become normative in the centuries after the exile. As Moshe Weinfeld observes, "During the period of the second temple one spoke not simply of the Land of Israel but of the city and the temple. Loss of the foundation for national life was not expressed in the formulas 'loss of the land' or 'exile from the land' as had been customary . . . in the period of the first temple, but in the formula destruction of the house of the temple or simply destruction of the house."[33] The land promise is now symbolized by the temple and city.

"I will glorify my glorious house"

The other great prophet of the exile was Isaiah or, more accurately, Second Isaiah because the book of Isaiah, like that of Ezekiel, is also a composite work. The first thirty-nine chapters belong to the time of the Assyrian conquest in the eighth century, long before the Babylonian exile, and do not concern us. But even the final section of the book, chapters 40–66, is not a unity. The first part, chapters 40–55, had its origin prior to the collapse of the Babylonian empire in 539 B.C.E., the later chapters were composed in the following generation, and chapters 60–62 may come from an even later period.[34]

Among the several themes that ring out from the pages of Second and Third Isaiah, the one that sounds the clearest is the future exaltation of Jerusalem. "O afflicted one, storm-tossed, and not comforted, behold, I will set your stones in antimony, and lay your foundations with sapphires. I will make your pinnacles of agate, your gates of carbuncles, and all your walls of precious stones. . . . In righteousness you shall be established, you shall be far from oppression, for you shall not fear. . . . This is the *inheritance* of the servants of the Lord" (Isa 54:11–17). So deeply have Second Isaiah's fulgent images of Jerusalem embedded themselves in the imagination of later generations, Christians as well as Jews, that it is easy to forget that he is speaking of a real city, not a celestial haven. The words that begin the prophecy, "Comfort, comfort my people, says your God. Speak tenderly to Jerusalem, and cry to her that her warfare is ended," are not a global message of consolation to the nations, but a very particular proclamation of hope to the Israelites that the desolate city will be "inhabited" and the wasted towns of Judah "shall be built" (44:26). The words spoken of Cyrus, the Persian king who had subdued the Babylonians, "He shall build my city and set my exiles free" refer to restoration of the actual city on the edge of the Judean desert (45:13).

During the period of the monarchy, the blessing of the patriarchs had been understood as a land promise in the strict sense of the term. "Behold, I have set the land before you; go in and take possession of the land which the Lord swore to your fathers, to Abraham, to Isaac, and to Jacob, to give to them and to their descendants after them" (Deut 1:8). In its earliest formulations the blessing made no mention of cities in the land. After Jerusalem had become an Israelite city it began to insinuate itself in the land tradition, at first remaining nameless. Thus when the book of Deuteronomy speaks of "possessing the land" it includes Jerusalem in the promise but omits the name, though the language it employs refers unmistakably to Jerusalem. When the Israelites are to pass over the Jordan "to go up to take possession of the land" which the Lord gave them, they are to go to the "place" which God will choose. Only in this place can they make offerings and offer sacrifices, for this is the place where God's name will dwell (Deut 12:5). The place of course is Jerusalem.[35]

Only in the exilic prophets does Jerusalem emerge out of the shadows to become the center of Israelite affection and hope. And Isaiah, like Ezekiel, reorients the blessing of Abraham so that it comes to center almost exclusively on Jerusalem, on Mount Zion. The promise to Abraham and, let it be noted, to Sarah now becomes the basis for the redemption of Zion: "Look to Abraham your father and to Sarah who bore you; for when he was but one I called him, and I blessed him and made him many. For the Lord will comfort Zion; he will comfort all her waste places, and will make her wilderness like Eden, her desert like the garden of the Lord; joy and gladness will be found in her" (51:2–3). Isaiah is faithful to the spirit if not the letter of the land promise.

Even in the final chapters of Isaiah, where the language is more futuristic, more utopian, more eschatological, the prophet does not sever the ties to the land tradition. Indeed he accentuates them. In chapters 55–66 the formula "possess the land" occurs three times, and in each case it has reference to the future Jerusalem. In one place both "holy mountain" *and* "land" appear, and the two terms associated with the acquiring of the land, "inherit" and "possess," are used. The prophet writes, "He who takes refuge in me shall *inherit* the land, and *possess* my holy mountain" (Isa 57.13).[36] In another place he again resorts to the formulaic language of the land promise to speak of the humiliation of Israel's enemies and the rebirth of Jerusalem: "Aliens shall stand and feed your flocks, foreigners shall be your plowmen and vinedressers; but you shall be called the priests of the Lord . . . therefore in your [or "their"] land you shall possess a double portion" (Isa 61:5–7). Later, when the book of Isaiah was translated into Greek, this verse was given an even more explicit link to the first appropriation of the land. It was translated "You shall possess the land a *second* time."

The link between the ancient promise and the future aggrandizement of the city is evident even in the famous passage in chapter 60 about the people that sat in darkness. There the prophet announces that the "glory of the Lord" will rise over Jerusalem, and nations will come to "your light and kings to the brightness of your rising." Isaiah pictures the wealth of the nations streaming to Jerusalem, young camels of Midian and Ephah, gold and frankincense, the building up of the walls of Jerusalem by foreigners, and a time of peace in the land. "Your [Jerusalem's] people shall all be righteous; *they shall possess the land forever,* the shoot of my planting, the work of my hands, that I might be glorified" (Isa 60:21). The prophet's message of hope is addressed to the descendants of Abraham and Sarah, not to the nations, and the original blessing of the patriarchs undergirds the people's future expectations.

Third Isaiah's exuberant language about the city is so majestic, so dazzling that it can easily blind readers to another feature of the future city. The city has a temple. There is of course nothing in Third Isaiah to compare to the final chapters of Ezekiel, yet Isaiah is no less zealous an apologist for the cult. His "prophetic-eschatological faith is focused on Temple and altar."[37] When he speaks of Zion and the holy mountain he is not simply speaking of the rebuilding of the city but also of the restoration of God's house and the offering of sacrifices on the mountain of the Lord. In the vivid picture in chapter 60 of God's glory rising upon Jerusalem, the prophet has in mind not only the city but also the temple: "I will glorify my glorious house." And several lines later, he mentions bringing wood from Lebanon "to beautify the place of my sanctuary" (Isa 60:7, 13). Elsewhere he speaks of "burnt offerings and sacrifices" that will be offered on God's altar (56:7). There could be no Jerusalem without a temple.

Isaiah's vision of the future, then, like that of Ezekiel, is centered on the city and the temple. What had formerly been attributed to the land as a whole is now transferred to the city and the holy mountain. From the time of the exile the city and temple become the driving force of Jewish hopes. Third Isaiah may use the image of a "new creation," but he is still thinking of a Jerusalem that is continuous with the Jerusalem of the past. Restoration and utopia are inextricably mixed. The form of Jerusalem may be more splendid, more glorious, and more enduring than any form the city had in the past, but it is still firmly fixed to the earth.

The sublime language and soaring images of Second and Third Isaiah, though anchored in the singular hopes of the Judean exiles for return and restoration, did, however, bring into existence something that was not there previously. George Steiner writes (not of Isaiah but of poets in general), "We cannot accurately conceive what it must have been like to be the first to compare the colour of the sea with the dark of wine or to see autumn in a man's face. Such figures are new mappings of the world, they reorganized our habitation in reality."[38] Isaiah's Jerusalem is unlike any city that ever existed. It will be a city in which "the Lord will be [the] everlasting light" (Isa 60:19), and "no more shall there be in it an infant that lives but a few days, or an old man who does not fill out his days" (65:20), for the time will come when mourners will receive a "garland instead of ashes. . . . The mantle of praise instead of a faint spirit" (61.3). The prophet sowed the seeds for a new cartography of hope, expanding the horizon of human expectation and kindling a fire that would not be quenched easily. In time his images would take on a life of their own. Yet, his vision of the future, like all eschatological hope within Judaism, finally had its origin in a very particular promise: the descendants of Abraham would one day possess the land given to them by God.

Zechariah's Holy Land

Although Ezekiel uses the term "holy" to describe the Temple Mount and the territory contiguous to the sanctuary ("holy district," as he calls it [45:3]), he does not actually use the term "holy land." The biblical writer who coined the term "holy land" was the prophet Zechariah.

In 538 Cyrus issued a decree that made it possible for the exiles in Babylonia to return to Jerusalem and begin the arduous task of reestablishing life in their former home and rebuilding the temple. On returning to Judea, however, the exiles suffered frustration and defeat. Their crops failed, food was scarce, and they lacked the resources to begin building. Further those who had remained in the land opposed their plans. Twenty years after the exiles' return the temple site remained empty and forlorn. In this setting two new prophets, Haggai and Zechariah, emerged,[39] and in them one detects a growing restiveness and discontent, as the dream the exiles had carried with them from Babylonia had begun to die. The only way to revive it, according to Haggai, was to bend all efforts toward rebuilding the temple and restoring the cult to its rightful place in the lives of the people. Haggai reproves the people because they devoted themselves to their own needs and neglected the sanctuary. The people make excuses, according to Haggai: "The time has not yet come to rebuild the house of the Lord." They "busy themselves each with his own house" while the house of the Lord "lies in ruins" (1:2, 9). In the prophet's view, the temple of the Lord must take precedence over everything else because only there can God show forth his glory. "On that day" God will usher in a new age, and his servant Zerubbabel will rule as the Messiah.

When Zechariah began to prophesy a few years later work on the temple had begun in earnest. Yet he too is impatient. He sounds a note that will be heard again and again in later Jewish writings: "How long, O Lord of hosts, will you have no mercy on Jerusalem and the cities of Judah?" (1:12).[40] It is in this context, the hope of restoration, that Zechariah uses the phrase "holy land" or "holy ground."[41] "Sing and rejoice, O daughter of Zion; for lo, I come and I will dwell in the midst of you, says the Lord. And many nations shall join themselves to the Lord in that day, and shall know that the Lord of hosts has sent me to you. And the Lord will inherit Judah as his portion in the *holy ground,* and will again choose Jerusalem" (Zech 2:10–12).

In this passage, as in the book of Ezekiel, holiness is associated with the presence of God's glory in Jerusalem.[42] The idea of holy land is an extension of the sanctity of the temple. Jerusalem, says Zechariah, will be called the "mountain of the Lord of hosts, the *holy* mountain" (8:3). Jerusalem is the place where God dwells (8:3), and his presence serves as a shield against her enemies (8:20-22). In a later addition to the book of Zechariah a section was appended that extended the sanctity of the city to everything that is found in the city, as would be the case in the Temple Scroll from Qumran.[43] Even the bells on horses will be inscribed "Holy to the Lord," and pots in the temple will be "sacred to the Lord of hosts." And "on that day" there will be no "merchants" in the house of the Lord (14:20–21).

Like Ezekiel, Zechariah uses the traditional formulas associated with the promise of the land, but he has centered them solely on Jerusalem and Judah, the new political entity that had come into being after the exile, rather than on the land as a whole. The land that earlier tradition had envisioned and that Ezekiel had reaffirmed is now a thing of the past.

Once the term *holy* was introduced it was inevitable that it would gain currency, not as a replacement for *the Land of Israel* but as a way of designating the character of the land and Israelite hopes for its future. In

Zechariah we hear in the term its future echoes. *Holy land* was a restorationist symbol to signify all that Israel hoped for after the terrible calamities of the sixth century. It may also reflect the rhetorical need to convince people of the necessity of return. The exile had taught Israelites that they could live in other lands. Though the term *holy land* first appears in Zechariah, its true artisan was Ezekiel. His conception of the holy mountain on which stood the temple sanctioned the use of sacral language to depict the land as a whole. In Ezekiel's vision it was not only the people of Israel who were in exile; God's glory had also departed Jerusalem. And as he looked to the future he envisioned a day on which not only the exiles would return from the East, but also God's glory would return "by the gate facing east" to enter the inner court and fill the temple. *Holy land* has its origins in the eschatological vision of the exilic prophets.

2 Within My Holy Borders

In the roll call of heroes in the chapter "Let us now praise famous men" of the Wisdom of Jesus ben Sirach (Ecclesiasticus), the first to be honored are "those who ruled in their kingdoms and were renowned for their power" (chap. 44). Ben Sirach has words of praise for sages who were "wise in their words of instruction" and poets who "set forth verses in writing"; but he offers his highest accolades to kings and leaders of the people: Abraham, Moses and Joshua, David and Solomon, Rehoboam and Jeroboam, Hezekiah and Josiah, Zerubbabel and Nehemiah. Even the prophets who are named, Samuel, Elijah, and Elisha, and the priests, Aaron, Phinehas, and Simon, son of Onias, were political as well as spiritual leaders.[1]

As ben Sirach looked back on Israel's history his gaze fixed on those leaders who had molded the Israelites together as a people and preserved and protected the nation in the land. At the beginning he places Abraham (not Adam), to whom was given the original promise that the nation would be blessed and would "inherit from sea to sea and from the River to the ends of the earth," and at the end of the catalogue stands Simon son of Onias, high priest, who by refurbishing the walls of the temple and hewing out a cistern for water saved his people from ruin and fortified the city against siege (chap. 50). Israel's spiritual patrimony was displayed in the heroic deeds of kings and in the prudent stewardship of its priestly regents. For the Israelites, religion was visible not only in the rhythms of communal life, governing the observance of days and times and seasons and regulating the offering of bulls, lambs, and turtledoves, it was also evident in the political destiny of the community. The fortunes of the people in the land and the fate of the city of Jerusalem were always at the center of Israel's religion. The memorable events in Israel's history, according to ben Sirach, were the conquest of the land (Joshua), the gathering of the tribes as a people (Samuel), the raising up of kings (David), the building of a house for God in Jerusalem (Solomon), the defense of the city (Hezekiah), the purifying of the temple (Josiah), the regaining of the land, and the rebuilding of the temple (Zerubbabel and Nehemiah); and Israel's hope for the future was that one day the "tribes of Jacob" would receive "their inheritance" (36:11).[2]

Among the peoples of the ancient Near East the Israelites were not unique in their attachment to a particular land; neither were they the only nation to suffer the trauma of deportation and exile in foreign countries. Other peoples whose religion was yoked to place were forced to adapt to diasporic existence in foreign lands.[3] In time, most peoples shook loose their moorings to the native land. But Jews who lived outside of Judea continued to maintain ties to Jerusalem, through pilgrimage, for example,[4] even while setting down deep roots in their adopted communities. This situation, observes Elias Bickerman, was "without analogy in antiquity."[5]

Although life in the diaspora had become a permanent and, for some, comfortable way of life that eroded the desire to return, Jewish tradition made the loss of the land and the exile a central fact of Jewish self-understanding even after the return of exiles from Babylonia. "They were carried away captive," writes ben Sirach, "from their land and were scattered over all the earth" (48:15).[6] The memory of the destruction of Jerusalem and the seizure of Jewish captives by the Babylonians breaks into Jewish consciousness again and again, reminding Jews of the period *before* the exile, when Israel lived in its own land under its own kings. The period of the monarchy served "as a model for national revival and as the focus of hopes for the future."[7] There is no more lachrymose moment in Israelite history than the day when Zedekiah, the last Jewish king, after being forced to watch the slaughter of his children, was "bound in fetters" (2 Kings 25:7) and taken captive to Babylonia. It was a picture one did not easily forget.

For the Jews redemption has always been understood as an event "that takes place publicly, on the stage of history," writes Gershom Scholem. "It is an occurrence which takes place in the visible world and which cannot be conceived of apart from such visible appearance."[8] Just as historical events had brought Israel into bondage, so new events, it was believed, would bring about Israel's deliverance. History was the nursery of hope. But redemption was also imagined as an event in *space* as well as in time. Genuine deliverance could occur only "within my holy borders," as the apocalypse of 4 Ezra puts it (13:48), in the "city of the Kingdom," as a Jewish liturgical poet would express it centuries later.[9] Jewish hope included of necessity a territorial dimension, and territory requires political authority. In the words of the Temple Scroll, "You shall not put a foreigner over you who is not your brother."[10]

After the calamities of the sixth century Jewish life and institutions in the land had never been fully restored even though many Jews had returned to Judea and the temple was rebuilt.[11] What the exilic and postexilic prophets had proclaimed with boundless confidence could hardly be identified with the condition of Palestinian Jewry during the centuries after the exile.[12] Though Jews were living in Jerusalem they continued to hope for something grander and more glorious, "just as the prophets said" (Tob 14:5).

In the course of time this hope would undergo many mutations, and its form would vary from place to place and from writer to writer.[13] Yet like a river that periodically overflows its banks, creating for a time new pools or even new channels, only to return to its original bed, Jewish hope took to itself new features as the social and political circumstances altered but did not meander far from the course that had been set in the generations after the exile. Its goal, restoration and "possession of the land," remained a political as well as a spiritual ideal.[14] Centuries later, when the land had been transformed into a Christian holy land, this hope would reappear with fresh vitality. In the tumultuous centuries from the end of Persian rule (fourth century B.C.E.) to the Bar Kochba revolt in the second century C.E. the belief was adapted to the conditions of Jewish life. Whether Jews spoke of the Land of Israel as the holy land or homeland or our land or *the* land, they never abandoned the conviction that it was their destiny as a people to dwell in this land.

Palestine and the West

Prior to the fourth century Palestine lay within the orbit of the great eastern empires, Egypt, Assyria, Babylonia, and Persia. But in 336 B.C.E., at the age of twenty, Alexander (later to be called the Great) succeeded to the throne of his father, Philip II, in Macedonia in the Balkans. Within a few years he had brought the fractious Greek states under his dominion and promptly began to march eastward across the Hellespont into Asia Minor to meet the Persians face to face. Challenged by the approaching army of Alexander, the Persians, commanded by the timorous Darius III, collapsed, and by 332 Alexander had reached Palestine, first laying siege to Tyre, then moving down the coast to Acco, Ashkelon, and Gaza to meet the soldiers he had sent ahead to occupy Egypt.

For the first time in its history greater Syria came under the sway of a power from the West, a political fact that would shape the course of events in the Middle East until the Muslim conquest in the seventh century C.E. and beyond. As a consequence Palestine was joined to the West, first through the Hellenistic kingdoms of the Ptolemies and Seleucids, later through the Romans. Unlike the peoples further east and the civilizations centered on the Tigris and Euphrates rivers (present-day Iraq), the people of Palestine became part of our history, the history of Greece and Rome and of Christianity, not simply a distant chapter in the fortunes of the ancient Near East. For the Jews living in Judea the arrival of the Greek-speaking Macedonians meant they had to learn to accommodate to yet another rule from abroad with its new language, its alien way of life, its rational approach to city planning, its system of education, even its new ways of conducting war, for example, the deployment of phalanxes of infantrymen.

After Alexander's death his generals met on the battlefield to decide the fate of the conquered lands, and in 301 Palestine became subject to the Ptolemies of Egypt. They would govern the area for only a hundred years. In 200 B.C.E. at the battle of Panias, near the source of the Jordan River, the Ptolemies were defeated by the Seleucids, another Hellenistic dynasty whose capital was at Antioch in Syria. When the Seleucids gained control of Palestine, the Jewish population was centered in Judea, the area of the former Persian province of Yehud. On the coastal plain, in the region east of the Jordan, and in Samaria and further north the

Hellenistic monarchies had established Greek city-states whose language, customs, and religion differed from those of the Jews living in Jerusalem and environs. In contrast to the Persians, whose rule in Palestine had left few traces on Jewish life, the Greeks would leave a lasting imprint on the people and the territory.[15]

Prior to the victory of the Seleucids the Jews had been able to pursue their way of life without disruption, but with the accession of Antiochus IV (Epiphanes) to the Seleucid throne in 175 C.E. a new policy was put into effect. He proscribed the observance of the Sabbath, circumcision, the keeping of the annual festivals. In the words of the Roman historian Tacitus, Antiochus sought to "rid [the Jews] of their superstitious way of life and to initiate them into the traditions of the Greeks" (*Hist.* 5.8). Resolute in his goal to integrate the Jews fully into his kingdom, Antiochus set out to transform Jerusalem into a Greek city-state. "No harsher trial ever tested the monotheistic faith of the Jews," writes Jonathan Goldstein.[16]

Antiochus's program was not simply the capricious plan of a foreign king; it exposed a growing fissure within Jewish society. For some Jews Greek ways were not unwelcome, and when Antiochus came to the throne he found ready supporters in Jerusalem.[17] According to our sources, which are often hostile to Greek sympathizers among the Jews, the chief villain on the Jewish side was Jason, the brother of the high priest Onias III.[18] Jason offered the king a large sum of money to be appointed high priest. Once he had gained the office he began to build a gymnasium (the symbol of Greek culture) in Jerusalem, establish a program for training young men in Greek ways, and "shift his countrymen over to the Greek way of life" (2 Macc 4:10). He even introduced the practice of wearing a Greek headdress, the broad-brimmed hat associated with the god Hermes, a sign, like any headgear, of cultural and religious allegiance. It would be, I suppose, like a Jew living in Syria wearing the kefiah of the Arabs.

Breaking Faith with the Land

One of our sources for the events surrounding the hellenizing of Jerusalem is the book of Second Maccabees, a work written in the latter part of the second century B.C.E. by a Jew living in the diaspora. It was based on a longer work by a man named Jason of Cyrene (the province adjacent to Egypt on the African coast), and the abridgment may have come from Alexandria. Second Maccabees is the first Jewish writing to use the term *holy land* since the prophet Zechariah and the first in which the term occurs in Greek.

The phrase occurs at the beginning of the book in a letter written by Jews in Jerusalem to the Jewish community in Egypt.[19] The letter reads as follows:

> To our brothers the Jews of Egypt, greeting, your brothers the Jews in Jerusalem and in the land of Judah. A good peace may God make for you, and may He be good to you, and may He remember His covenant with His faithful servants Abraham, Isaac, and Jacob. May he give you all a heart to revere Him and to do His will wholeheartedly and with a willing spirit. In the reign of Demetrius in the year 169 [143 B.C.E.] we Jews wrote to you, "In the affliction and in the distress which came upon us in the years from the time that Jason and his followers *rebelled against the holy land and the kingdom* and set fire to the temple gateway and shed innocent blood we prayed to the Lord, and He hearkened to us. We brought animal sacrifices and fine flour, and we kindled the lamps and laid out the showbread." And now we ask you to celebrate the Days of Tabernacles in the month of Kislev. (2 Macc 1:1–10)[20]

The ostensible purpose of this epistle was to inform the faithful in Egypt of the approaching festival, "the Days of Tabernacles in the month of Kislev." The festival in question was a commemoration of the rededication of the Temple (Hanukkah) after the victory of the Maccabees. The letter, however, is more than a gentle admonition to observe the festival, which had been inaugurated only a few decades earlier. More to the point, the festival centered on the temple cult in Jerusalem and may not have been observed by Jews in Egypt. The language of the letter—urging its recipients to remember the covenant, to revere God wholeheartedly, to keep the commandments—intimates that the Jews of Egypt needed some prodding to join their fellow Jews in Judea in celebrating the Hasmonean victory and the resumption of offerings in Jerusalem.

In apparent disregard for the prerogatives of Jerusalem, the Jews in Egypt had built a temple in Leontopolis. In their view the religion of Israel was transportable to another land. By constructing an alternate temple and instituting animal and vegetable offerings outside of Jerusalem, indeed in a foreign land, the Jews of Egypt spurned Jerusalem, its temple, its priests, and the land itself. From the perspective of the Jews in Jerusalem, "firm partisans of Jerusalem as God's elected place,"[21]

Egyptian Jewry's rebuff of the holy city broke faith with the covenant. According to the book of Deuteronomy sacrifice should be offered only in the place that God will choose (Deut 12:4). Hence the issue in the letter is not simply obedience to the Torah, but recognition of the uniqueness of Jerusalem and the Land of Israel. Its exhortation is not a pious preachment to be good and faithful Jews, but a very specific reproof, even censure, for their recusant devotion.

To make certain that the recipients of the letter get the point, the Jerusalemites refer to a letter they had written twenty years before about the behavior of Jason during the reign of Antiochus. In this letter it was said that Jason "rebelled against the holy land and the kingdom." In his magisterial commentary on 2 Maccabees, Jonathan Goldstein has proposed that Jason's chief sin was to support a schismatic temple located outside of Jerusalem.[22] By acknowledging the legitimacy of an altar outside of Jerusalem, Jason rebelled against the sanctity of the land. His crime was to spurn the place God had chosen.

In the letter to the Jews in Egypt the term *holy land* is not simply a description of a territory. To be sure, it designates the territory of Judea, that is to say, Jerusalem and its environs, but it presents Judea as a place toward which certain attitudes are appropriate (or inappropriate). Like the covenant, the idea of a holy land implies obligations and responsibilities. This can be seen by contrasting "holy land" with the other geographical expression in the letter. In the greeting the senders identify themselves as Jews from Jerusalem and the "land of Judea." This phrase designates a commonly recognized region, the country in which the writers were living, the country of Judea, just as one might refer to Achaea as the country of the Achaeans or Scythia as the country of the Scythians. "Land of Judea" is a territorial and geographical designation *tout court* without symbolic overtones, except of course the historical associations that Judea had in Jewish tradition. "Holy land," however, designates this same territory from the perspective of its spiritual quality, the land in view of its purpose and end.[23]

The term "holy land" is used here in the context of a debate among Jews about the prerogatives of Jerusalem and Judea. The letter ends with a report that after Jason's rebellion, sacrifices in the temple in Jerusalem were resumed, the lamps rekindled, and the showbread laid out. With the restoration of worship in the temple, Jerusalem was again able to fulfill its appointed role in Jewish life. Jason's sin—and, by implication, the sin of the Jews of Egypt—was that he did not "keep faith with the land."[24] The first time, then, that the term occurs in Greek Jewish literature it carries overtones that hearken back to the rebuilding of Jerusalem and restoration of worship in the temple. Though coined to remind the Jews living in the diaspora of the central place of Jerusalem in Jewish life, one can already hear reverberations of the future, when Jews would use the same term to support claims about the Land of Israel in discussions with non-Jews.

A century and a half later Philo of Alexandria uses the term to express his outrage that pagans had desecrated the Holy Land by building an altar to the emperor Gaius. In Jamnia, a city in Judea populated by Jews and non-Jews, the "foreigners" [non-Jews], says Philo, were continually provoking and subverting the ancestral traditions. When they learned of an imminent visit by the emperor Gaius, the non-Jewish residents constructed an altar of clay bricks to venerate him, knowing full well that it would rankle and incite the Jews. As soon as the Jews heard about the altar they banded together and tore it down because its presence "obliterated the sanctity that was appropriate to the *holy land*."[25]

For the authors of the letter to the Jews of Egypt the sanctity of the Land of Israel had to do with the celebration of Jewish festivals, but once the term came to be used with reference to non-Jews it took on new shades of meaning. The only worship that was fitting in the holy land was the worship of the God of Abraham, Isaac, and Jacob, and this worship was to be found only among the Jewish people. When claims about the sanctity of the land were made to non-Jews, especially to those living in Palestine, they were inevitably accompanied by statements about Jewish tenancy in the land and claims about ownership. This can be seen in the appropriation of Hellenistic ideas of fatherland or homeland during this period.

The Land of Israel as Homeland

After being imprisoned by Aretas, the Arab ruler in Petra, the high priest Jason, according to the author of 2 Maccabees, fled from city to city, "hated as a rebel against the laws, and abhorred as the executioner of his *country* and his fellow citizens." Finally he was "cast ashore in Egypt," and the one who had "driven many from their own *country* into exile died in exile" (2 Macc 5:8–9). In this passage the term for country in Greek is *patris,* "fatherland" or "homeland." The term "fatherland" designates a person's native city or country, the place where one was born and reared, the place called home. It refers to the land of one's ancestors, the territory in which one's people have lived for generations or centuries, the land that belongs to a people by tenancy. In Greek the usual term is *fatherland*, but the best English equivalent today is *homeland* or *native land.*[26]

A striking illustration of the appropriation of the language of the Hellenistic world occurs in the conclusion of a speech of Judas Maccabeus addressed to his army as they prepared for the first great battle of the war against the Seleucids. According to 2 Maccabees, he urged them to keep before their eyes the outrage the gentiles had committed against the "holy place" and their efforts to overthrow the "ancestral way of life." "With these words he filled them with good courage and made them ready to die for their laws and their homeland" (8:21). This speech prompts one to think less of biblical religion than of the speeches in Herodotus or Isocrates rallying the troops as they prepared for battle, Horace's famous line "Dulce et decorum est pro patria mori" [It is sweet and fitting to give one's life for the fatherland], or, in a less bellicose context, "pro deo et patria" awards in our day. A useful parallel from Greek antiquity is the speech of Hektor rebuking his fainthearted fellow soldier Polydamas in book 12 of the *Iliad*: "You—you would have had me put my faith in birds whose spreading wings I neither track nor care for, [an omen had seemed to go against the Trojans] whether to the right hand sunward they fly or to the left hand westward into darkness. No, no, I say, rely on the will of Zeus who rules all mortals and immortals. One and only one portent is best: *defend our fatherland*!" (*Il.* 12:243).

Jewish use of the term follows conventional Greek practice closely. As Antiochus Eupator advanced against the Jews, according to 2 Maccabees, Judas Maccabeus ordered the people to call upon the Lord to come to their aid lest they be deprived of "the law and the fatherland and the holy temple" (2 Macc 13:11). Menelaus, Jason's successor, is said to be "traitor to the laws and to his fatherland."[27] In these passages "law" and "laws" no doubt refers to the Torah, the revealed will of God, yet it also has Hellenistic overtones. It designates those customs and traditions which set off one people from another, the specific religious traditions that formed a people's way of life, its national institutions. Greeks had their laws, the Egyptians theirs, the Scythians theirs, the Libyans theirs. Jews were seen as a people defined by land and customs, a unique *ethnos* or nation, and fellow Jews were designated kinsmen (2 Macc 4:10).

By adopting Greek notions of fatherland and of ancestral customs associated with a particular land, Jews were able to express their relation to the land in a new way. The Scriptures had on occasion used phrases such as "our land" (Ps 85:9; Mic 5:5), meaning the land God had given Abraham's descendants and the place where God's glory was revealed; in the Hellenistic period such language carried with it the idea of ownership. When Judas Maccabeus wished to pass through Ephron east of the Jordan to Judea he said, "Let us pass through *your* land to go back to *our* land" (1 Macc 5:48).[28] The land was the country of one's birth, the resting place of one's ancestors, and hence a place to love and cherish. In an emotional letter to the emperor Gaius, King Agrippa (according to Philo) described his affection for the land of his people as follows: "All men, my emperor, have planted in them a passionate love of their native land and a high esteem for their own laws; and on this there is no need to instruct you, who love your native city as ardently as you honor your own customs. . . . As you know I am by birth a Jew, and my native city [*patris*] is Jerusalem in which is situated the sacred temple of the most high God."[29]

As the Land of Israel came to be viewed as a native land, Jews learned to legitimate their residency in the land *without* reference to the land promises in the Scriptures. The right to possess the land rested on tenancy, on having lived on the land for as long as anyone could remember. Commenting on the shift in sensibility, Joseph Heinemann writes, "On this foundation [the idea of native land] it was possible for [Jews] to discover a new basis for the traditional sentiment that existed between the people of Israel and the land of Israel, not by virtue of any distinctive character of our land, in the fashion of the sages, but by virtue of the attachment between it and its inhabitants, a general attachment such as that which would apply to any land and its inhabitants."[30]

The adoption of a new vocabulary to speak about the land and people, did not, however, mean that the traditional language was forgotten. The new merges readily with the old as can be seen in an instructive passage from 1 Maccabees. During the reign of Simon (143–135 C.E.), Antiochus VII had made an alliance with the Jews to aid him in his struggle against his rival Trypho. Simon sent silver and gold and military equipment as well as two thousand "picked men" to fight for him. But Antiochus refused, and he turned on Simon and claimed that he "had taken possession of many places in my kingdom." Jerusalem, Gaza, and Joppa, he says, are "cities of my kingdom" (1 Macc 15:28–29). When Athenobius, the emissary of the king, came to Jerusalem, he reported to Simon what Antiochus had said. To which Simon replied, "We have neither taken foreign land nor seized foreign property, but only the *inheritance* of our fathers, which at one time had been unjustly taken by our enemies. Now that we have the opportunity, we are firmly holding the *inheritance* of our fathers" (1 Macc 15:33–34). Though many Jews had begun to view the land in Hellenistic terms as their homeland, they nevertheless justified their claims appeal to the inheritance promised to the descendants of Abraham. Political claims did not rest simply on tenancy or might of arms but on the spiritual patrimony of the people of Israel.

Defense of Jewish Claims to the Land

In the Hebrew Bible the land is at once a gift and a territory that had to be conquered and its people displaced. At points the biblical writers were embarrassed by these apparently conflicting facts, but only in the Hellenistic period did the discomfiture become acute. As the land began to be understood as a homeland or native land, some Jews downplayed the role of the conquest in acquiring the land. This is hinted at in the passage cited above from 1 Maccabees ("we have not taken *foreign* land"), but in other works it is more pronounced.

The most flagrant revision of the biblical history occurs in the book of Jubilees, a work written in the second century B.C.E. Sometimes called the little Genesis (though it is in fact longer), Jubilees is a rewriting of the books of Genesis and Exodus (up to Exodus 12) by a Jew who lived in Palestine and wrote in Hebrew. The original Hebrew version is no longer extant, though passages from it were found at Qumran; the book has come down to us in several versions, in Greek, Syriac, Arabic, and Ethiopic. Of all the Jewish books written from the time of the Hasmonean victory until the destruction of the Second Temple, Jubilees is most profoundly concerned with Jewish rights to the land. From the opening of the book, where the promise to Abraham, Isaac, and Jacob is stated—"I will give to your posterity a land flowing with milk and honey" (1.7)—to its closing paragraphs, where the author speaks of the children of Israel entering "the land which they will possess"(49.18), Jubilees asserts the inviolability and perpetuity of the land promise. The land was given to Shem and his children "to occupy it forever" (8:17).[31]

Although the narrative of Jubilees follows the book of Genesis, the book reflects later Jewish traditions and institutions, for example, the centrality of Jerusalem and the temple, the Mosaic Law, especially the observance of the Sabbath and the celebration of the festivals (marked according to a solar calendar composed of twelve months of thirty days), the ingathering of the exiles (1:15 ff.) Like Ezekiel, Jubilees situates Mount Zion not only at the center of the *land* but at the navel of the earth. Noah knew "that the garden of Eden was the holy of holies and the dwelling of the Lord. And Mount Sinai is in the middle of the desert and Mount Zion is in the middle of the navel of the earth. The three of them—the one facing the other—were created as holy places" (8:19). A few centuries later this same tradition would appear in the Mishnah and other rabbinic texts.[32]

In spite of its ringing reaffirmation of the promise of the land to Abraham, Isaac, and Jacob and their seed, the book of Jubilees repeatedly calls the land "land of Canaan."[33] This is puzzling in a work written to challenge the notion that the Canaanites had any right to the land. Here is the author's explanation of the name land of Canaan:[34] Noah had three sons, Ham, Shem, and Japheth, and Canaan was the son of Ham, grandson of Noah. After the great flood Noah celebrated a happy feast, offering bulls and rams and lambs to the Lord, and he became drunk. He entered his tent and fell asleep and his son Ham saw his nakedness; Shem and Japheth, however, covered their father's shame. When Noah awoke from his drunkenness he knew what his son Ham had done. He cursed Canaan, Ham's son, and blessed Shem, the father of the Israelites.

Later the earth was divided among the three sons, each according to his inheritance. To Shem Noah gave the land from Lebanon to the river of Egypt, that is, the territory between the Jordan River and the Mediterranean Sea. To Ham he assigned the territory to the east extending as far as the Garden of Eden. To Japheth he gave the regions bordering the Mediterranean Sea, that is, Italy and North Africa. In allotting the several lands to his children, Noah made them swear an oath that anyone who seized a portion of the land assigned to his brother would be cursed.

Ham was satisfied with his portion and went there to live with his family. But Canaan coveted Shem's land, "the land of Lebanon as far as the river of Egypt," for he saw that it was "very beautiful." He refused to live in the "land of his inheritance" and dwelled instead in the land west of the Jordan up to the "shore of the sea." Noah and his sons rebuked Canaan for his insolence and presumptuousness: "You have settled in a land which is not yours nor did it come forth for us by lot. Do not do this, because if you do this, you and your children will fall in the land and be cursed with rebellion." But Canaan would not listen to his father and brothers and "settled in the land of Lebanon [land of Shem]." For this reason, concludes the author of Jubilees, "that land is called Canaan" (10:34).

The point of this fictitious and fanciful story is that the land of Israel received the name land of Canaan as a result of thievery and usurpation. Its rightful tenants are not the Canaanites, the sons of Canaan, but the Israelites, sons of Shem. The name land of Canaan is malapropos and anachronistic.

A less elaborate effort to defend and legitimate Jewish claims to the land can be found in the Wisdom of Solomon, a work written by a Hellenistic Jew living in Alexandria in the first century B.C.E. The author of this work is also embarrassed by the Israelite conquest of Canaan, but his way of justifying the occupation and displacement of the Canaanites was to reproach them for disfiguring and staining the holy land with their sins. "Those who lived long ago in your *holy land,* you hated for their detestable practices, their works of sorcery and unholy rites, their merciless slaughter of children, and their sacrificial feasting on human flesh and blood" (12:3–5). As David Winston observes in his commentary, this passage is intended "to justify the Israelite conquest of Canaan."[35] This land is unlike other lands; it will welcome only certain inhabitants. "These initiates [Canaanites] from the midst of a heathen cult, these parents who murder helpless lives, thou didst well to destroy by the hands of our fathers, that *the land most precious of all to you* might receive a worthy colony of the servants of God" (12:7).[36]

In the Wisdom of Solomon the term *holy land* legitimates Jewish claims that the land is "our" land. By their idolatrous and immoral behavior the Canaanites forfeited their right to the land.[37] This land, unlike other lands, was "most precious" to God and would receive only a certain people, a colony that was worthy of it. There had to be a symbiosis between the land and its people. To call the land "holy land," then, is to assert that the Jews have a unique relation to the land and a singular claim to live in the territory.[38]

To avoid the embarrassment that the Jews had not dwelled in the land from time immemorial and had occupied the land of the Canaanites,[39] some writers went so far as to claim that the land was uninhabited before the arrival of the Jews. There is evidence from this same period, observes Moshe Weinfeld, that some Jews defended the possession of the land not as the conquest of a territory inhabited by others but as the "taking of an uninhabited territory."[40] Where the idea that the land was uninhabited or desolate arises is uncertain, but it is first mentioned in a Greek writer, Hecateus of Abdera about 300 C.E. Hecateus says that after the Jews lived in Egypt they "were driven into what is now called Judea . . . which was at that time *utterly uninhabited.*"[41] Hecateus could hardly have derived this interpretation of the return from Egypt from the Bible. For this reason it has been suggested that he came to his view by contact with Jews who were interested in justifying Jewish claims to the land.[42]

Whatever the source of Hecateus's views, it is clear that an apologetic tradition to justify Jewish claims to the land of Canaan was being forged during the Hellenistic period. It was first adumbrated in the book of Jubilees, drawn on somewhat later by the author of the Wisdom of Solomon, and later elaborated in the rabbinical tradition. In some midrashim (rabbinic reflections on the Bible), quite in opposition to the biblical text, Joshua is presented not as a conqueror, but as a peacemaker.[43]

The presence of the name Land of Canaan in the biblical text long after Jews had adopted the name Land of Israel vexed later Jewish interpreters. Regarding the phrase "when you shall come into the land of Canaan," (Lev 14:33) one interpreter exclaimed, "Seven nations dwelled in the land and yet it says 'the land of Canaan!'"[44] In a midrash on Exodus 13:11, "When the Lord brings you into the land of the Canaanites," one rabbi agreed that the name land of Canaan is appropriate—but for the following reason: "When Canaan heard that the Israelites were entering the land, he stood up and bowed down before them. The Holy One, blessed be He, said to Canaan, 'You bowed before my children, and for that reason I will call the land by your name and I will give you a beautiful land as your own land. And what is that land? It is Africa!'"[45]

With the Canaanites safely banished to Africa, according to this view, the Jews could claim the Land of Israel as their own. So widespread was this tradition that some thought the Phoenicians in North Africa were fugitives from Palestine, that is, Canaanites who had been driven out when Joshua conquered the land. In the sixth century C.E., Procopius, the historian of emperor Justinian, reports that he had seen an inscription in Mauritania which read, "We fled from before Joshua, son of Nun, the robber." The presence of Phoenicians in North Africa is thus related to the expulsion of the Canaanites from Palestine at the time of Joshua. How this tradition made its way to the Byzantines and what the course of its wanderings over the centuries is unknown. It may however go back to the Hasmonean period and to charges against the Jews that they had no right to the Land of Israel.[46]

The Coming of Rome

Under the rule of the Hasmoneans the tiny Jewish state extended its hegemony over much of Palestine, and the name Judea came to designate the entire region. "The interior above Phoenicia as far as the Arabs, between Gaza and Antilebanon, is called Judea," wrote Strabo the Greek geographer (*Geog.* 16.2.21). But the Jewish kingdom was too tiny and too divided within itself to endure long in that tumultuous region. Even if it could have defended the enlarged territory acquired under Alexander Jannaeus and kept its neighbors in check, it could not halt the relentless expansion of the new power from the West into the eastern Mediterranean.

As the Hasmonean kingdom was claiming new territory in Palestine, Rome had begun its inexorable movement eastward. During the second and first centuries before the common era, this Italian city-state methodically subdued the peoples of the Mediterranean world one by one: Greece, the kingdoms of Asia Minor, Syria, Palestine, and Egypt. In 64

B.C.E. Pompey occupied Antioch in Syria, and within a few months the Roman legions had set up camps in Judea. As the Romans advanced on Jerusalem most Jews submitted without resistance, but some took refuge on the Temple Mount in a futile and final effort to defend the city. In the summer of 63, after a siege of three months, Pompey's soldiers breached the walls from the north and conquered the city either on the Day of Atonement (according to Jewish tradition) or on a Sabbath (according to a Roman historian).[47] Pompey inspected the Holy of Holies himself but did not plunder the temple, and the cult continued without interruption under Roman rule. Judea was granted autonomy, its territory reduced (the coastal cities and Transjordan were placed under another jurisdiction), and it became subject to the Roman provincial administration in Syria.

After eighty years of Hasmonean rule the Jews were again ruled by a foreign power. Authority was placed in the hands of the high priest, Hyracanus II, but he was not allowed to bear the title king as the Hasmonean had done (illegitimately according to some Jews). When Pompey returned to Rome in triumph, he paraded the defeated Hasmonean king Aristobulus before the populace of the city. Jews witnessed the sad spectacle of a Jewish king being carried off in shackles to be humiliated in a capital far from the homeland. Historical forces had again conspired against Jews and shattered the dream of an enduring Jewish kingdom in the land of Israel. Jews readily recalled the ancient promise to Abraham: "You chose the descendants of Abraham above all the nations, and you put your name upon us, Lord, and it will not cease forever" (Pss Sol 9:9). As in previous ages the Abrahamic blessing took on a new pertinence as it was filtered through the torrent of events that overwhelmed the nation. The Psalms of Solomon, from which this passage is taken, is a collection of religious poems written in Palestine shortly after the Roman conquest of Jerusalem. In them the hope of redemption and restoration, of reclaiming the land and city is stated with uncommon fervor and poignant realism: "Raise up for them their king, the son of David, to rule over your servant Israel in the time known to you, O God." With fresh vigor the hope of a royal Davidic Messiah breaks forth.[48] The Messiah, a mighty warrior, will drive out those who have "laid waste *our land*" (Pss Sol 17.11).

A View from the Diaspora

Jews living outside of the land of Israel looked to the holy land with affection and with hope. In the years immediately before the destruction of the Second Temple in 70 C.E., the most instructive writer was Philo, the Jewish philosopher who lived in Alexandria in Egypt. His writings lend themselves to an interpretation of Judaism shorn of its national and particularist features. Philo did not consider the land of Israel his homeland; homeland was the place where one was born and raised (*Cont.* 18), and his home was Alexandria, not Palestine.

When Philo recounts the story of Abraham's journey to the promised land he praises him not because he was going up to his native land, but because he possessed the spiritual courage to abandon family and tribesmen for a strange land.[49] Abraham did not "yield to the charms of kinfolk and country" but cheerfully obeyed God's command. Abraham gave no thought to "fellow tribesmen, or citizens, or schoolmates, or comrades, or kinfolk on the father's or mother's side, or fatherland, or ancestral customs, or community of nurture or home life" (*Abr.* 60–67). Indeed for Philo pilgrimage to Jerusalem is a "sojourn in a strange land" (*Spec.* 1.68–69).

In the view of many contemporary scholars, Philo's philosophical understanding of Judaism had no place for the holy land. A distinguished modern interpreter, Samuel Sandmel, wrote, "It cannot be overstated that Philo has little or no concern for Palestine."[50] In support of this view he cites Philo's statement "Entrance into the land is entrance into philosophy. This is the good and fertile and that bears fruit, which produces the divine plants, the virtues" (*QE* 2.13). Abraham's migration is an allegory of a soul that loves virtue in search of the true God (*Abr.* 68).[51]

But there is another side to Philo.[52] As we have already seen, Philo reports, with sympathy, that his fellow Jews were outraged at the profanation of the holy land by supporters of Claudius. Even so it does come as something of a surprise to discover that Philo uses the phrase "holy land" more frequently than any other Jewish writer of antiquity. The term occurs at least eight times in his writings. In places he uses the term simply as a description of the territory that belongs to the Jews. They live, he writes, "not only in the *holy land* but everywhere throughout the habitable world" (*Legat.* 331; also *Legat.* 206). But as we have seen, the term can also designate the character of the land, the sanctity that is appropriate to the land (*Legat.* 202).

Philo has much more to say. Even though he does not consider the Land of Israel his homeland, he believed the Jews have a proprietary claim on the land. He calls it "their land" (*Spec.* 2.171) and "land which the people were given to dwell in" (*Spec.* 2.162). It is the "ancient ancestral land" (*hypothetica* in Eusebius *PE* 8.6, 355). And though Jews who live in the diaspora consider the lands in which they were born their homelands, nevertheless, says Philo, they "hold the Holy City where stands the sacred Temple of the most high God to be their *mother* city" (*Flaccum* 46).[53]

For Philo the land of Israel was more than a spiritual idea.[54] It was a place to which Jews from all over the world looked for inspiration and comfort. The act of pilgrimage, for example, was not only a spiritual discipline or a religious duty; it was a social rite that united the people and created in them a sense of unity. Many come from all over the world to Jerusalem, some by land, others by sea, all to "enjoy a brief breathing space in scenes of genial cheerfulness. Filled with comfortable hopes they devote their leisure, as is their duty, to holiness and the honoring of God. Friendships are formed between those who did not know each other, and sacrifices and libations are the occasion for reciprocity of feeling and constitute the surest pledge that they are all of one mind" (*Spec*. 1.66–70).

Jerusalem not only united the people like children of a common mother; it also gave them a common destiny. One day the Jews will be reunited in Jerusalem. The Jews, he writes, will not "continue forever dispersed over islands and continents and living in the lands of others as strangers and vagrants, open to the reproach of lying in wait to seize the goods of others" (*Spec*. 2.168). In a remarkable passage at the end of his work "On Rewards and Punishments" Philo envisions a day when the Jewish people will return from exile in the lands where they have been scattered to build anew a Jewish nation in the holy land.

> For even though they live in the furthest parts of the earth in slavery to their enemies, who made them captives . . . one day all will be freed. . . . When they have gained this unexpected liberty, those who now were scattered in Greece and in other lands over islands and continents will arise from every region, and, with one impulse, they will set out for the appointed place, guided in their journey by a divine and superhuman vision unseen by others but manifest to those who are returning home. . . . When they have arrived, the cities which a short time lay in ruins will be filled with people once more; the desert will be inhabited; the barren land will become fruitful; the prosperity of their fathers and ancestors will seem meager, so lavish will be the abundant riches in their possession. . . . Everything will suddenly be reversed, God will return the curses against their enemies, enemies who rejoiced in the misfortunes of the nation and mocked and railed at them when they said they had an inheritance which nothing could destroy. [*Praem*. 163–72]

In this passage Philo writes as though he had Ezekiel 36 open before him.

As much as Philo set out to highlight the spiritual aspects of Jewish tradition, he did not abandon its material features. Just as he never lost the realism of the food laws even while allegorizing their details, so he never surrendered the territorial features of the land tradition. The holy land beckoned Jews from all over the world, not simply as a place to visit on pilgrimage but as a lodestar of Jewish destiny. "There can be little doubt that Philo was unable to make a clean sweep of all the terrestrial aspects of Jewish messianism in spite of his overall attempt to depoliticize and psychologize the traditional concept," writes David Winston, one of Philo's most astute present-day interpreters.[55]

Jerusalem Below and Jerusalem Above

Within a generation of Philo's death, the city of Jerusalem was in ruins, the temple looted and burned, the Sanhedrin dissolved, and thousands of Jews forced to flee to other parts of Palestine, to cities across the Jordan, and to other provinces within the empire. In Israel's long history few events were more calamitous than the destruction of Jerusalem and the leveling of the temple by the Romans. In later Jewish tradition the day (Ninth of Ab in the Jewish calendar) was marked by public mourning and lamentation. When the month of Ab arrives, according to the tractate on fasting in the Mishnah, "gladness must be diminished" and none "must eat flesh nor drink wine" (*m. Ta'an.* 4.6–7). Rome's victory over the Jews deprived the nation of its chief religious and national institution, the temple. So fixed were its daily rituals that the times of the day were marked by them. When the daily offering ceased in 70 C.E., 'the people were terribly despondent" (*BJ* 6.94). But this rite was only one of many activities that took place in the temple. Numerous other obligatory sacrifices as well as private offerings, the bringing of first fruits, offerings after childbirth, sacrifices for ritual cleansing or healing, and pilgrimage festivals depended on the temple. So central was the temple that in time pilgrimage would resume without any halakhic basis, that is, without foundation in traditional ritual law; instead it became a mournful occasion to view the ruins of the temple, lament Israel's misfortunes, and recall the glorious days of old.[56]

Without the temple Jewish life as it had been practiced for centuries was unthinkable. In the words of Gedaliah Alon, "Not only did it wipe out a symbol of national pride for Jews at home and abroad and tarnish their image in the eyes of the nations; not only did it shake the very foundations of the Jew's belief in his religion and in the future of [the] people; it cut deeper. It rendered impossible the practice of whole areas of religion, specially in the field of communal ritual. With the altars gone, the nation was confronted by a gaping vacuum, one which generations of survivors had to fill, and fill quickly, if the people as a people was to live on."[57] With unrestrained lamentation and fervent prayers Jews mourned the destruction of Jerusalem, an outpouring of grief that surpassed anything that had been heard in Israel since the capture of the city by the Babylonians in the sixth century.[58]

Among the several lamentations written in the decades after the loss of Jerusalem to the Romans two stand out, 4 Ezra and 2 Baruch. Neither of these works has come down to us in the original language, but even in translations of translations the disconsolate sorrow and deep pathos of the moment reverberate plaintively from their pages. In one of the most poignant passages 4 Ezra tells a parable about the grief of a mother whose son had died on his wedding night. Ezra rebukes the woman for thinking that her personal grief is greater than the lament of God's people: "You most foolish woman, do you not see our mourning, and what has happened to us? For Zion, the mother of us all, is in deep grief and great humiliation. . . . You are sorrowing for one son, but we, the whole world, for our mother" (10:9). The woman responds that she has "lost the fruit of [her] womb," the son whom she "brought forth in pain and bore in sorrow." Ezra tells her to go to her husband in the city and promises that she will receive back her son. But she refuses, and Ezra returns again to the city in mourning: "Our sanctuary has been laid waste, our altar thrown down, our temple destroyed; our harp has been laid low, our song has been silenced and our rejoicing has been ended; the light of our lampstand has been put out, the ark of our covenant has been plundered, our holy things have been polluted" (10:19ff).

Second Baruch, written about the same time as 4 Ezra, in the last decade of the first century, is also a plaintive threnode, and, like 4 Ezra, it presents the destruction of the city at the hands of the Romans under the guise of the capture and pillaging of Jerusalem by the Babylonians in the sixth century. After the captives have been taken into exile Baruch, who has remained in Judea, comes to the front doors of the temple and raises this lament over Zion: "Blessed is he who was not born or he who was born and died. But we, the living, woe to us, because we have seen those afflictions of Zion, and that which has befallen Jerusalem" (10:6–8).

These works echo the sorrow and grief at the time of the destruction of Solomon's temple many centuries earlier. The Lamentation of Jeremiah began, "How lonely sits the city that was full of people! How like a widow has she become, she that was great among the nations. . . . She weeps bitterly in the night, tears on her cheeks. . . . The roads to Zion mourn, for none come to the appointed feasts. . . . From the daughter of Zion has departed all her majesty" (chap. 1). Like the author of Lamentations, the authors of 4 Ezra and 2 Baruch not only mourn the loss of life, the personal suffering of the inhabitants of Jerusalem, and the social consequences of the war, but also recognize "the spiritual significance of the fall of the city."[59] Ezra's catalogue of woes mentions the sanctuary, the altar, the temple, and covenant (10:19–22). Why, the author asks, "has the Law of our fathers been made of no effect and [why do] the written covenants no longer exist?" (4:23–24).

Though the human suffering was great in the sixth century, lamentation was less an occasion to mourn personal loss than it was a public and religious duty. For what was being mourned was not simply a city, but the "loss of the inheritance" (Lam 5:2). In the first century the sentiments are similar: "Those who hate you will come to this place and pollute your sanctuary and carry off your *heritage* into captivity" (2 Bar 5:1). Likewise in the final lines of 4 Ezra, the tragedy is seen as a revocation of the land promise. The land "which was given to you for a possession in the land of Zion" was taken away from you, writes Ezra (14:31).[60]

As Ezra meditates on the events that have overtaken Jerusalem and ponders God's justice and the power of evil in the world, his book begins to sound like an essay on theodicy. Why did God allow wickedness to take root within the heart of human beings? Has the evil begun by Adam become a permanent presence in human life? How can human beings account for such suffering in a world created by a good God? Fourth Ezra is a treatise on the problem of evil, but its questions are prompted by what happened to Zion, the "one region from among all the lands, one lily from all the flowers, one river from all the depths of the sea" (4 Ezra 5:23–28).

Just as Ezra's lamentation was prompted by what happened to Jerusalem, not to humankind in general, so salvation was seen not as the salvation of the world but as the deliverance of Israel. Redemption will take place within the holy land, in the words of Ezra, "in my land and within my holy borders" (9:8, 13:48). Baruch is more explicit: "And the holy land will have mercy on its own and will protect its inhabitants at the time" (71.1).[61] The Land of Israel is the arena of God's activity, both for good and for ill, and in recounting the "bright waters" and the "dark waters" in Israel's past, Baruch makes the ebb and flow of events in the Land the basis of his narration: the conquest of the land, the building of Zion under David and Solomon "when the land received mercy," the time of

Hezekiah when "Zion was saved, Jerusalem delivered from its tribulations and those in the holy land rejoiced," and the reign of the king Josiah, who "purified the land from idols" (chaps. 57–72).[62] The land is the place where God's presence shielded and guided the Jewish people.[63]

Likewise the final redemption will be centered on a city. When the word of the Lord came to Baruch announcing that God will bring evil on the city, Baruch said he did not want to see the "destruction of [his] mother." If the city is destroyed and the land occupied by those who hate Israel, who will speak about God's deeds or hearken to the Law? Baruch, quoting Isaiah, asks, Do you think that this is the city of which God said, "On the palms of my hands I have carved you"? [Isa 49:16]. No, he answers, "it is not this building that is in your midst now; it is that which will be revealed, with me, that was already prepared from the moment that I decided to create Paradise" (2 Bar. 4).

What does Baruch intend by this oracle? One answer is that he despaired of the actual restoration of the city and temple and wished to reorient people's hopes to a heavenly city.[64] But Baruch does not speak of a heavenly city; his term is a "city that has been prepared," a city that has been "made ready." This city, according to Baruch, was built and fashioned by God at the time of creation. It has been in existence "from the moment that [God] decided to create Paradise." In the Mekilta, a midrash on Exodus, the temple is presented in much the same way.[65] It was fashioned by God at creation and existed with God. Later God showed this temple as well as the "order of sacrifices" to Abraham. In 2 Baruch God showed the city to Adam "before he sinned," and later he showed it to Abraham, and even later to Moses on Mount Sinai. The difference between the two cities is that the prepared city was not made by human beings. It was "graven on the palms of [God's] hands," and exists with God.[66]

Without a Jerusalem below there can be no talk of a Jerusalem above. As the Midrash makes clear, God's first and greatest love is the Jerusalem below. For this reason God carved into the palms of his hands another Jerusalem, the Jerusalem above, to insure that the Jerusalem below would never perish. The two Jerusalems are inextricably bound together, as can be seen in another midrash from the third century. The rabbis were puzzled over the meaning of an enigmatic text in Hosea: "I am God and not man, the Holy One in your midst, and I will not come into the city" (Hos 11.9). Does this verse mean, they asked, that because the Holy One is in the midst of the city one cannot enter it? Rabbi Yohanan explained, "The Holy One, blessed be He, said, 'I will not enter the Jerusalem above until I can enter the Jerusalem below. Is there then a Jerusalem above? Yes, for it is written.' Jerusalem, you are builded as a city that is compact together." His interpretation turns on a play on words: the Hebrew for "compact together" is formed from a root that also means "companion."[67] Hence the text from the Psalms means that Jerusalem, the city in Judea, has a companion, a city in the heavens. Neither city exists independently of the other. God will not enter the Jerusalem above until the Jerusalem below is rebuilt.

In some Jewish writings from this period there are intimations that a heavenly Jerusalem would take the place of the earthly Jerusalem.[68] Second Enoch, for example, envisions an inheritance located in an eternal and heavenly world: "I shall go up to heaven to the uppermost Jerusalem to my eternal inheritance,"[69] and the Sibylline Oracles also describe "a great triumphal entry into the heavenly city." But the idiom of Jewish eschatology remained historical and territorial, its apocalyptic and utopian visions merging with the prophetic hope of restoration. In 2 Baruch the city would one day descend to earth in the holy land, the land of the Jewish memory and destiny, and it will be located at the same place where Jerusalem has always stood. In apocalyptic writings from the early Byzantine period and in later midrashim, this scenario is elaborated in greater detail. As one anonymous author put it, "You [God] will make Jerusalem come down from the heavens and you will not destroy it for ever, and Israel's exiles shall enter within her and they shall dwell there in security."[70]

A Very Particular Hope

However one interprets the apocalypses written immediately after the destruction of the Second Temple, the hope of restoration did not die. A messianic movement of exceptional vigor, though limited success, arose that hoped to deliver the land from foreign rule. Emperor Hadrian, who had been governor of Syria under his predecessor Trajan, was born on the western extremity of the empire in Spain, but during his reign he traveled widely in the eastern provinces laying the foundations for buildings and temples, celebrating games, displaying the emblems of Greco-Roman civilization. He was a civilized and intelligent man, a lover of Hellenic culture, gifted in music and the arts. As part of his program to enhance Greek civilization in the eastern lands, he enlarged and remodeled a number of cities in Palestine, including Gaza on the Mediterranean coast and Tiberias on the Sea of Galilee, along the Greek model and laid plans to transform Jerusalem into a Roman colony with a temple to Jupiter Capitolinus to replace the ruined temple of the Jews.

In 131–32 C.E. a revolt broke out among a band of Jews in Palestine led by a man named Simon Bar Kochba. The immediate occasion for the revolt is uncertain, but it seems to have been kindled by Hadrian's plan to build a pagan city on the site of Jewish Jerusalem. Hadrian, writes the Greek historian Dio Cassius, stirred up a war by founding in place of the Jerusalem that had been destroyed a city "named Aelia Capitolina, and by setting up another temple to Jupiter on the site of the Lord's temple, for the Jews thought it an outrage that any foreigners should be made citizens of *their city* and that foreign temples should be set up in it" (*Hist.* 69.12). The revolt quickly won support among some of the Jewish populace, especially in Judea. Bar Kochba, a wily and intelligent leader, practiced a kind of ancient guerrilla warfare, hiding out in abandoned forts and caves, avoiding pitched battles with the Romans, and rallying the populace against the heathen invaders. Bowersock calls him a "pious thug."[71]

According to an ancient tradition within Judaism, the renowned Jewish rabbi Akiva recognized Simon as the Messiah, identifying him with the "star" (*kochba*) in Numbers 24 that would rise up to crush Israel's enemies. "A star [*kochba*] shall come forth out of Jacob, and a scepter shall rise out of Israel; it shall crush the forehead of Moab, and break down all the sons of Seth. Edom shall be disposed, while Israel does valiantly" (Num 24:17–18). Akiva interpreted the word *star* in the text to refer to Bar Kochba, reading it as "Kochba shall come forth out of Jacob." When Rabbi Akiva would see Bar Kochba, he would say, "This is the King Messiah." Rabbi Yohanan B. Torta, however, said, "Akiva, grass will grow between your cheeks and he [the Messiah] still will not have come" (*j. Ta'an.* 4:8;68d). If this tradition that identifies Bar Kochba with the passage from Numbers (which had been interpreted messianically) goes back to Akiva in the second century, writes Peter Schaefer, "one cannot help ascribing to it a politically explosive quality, for it is certainly not a mere academic play on words."[72] For Akiva was not an apocalyptic visionary; he expected a historical redemption and the return of Jews to Jerusalem.

In coins minted during the revolt and in the recently discovered documents, Bar Kochba revived the title *Nasi*, prince or ruler of Israel, a title that is used today for the president of the State of Israel. In the rabbinic period Nasi was the title of the leader of the Jewish people, the patriarch—for example, Judah ha-Nasi—as well as a title for the king who would rule Israel in the messianic age.[73] It is based on Ezekiel 37: "David my servant shall be king [*melek*] over them; and they all shall have one shepherd . . . and they shall dwell in the land that I have given to Jacob my servant in which your fathers have dwelt. . . . And my servant David shall be their prince [*nasi*] forever" (Ezek 37:24–25).

Some of the ancient sources indicate that during the Bar Kochba revolt the Jews occupied Jerusalem, but that is unlikely. "The archaeological evidence, as it stands . . . is not in favour of a Jewish reoccupation of the capital."[74] The revolutionaries did, however, mint coins, some bearing the image of a star and a temple, with the legend FOR THE FREEDOM OF JERUSALEM or YEAR 1 OF THE LIBERATION OF ISRAEL or YEAR 2 OF THE FREEDOM OF ISRAEL. These legends do not, however, imply that the revolutionaries actually took the city; more likely they signify something such as fighting for the "freedom of Jerusalem."[75] They no doubt gained control of sections of Judea, but they did not penetrate into the Galilee or into other parts of Palestine.

The revolt was put down quickly. By 135 C.E. the Romans had hunted down the last of the rebels at Bettir, not far from Jerusalem, and sold many Jews into slavery. To put a definitive end to Jewish hopes about restoration the Romans built a new city named Aelia Capitolina on the site of Jewish Jerusalem. Aelius was Hadrian's family name, and Capitolina, the temple dedicated to the gods of the Mons Capitolium in Rome, was the most sacred shrine in the Roman Empire. The name was still being used in the tenth century, long after the Arab conquest of Jerusalem. A statue to Hadrian was set up on the site of the Jewish temple, but the ruins of the temple were left untouched, a fact that would echo back and forth in Jewish and Christian memory until the arrival of the Muslims in the seventh century, and beyond. Jews came to Jerusalem to mourn the loss of the temple, and Christians made pilgrimage to the site to see proof of the demise of Judaism with their own eyes. Roman desecration of the site of the temple "declared to the world the impotence and rout of Judaism, the Capitol proclaimed the victory of Rome and its gods."[76] Jewish Jerusalem, it seemed, was extinct.

For the Romans Jerusalem had long been displaced by Caesarea as the chief city of Palestine. Formerly Strato's Tower, the city had been rebuilt by Herod the Great on a lavish and opulent scale late in the first century B.C.E. and given a new name, Caesarea. Its natural advantage of being located on the coast was complemented by the construction of a magnificent man-made harbor that was to make the city the commercial and, later, administrative center of the region. Many Jews settled in Caesarea, and during the early centuries of the Roman period it became a more important Jewish center than Jerusalem. By the second century it also had a significant Christian minority, and *its* bishop, not the bishop of Jerusalem, was the metropolitan, the presiding bishop in the region. Only in the fourth century, with the building of Christian Jerusalem, did the ancient holy city of the Jews regain its former glory as the heart of the holy land.

For the Jews, however, Jerusalem lived on not only in memory but also in hope. Among the petitions of the daily prayer recited since antiquity in the synagogue, one is a prayer to God as "the [re]builder of Jerusalem": "Have compassion, O Lord our God, in your abundant mercy, on Israel your people, and on Jerusalem your city, and on Zion, the abode of your glory, and upon the royal seed of David, your justly anointed. Blessed are you, O Lord, God of David, [Re]builder of Jerusalem."[77] From prayers as well as dreams we learn what we lack. After any thought of driving out the Romans had been abandoned, the Jews still clung to their ancient belief that there could be no full and God-pleasing Jewish life without the temple, without the city of Jerusalem, indeed without Jewish hegemony in the land.[78]

The blessing of Abraham had brought forth the dream that it was the destiny of the people of Israel to live securely in the land of Israel under their own rulers. For centuries, though buffeted by bewildering political and cultural changes that had altered the shape of Jewish life, Jews clung to this hope. Now under the new conditions imposed by Roman rule it lived still. Like Aeneas in Virgil's *Aeneid,* the Jews wished to "establish city walls and a way of life" (*Aeneid* 1.264). In time this dream would be challenged anew, not by the swords and spears of Rome (for whom the land was only another territory to be conquered and ruled), but by the ploughshares and pruning hooks of the Christians.

For the Jews redemption could occur only "within my holy borders." The term *holy land* was one way of asserting the territorial dimension of the Jewish tradition. In the Roman world the only people who used the term *holy land* were the Jews, and those who lived alongside of them in the great cities of the Roman Empire knew that this people nurtured a very particular hope. Jews, wrote Tertullian in North Africa at the end of the second century, consider the "special soil of Judea" to be the "holy land [*terra sancta*] itself" (*Res.* 26.10). They believe that their Messiah will come "to regather only the Jewish people from the dispersion," to return them to their "former condition," "restore [their] land," and rebuild the "cities and territories" of Judea as it was described in the prophets (*Marc.* 3.24). The Jews, reports another Christian living in Rome in the third century, live "in hope of a future coming of the Messiah." Their Messiah will be a "king over them, a warlike and powerful man, who will gather the entire nation of the Jews . . . and will establish for them Jerusalem as his royal city . . . and establish the ancient traditions as a nation exercising royal and sacerdotal prerogatives and they will dwell securely for a long time."[79]

3 Blessed Are the Meek for They Shall Possess the Land

Among the chief cities that were the stage for early Christian history—Jerusalem, Antioch, Alexandria, Rome, and Constantinople—only Jerusalem could claim a tangible link to Jesus of Nazareth. As a child Jesus journeyed to Jerusalem on pilgrimage with his parents, and as an adult he was baptized by John in the desert east of Jerusalem, the country of Judea, as it is called by the evangelist Mark (1:5). He spent time with his friends Mary, Martha, and Lazarus in Bethany, a village directly east of the city, and a memorable incident in his ministry, the overturning of the tables of money changers in the temple, took place in Jerusalem. His last days were spent in the city, and, shortly before his arrest, he celebrated Passover there with his disciples. Outside its walls he met his death, and in Jerusalem his followers first gathered to form the Christian church.

For Jesus and his disciples, as for other Jews, the city of Jerusalem and the temple were the most palpable symbols of Jewish life and religion. Jerusalem was the "holy city,"[1] and the account of Jesus' life and ministry presented in the Christian gospels, our chief sources for his life, culminates in Jerusalem. Although Jesus spent most of his years in Galilee and taught in its towns and villages, he believed that his destiny lay in Jerusalem, the only place his mission could be accomplished. When he thought his "time had come" he set his face resolutely toward the city of David and the Hebrew prophets. "Behold we are going up to Jerusalem," he tells his disciples (Mark 10:33). Jesus loved Jerusalem,[2] and even his words of judgment, like the maledictions of the prophets, are edged with compassion and tenderness. "How often would I have gathered your children together as a hen gathers her brood under her wings, and you would not! Behold your house is forsaken and desolate. For I tell you, you will not see me again, until you say, 'Blessed is he who comes in the name of the Lord'" (Matt 23:37–39).

Just as Jesus' mission would reach its fulfillment in Jerusalem, so the final drama of history would take place in the holy city. According to the gospels the catastrophic events that will usher in the end of the age will unfold in Jerusalem and Judea (Matt 24:16 and Luke 21:20). When Jesus told his disciples, as he was eating the Passover meal with them, "Truly, I say to you I shall not drink again of the fruit of the vine until that day when I drink it new in the kingdom of God" (Mark 14:25), they envisioned a kingdom located in Jerusalem.[3] According to the Acts of the apostles, after his resurrection Jesus charged his disciples "not to depart from Jerusalem" (Acts 1:4), and it was there that they awaited his coming. Later when Jesus appeared to them, they asked him, "Lord, will you at this time restore the *kingdom to Israel?*" (Acts 1:6).[4]

As any student of the gospels knows, the phrase "kingdom of God" is the most characteristic mark of Jesus' message. Like every other aspect of Jesus' life and teaching, it has been the object of intensive scrutiny for generations, indeed centuries. More often than not the result of such studies has been to divest the term of its historical and geographical overtones. *Kingdom of God* is thought to refer neither to an event in time nor to a specific place but is seen as a metaphor for a spiritual, and often highly individual, truth.[5] *Kingdom* does not mean kingdom.

What is true of the phrase *kingdom of God* is even more true of the term *land.*[6] This is evident in the translation of the third beatitude in the Gospel of Matthew. The conventional translation is, "Blessed are the meek, for they shall inherit the earth." But the beatitude might be translated, "Blessed are the meek for they shall possess the land." These words, however, grate on the ears like a familiar melody played out of tune. Yet, the term translated as "earth" in the beatitude is the word usually translated as "land" in the phrase "possess the land" elsewhere in the Bible. In the NRSV translation of the psalm on which this beatitude is based, it is translated as "land," not "earth": "but the meek shall possess the *land* and delight themselves in abundant prosperity" (Ps 37:11).[7]

The phrase "inherit the earth" [or possess the land] is the same formula used in the patriarchal narratives to designate the land given to Abraham and his descendants (Gen 15:7): "Behold, I have set the land before you; go in and *take possession of the land* which the Lord swore to your fathers, to Abraham, to Isaac, and to Jacob, to give to them and to their descendants after them" (Deut 1:8). If the word in this phrase is usually translated "land," why should it be translated as "earth" in the beatitude? Has Jesus (or Matthew) emptied the phrase of all of its traditional associations? As the Christian preacher John Chrysostom observed in the fourth century, "What sort of land does he mean? Some say [the term] designates a spiritual land, but we never find the term "land" used [in the Bible] in a "spiritual sense" (*hom.* 15.3 *in Mt.* 5:1–2; *PG* 57, 226c).

Of course translation is interpretation, and the translation "earth" rather than "land" (which is retained in the NRSV) is no doubt intended to help solve the perplexing problems associated with this beatitude.[8] But even if we cannot be certain of its origin, or of its original place in the beatitudes (if any), or of the precise meaning of the term "meek," I suspect that the difficulties presented by this beatitude arise less from these questions than from the implications of translating the term as "land."[9] For in the traditional phrase "possess the land," the term "land" designates a very specific land, the land of Israel. "Possess the land" does not sound like the kind of thing Jesus or early Christians would have said. Hence the beatitude is translated with the anemic and opaque expression "inherit the earth." "Land" is too particular, too territorial, too national, yes, too Jewish. If, however, one interprets Jesus within, rather than against, his Jewish world, the translation "possess the land" merits consideration. As we have seen, it is a recurring refrain in Jewish history, and in Jesus' time it was one way of designating the messianic kingdom centered in Jerusalem. "Inherit the earth" captures neither the spiritual nor the territorial overtones of the phrase.[10]

A Temple Not Made with Human Hands

That Jerusalem was central to Jesus' vision of the future can be glimpsed in two incidents recorded in the gospels: his entry into Jerusalem several days before his death and the overturning of the tables of the money changers in the temple.

Jesus' triumphal entry into Jerusalem took place at the end of his final journey to the city after he had told his disciples that his mission could be fulfilled only there. On arrival at the Mount of Olives overlooking the city, he instructed his disciples to find a colt that would be tied up and bring it to him. When they brought the colt the disciples put their garments on it, and Jesus sat on the animal. Then he went into the city, and, according to Mark, his followers cried out, "Hosanna. Blessed is he who comes in the name of the Lord. Blessed is the *kingdom* of our father David that is coming! Hosanna in the highest" (Mark 11:1–10).

In Matthew and Luke, the words about the kingdom of David are shouted by the crowds as they greet Jesus. But in Mark, the speakers are not so clearly identified. The text simply identifies them as "those who went before and those who followed," which may mean only Jesus' disciples. If it was only the disciples, not the crowds, who made the identification with the restoration of the kingdom of David in Jerusalem, their words may reflect how they understood Jesus' message before the resurrection.

According to the Gospel of Luke, the disciples were discouraged after Jesus' death (the Messiah was not supposed to die) because they had hoped he would be the one to "redeem Israel" (24:21). At the beginning of Acts, shortly before Jesus' departure, the disciples asked, "Lord, will you at this time restore the kingdom to Israel?" And in one of the first Christian sermons, preached in Jerusalem, Peter says that the time had come for the restoration announced by the prophets (Acts 3:21). Hope of restoration and the establishment of a kingdom in Jerusalem were not, it seems, foreign to early Christian tradition. At the very beginning of Luke, when Mary learns that she will give birth to Jesus, the angel says, "He will be great, and will be called the Son of the Most High; and the Lord God will give to him the throne of his father David, and he will reign over the house of Jacob for ever; and of his kingdom there will be no end" (Luke 1:32–33).

Just as a Jew visiting Jerusalem today heads to the Western Wall on arriving in Jerusalem, Jesus made his way to the temple. Once inside the temple, however, he did nothing but "look around at everything," as though he were casing the place, a curious detail that has the ring of authenticity. Jesus already knew what he planned to do, and, before executing his plan, he went to observe the physical arrangement of the site and to discover how to make a swift exit.

The following morning he returned to the temple: "And they went into Jerusalem. And he entered the temple and began to drive out those who sold and those who bought in the temple, and he overturned the tables of the money-changers and the seats of those who sold pigeons; and he would not allow any one to carry anything through the temple. And he taught, and said to them, 'Is it not written, "My house shall be called a house of prayer for all the nations?" But you have made it a den of robbers'" (Mark 11:17).

Jesus' fury at the money changers and pigeon dealers in the courtyard has long puzzled commentators. The incident usually goes by the name the cleansing of the temple, suggesting that the purpose of Jesus' gesture was to purge the temple. What precisely this means is, however, left unclear, and one suspects that behind this interpretation lurk Protestant notions about pure worship unencumbered by external rites. Jesus, writes a prominent New Testament scholar, wished to "restore the temple service to its original purity."[11] But what was this original purity? The temple, like other sanctuaries in antiquity, was and always had been a place for sacrifice, and sacrifice required suitable animals, sheep and birds that were pure and without blemish. If a person brought an animal from home, and, on inspection, it was discovered to have a blemish, it could not be used for sacrifice. Buying and selling of animals made the temple cult possible; without such trade it would have been difficult for the temple to function properly.

The idea that the temple needed to be cleansed (a term that does not occur in the text) may mask a view that finds the very idea of animal sacrifice offensive. Sacrifice however was the business of the temple. E. P. Sanders proposes a more plausible explanation. In his view Jesus had no thought of cleansing the temple; his action was a symbolic gesture signaling a more radical critique.[12] Jesus anticipated a new temple made by God that would come down from the heavens. At Jesus' trial several witnesses were reported to have heard Jesus say, "I will destroy this temple that is made with hands, and in three days I will build another, not made with hands" (Mark 14:57)

Jesus' prophecy about the new temple "not made with hands" as well as his action of overturning the tables of the money changers must be set within the framework of Jesus' message that the kingdom of God was at hand.[13] Immediately before Jesus had entered Jerusalem his disciples greeted him with the words, "Blessed is the kingdom of our father

David." One way of signaling that the kingdom was near and a new temple imminent was to flout the institutions that supported the present temple. Jesus' gesture is without parallel in Jewish antiquity.[14] But the eschatological ideas that supported the gesture do have parallels. Some Jews in this period believed that at the end of days a new and more glorious temple would take the place of the present building. The idea of a new temple was adumbrated in the Temple Scroll. It also appears in an early midrash on the prophecy of Nathan to David in 2 Samuel 7, a prophecy that includes the words "And I will appoint a place for my people Israel, and will plant them, that they may dwell in their own place and be disturbed no more. . . . I will raise up your [David's] offspring after you, who shall come forth from your body, and I will establish his kingdom." The midrash speaks about a future temple as the "house where there shall not enter any one in whose flesh there is a permanent blemish, but only those who hallow God's name and God shall be seen over it continually, and strangers shall not make it desolate again, as they desolated at first the Sanctuary of Israel because of their sins."[15]

According to this midrash, the future house, to be built in the "last days," will be made by God. The temple is a sanctuary which "[God's] hands have established." The author distinguishes between the "sanctuary of Israel" and the future "sanctuary of the Lord." Unlike the present temple the sanctuary of the Lord will endure forever. David Flusser, the Israeli scholar, has noted the parallels between this midrash and the charge that Jesus had prophesied that there would be a new temple "not made with hands" (Mark 14:58). "In both," he writes, "the expectation of a new temple is linked with a negative attitude to the existing sanctuary."[16] In Flusser's view the words of Jesus may belong to a similar tradition of interpretation.

The incident in the temple courtyard is only one event in the life of Jesus. Whether it can serve as the key to unlock the secrets of Jesus' life and ministry is unlikely. Yet, when it is set alongside other passages—for example, his promise that he will not drink wine with his disciples until he drinks it with them in the kingdom of God, the choosing of *twelve* disciples, as well as statements that his disciples expected the restoration of Israel—it helps us to place Jesus' life more firmly within the context of Jewish history. It is most improbable that Jesus' conception of the kingdom of God was wholly divorced from the Jewish hope of the restoration of Jerusalem. As G. B. Caird reminds us in his little-read essay "Jesus and the Jewish Nation," "The Gospels contain a very large amount of material which links the ministry and teaching of Jesus with the history, expectations and destiny of the Jewish nation."[17]

Within the framework of Jewish tradition, the phrase *possess the land* was emblazoned on a restorationist banner. It hearkened back to the covenant with Abraham and looked forward to the establishment of a new Jerusalem. Much that one would expect to find in a prophet of restoration is absent from Jesus' teaching. He neither calls for "national repentance" nor urges a return to the observance of the Law.[18] Jerusalem, however, was part of his eschatological vision, and he anticipated the day the city would welcome him, not with stones, but with blessings: "Jerusalem, Jerusalem," he said, "I tell you, you will not *see me again* until you say, 'Blessed is he who comes in the name of the Lord'" (Matt 23:39).

Entering into the Promised Rest

The only book of the New Testament that gives a prominent place to the promise of the land is the book of Hebrews.[19] Its author coined the phrase "promised land" (or "land of promise" as it occurs in Greek [Heb 11:9]), a phrase which is not found in the Hebrew Bible or in its Greek translation. Further, Hebrews is the only early Christian writing (except for Acts, and that only in a citation from Isaiah) that uses the old term "rest" to designate the land promised to the Israelites (Heb 3:11, 18, chap. 4 passim).

In later Christian tradition the passage about the "heavenly Jerusalem" in Hebrews 12 became one of the building blocks of a "spiritual" eschatology. As we shall see in the next chapter, this text, along with Galatians 4, was used by Origen and other Christian thinkers to defend the belief that after death Christians were destined to live in a heavenly city. But the eschatology of the book of Hebrews is not confined to chapters 11 and 12, the passages most cited by later Christian interpreters. A narrow preoccupation with these chapters deflects attention away from the rest of the epistle. In Hebrews, the promised inheritance is not simply part of the final chapters; it is one of the primary themes of the epistle as a whole. The book of Hebrews is the first systematic effort by a Christian to interpret the land tradition in light of the new circumstances that came into being after the death and resurrection of Christ.

The theme of inheritance is announced at the very beginning of the book of Hebrews. In days of old God spoke through the prophets but "in these last days" he has spoken by a Son whom he has made an "heir." His disciples will "*inherit* salvation" (1:14). The nature of the inheritance is at first left undefined; later in the epistle, however, the author says that what is inherited are the "promises" (6:12; also 6:19), and immediately he explains what he means by promise. *Promise* refers to the "promise to Abraham" (6:13) that his seed would be multiplied. Once the author of

Hebrews has introduced Abraham and his descendants, he turns to Moses and the Exodus and then, significantly, to Joshua, who was to bring the people to their promised "rest" (Heb. 4.8).[20] The term *rest* is a reference to the land of Canaan and is a synonym for inheritance of the land in the book of Deuteronomy: "You have not as yet come to the *rest* and to the *inheritance* which the Lord your God gives you. But when you go over the Jordan, and live in the land which the Lord your God gives you to possess . . ." (Deut 12:9–10). *Rest* had very concrete associations.[21]

The book of Hebrews has been read as an effort to transform the land promise, the promise of rest, into a spiritual concept that has no relation to the actual land of Canaan. In the book of Hebrews, writes one commentator, "the earthly Canaan has . . . absolutely no meaning."[22] Hebrews 4 was intended, writes another, "to prove that the rest is no longer Canaan but heaven."[23] There is of course some basis for this line of interpretation within the text of Hebrews. The "promised inheritance" belongs to a "new covenant" that is "eternal" (9:15). Its mark is the forgiveness of sins, obtained not through the offering of the blood of animals, but through the blood of Christ, who entered "not into a sanctuary made with hands, a copy of the true one, but into heaven itself" (9:24). But phrases such as "in heaven" have to be read in conjunction with other statements in the book. "Heavenly" does not of necessity designate a supernal realm. The "heavenly gift," for example, is something believers taste in this world (6:5). "Heavenly" and "eternal" (13:20) bear the sense of sure and certain, permanent and abiding, not otherworldly. In the second century, Justin Martyr contrasted the "temporary inheritance" obtained by Joshua with the "eternal possession" won by Christ (*dial.* 113), yet he had in mind an inheritance on earth.

According to Hebrews the promise to enter into the rest was still a thing of the future. Hence the author urges his readers to be firm in faith and patient in endurance, not to lose hope as they await the day they would receive a "better possession and an abiding one." After a "little while," he says, you will "receive what is promised" (10:36). By faith Abraham obeyed and went out "not knowing where he was to go. By faith he sojourned in the 'land of promise,' as in a foreign land, living in tents with Isaac and Jacob, heirs with him of the same promise" (11:9). For the first time in the Scriptures, the land is called the promised land. Yet in the very same sentence in which the term *land of promise* occurs, Hebrews seems to demote the land itself. Living in the land of promise is portrayed as "sojourning in a foreign land," a land where Abraham was unable to enjoy the rest he had hoped for. To emphasize the transitory character of the sojourn there he says that Abraham and Isaac and Jacob, all "heirs of the same promise," lived in tents. The text does not, however, say that the promised land was a *different* land from the one Abraham came to and lived in. Rather it states that while living there Abraham and his family did not find the stability and security they had hoped for. The promised land had not yet fulfilled its promise. They did not, in the language of chapter 4, find rest.[24]

At this point Hebrews breaks off the catalogue of heroes of faith (before Abraham the author had mentioned Abel, Enoch, and Noah) with a digression describing the inheritance for which they hoped. Abraham and others who died in faith did not receive "what was promised"; they only "greeted it from afar" for they were "strangers and exiles on the land [earth]." They were seeking a "fatherland," or in the translation of the RSV "homeland." Tempting as it is to take "homeland" to mean *a* land *other* than the land of Canaan, the author of Hebrews contrasts the homeland not with Canaan, but with the land Abraham had left. "If they had been thinking of that land from which they had gone out, they would have had opportunity to return" (11:15). The distinction he draws is between the land of promise, which is Canaan, and the land they left, Mesopotamia. "But as it is, they desire a *better* country, that is, a heavenly one." Better than what? Better than the country they left. There is no hint of a third country, that is, a country other than the land which Abraham left and the one in which he sojourned. One would not go far wrong to translate, "They desired a better land, a *holy land*" instead of a "better land, a heavenly one." They sought a good and pleasant land, a land blessed by God's goodness and bounty, where God would give peace and security, a land in which they would find rest. They desired a land to call their own, where they could settle and enjoy freedom from harm, where God could be called "their God," and they would have an abiding city. "Therefore God is not ashamed to be called their God, for he has prepared for them a city" (11:16).

Twice in this passage the author of Hebrews mentions a city. In each case the city is a symbol of permanence and security. It is a city with "foundations," and its "builder and maker is God." This city can only be Jerusalem. Like the city depicted in 2 Baruch and 4 Ezra, it is a "prepared city" (11:16), a city constructed by God. Many commentators, however, have taken the city to be a metaphor for a celestial city. One writes, "For the writer of Hebrews the 'city' of Abraham was clearly heaven itself."[25] But it is possible that the author has in mind a city that had been prepared beforehand by God, a city that one day would be unveiled and would majestically come down from the heavens to its resting place in the promised land.[26]

At the end of the roll call of heroes, the author of Hebrews comes finally to Jesus, the "pioneer and perfecter of our faith." And once again his discussion leads him back to the city, this time called Mount Zion to distinguish it from Mount Horeb, the place where the Torah was given: "You *have come* to Mount Zion and to the city of the living God, the heavenly Jerusalem." Jerusalem here designates less a future hope than a present reality. The author of Hebrews has begun to identify the "heavenly Jerusalem" with the new community that had come into being through the death of Christ, who, according to Hebrews, is the "mediator of a new covenant . . . that speaks more graciously than the blood of Abel" (12:24).

In the final chapter of the book, however, the city becomes a symbol of future hope.[27] "For here we have no lasting city, but we seek the city which is to come." Whatever fulfillment has already taken place in the gathering of the "first born" is not complete; there will be a more enduring city. The author has returned to the theme of chapter 11: Abraham was looking forward to a city that had "foundations" and whose "builder and maker was God."

The Land Promise and Early Christian Chiliasm

The book of Hebrews is elusive. It is easy to see how it provided warrant for a spiritual eschatology centered on a celestial city. Yet the prominence it gives to the promise of the land suggests that Jerusalem was more than a symbol of something else. That is the case for the other book of the New Testament that gives a large place to Jerusalem in its vision of the future: the Apocalypse, the Revelation to St. John, the final book in the Christian Scriptures. To this day it is one of the most popular books of the New Testament, yet from earliest times a cloud of suspicion has hovered over it. For Revelation envisions a future earthly city of Jerusalem, a golden and jeweled city, a "new Jerusalem coming down out of heaven from God" (Rev 21.2). In this city God will dwell and his people will suffer no harm. "He will wipe away every tear from their eyes, and death shall be no more, neither shall there be mourning nor crying nor pain any more" (21.4). As in the city of Ezekiel, out of this new Jerusalem will flow a river of living water and on its bank will grow all kinds of trees yielding twelve kinds of fruit, one each month. Unlike Ezekiel's city, however, this city will have no temple, for "its temple is the Lord God the

Almighty and the Lamb" (21.22). By its light will the nations walk and the city will need no light or lamp "for the Lord God will be their light, and they shall reign for ever and ever" (22.5).[28]

The Apocalypse is a vivid testimony to the perseverance of Jewish restorationist hopes within early Christianity. To be sure, the book of Revelation transforms these hopes in light of the reality of Christ. It begins with a vision of the glorified Christ "whose face was like the sun shining in full strength" (1.16), and its great theme is the victory of the Lamb of God (Christ) over the power of Satan and the forces of evil. Yet there can be no doubt that Revelation stands firmly within the restorationist tradition discussed in chapter 2; and its eschatology cannot be dismissed as a deviant tributary that wanders from the mainstream of early Christian hopes. The best-documented and most persistent eschatology in the first two Christian centuries was chiliasm, the belief that God would establish a future kingdom on earth centered in Jerusalem. The term *chiliasm* comes from the Greek word for "thousand" (*chilias*) and refers to the belief, first stated in the book of Revelation, that Christ would one day return to rule on earth for a period of a thousand years before the heavenly Jerusalem comes down from the heavens (Rev. 21).[29]

The Apocalypse is only one form of this tradition, however, and an idiosyncratic one at that. For the distinctive mark of the chiliastic tradition is not the idea of a thousand-year reign, but the belief that Christian hope is centered on a glorified Jerusalem that will come down from the heavens. The most articulate spokesmen for chiliasm in early Christianity were two outstanding Christian intellectuals, the philosopher Justin Martyr, who lived in the middle of the second century, and Irenaeus, bishop of Lyons in Gaul a generation later. Although Justin and Irenaeus knew the book of Revelation, their views of Jerusalem and the land promise go back to traditions that were formed independently of it.[30] The justification they give for their views rests on passages from the prophets about the restoration of Jerusalem, on sayings of Jesus about the future Jerusalem, and on the writings of Paul.

Justin was born early in the second century in Flavia Neapolis in Palestine, ancient Shechem (present-day Nablus), on the West Bank of the Jordan. In Christian history he is celebrated as a martyr and esteemed as an apologist who defended Christianity against its cultured critics. He was the first Christian thinker to write a book dealing specifically with the relation between Christianity and Judaism. This work, the *Dialogue with Trypho,* is an account of Justin's conversion to Christianity followed by a debate between Justin and a rabbi named Trypho (possibly Tarphon).[31] It is a long, leaden book, but it shows us what criticisms Jews brought against Christians, how Christians defended themselves, and what passages from the Septuagint were part of the debate. The discussion took place in Ephesus, where Trypho, according to Justin, had fled from Palestine at the time of the Bar Kochba revolt. As one would expect, the future of Jerusalem is one of the topics of discussion.

The Jew, Trypho, addresses Justin: "I realize, my friend, that you wish to be certain in all things by holding fast to the Scriptures. Tell me, then, do you really believe that this place Jerusalem will be rebuilt, and do you expect that your people will be gathered together and rejoice with the Messiah, with the patriarchs and the prophets, with the saints of our nation and those who have become proselytes before your Messiah came? Or have you simply acknowledged these things in order that you might seem to win the argument?" (*dial.* 80). As posed by Trypho, the question betrays some Christian editing, but the question itself is thoroughly Jewish.

Justin answers as follows: "I am not so devious a fellow, Trypho, that I say one thing and think another. I acknowledged to you previously that I and many others are of this opinion, and as you well realize, we believe that these things will take place." Where in the *Dialogue* Justin had discussed this point is uncertain, but near the beginning Trypho had asked Justin whether the Jews will "*inherit* [or possess] anything on the holy mountain of God" (*dial.* 25.6). It is not, however, until Trypho asks him directly about the rebuilding of Jerusalem that Justin states his views on the city's future. Expanding on his initial reply to Trypho Justin explains, "I and others who are 'right-thinking' Christians on all points are convinced that there will be a resurrection of the dead and a thousand year [period] in which Jerusalem will be [re]built, adorned and enlarged, as the prophets Ezekiel and Isaiah and others declare" (*dial.* 80.5).[32]

Elsewhere in the *Dialogue with Trypho* Justin mentions the promise of the land, and there, for the first time in Christian literature, the term *holy land* occurs. The passage deals with the conquest and allotment of the land under Joshua. Joshua (whose name in Greek was Jesus) had been appointed successor to Moses, writes Justin, and it was Joshua, not Moses, who led the people "into the holy land" and distributed it by lot to those who went with him. Likewise "Jesus the Christ will turn again the dispersion of the people and distribute the good land to each though not in the same way. For the former who was neither Christ nor the son of God gave them a temporary possession; but the latter after the holy Resurrection will give us an eternal possession." In Christ, God will "renew both the heaven and the earth and will cause an eternal light to shine in Jerusalem" (*dial.* 113.3–5). Just as Joshua once divided the land among the people, so the new Joshua, Jesus, will also distribute the land to his people.

Several chapters later Justin uses the term *holy land* in a similar context. In this passage he cites Zechariah 2:15 (LXX), the verse immediately before the passage in which Zechariah calls Judea and Jerusalem "holy land" (*dial.* 119). What interests Justin in this passage is the phrase "Many nations will flee for protection to the Lord and they will become to him a people." He wishes to show that the inheritance promised to Abraham will not be the possession of the Jews alone but will extend to all nations. According to the Scriptures Abraham will be the father of many nations, and with Abraham "we," writes Justin, "will inherit the *holy land* when we receive the *inheritance* for an infinite age, being children of Abraham on account of the same faith" (119.5). It is tempting to read this passage as an allegorical interpretation of the land promise. According to Justin, Abraham's departure from his homeland is not only the beginning of a journey to another land, it is also a spiritual transformation. As he leaves his former land he rids himself of his former way of life. Yet there is no hint in Justin that Abraham's goal is purely spiritual. The land itself is not allegorized. In every passage in which the term occurs in the *Dialogue* it refers to the actual land.[33]

Justin has a very particular and concrete sense of inheritance of the land. For Justin, Christian hope was centered on the establishment in Jerusalem of an "everlasting and imperishable kingdom" (*dial.* 117.3). Christians, the *spiritual* descendants of Abraham, are in fact "Israel," a claim that Trypho treats with disbelief. Justin had cited Ezekiel: "And I will beget people upon you, even my people Israel; and they shall possess you, and you shall be their inheritance." When Trypho heard these words he replied with astonishment, "What is this? Are *you* Israel? Does the prophet say such things about *you*?" (*dial.* 123.7). Justin answers this question in the affirmative, as he had Trypho's initial question concerning the rebuilding of Jerusalem.

The term *holy land,* then, enters the Christian vocabulary in the context of eschatology.[34] Within Jewish tradition eschatology and restoration were almost synonymous, and for Justin eschatology meant a future rebuilding of Jerusalem at the return of Christ. Christian hopes for the future were rooted in the land promise to Abraham and in the words of the prophets about the glorification of Jerusalem. To be sure, the hope of restoration was modified in light of the Resurrection of Jesus; there would be no temple in the restored Jerusalem. Yet Christian eschatology remained wedded to the earth, retaining the realistic features of the restorationist tradition. As Irenaeus would insist, the new Jerusalem would be located "under heaven."

The Promise to Abraham and Christian Eschatology

Irenaeus was born early in the second century in western Asia Minor, perhaps in the coastal city of Smyrna, modern-day Izmir.[35] As a young man, he had known Polycarp, a leading Christian teacher from the region who was old enough to serve as a direct link, if not to the first, at least to the second generation of Christians. Irenaeus also knew Papias, bishop of Hierapolis in Asia Minor, who was a companion of Polycarp and a disciple of a certain John. Papias, who was Polycarp's elder, claims to have received sayings of Jesus by word of mouth (*haer.* 5.33.4). After spending his youth in Asia Minor Irenaeus traveled to Rome, which, by the middle of the second century, had become a center of Christian intellectual life, a city in which teachers from all over the Roman world jostled for recognition. From Rome he moved to Gaul, where he became presbyter, and later bishop, of Lyons, a thriving city with a small Christian community. Though Irenaeus had lived and studied in Rome and had contact with the new theological ideas being forged in that city, on other matters he was traditional. He defended, for example, the old custom of celebrating Easter on the date of the Jewish Passover, 14 Nisan, whichever day of the week it fell, against the dictates of Victor the bishop of Rome (*h.e.* 5.23–25).

In the history of Christianity Irenaeus is celebrated as the premier opponent of Gnosticism. His work *Adversus Haereses* is a profound and detailed refutation of Gnosticism on the basis of the Scriptures and the core beliefs of the Christian movement, some of which receive their earliest formulation in his book. In the second century Irenaeus was the most articulate spokesman for Christian orthodoxy. In response to the Gnostic denigration of the material world, he argued that the supreme and transcendent God not only created the world of space and time, but also redeemed it through the life and career of an actual human being who was born of a woman at Bethlehem and lived a full human life like other human beings. In Christ God restored all things. Irenaeus's term for the process of restoration and renewal is "recapitulation," by which he means that Christ perfects humankind in God's image and likeness (*haer.* 3.16.6; 3.22.4).

As the final act in the process of recapitulation, Christ will establish a kingdom on earth. Only if the saints triumph within the same world in which they suffered will the restoration be complete and perfect and God will be "all in all" (1 Cor 15:28). Without such a "realistic" ending, that is, one that takes place on this earth, redemption can only be partial, unfinished. For if the saints do not rule over the powers that tyrannized them, restoration would be only spiritual and the saints would remain in servitude. It was therefore fitting, says Irenaeus, that "in the condition [that is, in the created world] in which they endured servitude, they should rule" (*haer.* 5.32.1). On that day all things will be restored to their original state and creation will be wholly subject to God and the rule of the righteous. For Irenaeus the establishment of an earthly kingdom is not an ornament in his theory of restoration, like a bright border that adorns a coat; it is an integral part of the garment of recapitulation itself.[36]

It is generally recognized that Irenaeus took the term *recapitulation* from Ephesians and developed his conception on the basis of the parallelism between Adam and Christ. What is not widely recognized is that he roots the original promise of restoration in the blessing of Abraham. With the coming of Christ, he writes, the "promise which God gave to Abraham . . . remains firm." At the very beginning of the biblical history, God told Abraham to lift up his eyes and look at the "land I will give to you and to your seed" (Gen 13:14–17). And again he told Abraham to go through the length and breadth of the "land I will give to you." With these words God promised Abraham the inheritance of the land, says Irenaeus. Abraham, however, did not receive the promise because he lived as a "stranger and a pilgrim" in the land, waiting patiently for its fulfillment. It was only among his descendants, "those who fear God and believe in Him," that the promise would be fulfilled (*haer.* 5.32.2).

Following Paul (Gal 3:6–9) Irenaeus says that the inheritors now include gentiles as well as Jews, that is, the land promise now extends to all who believe in God, not just to Israel "according to the flesh." But (and this is the key point) the promise itself is not spiritualized; its fulfillment will take place on earth. God said to Abraham, "I will give this land to your seed, from the river of Egypt to the great river Euphrates" (Gen 15). For this reason, continues Irenaeus, the Savior said, "Blessed are the meek for they will receive the land as an inheritance." In order to announce the "opening of the inheritance," the Lord also said to his disciples before his passion, "Drink of it, all of you; for this is my blood of the new covenant, which is poured out for many for the forgiveness of sins. I tell you I shall not drink again of this fruit of the vine until that day when I drink it new with you in my father's kingdom" (Matt 26:27–29).

In Irenaeus the land promise remains earthbound. "Without doubt," he writes, "when Christ speaks of drinking the fruit of the vine in the kingdom he is speaking of the inheritance of the land that he will renew and restore" (*haer.* 5.33.1). In his view Jerusalem remains Jerusalem, not a symbol, though "land" is extended beyond the land of Israel to embrace the earth as a whole.[37] Irenaeus cites, for example, a passage from the Psalms, "He who has renewed the face of the earth [land]" (Ps 104:30). This psalm, he says, has reference to the inheritance of the land and a "physical resurrection." It should not be understood to designate a "place above the heavens," for when Jesus speaks of drinking of the vine in the kingdom he means actually drinking, not a spiritual drinking "outside of the flesh" (*haer.* 5.33.1)

Irenaeus's conception of the kingdom of God has been formed by the Jewish restorationist tradition, as reinterpreted by Christians. He trots out a string of passages from the prophets that speak of the promise of the land, the return of the exiles, and the restoration of Jerusalem, some of which were used by Jews in the period of the Second Temple to sustain hope in a future restoration. He cites Ezekiel 37, "I will open your tombs and bring you forth out of your graves. . . . and I will place you in *your own land*" and "I will gather Israel from all nations . . . and they will dwell in *their own land*" (Ezek 37:12, 38:25, the latter a passage that is alluded to in the Temple Scroll in connection with the kingdom in the land).[38] He also cites a number of prophecies about Jerusalem, most notably the passage about the rebuilding of the city with gold and jewels (Isa 54:11–14) that is cited in the eschatological passage in Tobit (chap. 14) and will reappear later in Jewish apocalyptic texts.[39]

Some Christians (he has in mind the Gnostics) had interpreted the prophecies spiritually,[40] but Irenaeus explicitly rejects such a view. Pointedly he says, "If some are tempted to allegorize passages of this kind [about the rebuilding of Jerusalem, Isa 54:11–14 or 65:18] they will not be found consistent with the texts and will be refuted by the meaning of the words themselves" (*haer.* 5.35.1). In support he cites Baruch's word (5:3) that God's glory will be seen "under heaven."[41] But even more striking, he appeals to the words of Paul in Galatians 4: "The Jerusalem above is the mother of us all." According to Irenaeus, Paul meant that the Jerusalem below will be "rebuilt after the pattern of the Jerusalem above" (*haer.* 5.35.2).[42] He also cites the passage in Revelation 21 that the "holy city, the new Jerusalem" would one day come down from the heavens as a bride adorned for her husband. For Irenaeus Christian hope was fixed on a future Jerusalem located on this earth,[43] though it should be said that he is thinking of Jerusalem in eschatological rather than political terms.

It is a misnomer to label this belief chiliasm. A thousand-year reign was peripheral to the eschatology of Justin and Irenaeus. The term *chiliasm* implies that their views differ from other, presumably more orthodox forms of Christian eschatology. But Justin and Irenaeus were the voices of orthodoxy in the second century. On the basis of the sources that are extant they represent the great trunk of Christian tradition. Both Irenaeus and Justin were acute critics of deviant forms of Christian belief and practice, particularly of the Gnostics. Justin, according to the French scholar Le Boulluec, was the inventor of the Christian idea of heresy,[44] and he wrote a book "against all heresies." Not only do Irenaeus and Justin defend the Christian creed against any distortions, they also reproach as tendentious any spiritual eschatology. Irenaeus viewed with disdain those who allegorized the words of the prophets concerning Jerusalem. More magnanimous, Justin admits that there are "many who think otherwise," but "right-minded Christians" believe that Jerusalem will be rebuilt and enlarged.

Jerusalem, the Place of Jesus' Death and Resurrection

No matter how far back one can trace the eschatological hope of an earthly kingdom in Jersualem, chiliasm was not the way of the future. As we shall see in later chapters, chiliastic views persisted well into the fifth century (and have flourished in many periods in Christian history, including the present), but Christian devotion to Jerusalem, and with it the idea of a Christian holy land, was not to be grounded in the ancient promise of the land and the hope of restoration of Jerusalem. Although the term *holy land* was used by Justin, it did not take root among Christians in this period. It would be many centuries before Christians claimed it as their own.

There was, however, one fact about Jerusalem that was intractable: the chief events in Christ's life had taken place in the city and its environs. From the very beginning Christian belief was oriented to these events, to what *happened* to Jesus, not simply to his preaching of the coming kingdom of God. "For I delivered to you as of first importance," wrote St. Paul, "what I also received, that Christ died for our sins in accordance with the scriptures, that he was buried, that he was raised on the third day in accordance with the scriptures, and that he appeared to Cephas, then to the twelve" (1 Cor 15). Events take place in space as well as in time, and these events, what later tradition called the sacred mysteries, took place *in Jerusalem* or directly outside of the city. Jesus was buried in Jerusalem in a tomb close to the place of his crucifixion. These topographical facts embedded themselves deep within the Christian memory, so much that in the second century a Christian bishop would say that Jesus was crucified "in the middle of Jerusalem."[45] *Where* Jesus suffered and died and was buried helped to impose order on the memory of his life and laid a foundation for the sanctification of place.

When St. Paul says that "in the fullness of time" God sent forth his son "born of woman" he does not mention Bethlehem, yet from earliest times the place of Jesus' birth from Mary was not simply remembered, it was celebrated. In the Gospel of Matthew, when Herod asked where Christ was to be born, he was told, "In Bethlehem of Judea for so it is written by the prophet: 'And you, O Bethlehem, in the land of Judah, are by no means least among the rulers of Judah; for from you shall come a ruler who will govern my people Israel" (Matt 2:5–6). There is a "fullness of place" as well as of time. Few Christians could hear the story of Joseph going up "into Judea, unto the city of David, which is called Bethlehem" without wanting to see the scene of these wondrous happenings. Among all the hidden corners of the earth God has chosen to appear in Bethlehem of Judea. As early as the second century there are reports that Christians had begun to visit the "cave" in Bethlehem where Christ was born.[46]

The Christian church had its beginnings in the city of Jerusalem. In the book of Acts, the earliest narrative account of Christian origins, it is reported that Jesus' disciples and Mary and other women who were his followers gathered in a room in Jerusalem after his death. As they were offering prayers to God, the Holy Spirit descended on them like a rushing wind. Filled with the Spirit Peter went out into the streets and preached to the "inhabitants of Judea and all who dwell in Jerusalem." From this time there was a Christian community in Judea and Jerusalem, as the letters of Paul, written a generation earlier, confirm. Several times he mentions the church in Jerusalem and at one point refers to the "churches of Christ in Judea" (Gal 1:22). In Jerusalem the first Christian martyr, Stephen, met his death, and in the fourth century a great church was built in Jerusalem outside the Damascus gate to house his relics and honor his memory. The church in Jerusalem was a living link to the events that gave rise to the Christian faith and to those who had witnessed them. Only Christians living in Jerusalem could say that these things have been accomplished "among us."[47]

For the Christian holy land, memory will be a more potent force than hope. Yet had there not been hope and expectation centered on the restoration and renewal of Jerusalem, there would have been no message about the coming kingdom of God and no framework in which to view the life of Jesus and the beginnings of the Christian church. There would have been no claim of a singular birth in Bethlehem, the city of David, or of a "saving history" in Jerusalem the city of Jewish kings and prophets, or a community living "at the end of the age." But before pursuing the sanctification of place in early Christianity, I must look further at the chiliastic tradition or, more accurately, at its critics. For though chiliasm had deep roots within Christianity, it had manifest limitations. Only during the lifetime of Origen of Alexandria did these deficiencies become apparent.

4 Heavenly Jerusalem, the Mother of Us All

However tenaciously some had clung to the hope that Jerusalem would be restored in the holy land, when mighty Origen strode confidently into the arena of Christian debate in the third century, its adherents were forced to give way. With customary aplomb he wrote, "I plan to dispel the mistaken notion that the sayings about a good land promised by God to the righteous have reference to the land of Judea" (*Cels.* 7:28). Earlier in the century, Tertullian, the first Christian to write in Latin, and himself a chiliast, had eschewed the idea that the "soil of Judea" was the "holy land" (*res.* 26).[1] But it was Origen who laid to rest the dreams of an earthly kingdom.[2]

To his critics, Origen appeared to be more a Greek philosopher than a Christian intellectual; he wore only a veneer of Christian wisdom, playing the Greek, as the philosopher Porphyry put it (*h.e.* 6.19.7). However, on the topic of the holy land, as in so many others, Origen penetrated more deeply into the mind of the Scriptures than other Christians of his time. In his view, chiliasm compromised Christian messianism.

Among all the early Christian writers in the East Origen possessed the most fertile mind. According to Jerome he was the greatest teacher of the church after the apostles. His bold and audacious intelligence stretched Christian truth far beyond the horizons of its more pedestrian exponents. "God would never have implanted in our minds the love of truth if it were never to have an opportunity for satisfaction," he wrote (*princ.* 2.11.4). So daring were some of his speculations that a later generation of Christians condemned him as a heretic, depriving him of the honorific title St. Origen. Even today some deny him a place among the early teachers of the church.[3] Yet his ideas were enthusiastically embraced by Christians of every stripe in the generations and centuries that followed, and his style of biblical interpretation shaped all exegesis of the Scriptures for the next several hundred years.

Origen was born into a Christian family in Alexandria on the coast of Egypt at the end of the second century (ca. 185 C.E.).[4] He spent most of his youth and early manhood in his native city. A student of Clement of Alexandria, the urbane and learned Christian philosopher who presided over a private school in the city, Origen later headed up a "catechetical school" under the supervision of the bishop. During these years he traveled widely across the Christian world, to Rome in the West and Arabia in the East, and he studied pagan philosophy under the distinguished scholar Ammonius Saccas.

Origen, however, produced his most mature works in Caesarea, the famed coastal city in Palestine. That he chose to live in Caesarea rather than in Jerusalem is not surprising. Caesarea was the premier city in Palestine, capital of the Roman province of Syria Palestina, a city of refinement and learning.[5] It was called the daughter of Edom, that is, the daughter of Rome, by Jews. Like Alexandria it was thoroughly hellenized in its customs and culture. Its bishop was metropolitan of Palestine, an honor the bishop of Caesarea enjoyed until the see of Jerusalem was elevated to the status of a patriarchate at the Council of Chalcedon in 451 C.E. Jerusalem lay well off the main roads, far from the Mediterranean coast and Caesarea's spacious harbor, and it possessed neither the intellectual vitality nor the libraries that Origen required for his teaching and scholarship. Jerusalem had not yet acquired its aura of sanctity as the place of Jesus' death and Resurrection.

After a squabble with his bishop, Demetrius, in Alexandria, Origen was warmly received by Theoctistus, the bishop of Caesarea. His reputation as a teacher and scholar had preceded him, and Theoctistus invited him to preach in his church even though he was not ordained. Demetrius protested that "such a thing had never been heard of . . . that laymen should preach in the presence of bishops" (*h.e.* 6.19–18). On his first visit to Caesarea Origen remained only a short time, but several years later, on a return visit, he was ordained to the presbyterate (priesthood) by Theoctistus. Two years later (234 C.E.) he moved permanently to Caesarea. During the next two decades Origen established a Christian school in the city, and under the patronage of wealthy Christians he gathered a collection of books that would become (with the help of Eusebius, bishop of Caesarea, later in the century) the most famous Christian library in antiquity. From all over the Mediterranean world students journeyed to Caesarea to listen to his lectures and to learn to "practice virtue." As one admiring disciple observed, "He incited us more by what he did than by what he said."[6]

In Alexandria Origen had known Jewish thinkers, but Caesarea placed him closer to the center of Jewish intellectual life. In Caesarea he became acquainted with Jewish traditions of biblical interpretation and studied Hebrew under the direction of a Jew,[7] visited Jewish synagogues, and disputed with Jewish teachers.[8] Among the topics he discussed were the interpretation of Jerusalem in the Scriptures and the meaning of the biblical promises about the land. These disputes led him to formulate a Christian conception of the holy land that would set the direction of Christian thought on the topic for the next several centuries.

Political and Spiritual Exegesis of the Bible

More than any other Christian scholar in this period, Origen's intellectual enterprise was devoted to the interpretation of the Bible. Besides writing books on the Christian New Testament, for example, the Gospels of Matthew and John and the Epistle to the Romans, among others, he wrote a major commentary on the book of Genesis in thirteen books, a commentary on Isaiah in thirty books, another on Ezekiel in twenty-five books, as well as works on the Psalms, Lamentations, the Song of Songs, the books of Kings, Job, and others. He also preached on many other books of the Jewish Bible, submitting himself to the demanding discipline of expounding the biblical text verse by verse within the context of Christian worship.[9]

As a Christian interpreter of the "Jewish Scriptures"[10] Origen was presented with the challenge of finding spiritual significance for Christians in a book whose central theme was the relation of God to the people of Israel. Origen's assignment was made more difficult because the Septuagint, the Jewish Bible read by Christians, was a translation from the Hebrew made by Jews, and only in the synagogues could one find copies of the original Hebrew text. In a profound sense, Christians were dependent on the Jews for the book they now claimed as their own. "I have made it my business," Origen said, "to be informed on their various readings lest in controversies with the Jews I should quote to them what is not found in their versions" (*ep.* 1.5). Even though the Jews in Caesarea spoke Greek and used Greek in the synagogue,[11] Hebrew was still a living language that gave its speakers insight into the meaning of the biblical text as well as access to the traditions of interpretation that were handed on in Jewish communities. In Christian worship it may have been acceptable to read the Bible in Greek, but in discussions with Jews, arguments based solely on a translation put the Christian interpreter at a distinct disadvantage. It could be likened, I suppose, to an American scholar living in Germany who knows only English, yet claims to understand Goethe's Faust better than native-speaking German scholars.

Origen had begun to turn his energies to the interpretation of the Septuagint before arriving in Caesarea. In a work published shortly before he left Alexandria, *First Principles,* he surveyed the fundamental points of Christian teaching, setting forth those doctrines on which Christians agreed, calling attention to those about which there were honest differences of opinion. The final section of the book is devoted to matters of biblical interpretation,[12] and judging from what he says here as well as from his practice of exegesis in his homilies and commentaries, Jewish interpretations were very much on his mind as he went about his work.[13] What, for example, asks Origen, is one to make of the halakhic sections (matters of ritual law) of the Pentateuch? How are Christians to interpret the laws on sacrifices, the command to observe the sabbath, and other obligations prescribed by the Law of Moses? "What need is there to read these things in the churches?" he asks (*hom. 7.1 in Num.*).

According to the Scriptures the laws given by Moses were divine commands to be observed in perpetuity (cf. Exod 12:14), yet few of the laws given by Moses were applicable to the lives of Christians. What, for example, should one make of the "rites of sacrifices, the different kinds of victims, and the ministrations of the priests" described in Leviticus, asks Origen? "If I follow the 'simple sense' as some among us wish, without any recourse to the text's artifices and the obscurity of allegory, I, a man of the church living with faith and placed in the midst of the church, would be compelled by the authority of the divine precept to sacrifice calves and lambs and to offer wheat cakes with incense and oil" (*hom. 1.1 in Lev.*). Origen lays down the principle that "many of the laws" of Moses were not intended to be observed as they were written. Some are inapplicable in the present situation, others, for example, the prohibition against eating vultures (or ravens and owls), are irrational. Because this selection of birds appeared arbitrary, Origen concluded that the laws of Leviticus were not intended to be observed "according to the letter" (*princ.* 4.3.2).

The letter, that is, the actual wording of the text, cannot always serve as a trustworthy guide to interpretation. The interpreter must probe behind individual passages to discover the meaning of the text "as a whole."[14] What, however, is this whole, the larger context in which the individual passages are to be interpreted? In answer to this question one would expect Origen to set down a general philosophical or theological principle. Instead, he says that to understand the Scriptures one must begin with the history of Israel. The Scriptures, he writes, "tell us that God chose a certain nation on the earth." This nation was ruled by descendants of David and lived in a "*land* . . . given them by God called Judea whose metropolis is Jerusalem" (*princ.* 4.3.6). The Scriptures are a book about the people of God, the land promised to them, and the city of Jerusalem which stands at its center.

Within the Scriptures there are many "prophecies" (or "promises," as he calls them elsewhere [*princ.* 2.11]) spoken about Israel and Judea which predict "what is going to happen to them." When one reads these promises and realizes how grand and extravagant they are, the interpreter must ask whether they are spoken about this actual land, Judea, and this one people, the Jews, or whether they have a wider and more expansive application. Do they not, asks Origen, contain an "elevated sense"? Are the majestic promises of the Scriptures intended for this people alone and only for the land of Judea? Do they apply only to those who can trace their descent back to the patriarchs (4.3.7)? Origen's discussion of the principles of biblical interpretation is not simply an essay on exegetical rules in the abstract; his principles of interpretation have an "antiterritorial edge" to them. They are directed at an alternative exegetical tradition that took the promises in the Scriptures to refer only to the Jewish people and to the restoration of Jewish life in Judea.[15]

Even Jews who lived far from the land of Israel continued to eat the bitter bread of banishment. In Carthage in North Africa (modern-day Tunisia) Tertullian knew Jews who applied the image of the dry bones in

Ezekiel 37 to the "condition of the Jews," hoping that one day the "whole house of Israel" would be "gathered together, reconstructed bone upon bone, reincorporating the sinews of power and the nerves of royal rule, and be led out, as from tombs, that is from the most sorrowful and hateful dwelling places of captivity, to breathe again the air of rejuvenation and to dwell from that time on in their own land of Judea" (*res.* 30.2).

Tertullian wrote this passage early in the third century, about the same time that Origen was writing *First Principles*. For him as well as for Origen the Jewish hope of the restoration of Judea presented a theological and exegetical challenge. Were the prophecies in the Scriptures to be interpreted with reference to the future reestablishment of Jewish rule in Jerusalem, or could they have reference to the new Christian community? For Tertullian, as for Origen, the interpretation of the Bible could not be divorced from the present condition of the Jewish nation and the future of the people in "their land." For the Jews, says Tertullian, apply the passage from Ezekiel to the "condition of Jewish affairs." When the Scriptures speak about the "resurrection of the body" (in Ezekiel) the Jews believe there will be a "restoration of Jewish polity" (*res.* 30.4).

In the Jewish view, the promises in the Scriptures, then, have a very specific referent: they speak about the land of Israel and the future of the Jewish people in the land.[16] Origen, however, believes that if the prophecies are interpreted in this way they are emptied of their spiritual content. Origen appeals to two texts in the Christian Scriptures that seem to divest Jerusalem of its historical and hence political significance. They are Galatians 4:26, "The Jerusalem above is free and she is our mother," and Hebrews 12:22, "You have come to Mount Zion and to the city of the living God, the heavenly Jerusalem." These texts show that when the Scriptures speak of Jerusalem they do not have in mind the city in Judea that was once the capital of the Jewish nation; Jerusalem, according to Origen, does not designate a future political center but a spiritual vision of heavenly bliss.

In his use of Galatians 4 and Hebrews 12 Origen breaks with earlier Christian tradition. Irenaeus and Tertullian had cited Galatians 4 to support a belief in a future Jerusalem on earth.[17] In Origen's view, Paul is speaking not of a model for a city that will one day exist on earth but of a city in the heavens that will take the place of the earthly Jerusalem. Only this city can be the "mother of us all." Therefore the prophecies concerning Jerusalem designate a "heavenly city" and an "entire region containing the cities of the 'holy land.'" The prophets, writes Origen, were speaking about a "heavenly country" (*princ.* 4.3.8).[18]

It is possible that Origen debated the meaning of Jerusalem with a contemporary rabbi, Yohanan ben Nappaha, a native of Sepphoris in Palestine.[19] One of his sayings, a comment on a passage from the Song of Songs, is very close to the position Origen wished to refute. The text under dispute was Song of Songs 1:5: "I am very dark and comely, O daughters of Jerusalem." According to Rabbi Yohanan, some interpreters had taken the words "daughters of Jerusalem" to mean "builders of Jerusalem." How one can get *builders* out of *daughters* may seem a mystery, but Rabbi Yohanan's logic is unassailable. The Hebrew term for *daughters* is the same as the term for *builders* if the builders are female. On this foundation Yohanan built his interpretation that the passage from Song of Songs is speaking about the rebuilding of Jerusalem: "One day Jerusalem will be made into a metropolis for all nations and draw [all peoples] to her as a stream to honor her" (*Song of Songs Rab.* 1.5.3).[20] Though Yohanan's statement is cryptic, the words he chooses suggest he is referring to the hope of restoration as proclaimed by the prophets. "Metropolis" designates Jerusalem's future role as the "mother city," the city that will draw all Jews to her, an interpretation of which Origen is aware (*princ.* 4.3.6).[21]

In his commentary on the Song of Songs Origen takes quite a different approach to this passage. The verse "I am black and beautiful, O daughters of Jerusalem" prompts him to think not of the "builders of Jerusalem," but of the Queen of Sheba, who was black and beautiful. According to the Scriptures she had come from the ends of the earth to gain wisdom from Solomon. Origen takes her to be a symbol of the gentiles who are welcomed in Jerusalem even though they are not daughters of Jerusalem [that is, genuine Hebrews]. "She came to Jerusalem then," writes Origen, "to the vision of Peace, with a great following and in great array; for she came not with a single nation, as did the synagogue before her that was made up only of Hebrews, but with the races of the whole world, offering worthy gifts to Christ, fragrant spices . . . and gold." Hence the Jerusalem to which she comes cannot be the earthly Jerusalem because she would not be welcomed there. "This black and beautiful one comes to the heavenly Jerusalem and enters the vision of peace."[22]

Whereas Rabbi Yohanan believed that the heavenly Jerusalem could be entered only through the earthly city,[23] Origen's interpretation bypasses the earthly city and speaks only of the Jerusalem above. At the next verse in the commentary (1:6) he cites Galatians 4:21–26 in its entirety, and from Paul he deduces that the Song of Songs is speaking about the heavenly Jerusalem, the "free Jerusalem" which calls everyone through faith. This Jerusalem, Origen concludes, is Paul's mother and the mother of all believers. "She it is who is the *mother of us all*" (*comm. in Cant.* 1:6).[24]

The point at issue between Rabbi Yohanan and Origen is not whether there is a heavenly Jerusalem, but whether the heavenly Jerusalem is of necessity *paired* with the earthly Jerusalem. Will there come a day when all people will stream to Jerusalem "to honor her"? Rabbi Yohanan, like other Jews in his day, believed that one day Jerusalem would be restored as in former times. And this is the view Origen is contesting in this passage from *Contra Celsum* cited at the beginning of this chapter. "Moses taught that God promised a *holy land* which was 'good and large, flowing with milk and honey' to those who lived according to his law. And the good land was not, as some think, the earthly land of Judea."[25] In Origen's view the promise of the land signifies a spiritual conversion, that is, a return of "those who have gone astray." For when the psalmist spoke of the "city of our God" and the "holy mountain" he had in mind the heavenly Jerusalem, not an earthly city. To round out his argument Origen also cites Psalm 37, a text which, as we have seen, was also understood by Jews to signify the hope of restoration in the holy land. When the psalmist says "the meek shall possess the land and delight in much peace" he is referring to the "pure land in the pure heaven," not to a place located on the earth.

The Jewish Patriarch and Jewish Institutions in Palestine

Origen's insistence on a "spiritual," as distinct from a historical or political, interpretation of the prophecies was prompted in part by the renewal of Jewish life in Palestine in the third century and the growing self-consciousness of Jews about their claims to the land. By Origen's day, the unhappy memories of Bar Kochba were beginning to recede into the past, and the hardships that came in the wake of the several wars with the Romans were giving way to new economic growth.[26] It must be remembered that the Jews were a visible minority of the population of the Roman Empire at the time of Augustus (perhaps 7 percent), and though their numbers declined during the first two centuries, they remained a significant presence in most cities, particularly in the eastern empire. From the time of Septimius Severus (193–211) relations with Rome improved, and citizens of the empire looked on the Jews with new interest and respect.[27] At the same time a new generation of leaders had begun to give fresh spiritual and political direction to the Jewish people. Among these leaders the most resourceful and farsighted was the wise and prudent Judah the Prince. During his lifetime the disparate traditions of

Jewish learning were compiled to form the Mishnah, and the *beth din* (Jewish high court) came to exert wide influence over Jewish life. Judah was also a political figure who was treated with respect by Roman authorities (*b. Ber.* 16b). "Since the days of Moses," it was said "no man had combined in one person religious learning and political greatness" (*b. Sanh.* 36a).[28]

The office of patriarch, which had been established in the second century after the Bar Kochba revolt, served as an official liaison with Roman authorities, and the patriarch exercised a loose jurisdiction over Jews within the empire. The patriarch presided over the Jewish court, served as head of the academy (the institute for rabbinical education), and was responsible for determining the calendar which set the date of Jewish festivals, an important function in the ancient world. He was empowered to declare fast days, to make and annul bans, to appoint judges. He had the privilege of raising funds from Jewish communities throughout the Roman world. By the beginning of the third century the patriarch was the most visible representative of the Jewish people in Palestine.

For the Jews the office of patriarch was not only a source of pride; it was also a symbol of the continuation of national life within the land of Israel.[29] Origen acknowledged that the patriarch "differed little from a true *king*." It is not uncommon, he writes, that when "great nations" become subject the victors would allow the captives to "use their own laws and courts of justice." Those who have experience with the Jewish ethnarch, Origen observes, know how great his power is. He even conducts trials and condemns the guilty to death.[30] Some believed that the patriarch descended from the tribe of Judah and, for that reason, had a legitimate claim on the title king. Rabbi Judah the Prince, according to some sources, claimed descent from David.[31] Hence the existence of the office of patriarch could be seen as evidence of the survival of the monarchy. The title used by Judah, *Nasi* (prince), was the same as that used by Ezekiel of the future messianic ruler.[32]

It is ironic that Origen is a prime source (though not the only one) for our knowledge of the Jewish patriarch. For in his book *First Principles* and elsewhere he is at some pains to disprove the legitimacy of the office. Indeed, it is of the utmost importance for Origen's hermeneutical program that no vestiges of Jewish national life exist within the Land of Israel. "It is perfectly clear from history and from what we see in our own day, that, since the time of Jesus, the Jews no longer call anyone king, and all the institutions in which the Jews took such pride, I mean those connected with the temple and the altar of sacrifice and the rites which were celebrated and the vestments of the high priest, have been destroyed" (*princ.* 4.1.3).

Origen's judgment that Jewish national institutions had vanished from the land rests, in part, on his knowledge of the history of the Jews and on his observation of their present situation. The link between the patriarch and the Jewish kings of old *was* tenuous; the present patriarch may have had powers like a king but he was *not* a king. What Origen sees, however, is filtered through his Christian conviction that the messianic prophecies had been fulfilled in Jesus of Nazareth. One prophecy was of particular significance: the famous text in Genesis 49:10 about the "scepter of Judah." "The scepter shall not depart from Judah, nor the ruler's staff from between his feet *until* he comes to whom it belongs [or "Shiloh comes"]; and to him shall be the obedience of the peoples."[33] Jews acknowledged this passage was messianic. "The Messiah's name is Shiloh. For it is written, 'until Shiloh will come'" (*b. Sanh.* 98b). What struck Origen about the passage was that it said Jewish rule must depart from Judea before the Messiah will come, for the text says that one day "princes [that is, Jewish rulers] will cease in Judea." Jews, on the other hand, read the prophecy positively. The phrase "ruler's staff" was taken to refer to the patriarchs (thought by some to be descendants of Hillel), who symbolized Jewish claims to the Land of Israel (*b. Sanh* 5a). In this view Jewish rule in the land had *not* ceased; hence the prophecy was not yet fulfilled and the Messiah was still to come.

For Origen, then, disputes with the Jews about the interpretation of the Bible were not simply exegetical debates: they were debates about the future of Jewish life and institutions in the Land of Israel.[34] Even Tertullian in North Africa realized the importance of this point for Christian apologetics. In a work written "against the Jews" he observes that "none of the people of Israel remain at the present time in Bethlehem" (*ad. Iud.* 13.4). Today Jews can see the Land of Israel only "from afar." Here, as in the passage cited earlier, Tertullian continues to use the phrase "your land," that is, the land of the Jews, to designate Judea.[35] When Tertullian says that Jews look at Jerusalem from afar, he may be referring to the emergence of a new form of pilgrimage in Judaism. Now that the Jews were prohibited from living in the city of Jerusalem, they came to the city to view its remains from a distance and to lament its destruction.[36] Later writers, both Christian and Jewish, describe the scene of Jews weeping at the sight of the stones of the temple.[37]

Origen had also seen Jews weeping in Jerusalem. He noted, however, that their mourning was tempered by hope. They believed that one day their "inheritance" would be restored to them (*hom. 17.1 in Jos.*). This topic comes up in Origen's *Homilies on Joshua,* a book whose theme is the conquest of the land given as an inheritance to the Israelites.[38] The beginning of Joshua reads, "And it happened after the death of Moses the Lord said to Jesus (Joshua) the son of Nun, Moses' minister, 'Moses my servant is dead; now therefore rise up, cross the Jordan, you and your people, and go into the *land* that I am giving them. Every place on which the sole of your foot treads, I will give to you as I promised to Moses'" (Josh. 1:1–3). Origen asks the obvious question, "Which land?" He realized, of course, that the land promised to Moses was the actual land of Canaan, that is to say, the territory the Jews continued to claim as their own. But now that the temple was destroyed and the cities and villages in Judea were abandoned ("those described in this book" [Joshua]; (*hom. 17.1 in Jos.*), *land* requires an "elevated sense." Which land, then, is intended? The text (Josh 1:3), Origen notes, reads "given to *you,*" not "given to Moses." Playing on the name Joshua/Jesus (the names are identical in Greek) he continues, "You see that when Moses died, God gave the land to the people through Jesus (Joshua). Which land? That one, no doubt, of which the Lord says 'Blessed are the meek for they will possess the land as an inheritance'" (*hom. 2.2 in Jos.*). Unlike Irenaeus, who took the beatitude to refer to an earthly kingdom, Origen interprets it to refer to a "sublime region." The land God gives as an "inheritance" is located on high in the presence of Christ on the right hand of God (*hom. 2.3 in Jos.*).[39]

In the one place in the *Homilies on Joshua* in which Origen uses the phrase *holy land* the term designates the inheritance of a heavenly land, the land spoken of in the beatitude and in Psalm 37: "Blessed are the meek for they will receive [the land] as an inheritance" (*hom. 25.4 in Jos.*). Although we have no commentary of Origen on the beatitude, his homily on Psalm 37 is extant. From the way Origen approaches the interpretation of the Psalm it is clear that he is preoccupied with the same question posed in the commentary on Joshua. Which land does the psalmist have in mind? The matter under discussion in the psalm, says Origen, is the nature of the "future promise." When the psalmist says, "He will exalt you to possess the land," he is speaking of the "hope of inheritance" promised to the meek and the righteous. The psalm distinguishes "the land below," the land in which we now live, from the "land above," which is promised to the just as an inheritance. In answer then to the question Which land? Origen replies that the psalm has reference to a heavenly land, a land located above the earth, a "good land, holy land, great land, land of the living, land flowing with milk and honey" (*hom. 5. in Ps.,* 36; *PG* 12, 1362–63).[40]

Jewish Messianism and Christian Chiliasm

In these debates over the meaning of the holy land the central issue was the nature of messianism. This is not always apparent because Origen's interpretation is disciplined by the text that is before him. But in *First Principles,* where he addresses the larger issues of interpretation, his theological commitments become clearer. Again the issues are posed by the Jewish critics. They claim, says Origen, that Christians have misrepresented the prophecies that spoke of the Messiah. The Jews do not believe that Jesus is the Messiah because "they think that they are keeping close to the language of the prophecies that relate to him." In their view the prophets spoke of things that were to take place in the course of history. When the Scriptures speak of "release of captives" or building a "city of God" they mean that these things will happen in space and time, that there will be an actual release of captives and the real building of a city. When Isaiah speaks about the wolf feeding with the lamb and the leopard lying down with the kid, and the calf and bull and lion feeding together led by a little child, he anticipates that these things will one day take place and will be visible for all to see.[41] Because "they see none of these events actually happening during the coming of him whom we believe to be Christ," the Jews do not accept him as Messiah. "Contrary to the Law," they say, "Jesus called himself the Messiah" (*princ.* 4.2.1).[42]

What made these challenges on the part of Jews particularly vexing to Origen was that some Christians sided with the Jews, not by denying that Jesus was the Messiah, but by adopting a Jewish interpretation of the prophecies about the future of Jerusalem. On the basis of the book of Ezekiel (and Revelation), Tertullian, a chiliast, concluded, "We profess that a kingdom on earth has been promised to us" (*Marc.* 3.24).[43] Even in the middle of the third century adherents of this view could be found within the church. A well-known chiliast from this period, bishop Nepos, who lived in the Fayyum in Egypt, wrote a book entitled, significantly, *Refutation of the Allegorists,* and in it he interpreted the ancient prophecies "in a more Jewish way" (Eusebius, *h.e.,* 7.24.4). Nepos was neither a heretic nor a crazy on the fringe; he was a respected and admired Christian leader. As Dionysius, bishop of Alexandria, acknowledged in his book against chiliasm, *On Promises,* "I approve and love Nepos for his faith and industry, his diligent study of the Scriptures, and his abundant psalmody, by which many of the brethren have till this day been cheered; and I am full of respect for the man, all the more because he has gone to his rest already. But truth is dear and to be honored above all things" (*h.e.* 7.24.4).

Nepos did not stand alone.[44] Dionysius had visited the region where Nepos was bishop and discovered that the teaching that "there would be a kingdom of Christ on earth" had long been prevalent in the area and, according to Dionysius at least, had caused divisions within the church. Besides hoping for an earthly kingdom, Nepos also believed that one day there would be "festivals and sacrifices and slayings of victims." This suggests that he envisioned not only a restoration of Jerusalem but also a rebuilding of the temple![45]

From Origen's perspective, Christian chiliasm and Jewish messianism were of a piece.[46] Though chiliasts "believe in Christ," they "understand the Scriptures in a Jewish sense" (*princ.* 2.11.2). They envisage "an earthly city of Jerusalem that will be rebuilt with precious stones laid down for its foundation and its walls erected of jasper and its battlements adorned with crystal." They try to prove this on the basis of prophetic authority "from those passages of scripture which describe the promises made to Jerusalem," but they also appeal to the words of Jesus: "From the New Testament, too, they [the chiliasts] bring forth the word of the savior, in which he promises to his disciples the joy that comes from wine, 'I will not drink of this cup until the day that I drink it new with you in my Father's kingdom.'"

On the surface, Origen's case against the chiliasts is that they confuse physical desires, the dream of an earthly kingdom, with spiritual yearnings. But, if one probes a bit, it is clear that what disturbs him is that if the chiliasts are correct, the promises of the prophets cannot have been fulfilled in the coming of Christ and hence the messianic age has not yet begun. Origen cheerfully acknowledges that in Christ the prophecies were not fulfilled in the way they were *thought* to take place. "None of these things that have *taken place can be seen with the senses*," as he puts it (*princ.* 4.2.1). Yet something had happened (and was seen) when Jesus of Nazareth appeared in Judea. In Origen's view his opponents have much too narrow a sense of what it means for something to happen. The ancient prophecies inevitably look different when the interpreter is faced with events that seem to correspond, however unexpectedly, to what the prophets envisioned. History, even sacred history, seldom follows a predetermined pattern.

In the end Origen repudiated chiliasm and Jewish messianism as well as the idea of a holy land located on earth, not because he preferred allegory to history, but because he was attentive to a new set of historical events. If Jesus of Nazareth was the Messiah, the prophecies about the messianic age had already been fulfilled, and it was the task of biblical interpreters to discover what the scriptural promises meant in light of this new "fact."[47] For Origen the essential feature of the holy land was not its location but its quality and character. Yet, in pointing to the historical events that had already occurred, the history of Jesus of Nazareth, as a key to a new understanding of the promises in the Scriptures, Origen planted the seed of a new Christian conception of the holy land. For Jesus did not appear among men and women as a phantom or apparition, a spiritual being to be grasped only with the mind's eye. He had lived as a human being on earth among other human beings; he was a creature of time and space, born not only at a particular time in history but also in a specific place. The point was not lost on Origen: "Human understanding is astonished and . . . cannot grasp how one is to conceive and understand that awesome divine majesty, that Word of God itself, that Wisdom of God in whom all things visible and invisible have been created . . . , could exist within the circumscribed limits of a man who *appeared in Judea*" (*princ.* 2.6.2). As vigorously as Origen contested the idea that Judea was a holy land, he discerned, with characteristic prescience, why Judea would one day have a singular place in Christian piety and thought.

Eusebius and Jewish Claims to the Land

Origen's ideas about Jerusalem were appropriated by his worthy disciple Eusebius, bishop of Caesarea at the beginning of the fourth century. As we have seen, Origen's attitudes were formed not only by texts from the Scriptures that spoke of a heavenly city, but also by disputes with Jews in Palestine about the future of Jerusalem and the cities of Judea. What we have observed in Origen is corroborated two generations later in Eusebius's exegetical writings, particularly his commentary on Isaiah. Eusebius is known to most students of early Christianity as the author of the first ecclesiastical history, an account of Christian origins and early history up to the conversion of Constantine, the Roman emperor. But he wrote widely on other topics: theology, in defense of Christianity to pagans and Jews, a life of Constantine, a book on biblical place names (*Onomasticon*), several other biblical studies, a commentary on the book of Psalms (fragmentary), and a complete, verse-by-verse exposition of the book of Isaiah.[48]

For Christians Isaiah was the prophet par excellence. More than any other biblical writer he had spoken with greatest perspicacity about the coming of the Messiah. Passages from the book of Isaiah are the staple of Christian writings dealing with the Jews, as in Justin Martyr's *Dialogue with Trypho*. Origen was the first to attempt a commentary on Isaiah, but he reached only chapter 30, verse 6. It took him thirty books to deal just with these chapters, so it is no wonder that he did not complete the work. When Eusebius set himself to the task (with a much more modest book in mind) he had Origen's manuscript at hand, and his exegesis adheres closely to the principles laid down by Origen.

Eusebius, however, is no epigone; he did not simply plunder Origen's work to serve his own ends.[49] Eusebius's commentary was written late in his life, sometime after the Council of Nicaea in 325 C.E., when the Roman emperor had become a Christian and was a patron of the church. In his commentary, Eusebius uses the triumphant imagery of Isaiah about the messianic age to describe the reign of the new Christian emperor, an interpretation that was unimaginable in Origen's day. Origen thought it improper even for Christians to serve as magistrates in the cities of the Roman Empire (*Cels.* 8.75).

Yet in other respects Eusebius's agenda is similar to that of Origen. Like Origen he lived in Palestine and had contacts with Jews who saw in Isaiah's promises the foundation for their hopes of the restoration of Jerusalem. Just beneath the surface of Eusebius's commentary runs a persistent polemic against a Jewish interpretation of the book, and, at times, it splashes openly on to its pages. It is as though the words of the prophet are keys of a player piano, and every time a certain combination is struck the same notes are sounded. In Eusebius's case the note that sounds continuously throughout the book is the passage from Hebrews 12, "You have come to Mount Zion and to the city of the living God, the heavenly Jerusalem," and the terms and phrases that trigger his citation of that text are, among others, *land, Jerusalem, cities of Judah, Mount Zion, return, possess the land, Israel my inheritance.* Where the text of Isaiah could possibly be understood to refer to a return of the exiles, to the repossession of the land, or to the restoration of Jerusalem, Eusebius offers arguments against what he calls a "somatic," that is, an interpretation that sees the text in terms of the political history of the Jews in Eretz Israel.[50]

Eusebius's comments on Isaiah 2, an oracle concerning Judah and Jerusalem, are typical of his exegesis of Isaiah as a whole. The text reads, "The word which Isaiah the son of Amoz saw concerning Judah and Jerusalem. It shall come to pass in the latter days that the mountain of the Lord shall be established as the highest of the mountains, and shall be raised above the hills" (Isa 2:1–2). This passage, says Eusebius, follows a section condemning the "people of the circumcision" (14.26) and inaugurates a section on the calling of the gentiles. Some (the Jews) apply the prophecy to the "people of the Jews" as though it referred to "their land" (15.31–32).[51] They take the passage "in a bodily sense" to signify the "land of Palestine" (16.12–13), but the correct interpretation is to refer it to the "Jerusalem above which is the mother of us all" (16.15–16). A similar argument appears at Isaiah 4:2, "The fruit of the land shall be the pride and glory of the survivors of Israel." This text, says Eusebius, speaks of the "entire earth and the whole world." The "survivors" who will be called "holy" (4:3) are those who are worthy to "be recorded for life eternal in the 'heavenly Jerusalem' (Heb 12:22)" (26.36–27.5).

From numerous observations in the commentary, it is evident that in Eusebius's day Jews continued to anticipate the time when Jerusalem would again be a world metropolis. In his discussion of Isaiah 5:1, "Let me sing for my beloved a love song concerning his vineyard," Eusebius remarks, "Some say that this passage refers to the land of Judea." They offer this interpretation, continues Eusebius, because Judea is "fertile and fruitful," and they interpret the reference to a hill in the text to signify "the royal metropolis that will be established in this same Jerusalem" (29.14–17).

The term *Jew* in Greek (*Ioudaios*) and the word for Jewish religion, *Judaism* (*Ioudaismos*), were derived from the name for the region, Judea. Since the link between the term *Judea* and the Jewish people was self-evident (to pagans as well as to Christians and Jews), Christian interpreters were hard-pressed to show that biblical references to the "land of Judea" did not legitimate Jewish claims to the land. Psalm 76:1 reads, "In Judah [Judea] God is known, his name is great in Israel." In response to Jewish interpretations of the text, Eusebius claims that the psalm was referring not to Judea but to the "true Israel," a spiritual entity. The Jews, says Eusebius, appealing to the similarity between the name for Judea and the name for Jews, take the text in a "physical and bodily sense." For them, Judea "means nothing more than the land of Palestine, and the place of God is earthly Jerusalem" (*PG* 23, 876d).[53]

In Eusebius's disputes with the Jews over Judea and Jerusalem, he always contrasts Judea and Jerusalem with the heavenly city or, as in the passage cited above, with the new Roman colony Aelia Capitolina, never with Christian Jerusalem.[54] His *Evangelical Demonstration* was written two decades before the discovery of the tomb of Christ in Jerusalem and the construction of the Church of the Resurrection over the site of the tomb, so it is hardly to be expected that Eusebius would mention these things. Yet the reader of the *Demonstration* would never know that in Eusebius's day Jerusalem was a Christian center with its own bishop, a community of Christians extending back to apostolic times, and, even more to the point, that it had already become a place of pilgrimage. For

Eusebius, Christian Jerusalem lay in the future. He speaks of pilgrims to Bethlehem (*d.e.* 1.1; 4),[55] but the only pilgrimage to Jerusalem he mentions is "negative" pilgrimage, visiting Jerusalem for the purpose of viewing with one's own eyes the ruins of the city and temple.[56] "Believers in Christ," he writes, "gather from all parts of the world, not because of the glory of Jerusalem, nor to worship in the ancient temple at Jerusalem, but that they may know that the city was occupied and devastated as the prophets foretold, and that they may worship at the Mount of Olives opposite the city" (*d.e.* 6.18; 288d).

At this stage in Eusebius's life there is no hint that Jewish Jerusalem might be contrasted with a new Christian Jerusalem. The idea of a Christian Jerusalem was so new and so little rooted in Christian piety that Eusebius could make no place for it in his disputes with the Jews. Perhaps he realized that if he appealed to the emerging devotion of Christians to Jerusalem he would undermine the arguments he had leveled against Jewish attachment to the land. In this respect Eusebius is very traditional—not to say old-fashioned—at least in the *Commentary on Isaiah* and in the *Evangelical Demonstration*. He was, however, to prove a Janus-like figure who could look in two directions at the same time. More than any other early Christian thinker Eusebius was able to adapt his thinking to the new things that happened in his day. With the discovery of the tomb of Christ in Jerusalem, he began almost at once to integrate the new facts about Jerusalem into his religious and theological outlook. Like Ezekiel centuries earlier Eusebius was the first to discern the profound shift in devotion that was taking place in his day and to lay the foundations for a Christian idea of the holy land. This other Eusebius, this Ezekiel revenant, was devoted to the "new Jerusalem set over against the old," whose center was the tomb of Christ, located not in the heavens but in Judea.

5 A New Jerusalem Facing the Renowned City of Old

After the defeat of Bar Kochba in 135 C.E. the Romans plowed over the city of Jerusalem. Following an ancient rite for the founding of a new city, they yoked an ox and a cow to a curved plow, traversed the future city's boundaries, and where the earth formed a furrow marked out the location of its walls. When the outline had been traced in the soil they suspended the plow at the site of the principal gate.[1] Dio Cassius, a Greek historian, recorded the event: "At Jerusalem Hadrian founded a city in place of the one which had been razed to the ground, naming it Aelia Capitolina, and on the site of the temple of God he raised a new temple to Jupiter" (69.12). Named after the emperor's family, Aelius, and the gods of the Mons Capitolinus in Rome, Jupiter Optimus Maximus, Juno, and Minerva,

Aelia Capitolina was henceforth to be a Roman colony, displacing the ancient city of the Jews.[2]

Every effort was made to sever Jerusalem's ties with the past and to erase signs of the city's ancient glory as the seat of Jewish kings.[3] According to Dio the Jews were driven from the city and replaced by gentile settlers (69.12.21). Once Hadrian had "destroyed the temple of the Jews in Jerusalem," writes an ancient chronicler, he built public baths, a theater, a temple to the Capitoline gods, a sanctuary to the nymphs, a large ceremonial gate, a public esplanade, and other features of a Roman city.[4] Stones from the Jewish temple were used to build the theater and to construct the city wall.[5] The temple mount itself was turned into a "Roman farm," and Eusebius had seen "bulls plowing there, the sacred site sown with seed" (*d.e.* 8.3; 406c; cf. 4.13; 273d). At the place that would later be identified as the site of Jesus' tomb, a Roman temple was constructed.[6] Coins minted for Aelia Capitolina bore the names of pagan deities: Jupiter, Dionysius, Sarapis, Astarte, the Dioscuri.[7] On pain of death Jews were prohibited from entering the city (Dio Cassius 69.12; Justin, *apol.* 1. 47) and were forbidden even from "gazing on the soil inherited from their fathers" (*h.e.* 4.6.3).

So thoroughly had the Romans expunged Jerusalem from memory that in the early fourth century a Roman magistrate in Caesarea did not recognize the former name of the city when a Christian identified it as his home.[8] In the persecution under Diocletian a Christian was brought before the local judge in Caesarea, located only sixty miles from Jerusalem. When he was asked what his home city was, he answered, "Jerusalem." (According to Eusebius he meant the heavenly Jerusalem.) Puzzled, the magistrate inquired where this city was located. At first the Christian refused to answer, but then he identified it as the "fatherland of the pious [that is, Christians] . . . lying toward the East." Whether Eusebius's editorial gloss that *Jerusalem* designated the heavenly Jerusalem is correct or not, the name Jerusalem was unfamiliar to the magistrate.

Together, it seems, Romans and Christians had conspired to obliterate the memory of Jewish Jerusalem, the Romans by founding a new city dedicated to the gods of Rome, the Christians by directing people's affection to the heavenly Jerusalem.[9] Jerusalem had become Aelia, a name that would live on in Roman and Christian memory long after the city had regained its former name. As late as the tenth century, a Christian chronicler in Alexandria writing in Arabic, the new language of the Christian East, still knew the name Aelia.[10]

The efforts of Eusebius and Origen to demote the earthly city of Jerusalem in favor of a heavenly city were, however, already being undermined by quiet developments taking place in Palestine. During Origen's lifetime Alexander, a native of Cappadocia in Asia Minor, journeyed to Jerusalem "for prayer and investigation of the *places*" (*h.e.* 6.11.2). Shortly afterward another Cappadocian, Firmilianus by name, also visited Palestine "for the sake of the holy *places*" (Jerome, *vir. ill.* 54). These are the earliest-known Christian pilgrims to Palestine.[11] The first to write an account of his pilgrimage was a pilgrim from Gaul in the early fourth century.[12]

There were reasons other than pilgrimage to visit Palestine. From the time of Jesus Jerusalem had been the home of a Christian community. Unfortunately its early history is shapeless and obscure. None of its earliest documents, for example, letters to the churches in Asia Minor and Greece, are extant.[13] At an early date the Christians, like other Jews living in Jerusalem, suffered the cataclysm of the war with the Romans, and some (perhaps most) fled to Pella, a Greek city across the Jordan River (*h.e.* 3.5.3).[14] Some Christians, however, remained in Jerusalem after the war. Eusebius reports that until the time of Hadrian the church in Jerusalem was composed of "believing Hebrews," that is, Jewish Christians (*h.e.* 4.5.2). Eusebius provides a list of bishops for the city, as he did for other Christian centers, for example, Antioch and Rome, but like some episcopal lists from this period it is too symmetrical, too tidy, and apparently contrived. Exactly the same number of bishops presided over the church from the beginning to Hadrian as ruled from Hadrian to Narcissus in the late second century (*h.e.* 5.12.1–2). The first fifteen are Jewish, the next fifteen are gentile.[15]

When Jerusalem (or Aelia) comes clearly into view in the second century its bishops are leading figures in the Christian world. At the end of the second century a synod was held in Palestine to adjudicate whether Easter should be celebrated on the day of the Jewish Passover or on the Sunday following. The presidents of this synod were Theophilus, bishop of Caesarea, and Narcissus, bishop of Jerusalem (*h.e.* 5.23.3). It is unlikely that the church that emerges in Jerusalem after Bar Kochba was a new foundation composed only of gentiles who settled in the city after it became a Roman colony and who had no links to earlier generations of Christians living there.[16]

Christianity in Palestine was not confined to Jerusalem. In the first century there were Christian groups in Joppa and Caesarea (Acts 10:5, 24; 23:23, 33) on the coastal plain, where Christianity had its initial success. Early in the fourth century, when Eusebius recounts the trials of the martyrs of Palestine, among the cities that were home for Christian martyrs, those on the plain predominate: Diosopolis (Lydda), Gaza, Caesarea, Tyre, Ascalon, Jamnia, Eleutheropolis (Bet Gubrin). He also mentions Phaeno, a city in the Negev desert, and Scythopolis (Beth Shean), a Greek city south of Tiberias in the Jordan valley, and Gadara east of the Jordan River.[17]

The list of cities whose bishops were in attendance at the Council of Nicaea, the first great Christian synod, convoked in Asia Minor in 325 C.E., confirms that Christian strength lay outside of Judea and Galilee.[18] Not all manuscripts of the council agree, but the following cities appear in all: Caesarea, Nicopolis (Emmaus), Lydda, Jamnia, Eleutheropolis, Ashkelon, Ashdod, Jericho, and Scythopolis. Some lists include Neapolis (Schechem) and Sebaste (Samaria), others Gaza, Aila (Eilat) and Maximiniapolis, and still others Capitolias and Gadara east of the Jordan. Noticeably absent is the name of any Christian bishop from central Galilee. The only city mentioned from Galilee is Maximiniapolis, and it lies on the southern edge. Maximiniapolis, home of the Sixth Roman Legion, was composed almost wholly of new settlers from outside Palestine. Not until the middle of the fourth century is there evidence of a bishop in Tiberias, and the first mention of a bishop of Diocaesarea (the home of the Jewish patriarch) does not occur until the sixth century. Christians had not yet penetrated the Jewish areas.[19]

Constantine, Builder of Churches

By the beginning of the fourth century Jerusalem, which had lived in the shadow of Caesarea, began a swift rise to honor and authority. It was no doubt inevitable that its unique status as an apostolic city and the scene of Jesus' death and Resurrection would give it a singular place in the Christian world—but developments in the fourth century hastened its aggrandizement. The Council of Nicaea declared that Jerusalem (the bishops call the city Aelia), though subservient to Caesarea in the ecclesiastical structure, was to be esteemed first honoris causa: "Since custom and ancient tradition have established that the bishop in Aelia be honored, let him have the succession of honor, preserving, however, the proper right of the metropolis [Caesarea]" (*Nicaea,* Canon 7). Both the bishop of Aelia, Macarius, and the bishop of Caesarea, Eusebius, were in attendance at the council.

The Council of Nicaea was convoked by the emperor Constantine, the first Roman ruler to embrace the Christian religion. After exemplary service as a young military officer in Persia (ca. 290 C.E.) and another stint on the Danube, he returned to the imperial court in Nicomedia.

From there he was summoned to Gaul, where he joined his father, the *augustus* of the west. On his father's death in 306 at York the army acclaimed Constantine as emperor, and he assumed the rule of Britain, Gaul, and Spain. At first he accepted the title augustus but later prudently relinquished it when Galerius, the senior emperor in the West, offered him the lesser office of caesar. This meant that he was one of the two subordinate emperors (the two senior emperors were called augusti) responsible for the Roman provinces north of the Alps.

Sometime during this period Constantine made a slow turn toward Christianity. How and why he embraced the new religion remains a mystery. His father was a pagan who had tolerated the persecution of Christians in his domain, but when Constantine succeeded his father, he put an end to persecution. Soon he was seeking the counsel of Christian bishops. Six years later, after defeating the Franks, on his march south to Rome to challenge the emperor Maxentius, his resolve becomes visible for the first time. The night before the battle at the Milvian bridge Constantine had a vision of a cross (or the Greek letters chi-rho, signifying Christ). Constantine, it seems, was already thinking Christian thoughts. When he awoke the next morning, bishop Osius of Cordova, who was traveling with him, confirmed that the symbol represented Christ. At once Constantine acknowledged the protection of the new divinity. Ordering the removal of the pagan standards in his army, he led his troops into battle under a Christian banner.[20]

After defeating his rival Maxentius, Constantine publicly displayed his allegiance to the God of the Christians. When he arrived in Rome he refused to go to the Capitol, as was customary, to offer sacrifice in thanksgiving to the Roman gods for his victory. For this gesture he received the adulation of Christians and suffered the obloquy of pagans (Zosimus 2.29.5). Constantine was, however, not sole emperor of the Roman world; Licinius ruled as augustus in the East. In Constantine's domain, Rome and the West, the emperor's loyalties were evident. His soldiers were allowed to attend church on Sundays (*v.C.* 4.18.3), and he kept bishops in his company. A Christian symbol appeared on his helmet.

For centuries Roman emperors had used their office as well as the resources of the imperial treasury to build and endow sacred edifices. The first Roman emperor, Augustus (d. 14 C.E.), had built a temple to Apollo on the Palatine, another to Jupiter the Smiter and Jupiter the Thunderer on the Capitoline hill, another to Minerva and Queen Juno on the Sacred Way, to mention but a few of his endowments. In the *Monumentum Ancyranum,* a self-congratulatory account of his accomplishments, Emperor Augustus boasted that he "repaired eighty-two temples of the gods in the city."[21] Nero, it is reported, gave one hundred thousand sesterces to the shrine at Delphi after receiving a favorable reply. Elagabalus built temples at Taurus and Nicomedia as well as new shrines in Rome. And in the decade before his defeat at the Milvian bridge, Constantine's foe Maxentius had built a new temple to Venus.

Almost at once Constantine initiated a building plan of his own that would continue unabated until his death in 337.[22] Constantine's building program differed in one significant respect from that of former emperors: it featured churches. In Rome, where emperors had formerly constructed temples to Jupiter or Apollo or Venus, Constantine built basilicas to Christ and shrines to the martyrs. Pagans thought Constantine's zeal to build "memorials to human corpses" ignoble and demeaning (*laud. C.* 11.3).[23] The first, begun almost at once, was dedicated six years later to St. John (S. Giovanni in Laterano). Constantine's churches were not private structures, but public buildings, lavishly endowed, requiring thousands of gold solidi for maintenance alone.[24]

Before Constantine could launch a building program in the eastern provinces, he had to rid himself of his rival the augustus of the East, Licinius. In a war of attrition stretching over the next decade, Constantine occupied, piece by piece, the territory ruled by Licinius. The decisive battle took place in 324 at Chrysopolis, near Chalcedon across from Byzantium in northwestern Asia Minor. In triumph Constantine marched into Nicomedia the sole emperor of the Roman world. As he entered the capital of the East, his mind had already begun to think of founding a new Christian capital.

The new city, Constantinople, named after the victorious emperor, was constructed on the site of an ancient Greek city called Byzantium on the eastern tip of a promontory extending into the Bosporus on the European side. Wishing to build a city to honor the God of the Christians, Constantine resolved that it would be untouched by pagan worship. He embellished it with numerous sacred edifices, memorials of martyrs on a grandiose scale, and other buildings of the most splendid kind, not only within the city itself but in the surrounding territory. He venerated the memory of the martyrs and consecrated the city to the "God of the martyrs" (*v.C.* 3.48). By 330, only five years after work was begun, building had progressed to the point that the city could be dedicated. Constantine chose 11 May 330, the festival of St. Mocius, a Christian who had been martyred in Byzantium during the reign of Diocletian, the last great pagan emperor and persecutor. The symbolism was apparent. Purged of its ancient idolatry, Byzantium would no longer honor the Roman deities worshipped during the reign of Diocletian. The city was adorned with figures from biblical history, and a jeweled cross hung in the imperial palace.[25]

The Sacred Cave in Jerusalem

As grand and sumptuous as Constantinople was to be, it was soon to have a rival in Palestine. For Constantinople, though designed as the new capital, the home of the emperor, and the premier Christian city, was created ex nihilo. It was a city without history, a place that invoked no past. Like pebbles on a seashore, its stones bore no memories, a work of the imagination transformed into wood and stone. Jerusalem was the work of God, and its stones displayed the grainy texture of the city's past. In turning his attention to Palestine, Constantine aimed not simply to rebuild a city, but to construct a "memorial" of what God had done there (*v.C.* 3.25).

When Constantine first envisioned a Christian Jerusalem is unknown. It is possible that Macarius broached the matter at the Council of Nicaea. If Constantine was endowing churches in other cities across the empire, Jerusalem could hardly be overlooked. Yet Jerusalem had played only a minor role in Christian piety up to this point; it was venerated more as a symbol of the Jerusalem above than as a historical site or spiritual center in its own right.[26] There had been some pilgrims to Jerusalem, but there was little there for them to see. The tomb of Christ was buried beneath tons of dirt, and over it stood a pagan temple. Some came to Palestine to see the cave in Bethlehem or the tomb of Rachel near Bethlehem or the tombs of the patriarchs in Hebron and other places mentioned in the Bible, but in Jerusalem itself the preeminent site was hidden from view.

What we know of Constantine's plan as well as of its execution comes from the Life of Constantine written by Eusebius, Constantine's ardent admirer. In this remarkable book, designed as much to lionize the emperor before his contemporaries as to instruct later generations of his exploits, Eusebius directed attention, for the first time in Christian history, to the religious and theological significance of space.[27] He was interested in Jerusalem not as a symbol of something else, that is, the heavenly Jerusalem, but because it is the site of the places associated with the life of Jesus. His account of the discovery and building of the Church of the Anastasis bristles with a sacral vocabulary that has few precedents in Christian literature before his time. The term *place* (*topos*) has become incandescent, afire with energy and potency. Reporting on Constantine's plan for Jerusalem, Eusebius wrote that Constantine's greatest concern was how he might adorn "this *holy place* . . . which from the beginning was *holy* . . . and now appears more *holy* because it has brought to light proof of the suffering of the Savior" (*v.C.* 3.30). Formerly Christians had spoken of virtuous men and women as holy, of the holy church or holy Scriptures. Now holiness is attributed to a place: the "most blessed place," the "saving cave," the "holy cave," the "most holy cave," the "most marvelous place in the world" (*v.C.* 3.31).

Eusebius's words to depict the holiness of the tomb are complemented by another vocabulary drawn from the lexicon of ritual purity. The cave where Christ was buried had been covered with "impurities." The entire area had to be cleansed because it had been "stained." The workmen were ordered to "dig to a great depth and to transport to a far distant place the soil that had been polluted by the foul impurities of demon worship." The object of this digging and transporting of dirt was not simply to prepare the ground for a new building, but to uncover and display what was already there. Indeed Eusebius says the place was holy even before the burial and Resurrection of Christ, "from the beginning," suggesting that he has integrated the historical event of the Resurrection into an older cosmogonic myth.[28]

Eusebius repeatedly identifies the place as a cave, a term that does not occur in the New Testament. In the Mediterranean world caves were sacred places whose darkness and inaccessibility made them particularly suitable places to encounter the divine.[29] Porphyry, the philosopher and literary critic who wrote several books against the Christians shortly before the time of Eusebius, wrote a little essay on the "cave of the nymphs" in Homer's *Odyssey*. Caves, according to Porphyry, are not simply holes in the ground, but sacred precincts where the divine and human meet. They serve as "icons" and "symbols" (*antr. nymph.* 6.9) of higher things, and even before temples were built, people recognized the holiness of caves and grottoes. Eusebius calls the cave where Christ was buried "the sacred cave" or the "most holy cave." Eusebius also designates the place of Jesus' birth a cave as well as the place of his Ascension on the Mount of Olives. "In this same region [Judea] Constantine uncovered three sites venerated because of the three *mystical caves*, and enhanced them with opulent structures." By building these churches Constantine announced the "saving sign to all" (*laud. C.* 9:17). In Eusebius's account the term *cave* seems intentionally to accent the sacral character of the places he describes.

Of course the presumption behind Eusebius's account is that the workmen knew where to dig and had in fact discovered the place of Christ's burial. But how did they know where to place their spades and how could they be certain they had uncovered the tomb? Eusebius seems aware of such doubts. He says that the discovery of the tomb was "contrary to every expectation" (*v.C.* 3.28), implying that it was discovered unexpectedly. But that seems unlikely. Eusebius's language may be less an expression of surprise than a stylized way of displaying astonishment and wonder that the location of the great miracle had actually been uncovered. It is more likely that the Christian community in Jerusalem had a sense of where the tomb had been located. It is unlikely the tomb was uncovered by chance. The contractors knew *in general* where to dig.[30]

Certainty about the location is an essential feature in Eusebius's account, for he imposes on the discovery a provocative theological claim. The tomb of Christ is not simply a memorial of the place where the sacred events occurred—that is, a hedge against forgetfulness—but also proof of the veracity of what happened there, a "sign" or "token" of the saving Resurrection of Christ. Eusebius's Greek term for *sign* means "evidence" or "proof." It recalls the word *sign* in the Gospel of John, a term used in connection with Jesus' miracles, for example, the turning of water into wine at Cana (John 2:11) or the healing of the official's son in Capernaum (John 4:54). Through these and other signs Jesus evoked faith in those who saw them (John 20:30). In the midst of his Life of Constantine Eusebius has inserted a book of signs, but unlike the signs in the Gospel of John, which were miracles, those in Eusebius's book are *places*. Looking at the cave, the observer sees a "likeness of the coming to life of the Savior . . . a visible and clear sign of the amazing things that took place there, bearing witness to the Resurrection of the Savior by a deed that spoke more loudly than any voice" (*v.C.* 3.28).[31]

On the face of it Eusebius's claim that the discovery of the place is proof of what happened there appears illogical. Does the identification of the place where a famous battle presumably took place verify *that* it actually occurred? Such evidence can only be circumstantial. Yet when sight is joined to memory, stones and dirt and caves do not remain silent. Without memory there can be no identification, but without sight memories are evanescent and ephemeral. As Maurice Halbwachs reminds us in a book on "collective memory," it is difficult "to evoke the event if we do not think about the place itself." A community's memory is more likely to endure "when it concentrates on places," for seeing impresses on the imagination what one learns through hearing.[32] When linked to oral tradition or written texts sight bridges the gulf between past and present.

In Eusebius's day for the first time—or at least for the first time since the tomb of Christ was covered over—sight begins to be a component of

Christian faith. As this new "fact" penetrated Christian consciousness in the fourth and fifth centuries, Christians realized that seeing the holy places was a way of "renewing the image" of what had happened, that is, re-presenting the saving events of the past in the present, of allowing believers through "memory" to "become spectators of history."[33] If there were no places that could be seen and touched, the claim that God had entered human history could become a chimera. Sanctification of place was inevitable in a religion founded on history and on the belief that God "became flesh" in a human being. The holy places and the tombs of the patriarchs and prophets as well as the sites in Jerusalem and Bethlehem became witnesses to the truth of the biblical history and of the Christian religion. It would take time for these ideas to work their way into Christian piety and thought, but the discovery of the tomb of Christ in Jerusalem helped to hasten the inevitability. By "exposing to sight" the tomb of Christ Constantine unveiled the "deeds of God."[34]

Sacred Space and History

Earlier Christian sources have much to say about time, but what they say about space appears to dethrone place as the locus of the divine presence.[35] The most famous passage is, of course, the word of Jesus in John 4: "Woman, believe me, the hour is coming when neither on this mountain nor in Jerusalem will you worship the Father. . . . God is spirit and those who worship him must worship in spirit and truth" (21–24). This sentiment is echoed in popular as well as philosophical writings from the earliest centuries. Origen criticized pagan piety because it associated the divine with particular places. We have no need to go to a shrine to "seek God," he wrote (*Cels.* 7.35); the gods do not dwell "in a particular place" (*Cels.* 3.34).[36] Origen was uncomfortable *even* with the phrase "holy city" in the Gospel of Matthew. In his commentary he disassociated the epithet *holy* from the actual city of Jerusalem, as he had eschewed the term *holy land* for Judea (*comm. ser. in Mt.* 27:53).[37]

Yet these reproaches of pagan piety do not tell the full story. From early times Christians gathered for worship at the places where the faithful departed had been buried.[38] Like Greeks and Romans who built shrines to mark the place where they buried their famous dead or celebrated the exploits of mythical heroes, Christians constructed memorials to their dead. Called *martyria* (places that bear witness), these rooms were erected over the site where the martyr had been buried.[39] The earliest Christian martyrium was the tomb of St. Peter in Rome. In a room above the tomb a niche was carved in the wall and before it was constructed a small shrine containing two columns with a stone plaque. Peter was believed to have died at Rome, and the monument of his death was venerated by the year 200.[40] Other martyria have been discovered at Salona on the Dalmatian coast and at Bonn in Germany. At Salona, the room included a small apse, a table, and a canopy over the tomb. At Bonn archaeologists uncovered a room with benches and a stone table (altar) where Christians gathered to commemorate the dead.[41] The purpose of these shrines was to provide a place for the celebration of Christian worship at the burial site of a holy person.[42]

Adopting the terminology of the early Christian funerary shrines to designate the tomb of Christ, Eusebius calls it a "*martyrion* of the saving resurrection." His point is that the tomb "bears witness [*martyromenon*] more clearly than any voice to the Resurrection of the Savior" (*v.C.* 3.28). Elsewhere in the same account he uses the term *martyrion* to designate the basilica that was constructed adjacent to the site of the tomb (*v.C.* 3.40). Similarly the churches built on the sites of the two "mystic caves," the place of Jesus' birth in Bethlehem and the site of the Ascension, were called martyria.

Yet the martyrion at the tomb of Christ differed from the shrines of the apostles and martyrs in one noteworthy respect. Unlike the other martyria it did not hold any human remains. In John Chrysostom's memorable words, "The whole world runs to see the *tomb which has no body.*"[43] For John, the fact that the tomb was empty was reason to visit it; for John Milton, it was evidence that pilgrimage was a debased form of piety: "Here pilgrims roam, that strayed so far to seek/ In Golgotha him dead who lives in Heaven."[44] Early Christians knew that what was being marked and venerated was not the resting place of relics, but an event, the Resurrection from the dead (*v.C.* 3.28). The martyrion in Jerusalem marked the "place of the Resurrection," wrote Cyril of Jerusalem (*catech.* 14.6). Because the tomb as well as the sites marking the place of Christ's birth and Ascension were memorials of events, they were fixed and immovable. Unlike the tombs of the martyrs, which could be located anywhere (at least theoretically), the holy places were stationary. Paradoxically, the emptiness of the martyrion in Jerusalem made the bond between place and memorial more intimate.[45]

Another way of putting the matter is that Eusebius's account in the Life of Constantine is confined to historical sites, that is, to the places where significant events took place in the life of Jesus of Nazareth: the cave where he was born in Bethlehem, the place where he suffered and died, the site of his Resurrection, and the mountain from which he ascended into heaven. Besides these places, Eusebius also discusses the oak of Mamre near Hebron, a holy place associated with the patriarch Abraham.[46] At Mamre God first appeared to Abraham and promised that he would be the father of many nations (*v.C.* 3.53). By including the church at Mamre, Eusebius not only claimed Abraham's tomb for Christians, but also extended his conception of the holy places to embrace the territory of biblical history. For Eusebius, holy place is not confined to the sites hallowed by Jesus' life and ministry; it is wedded to the sacred history of the Bible, including the history of ancient Israel and hence to the *land* of biblical history. Unlike relics, the tomb of Christ, the cave in Bethlehem, the oak at Mamre could not be transported. Holy places were beginning to create an idea of holy land.

A New "Temple" in Jerusalem

It was said that when Justinian completed the building of Agia Sophia in Constantinople he exclaimed, "Solomon, I have conquered you." No such words are attributed to Constantine, but Jewish Jerusalem was very much on Eusebius's (if not Constantine's) mind as the Church of the Anastasis was being built.[47] Eusebius says that at the very place where Christ was buried, at the life-giving martyrion "a new Jerusalem was constructed" (*v.C.* 3.33).[48]

In describing the future building to the bishop of Jerusalem Constantine declares that it will eclipse every other building in the empire: "Not only will the church be grander in every respect than all others, but the details of the building will be of such a sort that when it is built it will surpass the most beautiful buildings in every city." Constantine instructs Macarius to procure whatever is needed for the building for "it is fitting that the most splendid place in the world should be adorned in an appropriate manner" (*v.C.* 3.31). In its size, in the opulence of its materials, and in the grandeur of its decorations, the basilica constructed at the site was without rival. Eusebius wrote,

> The interior surface of the building was hidden under slabs of multi-colored marble. The exterior aspect of the walls, embellished with well-matched and polished stones, gave an effect of extraordinary beauty which yielded nothing to the appearance of the marble. As to its roofing, the outside was covered with lead, a sure protection against the winter rains; the inside of the roof was decorated with sculpted coffering, which, like some great ocean, covered the whole basilica with its endless swell, while the brilliant gold with which it was covered, made the whole *temple* sparkle with a thousand reflections. (*v.C.* 3.36)[49]

For the ancient Israelites Jerusalem was situated at the center of the world. "This is Jerusalem," wrote Ezekiel: "I have set her in the center of the nations, with countries round about her" (Ezek 5:5). The center around which everything took its orientation was the temple, the "most holy place," as the final chapters of Ezekiel make clear. By Eusebius's time this conception of concentric circles radiating out from the holy of holies was firmly established in Jewish tradition: "The land of Israel is holier than other lands. . . . The walled cities (of the Land) are more holy. . . . Jerusalem is yet more holy. . . . The temple mount is more holy. . . . The sanctuary is still more holy. . . . The Holy of Holies is still more holy for no one may enter it except the High Priest on the Day of Atonement" (m. Kelim 1.6).[50]

Whether the architects of the buildings at the tomb were aware of this tradition is uncertain, but the form of the shrine lent itself to such a conception. From the reports of pilgrims we know that in the original complex the tomb stood in the open air, a "vast space, open to the sky, paved with beautiful stones and surrounded on three sides by long porticos" (*v.C.* 3.35). Across from the tomb to the south and east was the hill of Golgotha, the place where Christ was crucified. How the rock of Calvary fitted into the overall plan of the courtyard is still unclear to architectural historians, but the proximity of the two holy sites, the place of Christ's death and the place of his Resurrection, set this place apart from every other place in the world. In the original plan the tomb stood in an indentation on one side of a courtyard, but later in the fourth century the square courtyard was made into a circle and moved so that the tomb was at its center. Around it were set twelve enormous columns interspersed by square pillars at twelve, three, six, and nine o'clock, and the area was covered by a circular dome, known as the Rotunda.[51]

Eusebius does not use the phrase *center of the earth,* but the idea was aborning and may lie behind some of his observations on the new building. *As early as* the third century Origen knew of a tradition "that the body of Adam, the first human being, was buried where Christ was crucified" (*Comm. Ser. in Mt.* 27:32–3). Perhaps this is why Eusebius says that the place of Christ's burial was "holy from the beginning." In the generations that followed Christians would draw out this spatial parallel between Adam and Christ, just as Paul had drawn out a historical parallel between the first Adam and the second Adam (Rom 5). Ambrose, writing later in the fourth century, brings the two primordial beings into intimate relation: "The place of that cross was in the middle [of the earth] that it might be visible to all, over the tomb of Adam, a point the Jews dispute. The first fruits of new life and death's beginning come together at this place."[52] In time the new Christian "temple" at the place of Christ's burial and Resurrection would be viewed, like Jewish Jerusalem, as the "center of the earth."[53]

Eusebius knew, of course, that the Temple Mount was the center of Jewish Jerusalem. The temple had been constructed on a massive platform at the easternmost part of the city, where today the Dome of Rock is located, overlooking the Kidron valley and looking over toward the Mount of Olives. The Church of the Resurrection was built in a completely different part of the city, indeed near the center of the new Roman colony, well to the west of the old Jewish center. Eusebius is quite conscious of this topographical fact: "A new Jerusalem has been constructed *facing* the one renowned of old. . . . Opposite this city the emperor now began to rear a memorial to the Savior's victory over death with rich and lavish magnificence" (*v.C.* 3.33). Eusebius wished to set off the new Christian city centered around the Church of the Anastasis from the old Jewish city centered on the Temple Mount. Yet he emphasizes that the new Christian temple is located in the ancient land of the Jews. Constantine built an "enormous house of prayer, a temple holy to the 'saving sign' in the Palestinian nation in the heart of the Hebrew kingdom" (*laud. C.* 9.16).

Not once does Eusebius mention Aelia Capitolina in his several accounts of the new building. For Eusebius, the relation of the new Christian city to biblical Jerusalem was much more significant than its relation to the Roman colony of Aelia. In his description of the discovery of the tomb he contrasted the polluted temple of Venus with the sacred site of Christ's Resurrection. The one was a "gloomy shrine to lifeless idols" and the other a monument of the "return to life" (*v.C.* 3.26). But when he describes the majesty and grandeur of the new temple, he contrasts Christian Jerusalem with the Jewish city.

In his earlier treatise, the *Evangelical Demonstration,* written before the discovery of the tomb of Christ and before any churches were constructed in Jerusalem, Eusebius had drawn a contrast between the present ruins of the temple and the splendor of the ancient city. Standing on the Mount of Olives one could look down on the "old earthly Jerusalem" which lay in ruins. The testimony of the rubble, however, was largely negative. From it one could learn that the "city was taken and devastated as the prophets foretold." Eusebius is thinking specifically of Ezekiel's statement that the "glory of the Lord went up from the midst of the city" (Ezek 11:23). Eusebius now applies his words to the destruction of the Second Temple at the hands of the Romans.[54] Just as in former times God's glory had fled the city, so now in our own days the "glory of the

Lord departed the former city" to rest on the Mount of Olives (*d.e.* 6.18; 288d).

The prophet Ezekiel had, of course, not only spoken of the departure of the glory of God from Jerusalem; he had also prophesied its return: "Afterward he brought me to the gate, the gate facing east. And behold, the glory of the God of Israel came from the east, and the sound of his coming was like the sound of many waters; and the earth shone with his glory" (Ezek 43:1–2). In Ezekiel the return of God's glory to Jerusalem was associated with the future building of a new temple; in Eusebius's account the new Jerusalem is identified with the new Christian temple. "Perhaps," he writes, "this is the new and second Jerusalem announced in the prophetic oracles" (*v.C.* 3.33). The glory of the Lord had again returned to the holy city; as the departure of God's glory was predicted by the prophets, so the building of the new temple was a fulfillment of biblical prophecy. No doubt Eusebius realized that in his earlier writings he had interpreted the oracles of the prophets to refer only to a future eschatological city. Hence the subtle qualifier "perhaps." Yet, as he now beholds the new Christian city rising over against the ancient city of the Jews, he applies the words of the prophets to the actual city being built in the Roman colony of Aelia Capitolina.[55]

Responding as he had throughout his life to a new turn of events, Eusebius has made yet another shift in his thinking. Now the earthly Jerusalem is beginning to clothe itself in the images of the eschatological city. The prophecies to which Eusebius appeals are the same ones that Christian chiliasts and Jews had used in constructing their visions of a glorious future. For Eusebius, however, the prophecies are being fulfilled in his own lifetime, not in a future eschatological city. His is a more radical interpretation of the prophets than that of the chiliasts.

Eusebius applies to Christian Jerusalem the metaphor of a river that flows from the center of the city and brings salvation to the world. "In the Palestinian nation in that very place," he writes, "as from a fount a lifegiving river gushed forth for all" (*laud. C.* 9; also 11). This river is an "ever-flowing fount, streaming forth, overflowing with salvation for all."[56] This language recalls the final chapter of the Apocalypse: "Then he showed me the river of the water of life, bright as crystal, flowing from the throne of God" (Rev 22:1–2). The source of the metaphor (at least within the biblical tradition) is much earlier. It occurs in Ezekiel: "Then he brought me back to the door of the temple: and behold water was issuing from below the threshold of the temple . . . and the water was flowing down from below the south end of the threshold of the temple. . . . And wherever the river goes every living creature which swarms will live. . . . And on the banks, on both sides of the river, there will grow all kinds of trees for food. . . . Their fruit will be for food, and their leaves for healing" (Ezek 47:1–12).[57] In contrast to his earlier works, in which he had identified this city with the heavenly city, Eusebius here applies the images of the eschatological city to the actual city in Judea, the new Christian city, at whose center stood the "new temple" of the Lord. Roman Palestine, like the ancient land of Israel, again had a holy temple in its midst.

Envy of the Temple

In a suggestive article entitled "Christian Envy of the Temple" (1959), H. Nibley wrote that Christians, no less than Jews, recognized the importance of a tangible bond between earth and heaven.[58] Although Christian apologists, appealing to Isaiah 66:1, "What is the house which you would build for me, and what is the place of my rest?", manufactured innumerable arguments against the Jewish temple, they believed that God's dwelling place was on earth as well as in heaven. Indeed the Christian doctrine of the Incarnation required as much, for it affirmed that God had taken up residence on earth in the person of Jesus of Nazareth. With the building of the Church of the Resurrection God's glory again dwelled in Jerusalem, and the new Christian temple commemorated this fact. By the end of the fourth century the church in Jerusalem had set aside a special day, called Encaenia [Renewal], to mark the discovery of the true cross and the dedication of the temple at the site. Egeria reports that the festival was celebrated "with all possible joy" and, following the model of the celebration in ancient Israel of the dedication of Solomon's temple, was observed for eight days. "You will find in the Bible that the day of Encaenia was when the House of God was consecrated, and Solomon stood in prayer before God's altar, as we read in the Books of Chronicles" (*itin. Eger.* 48.2).[59]

Whether it is proper to speak of Christian envy of the Jewish temple, as Nibley does, is moot, but the language Eusebius uses in his Life of Constantine suggests that the parallel between the ancient temple of the Israelites and the new temple, a "memorial of the Savior's resurrection," was not far from his mind. In the Life of Constantine he cites as a "prophetic word" a passage from the Psalms on pilgrimage to the temple. The Greek text reads as follows: "Let us worship at the place where his feet have stood" (Ps 132:7). Psalm 132 is one of the songs of ascent, sung by pilgrims as they went up to the mountain of Jerusalem to join in the pilgrim festivals. In the original Hebrew the psalm reads, "I will not enter my house or get into my bed; I will not give sleep to my eyes or slumber to my eyelids, until I find a place for the Lord, a *dwelling place* for the Mighty One of Jacob. . . . Let us go to his dwelling place; let us worship at his footstool."

In Eusebius's Greek translation the term *footstool* was rendered "where his feet stood." The reason for this translation is unknown, but it is obvious that its language lent itself easily to a Christian interpretation ("his" = Jesus' feet). Eusebius cites the psalm in reference to Helen, the mother of Constantine, who had visited Palestine shortly before her death in 329 C.E., at the time Constantine was initiating his building program in Jerusalem and environs. No doubt she came with the emperor's blessings.[60] In later tradition Helen was celebrated as the first Christian pilgrim, and Eusebius presents her act of piety as a model for future generations (*v.C.* 3.42).[61] In later tradition she was associated with the discovery of the true cross,[62] and for that feat Sir Stephen Runciman called her "the most successful of the world's great archaeologists."[63] In the fifth century she was accorded equal honor with her son Constantine in the building of the temple at the tomb which was called the New Jerusalem (Socrates, *h.e.* 1.17).

Eusebius also mentions Helen in connection with the building of churches at Bethlehem and on the Mount of Olives. By visiting the territory where Christ had sojourned, Helen had "venerated the saving places" (*v.C.* 3.42), thereby fulfilling the word of the prophet, "Let us worship at the place where his feet have stood." Up to this point in his account of Constantine's building projects in Palestine Eusebius has eyes only for Jerusalem. But now he says that "in this same *region*" other auspicious places were discovered. The first is Bethlehem, the "cave which was the first manifestation of the Savior, where he had undergone birth in human flesh." The second mystic cave is located on the Mount of Olives and is a "memorial of his ascension into heaven" (*v.C.* 3.41).

Although Eusebius's intention is to highlight these two specific holy places, he introduces for the first time in his narrative a territorial designation. The two mystic caves were located in the same *territory* in which the temple was located (*v.C.* 3.40–41). Eusebius extends the idea of a sacred place to include the region surrounding Jerusalem. In the vicinity of the "most holy place" could be found two other "holy places." In the next paragraph he also uses a territorial term, but now the word is not "region" but "land," the biblical term for the land promised to Abraham. Helen, in her travels to the cities and provinces of the East, wanted to "behold this venerable *land*" (*v.C.* 3.42). Only here, in this land, could she "venerate the saving places" the Savior had hallowed by his presence and fulfill the words of the Psalmist, "Let us worship at the place where his feet have stood."

Eusebius does not use the term *holy* land; indeed it may be that he shuns it, as had Origen, because of its traditional Jewish overtones. But his phrase "marvelous" or "admirable" land is a singular addition to the emerging idea of a Christian holy land. It suggests that the holy places do not exist in isolation from the territory that surrounds them, and that their unique quality as signs of the divine presence extends beyond the sites themselves to the surrounding area, as Ezekiel had shown. A century later monks will come to Judea "to live in *this* desert" (Cyril of Scythopolis, *Life of Euthymius* 6), that is, the desert surrounding Jerusalem. What area was included under the term *marvelous land* is of course not specified; Eusebius is not thinking of a territory with boundaries. But he surely includes the area immediately around Jerusalem, including the Mount of Olives, Bethlehem, and perhaps the oak at Mamre near Hebron. Whether he included his own city of Caesarea as part of this land, though, is unclear. Caesarea does not figure large in biblical history, yet it does appear in the book of Acts as the place of the conversion of the Roman centurion Cornelius (Acts 10.1–11) and the place where Paul stood trial before Felix, Festus, and Agrippa II (Acts 24–26).[64]

A New Ezekiel

Long before the discovery of the tomb of Christ Eusebius had written a book that bears the title *Onomasticon*. Its fuller title is "On the location and names of places among the Hebrews." According to the preface it included the following information: Hebrew names translated into Greek, a map (or description) of ancient Judea and the ancient tribal divisions among the Hebrews, a plan of Jerusalem and the temple, and the distances between the various cities.[65] The work is arranged according to the books of the Bible (intended to aid the Bible reader), but it could also serve as a handbook for pilgrims. Eusebius identifies obscure biblical sites and mentions places where memorials can be seen, for example, the tomb at Bethlehem, the terebinth at Hebron. Most important, he makes no apparent distinction between places in the Hebrew Bible and places in the Christian New Testament. At Jericho he mentions the tomb of Joshua, but also says that it is a city that the Lord Jesus honored with his own presence.[66] In modern terminology Eusebius's work might be called a gazetteer, a geographical dictionary of names and places. To a certain extent the *Onomasticon* was a modification of a work of Origen on the Hebrew names in the Scriptures. Eusebius's book, however, had certain original features: a map or description of ancient Judea and a plan of ancient Jerusalem and the temple. His purpose was historical and exegetical. He seems to have used a contemporary map of Roman roads of Palestine as well as other sources on the geography of Palestine, as his use of phrases such as "to this day" or "shown to this day" indicate.

But the work has a larger significance. By conceiving of the land of the Bible as a geographical territory in which Christians have an interest and in which Christian sites are mentioned along with ancient Israelite sites, Eusebius had begun to envision Palestine not as a Roman province but as a land whose character and identity were formed by biblical *and* Christian history. In the Roman province of Palestine Caesarea was the premier city, but in Eusebius's *Onomasticon* the center is Judea and Jerusalem. As Dennis Groh has observed, Eusebius brings together "biblical, Roman and Christian realities . . . in such a way that Christianity in his own day can be seen to be the successor of the biblical realities in the Roman world."[67] The biblical land was not only an ideal land or a place of past history; it was also a land where Christians lived. In several places Eusebius mentions villages that are "wholly Christian."[68]

It would be stretching the evidence to claim that Eusebius first imagined a Christian holy land. Yet, like Ezekiel eight centuries earlier, Eusebius set some of the foundation stones in place. Ezekiel had written, "This is the law of the temple; the whole territory round about upon the top of the mountain shall be most holy" (Ezek 43:12). In his description of the discovery of the tomb of Christ and the building of the Church of the Anastasis Eusebius gave the land a center, a holy place and sacred edifice, that made this land venerable and marked it off from all others.

Without the developments that took place in Eusebius's lifetime—the conversion of Constantine, his lavish endowments to build churches, the discovery of the tomb of Christ, the building of the Anastasis, Helen's fervor for the holy places, the construction of churches at Bethlehem, on the Mount of Olives, and at Mamre—Jerusalem and the land surrounding it would not have been catapulted so quickly to the center of Christian devotion. Yet Eusebius saw something that others had not yet discerned and had the theological sophistication and the religious imagination to portray what he had seen. The Christian holy land was, however, not the work of bishops or intellectuals: its artisans were the faithful who lived in the land and the pilgrims who came from abroad to worship at the holy places.

6 At the Very Spot

Unlike Islam, Christianity lays no obligation on the faithful to make pilgrimage. For the Muslim, pilgrimage is a sacred duty. In the words of the Quran, "Whoever can make the journey [to Mecca]" is obligated to do so (2.196; 3.97). By the end of the fourth century, however, pilgrimage to Jerusalem had become so widespread[1] that a Christian bishop had to remind fellow Christians that "where the Lord calls the blessed to possess the kingdom of heaven [in the beatitudes] he does not include among their good deeds going up to Jerusalem on pilgrimage; and where he speaks of 'blessedness,' he does not include this kind of devotion" (Gregory of Nyssa, *ep.* 2). Christians were not exempt from the lure of holy places.[2]

Once pilgrimage emerged as a form of devotion among Christians, it became an enduring feature of Christian piety.[3] In the early Middle Ages, when Muslims first observed Christians journeying to Christian sites under Muslim hegemony, it appeared to them that the command to make pilgrimage was a directive of Christian law: "Many times I have seen people coming here [Syria] . . . from those parts of the world [the West]. They mean no harm. All they want to do is to fulfil their *law*."[4]

No matter how zealously Christians took to heart Jesus' words "God is spirit, and those who worship him must worship in spirit and truth" (John 4:24) or the axiom "The God who made the world . . . does not live in shrines made by human beings" (Acts 17:24),[5] they have approached the holy places with burning hearts and shining faces. In the words of Stephen Graham, "The road from the Jerusalem of the tourist to the Jerusalem of the pilgrim is long indeed. The difference between the man surveying the Church of the Sepulchre with a handbook and the poor peasant who creeps into the inmost chamber of the Tomb to kiss the stone where he believes the dead body of his savior was laid, is something overwhelming to the mind."[6] To see for the first time the scenes of biblical history, to touch the actual places where Christ lived and died, to tread the same streets and roads that he walked releases unfamiliar and untutored affections.

To some, pilgrimage, with its many subsidiary forms of devotion, its commercialism, its vulgar reliance on touch and sight, seems to appeal only to the credulous and superstitious. It has been malevolently branded a form of "natural piety" that has little or no place in the higher spiritual religion of Christianity. John Calvin, the reformer, called it a form of "counterfeit worship," and many have agreed.[7] But as Samuel Johnson observed,

> [although] long journeys in search of truth are not commanded, to visit the place of great actions moves the mind in uncommon ways; curiosity of the same kind may naturally dispose us to view that country whence our religion had its beginning; and I believe no one surveys those aweful scenes without some confirmation of holy resolutions. That the Supreme Being may be more easily propitiated in one place than in another, is the dream of idle superstition; but that some places may operate upon our own minds in an uncommon manner, is an opinion which hourly experience will justify.[8]

In the formation of a Christian idea of holy land, pilgrimage plays a key role, especially during the fourth and fifth centuries, when the practice was in its infancy; and the piety of the pilgrims shaped Christian thinking about Jerusalem and the territory surrounding the city. Among the many interesting features that mark pilgrimage in this period two are particularly relevant to this book: the inclusion in the itinerary of pilgrims of holy places throughout the region, not simply those in Jerusalem, which created the idea of a sacred territory; and the intensification of devotion to place, and hence to tangible things, as seen in certain rituals, and with this the emergence of a sacramental notion of holy places.

Greek Holy Places

In antiquity pilgrims were a familiar sight.[9] At shrines and cult centers throughout the Mediterranean world they could be seen bringing their offerings, joining in sacrifices, fulfilling vows made in times of distress, seeking relief from pain or healing, giving thanks for benefits, participating in processions and banquets. At least two hundred sacred shrines were dedicated to the healing god Asclepius. His chief pilgrimage centers, Epidauros and Pergamon, were not unlike a sanatorium or spa where the infirm went to bathe, to drink mineral water, and to place themselves under the care of a physician. Often these centers included temples, fountains, and baths as well as a gymnasium, theater, hostel for pilgrims, rooms for incubation. Visitors would stay for several days, sometimes for weeks.[10]

At these and such other well-known shrines as Hierapolis in Syria, Delphi in Greece, and the island of Philae in Egypt, pilgrims from all over the Mediterranean world could be seen. To Hierapolis, the cult center of the goddess of Syria, came people from Phoenicia, Babylonia, Cappadocia, and Cilicia, says Lucian (*dea syria* 10).[11] He described the ritual of a pilgrim who was setting out to the shrine of the goddess of Syria at Hierapolis:

> Whenever someone is about to go to the Holy City, he shaves his head and his eyebrows. Then after sacrificing a sheep, he carves it in pieces and dines on it. The fleece, however, he lays on the ground to kneel on, and the feet and the head of the animal he puts on his own head. As he prays he asks that the present sacrifice be accepted and promises a greater one the next time. When he has finished, he puts a garland on his head and on the heads of those who are making the same pilgrimage. Then he sets out from his own country to make the journey, using cold water both for bathing as well as drinking, and he always sleeps on the ground, for it is a sacrilege for him to touch a bed before he completes the journey and returns to his own country. (*dea syria* 55–56)[12]

For this pilgrim the journey to Hierapolis required that he leave his home city and country to travel to another place. There were temples closer to home, but "none was greater than that in the holy city" (of Hierapolis), for it was there that the gods "appear to the inhabitants" (*dea syria* 10). Pilgrimage was rooted in a fundamental religious fact: the gods appeared at particular places and locales. In a way that is difficult for moderns to grasp, religion in the ancient world was wedded to place, as Walter Burkert reminds us: "The cult of the Greeks is almost always defined locally; the places of worship are fixed in ancient tradition and cannot be moved lightly."[13] Unlike the sacred space defined by a synagogue or a church or mosque, that is, religious space that was chosen or created by the construction of a building, the sacredness of a mountain or a grove or a cave was discovered or found. Its sacrality was given, and the building of an altar or a temple simply marked the location.[14]

Holy places not only drew people to them to pray, to fulfil a vow, to offer sacrifices, and to seek healing; they also provided a point of orientation, an axis or fulcrum, a center around which other points are located. At the shrine at Delphi the pilgrim could view a smooth, rounded stone, the *omphalos,* the navel of the world. Likewise at Claros, the site of an oracle in Asia Minor, there was a room in which had been placed a stone of deep blue marble. Around it were placed stone benches, and as the pilgrims stared at it they seemed to be sitting at the center of the earth. These sacred places created a zone or precinct extending out beyond the shrine itself. This land of Epidaurus was "sacred to Asclepius" and the "sacred grove of Asclepius was surrounded on all sides by boundary marks" (Pausanias 2.27.1). No birth or death was allowed to take place within the enclosure, and all offerings had to be consumed within its bounds. Usually only one entranceway was allowed, and in some cases it was marked by a ceremonial gate that set apart the sacred territory from the common or profane space that surrounded it.[15] In most cases the zone was limited to the immediate vicinity, a grove or a temple precinct, but in places it was extended to include a town or city or even a group of villages in the surrounding region.[16]

At the pilgrimage shrines, piety was nurtured not only by seeing and touching, by the proximity to holy places and holy things, but also by history and myth, memory if you will. "I will relate," writes Lucian, "the stories that are told about the 'holy place' and how the temple was built" (*dea Syria* 1). At the shrines could be found guides or hosts (*dea Syria* 56), whose task it was to recount the stories and myths associated with the site, to point out significant details, and to explain their meaning to the pilgrims and visitors (Dio Cassius 36.11). In his "Description of Greece,"

Pausanias, the geographer and traveler, provides many examples of the stories that were told at the pilgrimage centers as well as at other sites of historical interest.[17] In antiquity, no less than today, pilgrimage and tourism existed side by side, and for much the same reasons. Without memory, without historical (or mythical) associations, trees and stones and rivers and temples are dormant and inert.

For the Jew, pilgrimage centered on Jerusalem, the city that stood "in the center of the nations" (Ezekiel 5:5). In ancient Israel there had been other pilgrimage sites, Shiloh, for example, the setting for an annual pilgrimage in ancient Israel, but in the period of the second commonwealth, when the temple was standing, Jerusalem was the chief goal of Jewish pilgrims. "Three times a year all your males shall appear before the Lord your God at the place which he will choose [Jerusalem]: at the feast of unleavened bread, at the feast of weeks, and at the feast of booths" (Deut 16:16). Besides celebrating these pilgrimage festivals, pious Israelites traveled to the city to fulfill other ritual obligations, for example, at the birth of a child.

Pilgrimage to Jerusalem was a communal undertaking, a joyous and happy occasion as people from the same town or village traveled to the holy city in company with fellow Jews.[18] The historian Josephus says it fostered "mutual affection" among Jews. "For it is good that they should not be ignorant of one another, since they are members of the same race and share the same pursuits" (*Ant.* 4.203–04). Anthropologists have observed that the journey to the holy place and fellowship with other pilgrims are as important as the goal.[19] Often pilgrims would remain in Jerusalem for weeks and months, and hostels were built for that purpose. During their stay in the holy city they not only offered sacrifices in the temple, but also fulfilled other ritual obligations such as purification, and during their stay some engaged in study of the Torah. An inscription found on a building in Jerusalem reads, "For the reading of the Torah and the study of the commandments, and the hostel and the rooms and the water installations, for needy travellers from foreign lands."[20] Pilgrimage was much more than a visit to holy places; it was an occasion to renew friendship, to study, to forge and strengthen bonds of loyalty to Jerusalem and the Land of Israel.

Following the destruction of the Second Temple in 70 C.E., the ancient laws on pilgrimage could no longer be observed. Pilgrimage for the Jew had been a ritual act whose purpose was to offer prescribed sacrifices in the holy city. The loss of the temple and the occupation of the city by non-Jews did not, however, put a stop to pilgrimage. Though the traditional ritual obligations could no longer be fulfilled, Jews continued to return to the city. At first they may have continued to observe those laws that still seemed applicable, for example, the offering of the *Maaser Sheni,* the second tithe. This was an offering of produce that was supposed to be eaten in Jerusalem or "redeemed" by putting aside coins of the same value. For a time this practice was continued by Jews living in the vicinity of Jerusalem.[21]

Later, Jews came to Jerusalem—or at least to the outskirts of the city—for another reason: to mourn the destruction of the temple. This practice, visible even today at the Western Wall (the remains of the Second Temple from the time of Herod), had its origins in the generations after the Bar Kochba revolt. Attested by Christian as well as Jewish sources from the Roman and Byzantine periods, it became the most visible expression of Jewish devotion to the fallen city. A description of the practice is found in Jerome, the fourth-century Christian scholar who lived in Bethlehem. He often had occasion to view, in his words, the "pitiful crowd" of Jews who came each year on 9 Ab, the anniversary of the destruction of Jerusalem, to mourn the lost city. When they reached the summit of the Mount of Olives they wailed and lamented as they gazed at the ruins of the temple and remembered its altar.[22]

This lugubrious band of pilgrims presents quite another face when the observer is a Jew. To the Jews they were not a pitiful mob but a company of the pious engaged in a purposeful religious act with its own ceremony and formalities. Mourning the destruction of the temple was not simply the by-product of an occasional journey to Jerusalem: it was becoming a regular practice. A text from the Cairo Geniza, a storeroom in the Cairo synagogue discovered early in this century, describes the ritual to be observed on arriving in sight of the holy city:

> If you are worthy to go up to Jerusalem, when you look at the city from Mount Scopus [you should observe the following procedure]. If you are riding on a donkey step down; if you are on foot, take off your sandals, then rending your garment say: "This [our] sanctuary was destroyed. . . ." When you arrive in the city continue to rend your garments for the temple and the people and the house of Israel. Then pray saying: "May the Lord our God be exalted" and "Let us worship at his footstool. . . . We give you thanks, O Lord our God, that you have given us life, brought us to this point, and made us worthy to enter your house. . . ." Then return and circle all the gates of the city and go round all its corners, make a circuit and count its towers.[23]

From these fragments in the Cairo Geniza as well as several passages in the Talmud it is apparent that pilgrimage to the fallen city had become a distinct ritual. The rabbis debated, for example, what specific rites one should perform and at what places. Should one rend one's garments when one actually sees the holy city or not until one is able to see the ruins of the temple? Some said that there were two distinct rentings, one for the city and a second for the temple. "As soon as one reaches Mount Scopus he rends. Does he rend for the Holy Temple separately and for Jerusalem separately? The former ruling [he rends for the holy temple] obtains where one first encounters the site of the sanctuary and the latter [he enlarges it for Jerusalem] where one first encounters Jerusalem." The rabbis, ever practical, even discussed how one repairs the garment that has been rent! (b. *Moed Katan* 26a).[24]

After the destruction of the Second Temple, the fuel that ignited pilgrimage to Jerusalem was memory, but in it germinated dreams of future restoration. Even the Christian critic Jerome (as we shall see in the next chapter) knew that when Jews looked at the ruins of Jerusalem their thoughts turned at once to the ancient prophecies of the restoration of Jerusalem.[25] In the very act of lamenting the loss of the city and temple Jews voiced the certain hope that a new temple would one day rise from its ruins.

Jews also venerated places that marked the sites of significant events in the life of the people.[26] An early example is the account in the book of Joshua of the forging of the Jordan River by the Israelites before the conquest of Canaan. After the Israelites had passed through the river to dry ground and were safely on its opposite bank, Joshua ordered representatives of the twelve tribes to take stones out of the river and construct a monument in the river and in Gilgal, the place where the Israelites camped after crossing the Jordan. These stones were to be a "sign" to the people, a "memorial" so that when "in time to come" their children ask, "What do these stones mean?" their parents can tell them that here God cut off the waters of the river before the ark of the covenant.[27]

According to the book of Joshua, a cairn marked the place where God had performed this marvelous deed on behalf of his people. At a later period in Jewish history places where God had intervened in history were remembered with special prayers and blessings. In the treatise on blessings (m. Berakoth 9.1) in the Mishnah, there is a discussion as to where and when one should speak a blessing. "If one sees a place where miracles have been wrought for Israel, he should say, blessed be he who wrought miracles for our ancestors in this place."[28]

In the discussion of this passage in the Talmud, the rabbis distinguished between blessings that are incumbent on the people of Israel as a whole and blessings that are spoken only by individuals. If, for example, someone is attacked by a lion or a wild camel and is "miraculously saved," whenever that person passes that place again he should say, "Blessed be He who wrought for me a miracle in this place." But because the deliverance concerned an individual, only the person for whom the miracle was done is required to say a blessing.

The other type of blessing applied to all Israel. "If one sees the place of the crossing of the Red Sea, or the fords of the Jordan, . . . or the stone which Og king of Bashan wanted to throw at Israel . . . or the pillar of salt of Lot's wife, or the place where the wall of Jericho sank into the ground, for all these one should give thanksgiving and praise to the Almighty" (b. Berakoth 54a). These miracles God has done for Israel, and they should be remembered with a blessing by any Jew when viewing the place where the miracle took place.

Whether the deliverance was individual or corporate, the holiness of the place was created by the event that happened there; unlike a sacred grove it was not discovered. At such places the appropriate ritual action was not only prayer or vows or petitions for healing; the place required retelling the story of what happened there. In reciting the story, however, the pilgrim did not simply recall what happened to others in the past; the prayer acknowledged God's mercy in the present. By the ritual act of offering a blessing, blowing a ram's horn at Rosh Hashanah, or eating bitter herbs at Pesach, faithful Jews made the past part of their present. Invoking God's marvelous deeds at the very place where the events had taken place intensified and heightened the sense of participation in the marvelous deeds of old.

The Beginning of Christian Pilgrimage

Marcel Proust wrote, "The past is hidden in some material object (in the sensation which that material object will give us) which we do not suspect."[29] Memory is linked inescapably to tangible things that can be seen (or tasted or smelled), and it was to recollect and remember that Christians first set out, in the words of Origen, "to trace the footsteps of Jesus."[30] It is, however, misleading, indeed anachronistic, to call Origen a pilgrim, if by *pilgrim* one means someone who prays or engages in a ritual at a holy place. Origen's interest was as much historical and exegetical as it was religious. Several generations earlier another Christian thinker, a bishop from western Asia Minor, Melito of Sardis, had made a journey to the East, presumably Palestine, to the "place where these things had been proclaimed and accomplished." His purpose in going there was to obtain "precise information" about the books of the "Old Testament." He wanted to know the number as well as the order of the books that Christians shared with the Jews.[31] Like Origen, he was interested in Palestine because it was the land of the Bible and it could provide information that was not available elsewhere.

As noted in chapter 5, in the third century pilgrims had begun to visit Palestine "for prayer" and "investigation of the holy places."[32] But we have no firsthand account of an actual journey until the fourth century. This is the *Itinerarium Burdigalense,* the record of a Latin-speaking pilgrim from Bordeaux in Gaul who arrived in the East in 333 C.E., four years before the death of Constantine.[33] He made the long and arduous journey to Palestine by land, passing through northern Italy, down the Adriatic coast, across northern Greece and Macedonia, south to the Bosporus, which he crossed at Chalcedon, traveling across the spine of Asia Minor to Ancyra, then through the Taurus mountains to Tarsus, finally reaching Antioch in Syria. From there he traveled along the coast through Laodicea, Beirut, and Sidon to Palestine.

The record of this anonymous pilgrim's journey is a brief, almost stenographic account, noting where he went, what he saw, where he changed horses, distances from one place to another. His pilgrimage took him all over Palestine, not simply to Jerusalem and the scenes of Jesus' life, but also to obscure places, sometimes where little-known biblical events took place. His comments take this form: "Mount Carmel is there. There Elijah did his sacrifice"; "City of Jezreel; it was there that King Ahab lived and Elijah prophesied; there also is the plain where David killed Goliath"; "A mile from there is the place called Sychar, where the Samaritan woman went down to draw water, at the very place where Jacob dug the well, and our Lord Jesus Christ spoke with her."[34]

Jerusalem is presented in the same terse style. The pilgrim from Bordeaux mentions the pools built by Solomon (the pools of Bethsaida), the site of the temple, the place on the Temple Mount where the Lord was tempted, the statues of Hadrian, the column where Christ was scourged, Mount Sion, where, according to his report, seven synagogues stood, Golgotha, "where the Lord was crucified and about a stone's thrown from it the vault where they laid his body and he rose again on the third day." Here, he observes, without further comment, the emperor had built a "basilica," a "place for the Lord." He also mentions the new basilicas constructed on the Mount of Olives and at Bethlehem and also the basilica at Mamre, which he says was "exceptionally beautiful."[35] He went to

Jericho and saw the tree Zacchaeus climbed to see Christ, the spring of the prophet Elisha, the house of Rahab the harlot, the place where the Israelites placed the twelve stones, the place in the Jordan where the Lord was baptized by John.

It is easy to smile at this pilgrim's credulity. The house of Rahab standing in Jericho twelve hundred years later! Zacchaus's tree three hundred years old! Pilgrims were shown the waterpots used at the wedding of Cana, and in Arabia they could see the dunghill on which Job sat.[36] Yet even modern pilgrims are shown "Jacob's well" and the inn used by the good Samaritan on the road to Jericho. Like pilgrims of old, they often make the same circuit that this pious pilgrim traced, peering curiously at the scenes of biblical history to evoke images of the mighty heroes of ancient times. There is more here than credulity; these sights were narrow beams of light that penetrated the soul. In the aphorism of Cynthia Ozick, "A visitor passes through a place; the place passes through the pilgrim."[37]

What stands out in the account of the pilgrim from Bordeaux is not his credulity but his juxtaposing of minor biblical events and the places of the central mysteries of the Christian faith. The book exhibits almost no theological interest. It moves indiscriminately from one place to another. When he came to the Mount of Olives he wrote, "On the left is a vineyard where is also the rock where Judas Iscariot betrayed Christ; and on the right is the palm-tree from which the children took branches and strewed them in Christ's path. Nearby, about a stone's throw away, are two memorial tombs of beautiful workmanship. One of them, formed from a single rock, is where the prophet Isaiah was laid, and in the other lies Hezekiah, king of the Jews."[38] Like a contemporary biblicist for whom every word of the Bible is of equal moment, the pilgrim of Bordeaux has no hierarchy of place. If a site is mentioned in the Bible and it can be located, it is worthy of a visit.

It has been suggested that the pilgrim from Bordeaux was guided by a Jew or that his itinerary was planned by a Jew or that he was a Jewish Christian.[39] One scholar claimed even that he had never visited Palestine.[40] His route is puzzling; he sometimes turns back to visit places he could have seen when he was in the vicinity, and he makes few observations on the things he has seen. It is possible that the earliest Christian pilgrims followed paths that were well worn by Jews.[41] Except for the places in Jerusalem, the text makes no mention of sites associated with Jesus' youth and ministry. Apparently he did not visit Galilee; he mentions neither Nazareth nor Capernaum, two places that figure large in the gospel accounts of Jesus. In some cases he has access to information that is known only in Jewish tradition. He associates Job with the town of Aser, a topographical detail that is known only from Jewish sources. He says that Goliath was killed in the valley of Jezreel. According to the Hebrew Bible he was killed in the valley of Elah (1 Sam 17:2).[42]

For the pilgrim of Bordeaux pilgrimage meant visiting the land of the Bible.[43] In this respect he is more like Origen than later Christian pilgrims. His testimony is precious, for it shows that the first pilgrims traced an arc of holy places in Palestine that extended beyond Jerusalem and Bethlehem to embrace the territory of biblical history. Christian pilgrims did not come solely to see and touch the places hallowed by Christ's life; they were also drawn by the desire to see with their own eyes the land of the Bible. In this way the pilgrims helped create the idea of a holy land, as distinct from a series of holy places.

On the Very Spot

A much fuller account of pilgrimage to Palestine was written by an aristocratic woman from Spain named Egeria, and her narrative also rests on the terrain of biblical geography.[44] By the time Egeria visited the land in the late fourth century, Jerusalem was a bustling Christian city, filled with pilgrims, monks and nuns, clerics, and adventurers. Its new monuments at the holy places dazzled pilgrims from all over the world, and the elaborate liturgies celebrated in the chief churches thrilled visitors. Nevertheless, her pilgrimage, like that of the pilgrim of Bordeaux, was as much a quest to satisfy her intense curiosity about the land of the Bible as it was to worship at the holy places in Jerusalem and elsewhere. "You know how inquisitive I am," she wrote of her visit to the valley of Cherith, where Elijah had hid (1 Kings 17:3–6). She wanted to know from the monk who lived there why he had built his cell in that place [16.3].[45]

Egeria wished to see with her own eyes the places where the great events of biblical history took place. She visited the "holy mount of God," Mount Sinai, deep in the desert and difficult of access even today, Mount Horeb, where the prophet Elijah fled from the presence of king Ahab, the land of Goshen, Mount Nebo, where Lot's wife was turned into a pillar of salt. She had hoped to see the "actual pillar," but what she saw was only the place where it had stood. Disappointed, she wrote home, "The pillar itself, they say, has been submerged in the Dead Sea—at any rate we did not see it, and I cannot pretend that we did" (12.7). Before arriving in Jerusalem, she saw the tomb of "holy Job," Tishbe, the village from which the prophet Elijah got his name, and many other places. Like other pilgrims, she said her "first desire" was to see, and the verbs *see* and *was shown* run throughout her account as well as those of other pilgrims.[46]

In part Egeria's journey was a grand adventure, a sightseeing tour of biblical history, the breathless journey of one of the idle rich. As she moved from place to place she dreamed of the time when she could recount her exploits to her friends back home, very much like the modern pilgrim who is thinking of gathering relatives and neighbors for a slide show in the very act of taking pictures of the trip. But she always carried a Bible with her. "Whenever we arrived [at any place] I always wanted the Bible passage to be read to us" (4.3). At another site she wrote, "So there too we had a passage read from the Book of Moses" (4.5). The Bible was read not simply to remind the pilgrim of the details of the event that happened at the place; it was also part of a ritual involving prayer and a reading from the psalms, and in some cases an offering of the Eucharist. "When we reached this plain [where Moses blessed the Israelites before his death] we went on to the very spot, and there we had a prayer, and from Deuteronomy we read not only the song, but also the blessings he pronounced over the children of Israel. At the end of the reading we had another prayer, and set off again, with thanksgiving to God" (10.7). The parallels to Jewish pilgrimage are close. Egeria read the biblical account of what had taken place at the site; her company also offered a prayer and sometimes celebrated Holy Communion. "All there is on the actual summit of the central mountain (Sinai) is the church and the cave of holy Moses. No one lives there. So when the whole passage had been read to us from the Book of Moses (on the very spot!) we made the Offering [Eucharist] in the usual way and received Communion" (3.6). The phrase "in ipso loco" ("on the very spot" in John Wilkinson's felicitous translation) captures the thrill and excitement of the moment.[47] The experience was without parallel, and nothing could prepare people for it.

Of all the places in Palestine where Egeria paused to read the Bible, pray, and offer the Eucharist, Jerusalem stood apart. There the central events in Christ's life had taken place. By far the longest section of Egeria's book is devoted to the city of Jerusalem and the holy places contiguous to the city. When Egeria reaches Jerusalem her narrative changes character; her interest shifts away from seeing places to participating in the rituals that took place in the city. "I am sure it will interest you to know about the *daily services* they have in the holy places, and I must tell you about them" (24.1).

By the time Egeria arrived in Jerusalem, late in the fourth century, Christian worship in the city had begun to settle into distinctive patterns dictated by the presence of the holy places.[48] That Christians could gather for worship at the very spot where the saving events had taken place made a deep impression on the Christians living there as well as on pilgrims. Egeria writes, "What I admire and value most is that all the hymns and antiphons and readings they have, and all the prayers the bishops say, are always relevant to the day which is being observed *and* to the *place* in which they are used" (47.5). A few details can illustrate the practice. On Thursday of the "great week" (holy week), after services in the Martyrium (the great basilica) the congregation would return home for a short meal and then gather at the Eleona on the Mount of Olives. After psalms and readings and prayers they would proceed to the Imbomon, the hillock of the Ascension on the Mount. Early in the morning they moved to the place where Jesus had been arrested on Gethsemane, returning to the atrium of the chapel adjacent to Golgotha. On Friday the faithful came to this chapel to venerate the wood of the cross and to listen to the accounts of his passion. This was followed by services of prayer in the Martyrium and the Anastasis. On Saturday the paschal vigil took place in the great church, the Martyrium, and afterward the newly baptized were led to the Anastasis. The bishop went inside the screen of the aedicule and said a prayer for them. Then they returned to the church, where the congregation continued its vigil.

The development of stational liturgies, that is, rituals celebrated at particular places or stations, is the most visible evidence of the primacy of place in the spiritual outlook of Christians living in Palestine. From the beginning Christian worship had been oriented to time, to the "end time," the eschatological hope that was foreshadowed in the liturgy, and to "ritual time," the representing of the historical events of Christ's life, the suffering, death, resurrection within the context of liturgical celebration. Further, the narrative character of the gospels (recording Jesus' life from birth through death) indelibly imprinted on the minds of Christians the sanctity of time. For Christians in Jerusalem, however, the proximity of the holy places made possible a sanctification of space. The liturgy could now be celebrated not only according to the rhythm of Christ's life, birth, suffering, death, resurrection, but also *at* the Eleona (Mount of Olives), or the Imbomon ("little hillock," place of the Ascension), Golgotha, or the Anastasis (tomb): at the places where the events had taken place.

Stational liturgies are by their very nature public occasions. With the triumph of Constantine and the construction of new churches across the empire, public prayer found its home within the basilica, still an enclosed space. But in Jerusalem in the late fourth century the clergy and faithful flung open the doors of the churches and poured into the streets. Stational liturgies were mobile. John Baldovin, a liturgical scholar, writes, "[They] did not always take place at the same church" but "were celebrated in different sanctuaries or shrines."[49] Because the events that were celebrated (for example, Christ's betrayal and death) were interrelated and had taken place in different parts of the city, the congregation not only gathered at the place, but also had to get from one place to another, sometimes on the same day. Stational liturgies invited movement, and solemn ritual processions became a distinguishing feature of stational liturgies. On the high liturgical celebrations of the year Christians could be seen making their way through the streets of the city as they sang hymns and chanted psalms and paused for prayer. With the emergence of stational liturgies Christianity acquired a new visibility.[50]

These developments were taking place in Jerusalem at the same time that Christianity became recognized as the official religion of the Roman world. In an edict in 380 Emperor Theodosius I declared that Trinitarian Christianity would be the law of the empire. The conjunction is not accidental. For stational liturgies required not only that Christians have access to the holy places, but that suitable buildings be constructed at the shrines, that civic officials support and encourage this new public display of Christian piety, and that Christians control the streets. The liturgical ceremonies in Jerusalem gave ritual expression to the new status of the Christian religion. As Jonathan Z. Smith observes, the rise of stational liturgies "reflects the movement of an insecure Christianity from an essentially private mode of worship to an overwhelming public and civic one of parade and procession."[51] The implications were far-reaching. Space is never ideologically neutral. Jerusalem was becoming a Christian city, the city of the Christian God, and perforce a city of uncommon symbolic power for the Christian empire. As Jerusalem became a holy city it acquired a political as well as a religious character for Christians. If a hostile army should one day invade the city it would not only disrupt the public worship of God, but also threaten the stability of the Byzantine Empire.

When the Vietnam War Memorial in Washington was dedicated in 1982, men and women came from all over the United States, some traveling hundreds, even thousands of miles by car and bus to be present at the site. When they arrived they found a plain, low wall with nothing but long lists of the names of those who died in the Vietnam War engraved in black marble. Yet they came, and continue to come, to indulge in the simplest sort of human memorial, seeking out the name of a friend or loved one and running their fingers over the cold, stony texture of the engraved slabs. "I don't know what it is," said one veteran who stood for two hours at the wall. "You have to touch it. There is something about touching it."

"There's something about touching it." Without the images and impressions of touch and sight and smell, memory is formless and vacuous. Memories that are purely mental, that are not anchored in things, seldom endure.[52] This elementary truth was understood by the peasant who came to Jerusalem to kiss the wood of the cross, by Egeria, who celebrated the Eucharist at the holy places, and by learned theologians who had never seen Jerusalem.[53] No one expressed it more clearly in this period than Paulinus, a bishop from the city of Nola in Campania in southern Italy: "No other sentiment draws people to Jerusalem than the desire to *see* and *touch* the places where Christ was physically present, and to be able to say from their own experience, 'We have gone into his tabernacle, and have worshipped in the places where his feet stood'" (*ep.* 49.14). Paulinus reasoned that if one wished to recall someone or represent an event there was no better way than to "see the place" or to touch a fragment of something that person touched.

Paulinus's sentiments were echoed by Christians living all over the Mediterranean world, in North Africa, in Palestine, in Asia Minor, and not only in reference to the holy places in Jerusalem. By the end of the fourth century the tombs of martyrs and saints had become places of veneration, drawing Christians to see and touch the remains (relics) of holy men and women buried in their own regions. One bishop wrote, "When one touches the bones of a martyr, one shares in the holiness which is present in the grace inhering in the body."[54] Gregory of Nyssa said that he had buried some of the bones of a group of martyrs alongside his parents. Normally, he said, one does not like to go to a tomb, but at the tomb of a martyr one receives a "sanctifying blessing." "To touch the corpse itself, if ever good fortune would allow such an opportunity" is like touching the "living and blooming body itself, bringing in the eyes, mouth, ears and all the senses . . . as though [the martyr] were fully present" (*PG* 46, 739a-b).

As these statements suggest, devotion to the holy places in Palestine did not stand apart from other forms of veneration practiced at this time. A new tactile piety that attached itself to things, to bones and relics, to places and shrines, to sacred books, even to liturgical implements like chalices and veils, was evident all over the Christian world. In a letter to Theophilus, pope (patriarch) of Alexandria, Jerome urged that all who minister at the altars in the church show proper reverence for the "accessories" used in the liturgy. These things, he writes, are not "lifeless and senseless things devoid of holiness; from their association with the body and blood of the Lord they are to be venerated with the same awe as the body and the blood themselves." Elsewhere Jerome defends the veneration of the bones of martyrs. In kissing and adoring "ashes wrapped in a cloth" (the remains of a saint), he said, it is as though one "beheld a living prophet" in one's midst.[55]

This tactile piety, worship with the lips and the fingertips,[56] took many forms depending on the place or object that was venerated. Some pilgrims journeyed from Jerusalem down through the Judean desert to the Jordan River to bathe at the place where Christ was baptized.[57] Others took home objects—oil, water, earth, wood, stones—that bore a tangible relation to the place they had seen and touched. These objects, called blessings, allowed the pilgrim to maintain physical contact with the holy place or thing. Holiness was transmitted through touching. The blessing was "not a memento to evoke pleasant memories, as is a modern tourist trinket, but rather a piece of portable, palpable sanctity which possessed and could convey spiritual power to its owner."[58] Still others, dissatisfied with ersatz relics, tried to get the real thing. When the bishop of Jerusalem exposed pieces of the holy cross for veneration, he had to hold it firmly, and his deacons had to keep their eyes on the pilgrims lest, while kissing the cross, one would try to bite off a piece.[59]

For the pilgrim the holy places were not simply historical sites that invoked a memory of the past. Seeing was more than seeing, it was a metaphor for participation. Theodoret of Cyrus tells the story of Peter of Galatia, who went down to Palestine from Syria "in order that by *seeing* the places where the *saving sufferings* had taken place he might worship *in them* the God who saved us." Peter, Theodoret reminds us, did not believe that God was "confined to a place." He knew that God's nature was without limit. Nevertheless he went to Palestine to "treat his eyes with the sight of his desire." It was not enough that the eye of the soul enjoy God through faith. Peter's delight in the holy places was like the pleasure a lover receives from gazing on the clothing or the shoes of the beloved. Wounded with love for God and longing to see God's "shadow," Peter "took himself to those *saving places* where he could *see* the founts that gushed forth."[60]

In Christian discourse the terms *sign* and *symbol* designated things that could be seen and touched that pointed beyond themselves.[61] They were tiny windows that opened on another world. Among signs, the most important were water in Baptism and bread and wine in the Eucharist, but also oil for blessing, relics, and gestures such as the making of the sign of the cross. Signs were not simply pointers: they shared in the reality they signified. "With the inner eye one sees the whole power of the Cross in this tiny fragment," wrote Paulinus of Nola (*ep*. 31.1). Hence they deserved honor and veneration.[62]

At several places in his writings Gregory of Nyssa calls the holy places signs. On a visit to Jerusalem, made, in his words, "according to a vow," he rejoiced to be able to see the "*signs* of the Lord's sojourn in the flesh." In one place he calls the "holy places" [his phrase!] "saving symbols."[63] Now Gregory was a subtle, sophisticated thinker, the most rigorously intellectual of all the early Christian writers, and he chooses his words with care. In a dispute over the Christian doctrine of God Gregory had protested against the uncompromising intellectualism of a fellow bishop, Eunomius. One of his arguments against Eunomius rested on an appeal to the necessity of signs for Christian faith. According to Gregory, Eunomius transformed Christianity into a philosophical system in which "dogmatic exactness" was prized over all else. What Eunomius overlooked, said Gregory, was that Christianity was not solely a matter of the mind; it also invited "participation in sacramental practices and symbols."[64]

What did he mean by calling the holy places signs? These places, writes Gregory, had "received the footprints of Life itself"[65] and for this reason they are palpable reminders that God once walked this earth. Just as perfume leaves an odor in the jar after it has been poured out, so God has left traces of his presence in Palestine. As we are able to savor the fragrance that was once in the jar, so through the traces Christ left on earth human beings can participate in the living reality that was once visible in this land.[66] By visiting those places that bear the imprint of "life itself," the pilgrim was able to know the transcendent God who was beyond human comprehension.

There was, however, another side to Gregory. He was also an articulate critic of pilgrimage, a fact that has caused embarrassment to later advocates of the practice. In the letter in which Gregory had observed that the Lord gave no command to go up to Jerusalem, he also presented several other arguments against pilgrimage. There he states with exemplary brevity the classical theological case against sacralization of place: God is no more present in one place than in another. Even writers who praise and defend pilgrimage, for example, Theodoret of Cyrus in the passage on Peter of Galatia, always qualify their approval with a remark such as the following: "not as though God is confined to a place." In his letter on pilgrimage, however, Gregory develops the argument at greater length. What advantage, he asks, is there in being present at the places themselves? Can the Spirit not journey to Cappadocia (where Gregory lived)?

He is just as present on the altars of Cappadocia as in Jerusalem. There may be a smidgeon of Cappadocian chauvinism here, but the point is clear: change of place does not bring one closer to God.[67]

Later generations of readers had difficulty reconciling Gregory's statements on the holy places with this letter on pilgrimage. The letter has had a contentious history, especially since the Reformation. In the sixteenth century and in the generations following, it prompted an acrimonious dispute over the spiritual benefit of pilgrimage to the holy land. Edited and translated by the great Calvinist scholar Pierre du Moulin (d. 1658), the letter came to be used as evidence that pilgrimage was inimical to Christian piety.[68] In response to du Moulin, Jacob Gretser, a Swiss Jesuit, wrote a lengthy book in favor of pilgrimage.[69] Later another Calvinist theologian, Johann Heidegger, joined the debate with an equally weighty tome against pilgrimage.[70] In the eighteenth century the dispute shifted to the East and to the patriarch of Jerusalem. Chrysanthus (1707–31) wrote a long book defending pilgrimage, *History and Description of the Holy Land,* and in it he included a section on the authenticity and interpretation of the letter.[71]

I mention this debate because the letter of Gregory of Nyssa *is* puzzling in the light of his other statements. There can be no question that he had reservations about pilgrimage, especially for monks and nuns. And he also states with his usual lucidity the theological and spiritual perils of a piety that is attached to place. Gregory was a disciple of Origen, the great Platonist theologian, and among Greek Christian thinkers from this period he is the most philosophical. More than any Christian thinker from antiquity he gave philosophical expression to the belief that God was wholly transcendent. By definition God is boundless, without extension in space, beyond measure. So different is God from anything that when the mind contemplates God it "becomes dizzy and perplexed," as though it had stepped off the edge of a cliff and lost its footing.[72]

Gregory was, however, as much a theologian of the Incarnation as he was of transcendence: "There can be no doubt that God underwent birth in human nature."[73] As the eighteenth-century patriarch of Jerusalem, Chrysanthus, recognized, the key to understanding Gregory's devotion to the holy places was not only that God had become flesh but that God appeared at particular places. Consequently these places are unlike "other common places."[74] If God had once been present on earth in Jesus of Nazareth, the soil on which he walked, the cave in which he was born, the stones of the tomb in which he was buried bear the imprints of God's presence and are, in the words of John of Damascus, "receptacles of divine energy."[75]

Unlike such signs as the water of Baptism and the bread and wine of the Eucharist, the holy places were stationary. They might be moved closer to a good road by an enterprising monk or greedy merchant to make access easier, but in principle they were immovable. Objects associated with them could of course be transported, and once the flow of pilgrims began, people began to carry things back home from the holy land: water from the Jordan River, tiny boxes of oil from lamps in the churches, and so forth. As soon as there were pilgrims there were people to feed them and house them and sell them souvenirs and blessings.[76] But the holy places themselves could not be cut up and sold, carried about or transported.[77]

From Paulinus of Nola in Italy and Gregory of Nyssa in Cappadocia we can glimpse the tentative outline of a Christian theology of the holy places. But it is only from residents of Palestine that we can discern the lineaments of an emerging Christian idea of a *holy land*. The architects of a Christian holy land were not the pilgrims who came from all over the world to worship at the sacred sites, but Christians residing in the land: Eusebius, Cyril of Jerusalem, Jerome, Paula, Melania, Hesychius, the monks who lived in the Judean desert, Cyril of Scythopolis (Beth Shean), Sophronius, John of Damascus. Almost every Christian thinker who contributed significantly to the Christian understanding of the holy land lived, at least for part of his or her life, in the land.

Cyril, who was bishop of Jerusalem from 349 to 384 C.E., had the singular privilege of presiding over the church in Jerusalem in the decades immediately after the completion of the complex of new buildings begun during Constantine's reign: the circular shrine surrounding the tomb of Jesus (the Anastasis), the shrine of Golgotha, and the basilica (Martyrion) adjacent to the tomb. These buildings, wrote an ancient historian, were so splendid they could not be looked on "without exciting wonder" (Sozomen, *hist. eccl.* 2.26). In sermons preached in the basilica within a few feet of the actual places of Christ's death and Resurrection, Cyril took full rhetorical advantage of his unparalleled setting. Speaking of Calvary, "most holy Golgotha," as he calls it, Cyril proclaimed, "Others only hear, but *we* both *see* and *touch*" (cat. 13.22). Others have received the testimony of the prophets concerning the Lord, but only Christians in Jerusalem have the witness of holy places. *"Here* in this city of Jerusalem" the Spirit was poured out on the church, *"here"* Christ was crucified; *"here"* you have before you "many witnesses," the "place itself of the Resurrection," and "toward the East [Mount of Olives] the place of the Ascension" (14.23, also 4:14).[78] With no less exuberance Jerome, who lived in Bethlehem, also exclaims, *"Here"* [in Bethlehem] he was wrapped in swaddling clothes: *here* he was seen by the shepherds; *here* he was pointed out by the star; *here* he was adored by the wise men" (*ep.* 46.10).

In Cyril's sermons *here* refers to the city of Jerusalem and in some passages to very specific places, the tomb of Christ, Golgotha, the place of Christ's Ascension on the Mount of Olives, Mount Zion. But the holy places were not confined to Jerusalem and environs. "My beloved," he proclaims, "there are many testimonies of Christ." The first testimonies are God the Father, the Holy Spirit, the archangels, the Theotokos (the Virgin Mary). Then he mentions the apostles, the winds silenced at Christ's command, the loaves multiplied to feed thousands, and the grave clothes for his burial. Finally he turns to places: "The blessed *place* of the manger bears witness; Egypt bears witness . . . ; the Jordan River bears witness; the sea of Tiberias bears witness . . . ; the holy wood of the cross bears witness . . . ; Gethsemane bears witness; the Mount of Olives bears witness" (*cat.* 10.19). In this passage Cyril is beginning to think of the holy places not so much as a collection of individual sites bearing witness to discrete events but as a distinct geographical region located near the "center of the earth"[79] (*cat.* 13.28).

Jerome also presents a catalogue of holy places in Palestine (and Egypt),[80] but his list differs in one notable respect from that of Cyril. Cyril confined the list of testimonies to places mentioned in the gospels; Jerome's sacred topography included the sites of Israelite history. In part this reflects Jerome's historical interest. For him the Christian visitor to the land was like the studious Greek or Roman tourist who visited memorable sites in Greek or Roman history. "Just as Greek history becomes more intelligible to those who have seen Athens, and the third book of Vergil to those who have sailed from Troas by Leucata and Acroceraunia to Sicliy and so on to the mouth of the Tiber, so one will get a clearer grasp of Holy Scripture who has gazed at Judea with his own eyes and has got to know the memorials of its cities and the names, whether they remain the same or have been changed, of the various localities."[81]

Jerome's devotion to the land, however, was not only historical. In other places he speaks of the holy places as though they made the past present. In a letter to Marcella (who would eventually settle in the land), Jerome urged her to move to Palestine. When that day comes, he wrote, we shall "enter the Savior's cave and weep together in the tomb of the Lord with his sister and with his mother (John 19.25). We shall touch with our lips the wood of the cross. . . . We shall *see* Lazarus come forth bound with grave clothes, we shall *look* upon the waters of Jordan purified for the washing of the Lord." Jerome ends his letter with the erotic imagery of the Song of Songs: "I have found him for whom my soul longed; I will hold him fast and not let him go." He uses similar, though less emotional language to speak of the prophet Amos. "We shall *see* the prophet Amos upon his crag blowing his shepherd's horn." Realizing perhaps that his rhetoric was losing its footing in common sense, Jerome ends on a note of realism. "We shall see," he writes, "the tombs of Abraham, Isaac, and Jacob, *not* however their tents!" (*ep.* 46.13).

Though Jerome displays more tender feelings toward the sites associated with Jesus than to other places, he makes no clear distinction between them and the places of Israelite history. For Jerome as for the pilgrim from Bordeaux and Egeria, the sites from the Old Testament and the New Testament are yoked to create a single sacred geography. Just how deeply this biblical world had penetrated the consciousness of fourth-century Christians can be seen in another letter. Written about Paula, a Roman noblewoman and friend of Jerome's, it describes their journey up and down the land to visit "those places that are contained in the sacred books" (*ep.* 108.8).

Jerome begins his account in the northern part of the country at the port city of Zarephath, in modern-day Lebanon, fourteen miles north of Tyre. Here the prophet Elijah had raised the son of a poor widow and was fed by grain which was miraculously replenished (1 Kings 17:8–24). Here, says Jerome, Paula "adored her Lord and Savior" (*ep.* 108.8), illustrating how the collective memory of the Christian community was adapting the biblical sites to the beliefs and spiritual aspirations of the pilgrims. From there she went to Tyre, where Paul had once prayed (Acts 21:5), then to the valley of Megiddo, on to Caesarea to see the house of Cornelius, now a church, and to the house of Philip. From there she went to Lydda (Diospolis), to Arimathea, the village of Joseph who buried Jesus, to Emmaus, where Christ was known in the breaking of bread, to Gibeon, where Joshua fought, and to various other places before reaching Jerusalem. As in Jerome's other account, Israelite and Christian sites merge.

In Jerusalem Paula's emotions overwhelm her. Had it not been for her desire to visit the other places in the land, she would never have torn herself away, says Jerome. For when she saw the cross, she adored it "as though she beheld the Lord hanging upon it," and when she entered the tomb "she licked with her mouth the very spot on which the Lord's body had laid, like one athirst for the river she has longed for." From Jerusalem Paula headed south to Rachel's tomb near Bethlehem, to Bethlehem itself, where she kissed the manger, then on toward Gaza to pass the site where Philip read and interpreted the prophets to the Ethiopian Eunuch; next to the oak of Mamre, to Hebron, and other places in the region. She returned to Jerusalem and after some days of rest set out for Jericho, Bethel, the tombs of Joshua and Eleazar, Jacob's well near Mount Gerizim, the caves of the prophet Obadiah, Cana and Capernaum, Nain, and other sites in Galilee. Again she must have returned to Jeruslaem because from there she set out on the final leg of her journey to visit monasteries and Christian churches in Egypt.

Reading through these and other accounts, one is impressed not only by the fervor of the pilgrims, but also by the large number of sites that had been identified, "with whatever degree of accuracy," as J. N. D. Kelly quips in his biography of Jerome.[82] In Palestine holy places seem to spring up like mushrooms. Roman Palestine was being transformed as the number of Christians increased in the region. This is not to say either that Christians were the majority or even that the pilgrim sites were the exclusive preserve of the Christians. At the oak of Mamre, for example, pagans as well as Jews made pilgrimage to the site, and one pilgrim said that the shrine had a screen running down the middle: "Christians come in on one side and Jews on the other," and, he adds, "they use much incense."[83] But Christianity was in the ascendancy, and the continuous flow of pilgrims to shrines and churches all over the country, many following the same itinerary, helped create the sense that the entire region, not just the holy places, was set apart from the rest of the Christian world.

Living in the Land

The holy places were also vital centers of Christian life. As the liturgical scholar John Baldovin observes, the complex of buildings at Golgotha and the Anastasis was "not only a memorial but also the ecclesiastical center for the Jerusalem church, complete with baptistery and bishop's residence."[84] Not only was this the case in Jerusalem. Whenever Egeria reached a biblical site, she always found Christians living nearby, often monks and nuns: "And I cannot do enough to express my gratitude to all the holy men who so kindly and willingly welcomed so unimportant a person as me to their cells and, what is more, took me round all the biblical sites I kept asking to see."[85] Other pilgrims had similar experiences: "We came to Horeb, the mount of God, and as we were moving on in order to climb Sinai, we were suddenly met by a crowd of monks and hermits, singing and carrying a cross. They greeted us with great respect, falling on their faces to the ground, and we did the same and wept."[86] All over the country—on the coast, in the Negev desert in the south, in the Jordan valley, around the Sea of Galilee, and especially in Jerusalem and Judea—the evidence of the Christian presence was visible in new churches, in monasteries, in hostels constructed for pilgrims, and in the swelling population which came to profit from the new things happening in Palestine.

In this period we pick up the first hints that living in the land, not simply visiting the holy places as a pilgrim, conferred spiritual blessings. Again Cyril of Jerusalem is an early witness. The outpouring of the Holy Spirit on the day of Pentecost took place in this city of Jerusalem, Cyril reminds his hearers. "This honor belongs to *us,* and we speak, not about the good things that have happened to others but *among us*."[87] Others expressed the same idea. In a sermon on Stephen, the first Christian martyr, who was martyred in Jerusalem, Hesychius, a presbyter living in Jerusalem in the fifth century, declaimed, "*Among us* Stephen fixed his courtyards and his tents, *among us* he received the lot of his ministry and the part of his martyrdom. *Here* he had his altar of sacrifice and the bema of his blessing, the field of his teaching and the theater of his eloquence."[88] In Hesychius's sermon the accent is less on a specific site, for example, the tomb in Jerusalem, than it is on the city and its inhabitants. He is thinking not only about holy places, but also about the community of Christians that resides in the city and has resided there since the time of Stephen, that is, since the beginning of Christianity.

A few decades later, in a letter to the empress Eudocia, a pilgrim and booster of the holy places, Leo, the bishop of Rome, urged her to make her "place of habitation" in Palestine because only there could she see the "evidences" of Christ's passion and the "signs" of his wondrous acts.[89] If one saw these evidences, one would recognize that Christ lived the life of a human being. In theological parlance he was "true man." Leo was not an impassive observer. He was consciously using the holy places to support his theological position. Yet he had a point. Daily contact with the holy places works on the heart and mind, and without the witness of the places where Christ lived, Christian memory loses its anchorage in history.

For the first time Christians begin to draw parallels between the call of Abraham and the immigration of Christians from other parts of the world to Palestine. In his letter encouraging Marcella to come to Palestine, Jerome cites Genesis 12: "What are God's first words to Abraham? Go out he says from your land and from your kindred, and go to the land I will show you." Abraham followed the bidding of God so that he might "*reside* in a land of promise" (*ep.* 46.2). Elsewhere Jerome uses this text metaphorically to describe spiritual leave-taking, renouncing the world and forsaking family, home, and earthly goods.[90] Here too it carries that sense, but it also refers to an actual journey to Palestine, and it will be used in the same way by later monastic authors. An even more revealing comment occurs in a letter about the imminent invasion of Palestine by the trans-Caucasian Huns, who had desolated the Armenian highlands and parts of Syria. The populace was terrified, and some headed for Joppa to take the first boat sailing abroad. "I remained," writes Jerome, "at the place *I had settled* in the East because of my deeply rooted love of the holy places" (*ep.* 77.8). Bethlehem was Jerome's "resting place" because it was the "homeland [*patria*] of the Lord. . . . I dwell here because the Savior has chosen it" (*ep.* 108.10). He calls Bethlehem "our Bethlehem" (*ep.* 58.3).

Jerome defends the epithet *holy* for the city of Jerusalem. Against Origen, Eusebius, and critics in his own day, he insists that the phrase "holy city" in Matthew refers to the actual city of Jerusalem. With wintry disdain he scorns those who claim that "holy" can be applied only to the "heavenly" Jerusalem (*ep.* 46.7).[91] Christian artists lent him support. In the mosaic of Jerusalem set in the apse of the Church of Santa Pudenziana in Rome during Jerome's lifetime, we glimpse for the first time how the holy city had begun to imprint itself on the Christian imagination. In the center of the mosaic sits a bearded Christ on a throne with a nimbus about his head. On either side sit the apostles in two groups, among them Peter on one side and Paul on the other in the places closest to Christ. Behind each group stands a female figure, one representing the church from the gentiles, the other the church from the circumcision. Behind this group is a portico extending across the whole mosaic, and behind it stands a series of buildings that can be clearly identified as the new Christian buildings in the city, the Martyrium, the Anastasis, the Imbomon, and the Eleona church. Behind the buildings stands a mountain, and above it an enormous cross that reaches into the heavens. The mosaic depicts the triumphant Christ enthroned in the heavenly Jerusalem, but it does this by portraying the actual fourth-century city with "remarkable naturalism."[92] Imperceptibly the actual city of Jerusalem was being invested with celestial grandeur.

Although *holy city* had begun to be used by Christians to designate the earthly Jerusalem, the term *holy land* as a designation for the new Christian land did not become current until later. Here and there *holy land* crops up, but the occurrences are few.[93] It is missing in the pilgrimage accounts, Egeria does not use it, and it does not appear in the long letters of Jerome dealing with the land. In the few places where it does occur in Jerome's writings, the phrase carries no distinctively Christian overtones. In one letter he says that the Israelites carried the bodies of Joseph and the patriarchs from Egypt to the "holy land" (*ep.* 109.2). But the mention of holy land seems irrelevant to the topic under discussion and is used simply as a descriptive name. Similarily in his commentary on Ezekiel he uses the term *terra sancta* as a designation of the land Ezekiel describes in the final chapters (*Comm. in Hiezech.* 47. 15–17; *CC* 75, 720).[93] It is possible that the term *holy land* was used by Jews in Palestine and for that reason Jerome avoided it.[94] As we shall see in the next chapter, Jerome was engaged in a lively theological and exegetical debate with the Jews about the future of the land. In those disputes he expressed quite different views from those in his letters to pious and devout Christians.

A remarkable passage on the holy land from this period comes not from Jerome, but from his contemporary St. Augustine, who lived at the other end of the Mediterranean in North Africa. A friend of a certain Hesperius had gone on pilgrimage to Palestine and brought Hesperius a carton of soil from Jerusalem, "where Christ was buried and rose again on the third day." Augustine calls this soil holy land (*terra sancta*) (*civ. dei* 22.8). Hesperius placed it in a box in his bedroom, and its presence frightened away evil spirits. "Out of feelings of reverence" (he felt uncomfortable with the box of holy soil in his bedroom), he asked Augustine whether it would be acceptable to bury the soil and construct a small shrine at the spot.[95] Augustine had no objection, and soon people were trudging to the shrine for healing. When a young peasant who was paralyzed heard of the shrine, he had his parents carry him to the holy place. He left it walking on his own legs!

Here, as elsewhere, Augustine's piety collides with his theology. God, he wrote, does not limit his possession to a small part of the earth. When the Scriptures speak of "possess the land" (in the beatitudes), they have reference to a heavenly land, not one that can be tilled with a plow.[96] Yet Augustine tolerated, even approved, the transporting of soil from the holy land all the way to North Africa as a talisman against evil spirits and a balm for healing. Had Hesperius returned with a piece of the cross or a holy nail or a stone from the tomb, objects that had had physical contact with Christ's body, one might more easily understand Augustine's behavior. But dirt that could be scooped up anywhere? Christ's sojourn on earth, it seems, had sanctified not only the specific places where he lived and died, but the very soil of the land itself.

7 Your Ancient Ruins Shall Be Rebuilt

Early in the fifth century, a Jew living on the island of Crete in the eastern Mediterranean dreamed that he had been sent to deliver the people of Israel out of exile. Like Moses of old who had led the Israelites from Egypt through the Sea of Reeds to liberate them from Pharaoh's slavery, he imagined he would lead the Jews of Crete through the Mediterranean Sea to the land of promise. According to Socrates Scholasticus, a Christian historian who records the story, this Moses redivivus traveled around Crete for a year, preaching his message of redemption. So beguiling were his promises that some Jews sold their property, abandoned their businesses, and gave away their money.

When the appointed day dawned this new Moses directed his followers to a promontory and urged them to fling themselves into the waters below. Those who had arrived first leaped off the cliff, only to be dashed against the rocks or drowned. Some were rescued, according to Socrates, by Christian fishermen. Moses, however, slipped away, and when his followers realized they had been deceived, they abandoned the Jewish way of life and embraced Christianity.[1]

No doubt Socrates recounted this story to show the superiority of Christianity over its rivals, particularly Judaism. The power of Christ surpassed the power of Moses. Socrates is a careful historian; his information is often corroborated by other sources and by other historians of his time. In this case, however, he is the sole witness. Whatever the story's historical kernel, it bespeaks an awareness among Christians in the fifth century that Jews living in the diaspora yearned to return to the land of Israel and would enthusiastically follow a leader who promised to lead them home. What Socrates reports may be simply a historical fiction to embellish the success of the Christian religion or the unhappy tale of a luckless community seduced by a smooth-talking charlatan—but it may point to more.

A key to the story lies in the phrase "land of promise." This is a *Christian term* used to designate the land given to Abraham, Isaac, and Jacob. The phrase itself does not occur in the Hebrew Bible, though the idea is present in the story of Abraham. After God called Abraham to leave his country and go to the "land that I will show you," God appeared again to Abraham and said, "To your descendants I will give this land" (Gen 12:7). The phrase first occurs, as we have seen, in the New Testament book of Hebrews, where it designates the land to which Abraham journeyed. "By faith Abraham obeyed when he was called to go out to a place which he was to receive as an inheritance; and he went out, not knowing where he was to go. By faith he sojourned in the *land of promise,* as in a foreign land, living in tents with Isaac and Jacob, heirs with him of the same promise" (Heb 11:8–9).

By the fourth century Christian commentators on the book of Hebrews had identified the land of promise with a future heavenly land. Eusebius of Caesarea reflects the conventional view in his commentary on Isaiah 33:17: "Your eyes will see the king in his beauty; they will behold a *land* that stretches afar." This text, says Eusebius, refers to the "land of promise, the heavenly land" which the soul sees from afar.[2] In support of this interpretation he cites the beatitude "The meek will possess the land." "Land of promise" was a synonym for the phrase "land of the living" in Psalm 27 (v. 13) and hence referred to "eternal life." In Christian parlance the land of promise was a celestial country established by God, a place more splendid than any to be found on this earth, a land that awaited the saints after death.

The term, however, did have another meaning in this period. This may again be seen in Eusebius's commentary on Isaiah at 11:15: "The Lord will utterly destroy the tongue of the sea of Egypt; and will wave his hand over the river with his scorching wind." According to Eusebius, this passage refers to "Moses of old" through whom the "hand of the Lord delivered the Israelites out of Egypt and led them through the Red Sea and brought them into the *land of promise* which formerly belonged to other tribes." Here "promised land" refers to Palestine, the land to which the Israelites returned after escaping from Egypt and wandering in the desert.[3]

The attitudes of Christians to the land in the early part of the fifth century were shifting. On the one hand, as I noted in the previous chapter, Christians had begun to see the land of the Bible as a Christian land hallowed by the footsteps of Jesus and Christian history; on the other hand they had enough contact with Jews, particularly in Palestine and Syria, to know that Jews believed the land had been promised to them and would one day be restored to Jewish rule. In discussing biblical history a Christian could use the term promised land to designate the actual land in which the ancient Israelites lived; however, when the discussion turned to the present meaning of the term, especially in debates with Jews, they refused to apply it to the land of Judea. For the term *promised land* implied, as the story of Moses of Crete shows, that the land given to Abraham's descendants continued to hold out promise to the Jews. Hence Christian thinkers invoked the traditional idea that promised land designated a heavenly land.

By the beginning of the fifth century there could be little doubt that the future of the biblical land lay in the hands of Christians (that is, the Romans or Byzantines, as they came to be called). This historical fact, however, had not yet penetrated Christian consciousness, and what gives this period its particular interest is that we can trace the subtle changes taking place in Christian thinking as it did. We can also observe that ideas formed in the generations after the exile in Babylonia (discussed in chapter 2) remained very much alive among Jews in this period. A good place to begin is with Jerome, in particular, with a little-known letter he wrote to a Roman civil servant in Gaul named Dardanus.

Palestine Not the Promised Land

Claudius Postumus Dardanus, prefect of Gaul in the early fifth century, had long shown an interest in religious questions. Once he had written to Augustine to inquire about certain theological matters, and in 414 C.E. he wrote to Jerome to ask, "What is the land of promise [*terra repromissionis*]?"[4] From the way Jerome answers Dardanus's query, it appears that Dardanus had been discussing the meaning of the term with Jews, and, toward the end of the letter, Jerome addresses the Jews directly. The issue, as Jerome formulates it, was whether "land of promise" refers to the present land, that is, to Palestine, or to some other land. "The Jews assert," says Jerome in his reply to Dardanus, "that this land [Palestine] is the land of promise" (*ep*. 129.1).

As Jerome's statement intimates, the question posed by Dardanus requires an answer that is not simply historical. The pressing agenda was the relation between the promised land and the actual land in which Jerome was living, Judea in the Roman province of Palestina Prima. In his reply Jerome appeals to two biblical texts, one from the Psalms and the other the beatitude about "possessing the land." The phrase "land of promise," he writes, is a synonym for the term used by David in the psalm: "I believe I will see the good things of the Lord in the *land of the living*" (Ps 27:13). This land, the land of the living, is the same land that the Lord spoke about in the gospel: "Blessed are the meek for they will possess the land."[5] In Jerome's view, "land of promise" refers to a heavenly country (*ep*. 129.3), and most of the epistle is a defense of this interpretation.[6]

Jerome's initial argument is that when David wrote the verse "I will see the good things . . . in the land of the living" he was residing in Palestine. Not only did he live in the land, he was king and ruled over a mighty nation extending from Egypt to the Euphrates. How could David speak about receiving the land as a matter of promise when he already "possessed it as a result of his victories"? If David was living in the land of promise he would hardly refer to this land as a thing to be hoped for, a place to be obtained only at a future time. Therefore "the land of Judea . . . is not the land of the living" and cannot be the land of promise. Further, the beatitude of Jesus cannot be taken to refer to Judea. The meek and gentle are not the kind of people who possess a land. It is the common experience of humankind that the strong and mighty control the earth. If the meek are to possess the land, *the land* must designate a spiritual entity.

As fanciful as these arguments may appear, they do possess a kind of eccentric logic, at least from the Christian point of view. They restrict the meaning of the term either to the original promise to Abraham or to a heavenly hope that is only tangentially related to the descendants of Abraham. After Abraham and his descendants settled in the land, according to Jerome, it was no longer fitting to speak of the actual land (where the Israelites once lived) as a land of promise. In Dardanus's words, as rephrased by Jerome, "The land which the Jews possessed when they returned from Egypt had been possessed by their ancestors previously, therefore it is not a *promised* land but a *restored* land" (*ep.* 129.1).

After setting forth the main line of his reply to Dardanus, Jerome offers a series of ad hominem arguments against Jewish views of the land. Palestine, says Jerome, is much too tiny and desolate to be the promised land. When I first read this letter I was reminded of Mark Twain's quip in *The Innocents Abroad*: "The word Palestine always brought to my mind a vague suggestion of a country as large as the United States. I do not know why, but such was the case. I suppose it was because I could not conceive of a small country having so large a history."[7] With much greater sarcasm Jerome points out that the land extends only from Dan to Beersheva, hardly 160 miles in all. Even Israel's most powerful kings, David and Solomon, did not possess more than this tiny territory. Jerome excludes the coastal cities, Gaza, Ascalon, Gath, Accarus, and Azotum as well as lands of the Idumeans [Negev desert] in the south and the lands east of Jerusalem. "I am embarrassed," he says, "to mention the land's breadth, lest I might appear to give the pagans an occasion to blaspheme. From Joppa to our little village, it is only 46 miles, after which there is a vast desert, full of ferocious barbarians. . . . This, O Jew, is the length and breadth of your lands; yet you glory in these things and prattle about them to ignorant people in the different provinces" (*ep.* 129.4).[8]

Jerome ends this broadside against the Jews with a mordant line from the Latin bard Persius: "Throw your / Baubles to the crowd! I know you outside and in." These words are taken from one of Persius's satires about an indolent young man who gets by on his family name. Puffed up with his pedigree, he brags to his friends about his noble ancestors. You claim, writes Persius, that you are "a descendant (number one thousand) of some Tuscan / Ancestor, and parade once a year with the gentry, / In Purple, to salute your censor. Or throw your / Baubles to the crowd! I know you outside and in, / and I wonder—does shame have no hold on you?" (*Pers.* 3.28–30). Behind Jerome's words we can detect a voice we have met earlier, namely, that of Jews who took pride in their illustrious past, in the tales of kings and prophets, and who appealed to the glory of ancient Israel as a warrant for present Jewish claims to the land.

Undaunted by Jerome's marshaling of biblical passages, the Jews apparently rejoined with their own dossier of biblical texts. Chief among these is Numbers 34, a passage that lays down extensive borders for the land.[9] In this text Eretz Israel extends north to Hamath in Syria and eastward well beyond the Jordan River. To this claim Jerome replies that even within the "narrow limits of [their inheritance]," the Jews never had complete dominion. They were unable to expel foreigners from their cities, and, even more to the point, Jerusalem has not always been a Jewish city. The name Jerusalem is one among several, for once it was called Jebus, then Salem, third Jerusalem, and now Aelia. Further, to this day only ruins remain of the Jewish city and the temple. A seasoned polemicist, Jerome ends his exchange with more biting humor. I do not wish to "mock the land of Judea," he writes, but is it really a "land flowing with milk and honey"? It is more like a "land of thornbushes" than the "land of the living" (*ep.* 129.6).

Even Jews recognized there was some hyperbole in the phrase "land of the living." One rabbi asked, "Can the Land of Israel be the land of the living when people are dying there?" Yet, few Jews were that sardonic. They were more likely to say, "Behold, the land of the living must be none other than Tyre and its villages [or Caesarea and its villages], for there is plenty there and everything is cheap." On the other hand, the term "land of the living" did carry eschatological overtones among some Jews. The phrase "my portion is in the land of the living" was taken to refer to the "land whose dead will be the first to be resurrected in the days of the Messiah."[10]

In the hope that those buried in the land of Israel would be the "first to come to life" at the Resurrection of the Dead, Jews living outside of the Land of Israel began (in the third and fourth centuries) the custom of transporting the remains of their dead for reburial within the Land of Israel. Inscriptions on tombs name persons who lived their entire life outside of the land (in Syria, for example) who died in the country in which they were born and whose bones were carried by their loved ones to be buried in the Land of Israel. They would be the first to greet the Messiah, and burial in the Land of Israel was said to atone for sins. "If someone died outside of the land and was buried there, then he has two sins; if he died there and was buried here [in Eretz Israel], then he has one sin. Another said, 'Burial here atones for their death [outside of the Land].'"[11]

Only within the Land could a Jew assume the happy obligation of observing the Law to its fullest extent, that is, fulfill all the precepts of the Law including the agricultural laws. "Rabbi Simlai asked: Why did Moses our teacher long to enter Eretz Israel?. Did he want to eat of its fruit or to be satisfied from its bounty? No. For Moses said: 'Many precepts were commanded to Israel but they could only be fulfilled within Eretz Israel. I wish to enter the Land in order I might be able to fulfill all of them" (*b. Sotah* 14a).[12] Living in the land was thought to outweigh all other commandments, a principle beautifully illustrated in a story about a group of rabbis who were traveling outside of the Land. When the rabbis arrived at a city in Syria and realized they were outside of the Land of Israel, "they raised their eyes to heaven, wept, rent their garments and recited the biblical verse 'You shall possess [the Land] and live in it and you shall observe all the statutes and the ordinances' [Deut. 11:31–32]. Then they returned [to the Land of Israel], and when they came to their homes they said: 'The duty of dwelling in the Land of Israel is equivalent to all the other commandments of the Torah.'"[13]

It is apparent that Jewish views of the Land are very much on Jerome's mind as he responds to Dardanus's query concerning the phrase "land of promise." For Jews the Land of Israel continued to be viewed as their land and as a unique inheritance of the Jewish people. Jerome calls it "your land" (*ep.* 129.4). Galilee continued to be the home of a sizable Jewish populace, and Caesarea was a large Jewish center. The Jewish patriarch, a living symbol of former Jewish rule in the land who dwelled in the Land, retained the privilege of fixing the calendar (which was normative for Jews living elsewhere) and presided over the supreme Jewish court. Eretz Israel was still a center of Jewish learning. Even though the Land was under foreign rule, it was nevertheless an ornament to the Jewish people, and it bound all Jews together in familial and spiritual kinship. And, as the tale of Moses of Crete suggests, the Land of Israel continued to serve as a beacon of hope for Jews.

Biblical Prophecy and the Restoration of Jerusalem

When he began to study the Scriptures, Jerome, like most Christian biblical scholars, was dependent on the Greek translation of the Hebrew Bible called the Septuagint.[14] The Septuagint was used by Christians living in the eastern Mediterranean and was the basis for translation into other languages. In the early Christian centuries few Christians could read Hebrew, and the Septuagint was viewed as the authoritative Christian Bible. Jews, however, even in communities that prayed in Greek and read the Scriptures in that language, possessed Hebrew versions of the Scriptures, and in Palestine Hebrew scholarship flourished.

Even before moving to Palestine Jerome had begun to study Hebrew, and in one of his early works, *Hebrew Questions,* he expressed doubts about relying solely on the Greek translation of the Bible. When he settled in Bethlehem, his contacts with Jewish scholars deepened, and he realized that if his views on the interpretation of the Hebrew Bible (the

Christian Old Testament) were to receive a hearing, he would have to ground them in the original text. In 390 he began to translate the Bible from Hebrew into Latin. "With my eyes open I thrust my hand into the flame," he wrote in the preface to his translation of the book of the prophet Isaiah into Latin.[15] In the next twenty-five years Jerome would write a whole library of commentaries on the Hebrew prophets, and these works, written by a Christian scholar living in Palestine, offer us a lively portrait of conflicting views of Jews and Christians on the interpretation of the biblical promises about the land of Israel.[16]

I begin with the famous vision (as Jerome calls it) in Ezekiel 37 about the valley of dry bones. This text had been interpreted by Christians as a reference to the general resurrection at the end of time.[17] Ezekiel, however, gives the image of the bones a much more particular meaning: "Son of man, these bones are the *whole house of Israel*" (Ezek 37:11). Further, the text says that God will raise the people of Israel from their graves "and bring [them] home into the land of Israel" (37:12). In his exposition of this passage Jerome provides a Latin translation of the Septuagint as well as of the Hebrew text "lest," in his words, "the Hebrews bring accusations against us that the text has some error in its wording." The Jews, he complains, make fun of the Christians and try to show discrepancies in the Christian readings in their manuscripts. They interpret the text as a promise of their return to the land of Israel, for it teaches that they will live "not in another land but in that which God gave to his servant Jacob, in which their fathers, Abraham, Isaac, and Jacob and the other holy ones lived. Not only will they themselves dwell there, but also their sons and their descendants, as Vergil said, 'sons of his sons and those who are born from them.' And they will dwell there not for a short time but forever" (*Comm. in Hiezech.* 37; *CC* 75, 520–21). The Jews say that this text refers to the time of Zerubbabel in the sixth century B.C.E., but they *also* believe that it points to the "future advent of *their own* Messiah" (*CC* 516).[18] The vision of the dry bones was at once a reminder of God's gracious deliverance from captivity in Babylonia in the past and a prophecy of the future restoration of the house of Israel. In short, the words of Ezekiel embody a promise that is yet to be fulfilled.

Jews gave other prophetic oracles a similar interpretation. The prophet Isaiah announced, "Your ancient ruins shall be rebuilt; you shall raise up the foundations of many generations; you shall be called the repairer of the breach, the restorer of streets to dwell in" (Isa 58). Commenting on this passage Jerome wrote, "The Jews and friends of the letter that kills refer this to the rebuilding of the cities of Palestine. They claim either that this took place under Zerubbabel and Ezra and Nehemiah *or* they refer it to the end of time, to the reconstruction of Jerusalem and the laying of deep foundations around the cities and the buildings of walls so high that no enemy can enter and all foes will be barred from them" (*Comm. in Esaiam* 58:12; *CC* 73a, 672–73).

Isaiah 58 is a restorationist oracle that envisions the return of the exiles, the resettling of the cities of Judea, and the rebuilding of Jerusalem. The original setting of the prophecy was the sixth century B.C.E., when the Israelites were in exile and longed for the time they would return to the land. According to the Jews living in Palestine in the fifth century C.E., however, the oracle did not speak of the past alone; it also had meaning for present and future generations of Jews.

In the books of the major Hebrew prophets, Isaiah, Jeremiah, Ezekiel, Daniel, and of the minor prophets, Micah, Haggai, Zachariah, and others, there are dozens of so-called restorationist passages. These texts announce a time when the exiles will return to the land of Israel, Jerusalem will be rebuilt, Jews will rule the land, and sacrifices will again be offered in the temple. Here are a few examples chosen almost at random: Isaiah 35:10, "And the ransomed of the Lord shall return, and come to Zion with singing"; Ezekiel 36:8, "But you, O mountains of Israel, shall shoot forth your branches, and yield your fruit to my people Israel, for they will soon come home"; Amos 9:11–15, "In that day I will raise up the booth of David that is fallen and repair its breaches. . . . I will restore the fortunes of my people Israel, and they shall rebuild the ruined cities and inhabit them. . . . I will plant them upon their land, and they shall never again be plucked up out of the land which I have given them."[19]

Whenever Jerome comes upon one of these passages in his commentaries, unfailingly he reports that the Jews interpret the prophetic word to refer to a restoration of Jewish life in the land; his commentary on Ezekiel 28:25–26 is an example. The text reads, "Thus says the Lord God: when I gather the house of Israel from the peoples among whom they are scattered, and manifest my holiness in them in the sight of the nations, then they shall dwell in their own land which I gave to my servant Jacob. And they shall dwell securely in it, and they shall build houses and plant vineyards." This passage speaks of the time of God's vindication, when "the people of Israel, which had been dispersed among many nations, will return to its own land and God will be hallowed among them . . . and they will dwell in the land which he gave to their father Jacob; and they will dwell securely trusting in the Lord, and they will build houses, and plant vines, when his promises have been fulfilled." Some take this passage, says Jerome, to be referring to the time of Zerubbabel, when the Jews returned from exile in Babylonia to dwell in the "land of Judea"; others, however, believe it refers to the future and think that it will be fulfilled "in the last time," that is, in the Messianic age (*Comm. in Hiezech.* 28:2026; *CC* 75, 400).[20]

By the time Jerome wrote his commentaries Christian expositors were well informed about the historical setting of the Hebrew prophets. Because of the growing sophistication of Christian biblical scholarship (also because of the challenge of Jewish exegesis), Christian scholars realized that the words of the prophets could not be applied with impunity to Christ, as for example Barnabas and Justin Martyr had done in the second century.[21] The prophets spoke to their own age as well as to future ages. If Ezekiel lived in the sixth century B.C.E., whatever the future meaning of his prophecy, his words also had meaning in the historical circumstances of his own time.

The question, however, was whether the meaning of the prophets' words were exhausted by a strictly historical interpretation. In some cases all details of a text could be understood in light of the historical circumstances in which it was written, but other texts seemed to make room for a future that was as yet undisclosed. Since the age of the apostles Christians claimed that this future was being realized in their own time, in "these last days," as the New Testament put it (Heb 1:1; Acts 2:17). Christians scrutinized the biblical text to discover a word, a phrase, a chance detail that showed the prophet had spoken not only about his own time but about the future.[22] What one discovers in reading Jerome's commentaries is that Jews did the same. Jeremiah 31 is a good illustration: "Behold the days are coming, says the Lord, when the city shall be rebuilt for the Lord from the tower of Hananel to the Corner gate. . . . It shall not be uprooted or overthrown any more for ever" (38–40). The Jews take this text to refer to the "messianic reign in the land of Judea." They point to the tower of Hananel and the gate and say, "There the sanctuary of the Lord *will* be built and *will remain forever*." At the time of Zerubbabel, they explain, these things did not come to completion; hence the prophecy is transferred to the "time of the Messiah," who will come at the end of the world when the city of Jerusalem will be constructed with gold and precious jewels (*Comm. in Jer.* 31:38–40; *CC* 74, 323).

The key to this interpretation of Jeremiah is the term *forever*.[23] Just as Christians, to secure a foothold in the text for a Christian *interpretation,* seized on the historical fact that Jewish rule in Jerusalem had come to an end (it did not last "forever"), so the Jews now counter Christian exegesis with a similar argument. Let us grant, they say, that the words of the prophets were not wholly fulfilled in the sixth and fifth centuries B.C.E. That does not mean they were fulfilled at the time of Jesus. For many of the things promised by the prophets did not happen at the time of Jesus, and they have not happened since. The words of the prophets will be fulfilled only when the things they spoke of actually take place in the course of history, that is, when the people of Israel return to dwell in the land in safety and a new Jerusalem is reconstructed.

Behind this debate in Palestine in the fifth century lies, of course, the ancient hope of return and restoration. The prophets speak of a grander, more splendid, more enduring restoration than was achieved during the period of the Second Temple. As the early Christians had fastened on this "more" to apply the words of the prophets to the life of Jesus and the Christian community, so the Jews seized on the "more" to legitimate their hopes for a future fulfillment of the promises found in the Hebrew prophets. Paradoxically (from the Christian point of view), when the issues are framed in this way, it is the Christians who are the defenders of the old (what has already happened) and the Jews who look for signs of the breaking in of a new age.

Jerome's presentation of Jewish hopes about the land in his commentaries conforms closely to the messianism of earlier Jewish sources (discussed particularly in chapter 2): the Jews will return to Judea; Jerusalem will be rebuilt and the cities of Judea restored; Jews will again rule the land; a prince in the line of David will be king; the temple will be reconstructed, and sacrifices will again be offered; all the requirements of the Law will be carried out; circumcision will be observed in the Land of Israel, and the Sabbath will be kept; there will be prosperity and long life; people will build houses and live in them and plant vineyards and harvest their fruit; the nations of the world will serve Israel, who alone will live in the land.[24] The passage "I will pour out my Spirit upon the house of Israel" (Ezek 39:29) was interpreted as "The spirit of the Lord will be poured out on them that they might dwell in *their* land. On the day of the Lord only those who belong to the house of Israel will dwell in the Land, not the nations" (*Comm. in Hiezech.* 39:17–29; *CC* 74, 543.2021–23).[25] From Jerome's perspective the Jews have translated the spiritual vision of the prophets into a political hope. His most frequent reproach is that the Jews interpret the prophets "*carnaliter,*" in a carnal or earthly manner. Isaiah's words "They shall build houses and inhabit them; they shall plant vineyards and eat their fruit" are taken "*carnaliter,*" that is, they signify that Jerusalem and the cities of Judea will be restored to their original condition (*Comm. in Esa.* 65.21; *CC* 73a, 763). What Jerome means by *carnaliter* is *historically,* that is, the prophecies about the restoration of the land refer to the actual return of the Jews to the territory they once ruled and to the establishment of a Jewish kingdom in Jerusalem.

At no point in these commentaries does Jerome challenge Jewish exegesis by an appeal to the new Christian developments that had taken place in the fourth century and were continuing in his lifetime. Only in letters to Christians who wished to come to Palestine on pilgrimage does he speak of the religious significance of the actual city of Jerusalem. Apparently some Christians believed that Jerusalem was accursed because Jesus had been crucified there. In this view, only the heavenly Jerusalem, not the actual city in Judea, could be called the holy city. In response to these views Jerome defends the "religious significance of Judea" (*ep.* 46.4) and the appellation holy city as a designation for Jerusalem. Jesus, he reminds his readers, wept over Jerusalem.(*ep.*46.5). Today the city of Jerusalem, which had been venerated of old by the Jews, has been endowed with "much greater majesty than it possessed in former times. . . . Is the tomb of the Lord less worthy of veneration" than the ancient temple of the Jews? (*ep.* 46.5). "The entire mystery of our faith is native to this province and city," he exclaims. "As much as Judea is exalted above the other provinces, so much is this city exalted above all Judea" (*ep.* 46.3).

In Jerome's commentaries, however, there are no hints of these views. When Jerome engages in debate with Jews about the present meaning of the oracles of the prophets, he seldom strays far from traditional Christian views of Jerusalem as expressed by Eusebius and Origen. The city of Jerusalem is significant only as a symbol of the heavenly city or of the new spiritual reality of the church. That Christian and Jewish claims to the city and to the land might be in conflict has not crossed his mind.

"Blessed are you, O Lord, Rebuilder of Jerusalem"

After the defeat of Bar Kochba in the second century, Jewish hopes for a restoration of political institutions in Eretz Israel were less vocal than they had been earlier. But there is no reason to suppose they had been abandoned. The reader may recall the words of Hippolytus, the third-century Christian writer cited at the end of chapter 2. The Jews, he wrote, live "in hope of a coming of the Messiah in the future . . . who will gather the entire nation of the Jews and will establish Jerusalem as his royal city and restore the ancient traditions. The people will exercise royal and sacerdotal prerogatives and they will dwell securely for a long time" (*haer.* 9.30).

From Jewish sources we know that Jews continued to pray for the restoration of Jerusalem. The ancient prayers of the synagogue, used by Jews to this day, include one petition (out of eighteen) for the restoration of Jerusalem. The text of this prayer in the old Palestinian rite, as preserved in fragments found in a synagogue in Cairo, reads as follows: "Have compassion, O Lord our God, in your abundant mercy, on Israel your people, and on Zion the abode of your glory, and upon the royal seed of David, your justly anointed. Blessed are you, O Lord, God of David, Rebuilder of Jerusalem."[26]

The Tefilah, as this prayer was called, uses the phrase "Rebuilder of Jerusalem" as an epithet for God. Alongside other descriptions—"shield of Abraham," "who resurrects the dead," "who forgives readily," "who hears prayers"—God is identified by actions that relate specifically to Jerusalem and the Jewish people. These same accents appear in two other petitions in the prayer: "May it be your will, O Lord our God, to dwell in Zion, and may your servants worship you in Jerusalem." And the final petition: "Bestow thy peace upon Israel your people and upon your city and upon your inheritance." God is called the God of David for it is David's seed that will rule in the restored Jerusalem. When Hippolytus said that Jews hoped the Messiah would establish Jerusalem as his royal city he was reflecting what he had heard from Jews.

The prayer for the rebuilding of Jerusalem can be found at four different places in the traditional Jewish prayerbook: in the weekday Tefilah, in grace after meals, in the benediction after reading from the prophets in the synagogue, and in the benediction recited at the marriage ceremony.[27] This prayer rests on the biblical account that the land of Israel was promised to the descendants of Abraham and that one day the Jews would dwell in the land in peace and security. Until that day the promise to Abraham will not have reached its fulfillment. The rebuilding of Jerusalem will also mean the restoration of worship in the temple, as a passage from the Mishnah suggests: "Therefore, O Lord our God and the God of our fathers, bring us in peace to the feasts and pilgrim festivals which are approaching while we rejoice in the building of your city and rejoice in your worship; and may we eat *there* from the sacrifice and the Pesach offerings. . . . Blessed are you who have redeemed Israel" (*m. Pesachim,* 10.6).

A few years ago an ancient Hebrew inscription was found in Jerusalem with a portion of a verse from Isaiah 66: "You shall see and your heart shall rejoice; your bones [shall flourish] like the grass." This passage is taken from the glorious vision of the restored city in the final chapter of Isaiah. On that bright day the Lord will extend Jerusalem's prosperity, and the wealth of the nations will flow to her like an overflowing stream. As a mother comforts her children so will God comfort Jerusalem. This inscription is dated to the fourth or fifth century. Because it includes only a fragment of a biblical verse without commentary, its meaning remains elusive. Yet, in light of what we have learned from Jerome's commentaries, it may be a cryptic way of expressing Jewish hopes of restoration.[28] Words from the same vision of Isaiah, "They shall not build and another inhabit, they shall not plant and another eat" (Is 65:21–25), have expressed the hopes of modern Israelis. Some years ago I saw this text painted on a hut not too far from Gaza in the territory that was later returned to Egypt after the peace treaty between Israel and Egypt.

It is possible that events in the late fourth century kindled a fresh burst of Jewish messianism.[29] The most significant event was the plan of Emperor Julian (the Apostate) to rebuild the temple in Jerusalem. By restoring the Jewish temple Julian hoped to prove the mendacity of the Christian religion and expose Jesus as a false prophet. According to the gospels, the disciples once pointed out the buildings of the temple to Jesus, and he had said, "You see all these, do you not? Truly, I say to you, there will not be left here one stone upon another, that will not be thrown down" (Matt 24:1–2). Christian interpreters took this text to signify that the temple would never again be rebuilt. If the temple were ever reconstructed its existence would be definitive proof that Jesus spoke falsely.

How Julian's proposal was greeted by Jews is unknown except from what is reported in Christian and pagan sources.[30] According to these admittedly hostile accounts, "The Jews were seized by a frenzied enthusiasm and sounded trumpets" when they heard of the plan. Some donated money for the building. Others claimed that "one of their prophets had returned," and they taunted Christians that their rule would be restored (Rufinus, *h.e.* 10.38). Julian had, it seems, touched a sensitive nerve, and emotions ran high. A generation after his death Christian preachers were still discussing the matter from the pulpit. Jews, said John Chrysostom, went about "boasting that they would get back their city again." Julian's contemporary Gregory, bishop of Nazianzus, said that his intention was "to return the Jews to *their land,* rebuild the temple, and restore the authority of their ancient traditions" (*orat.* 5.3).

What Julian envisioned beyond the restoration of the temple can be only a matter of speculation. It is unlikely that he anticipated the restoration of Jewish rule in a province of the Roman Empire. Yet the rebuilding of the temple would certainly require the resettlement of Jews in Jerusalem and perhaps the establishment of some new type of Jewish social and religious, if not political, life in the land. Whatever his original idea, which no doubt took on a life of its own once it had come to the attention of Jews and Christians, his proposal may have spawned a fresh wave of messianic fervor among Jews and foreboding among Christians.

Julian's project was begun in the spring of 363, but shortly after the workmen began to dig, a powerful earthquake shook the city and other parts of the country, and the work came to a halt. At the time, Cyril was bishop of Jerusalem, but he says nothing about the undertaking. His silence is perplexing, and some have drawn from it the conclusion that the whole episode is a fiction. Recently, however, a letter about the events attributed to Cyril was found in a Syriac manuscript. Though it is unlikely the letter is genuine, it may have been written not too long after the events, perhaps about 400 C.E. In it the earthquake is presented as a fortuitous act of divine deliverance, a display of divine power before the Jews and the pagan emperor.[31]

According to this letter the earthquake took place on the day the workmen had begun to lay the foundations of the new temple. The air must have been electric with tension. Here, the city that so recently had seen the construction of the Martyrium and the Anastasis at the tomb, the "new Jerusalem set over against the old," now witnessed the rebuilding of a temple that was a symbol of all that the new religion had abandoned. With the ardent support of the emperor, and possibly with the help of Jews, workmen began laying the foundation for a building that was an offense to Christianity. On the day work began the Christians of the city gathered in the Martyrium, and after praying there they moved in procession to the Mount of Olives. As they proceeded through the middle of the city they recited psalms and prayed to the Lord that God's truth might be seen by the Jews. As the earthquake shook the city some believed the day of reckoning had arrived, and those who did not believe in Christ discovered that their clothes were marked with a cross, the sign of Christ's crucifixion.

Like other reports of Julian's plan to rebuild the Jewish temple, this one is overladen with legendary details. Yet the very existence of the letter is evidence of the impact of Julian's project on Christians in the early fifth century. No matter what Julian's arcane purposes, the possibility that a new temple might be constructed spread fear among Christians and created friction between the two communities in Palestine.

There is other evidence that messianic hopes sprang up from time to time among Jews during this period.[32] In the mid-fifth century Eudocia, the wife of the emperor Theodosius II, is reported to have looked with favor on Jews residing in Jerusalem and on pilgrimages to the city to pray at the ruins of the temple. Encouraged by Eudocia, some Jews living in Galilee were said to have written a letter to Jews in the diaspora announcing that the dispersion had come to an end and the reunion of the tribes would soon take place. The letter encourages them to go up to

Jerusalem for the feast of tabernacles because "our kingdom will be restored in Jerusalem."[33]

About the same time that these words were written a Jewish poet living in Palestine voiced similar hopes. His name is Yose ben Yose, and his works have been edited recently from an Oxford manuscript.[34] Exactly when Yose ben Yose lived is uncertain. His name is first mentioned by Saadia Gaon in the tenth century. Some scholars place him as late as the eighth century, and some as early as the fourth; his current editor, the Israeli scholar Aharon Mirsky, places him in the fifth century. He was from a priestly family and lived in Palestine.

Among Yose ben Yose's poems are to be found several liturgical pieces in the form of the *malkhiyyot,* a prayer for God's sovereignty inserted in the synagogue liturgy for New Year (Rosh Hashanah). These petitions come at the end of a series of prayers that begin with the blessing of the patriarchs and a recitation of God's acts of deliverance on behalf of Israel. The distinctive feature of the malkhiyyot is that they celebrate God's rule as king over humankind. The oldest form of these prayers date to the period of the Second Temple. They address God as the "Lord of all" and pray that God's name will be revealed in all the earth and among all people. "May all the inhabitants of the world realize and know that every knee must bend, every tongue must vow allegiance." In analyzing the language of this prayer, liturgical scholars have noted that it includes no petition for the establishment of God's kingdom in Israel. Its emphasis is on the world, on all flesh, on God's rule over all creation. It asks that God's reign be recognized and acknowledged by all peoples of the world. J. Heinemann writes, "All this strongly suggests that [these prayers were] composed against the background of the Temple service. Only while the Temple stood could it be stressed that the Divine presence dwells 'up on high' without explicitly stating that it also dwells in the Holiest of Holies."[35]

In the malkhiyyot of Yose ben Yose centuries later, the language of the prayers has changed significantly. The emphasis shifts away from the world to Israel and the city of Jerusalem. No longer is the poet concerned about idolaters who refuse to bend the knee to the God of all creation, the Lord of the universe; now the liturgy is preoccupied with God's presence in the city of Jerusalem. When Yose ben Yose composed his prayers, the rulers of the world—which is to say, the princes of the Roman Empire—were not idolaters (like the Romans), but Christians, who believed, as did the Jews, in the one God who rules over all. Hence the poems no longer ask that God's reign be extended over the whole world, but that God rule in Israel and in the city of Jerusalem:

Make for yourself a terrible name
As of old, may you prosper in the throne of your kingdom
Let the joy of all the land awake and rise up.
Establish your throne in the *city of the kingdom* [Jerusalem].[36]

Within the formal strictures of liturgical poetry, the malkhiyyot of Yose ben Yose reflect a shift in language and sensibility. Even those poems that do not specifically speak about Jerusalem use a distinctively new vocabulary that no longer highlights God's sovereignty over the world but his kingship in Eretz Israel. In one poem Yose ben Yose mentions the Byzantine, or Christian Roman, empire, using the old Hebrew word for Rome, Edom.[37]

Let the deliverers take our side.
Carry off the glory from Edom.
And place on the Lord the splendor of the kingdom.

According to Mirsky this is a prayer for the vindication of Israel against its Christian rulers. Even in poems that do not belong to the genre of malkhiyyot Yose ben Yose is fond of the term *kingdom*. He introduces it frequently in his poems, and it often designates an actual kingdom, a "kingdom of flesh and blood." *Kingdom* signifies Israel's deliverance from oppressive rulers in the land. At times *kingdom* is almost a synonym for *Eretz Israel*: "Stir up the land to carry off the servitude of the kingdom."[38]

Yose ben Yose is an unexpected witness to a new social and religious fact: Jews had begun to sense that the Christian Romans who ruled the Land of Israel worshipped the God of Abraham, Isaac, and Jacob and had a spiritual investment in the city of Jerusalem. Unlike the earlier Romans and previous conquerors, they were not idolaters; they claimed Jerusalem as their own, and in the city of David they had built a magnificent temple to the God of David and Solomon. In this temple, which took the place of the Jewish temple, Christians worshipped the *God of Israel,* prayed the psalms, and read the Jewish Scriptures (the Old Testament) as their own book. For the Romans, Jerusalem was the capital city of a conquered people, a place without spiritual significance; for the Christians it had become *the* holy city, the place where Christ had died and where one could find the memorial of his Resurrection. In this setting, Yose ben Yose's prayer, "Establish your throne in the city of the kingdom," embodied the hopes of the Jewish community that the Land of Israel would vomit forth the intruders and restore Jewish rule.[39]

Jewish Hopes and Christian Fears

For centuries Christians had appealed to the visible evidence of the ruins of the Jewish temple as certain proof that Christianity had triumphed over Judaism. One reason Christians went on pilgrimage to Jerusalem was to see with their own eyes the place where the famous Jewish temple had once stood. Even before the discovery of the tomb of Christ and the building of the Anastasis, Christians came, according to Eusebius, "from all parts of the world," to stand on the Mount of Olives and gaze over at the devastation on the Temple Mount, remembering that God's glory once dwelled there (*d.e.* 6.18; 288d). Only by actually visiting Jerusalem could one see that the city of the Jews was no more. This sight comforted and reassured Christians.[40]

Long after the construction of the new Christian buildings adjacent to the site of Christ's tomb, Christian pilgrims to Jerusalem continued to visit the Temple Mount. A generation after Jerome, an eminent bishop from Syria, Theodoret of Cyrus, traveled to Jerusalem to "see the desolation with my own eyes." Standing before the ruins, he recalled the ancient prophecies about the city (Matt 24 and Dan 9) and his "heart exulted." The Jews have been deprived of their famous house, he writes, "as those who visit it can see."[41] This same bishop, however, had heard disturbing rumors about Jewish hopes of restoring the temple and reestablishing Jewish life in the holy city. Theodoret was a historian as well as a theologian and biblical scholar, and he was well informed about Julian's aborted effort to rebuild the temple several generations earlier. Julian's project had cast a long shadow over Jerusalem for some time after his death. But Julian had lived almost a century earlier, and what Theodoret heard was more current.

Like Jerome, Theodoret of Cyrus was a zealous student of the Scriptures, though not as learned as Jerome (he seems not to have known Hebrew). Among his writings are a series of commentaries that systematically expound the books of the Bible verse by verse. Like Jerome he wrote commentaries on all the prophetic books, on Isaiah, Jeremiah, Ezekiel, and Daniel, and on the minor prophets.[42] Although his commentaries on the prophets are less polemical than Jerome's (at least on the surface), he too was conscious of an alternative Jewish exegetical tradition, and from time to time he presents Jewish interpretations for the purpose of refuting them. As is to be expected, Theodoret's dispute with Jewish interpreters occurs at some of the same passages that troubled Jerome and often takes the same form. Against Jewish claims that the prophecies should be interpreted by reference to the future history of the

Jewish people, Theodoret presents a "spiritual" interpretation that applies the text to Christ and the Christian church.[43]

Theodoret discusses Jewish interpretations on the future of the Land of Israel in his commentaries on Isaiah, Haggai, Micah, Daniel, and others, but the book that caused him the greatest perplexity was Ezekiel. Ezekiel expressed Jewish hopes with uncommon tenderness, and its final section, the grand vision of a new temple, had taken on new urgency since the time of Julian. A typical example of Theodoret's exegesis is his commentary on Ezekiel 37, the vision of the valley of the dry bones. What catches Theodoret's attention in this chapter is not so much the image of the reviving of dry bones (though he does observe that the bones are a type of the "resurrection of all") as the statements at the end of the chapter about the future of Davidic rule in the land of Israel. Ezekiel wrote, "They shall dwell in the land where your fathers dwelt that I gave to my servant Jacob; they and their children and their children's children shall dwell there forever; and David my servant shall be their prince forever" (Ezek 37:25).

From the way Theodoret approaches this passage it appears that Jews he knew claimed that signs of Davidic rule could still be found in the Land of Israel in the office of the Jewish patriarch. As noted in chapter 5, the legitimacy of this claim was debated at the time of Origen, and it reappears in Christian writers in the fourth century, notably in Cyril of Jerusalem and in Jerome.[44] By the middle of the fifth century, however, the patriarchate had been abolished by the Roman emperor. Perhaps the demise of the patriarchate was so recent that Jews still nurtured hopes that the office would be restored. In any case, in one of his writings Theodoret presents a debate between an orthodox Christian (himself!) and a "heretic" about the "legitimacy" of the patriarchate. The question centers on the interpretation of Psalm 89:4: "I will establish your [David's] descendants forever." At one point Theodoret asks whether the Jewish patriarch stands in the line of David. His opponent says yes, interpreting the text to mean that the rule of David had not come to an end; Theodoret, on the other hand, says that the passage does not apply to the patriarch because his sovereignty has come to an end. The text says that David's rule must last forever, hence the passage is to be referred to the rule of Christ.[45]

These same arguments appear in Theodoret's commentary on Ezekiel 37. The Jews agree with us, he says, that the words of Ezekiel "do not fit Zerubbabel" and cannot be applied to the return from exile in the sixth century B.C.E. That is, a strictly historical interpretation of the text is inadequate. Zerubbabel was not a king but an administrator, and his rule came to an end. Ezekiel, however, says that the rule of David would last forever. "If the Jews take the text to be speaking about an eternal rule of the house of David, let them show that the race of David still rules." Since Jews cannot bring forth evidence to support this claim (according to Theodoret), only two possibilities of interpretation remain: either the prophecy is false or one must interpret it christologically, that is, refer to the eternal rule of Christ who was born of the "seed of David." The Jews, as Theodoret acknowledges, could hardly agree that the prophecy is false; hence they claim that there continues to be a "rule of the Jews" in the land and that the "house of David exists and is known" (*Comm. in Hiezech.* 37:25; *PG* 81, 1197).[46]

To this point the debate seems a trifle inconclusive, Christians appealing to an eternal rule of Christ that is invisible and Jews claiming Davidic descent for a nonexistent patriarch. Theodoret, however, breathes a bit more easily when he reaches the next verse, "I will bless them and multiply them and will set up my sanctuary [temple] in the midst of them *forevermore.*" Here Theodoret appears to be on firmer ground. The temple and all the holy things associated with it have long since been destroyed. "Therefore since we do not *see* the outcome of these [prophecies] according to the Jewish interpretation," the prophecy must be given a spiritual interpretation and applied to Christ's eternal rule. Only such an interpretation accords with the "historical facts" (*PG* 81, 1197).[47]

Theodoret's most extensive discussion of the restoration of Jerusalem comes at the very end of his commentary on Ezekiel. The prophet, after setting forth in unprecedented detail the shape of the new city, ends his book with the words, "And the name of the city henceforth shall be, the Lord is there." The Septuagint translator, however, had read the Hebrew to mean: "And the name of the city . . . shall be its name." Theodoret observes that the city continued to be called Jerusalem even after it was rebuilt several times. "Name" here signifies "glory" and the prophet was referring to the time after the coming of Christ when Jerusalem would be famous among the gentiles (cf. Ezek 16:14).[48] Jewish interpreters, however, saw the text quite differently. For them Ezekiel prophesied the time when the Shekinah, the glory of the Lord, will return to the city, which is to say, to the Jewish temple. "*From the day* that the Lord's Shekinah [glory] rests upon it, the name of the city will be: The Lord is there."[49]

Theodoret begins his exposition of the final section of Ezekiel by reminding his readers that the city of Jerusalem had been built and rebuilt several times in the past, under Zerubbabel and Nehemiah, at the time of the Maccabees, and later by Herod. He makes no mention of Bar Kochba.

Today, however, he says, some Christians, bewitched by Jewish fantasies, believe "another building of Jerusalem has been promised and worship according to the Law of the Jews will be established there" (*PG* 82, 1248c). What Theodoret presents here as the opinions of Jews and judaizing Christians about the future of Jerusalem is of course similar to what we have learned from Jerome. Nevertheless it is significant that these ideas were circulating almost two generations later in northern Syria, not only in Palestine. What sets Theodoret apart from Jerome, however, is not what he reports about Jewish views, but what he reveals about his own attitude toward Jerusalem. For when Theodoret heard rumors about the building of a Jewish temple in Jerusalem, unlike Jerome, he thought at once of Christian Jerusalem, Jerusalem as it existed in his own day, not just of the heavenly Jerusalem. He writes,

> *Today* in Jerusalem there is the church of the Cross, the church of the Resurrection, the church on Mount Zion, the church in Holy Bethlehem, and many other churches. If the temple of the Jews were rebuilt, would these be destroyed, or would they continue to be held in honor? If they are honored, as they have been in the past, will they be revered by the Jews, or will they be scorned? . . . If the Jews do honor them, to which of the sacred edifices will they show greater respect? To that of the Cross, to the church of the Resurrection, or to the one that is going to be built [the temple]? If they show greater honor to that one [their temple], they would do so because they lack perfect knowledge. But if they prefer these [the Christian buildings], then the reconstruction of that one [the temple] would be superfluous. If, on the other hand, they give equal honor to the Christian building and to the temple, would they not offer sacrifices there [in the temple]? If this be so they would receive no benefit from the divine mysteries [Christian Eucharist]. How could they benefit from the divine mysteries along with gentile believers, when the [Jewish] Law prohibits mixing with gentiles?

The result of all this, concludes Theodoret, is that Christian rites and Jewish rites would be celebrated side by side, making conflict and strife inevitable. Christians would insist on their way of life and Jews on theirs (*PG* 81, 1252a–53c).

This remarkable passage, without parallel in Jerome or other Christian writers from this period, vividly and concretely portrays Jewish hopes for the future against the reality of Christian Jerusalem in the fifth century. Here there is no talk about a distant utopia; Theodoret imagines the Jewish temple as an actual building set in the midst of the

Christian churches of the city. So realistic is his depiction that one can envisage Jews and Christians living side by side and having to choose whose sanctuary they would enter and which rites they would celebrate. No doubt Theodoret projected on to Jerusalem his experience of living in the cities of Syria where Jews were numerous, and Christians were drawn to Jewish festivals and other practices, much to the dismay of Christian leaders.[50] But the point here is that he is speaking about Jerusalem, the new Christian metropolis.

Theodoret is the first Christian writer to sense that the building of Christian Jerusalem injected a new factor into Christianity's relation to Judaism. Jerome denounced Jewish appeals to the prophets as a basis for the future aggrandizement of the city of Jerusalem because the prophets spoke about spiritual matters, Christ and the church. This line of interpretation also appears in Theodoret. But in the passage from his commentary on Ezekiel he transposes the debate into a quite different key. The idea that the temple would be rebuilt and Jewish life established anew in Jerusalem was odious to Theodoret because Jerusalem was now a Christian city.[51]

In other ways Theodoret had begun to integrate the new Christian Jerusalem into his interpretation of the Scriptures. As we saw earlier, writers had used the verse from the psalm "Let us go up to the place where his feet have stood" as a warrant for Christian pilgrimage. Theodoret goes a step further; he interprets Christian pilgrimage to the holy city as the fulfillment of biblical prophecy. The famous oracle in Isaiah 60, "Arise, shine, for your light has come, and the glory of the Lord has risen upon you," includes the words, "Nations shall come to your light, and kings to the brightness of your rising." Theodoret says that this is fulfilled by the great throng of pilgrims that flock to the "city of Jerusalem to worship God not in the temple of the Jews but to see those famous places, that of the Cross, the Resurrection and the Ascension."[52] Theodoret's exegetical ingenuity helps one appreciate the change that was taking place in Christian attitudes toward Jerusalem by his time. Unlike earlier commentators he is willing to apply the oracles of the prophets directly to Jerusalem's churches and shrines and to Christian pilgrims to the biblical land. With the rise of Christian Jerusalem the prophecies could be applied historically, which is to say, literally—in Jerome's words, *carnaliter*—to the actual city, not only to spiritual realities or to the heavenly city.

In the second century Melito, the Christian bishop of Sardis in Asia Minor, had written, "The Jerusalem below was precious, but it is worthless now because of the Jerusalem above." Almost a century later Origen of Alexandria had disclaimed any identification between the holy land and the land of Judea. In disputes with Jewish rabbis he had insisted that it was the heavenly Jerusalem, not the earthly city, that was the "mother of believers." By the time Theodoret wrote his commentaries on the prophets, however, Jerusalem was a vibrant Christian metropolis, soon to be elevated to the status of a patriarchate. The city was home to a dazzling assembly of churches and shrines, and its holy places were visible signs of the power and majesty of Christ. Like a mother Jerusalem greeted its children from all over the world, offering them balm and healing within its walls. It had also begun to welcome holy men and women from Egypt, Syria, Armenia, Asia Minor, Greece, Italy, and elsewhere. These holy people, some of whom came to Palestine with the word of God to Abraham, "Go up to the land that I will show you," were the first to identify Palestine as the Christian holy land.

8 The Land that I Will Show You

Tertullian of Carthage boasted, “We [Christians] are not Brahmins or Indian ascetics who dwell in the wilderness and are recluses from communal life” (*apol.* 42). Nevertheless, Christianity, like other religions, offered hospitable soil for the cultivation of the ascetic life. In the mid-second century the physician Galen had observed that some Christians “refrain from cohabiting all through their lives” and others exercise “self-discipline and self-control in matters of food and drink,”[1] but the withdrawal of pious men and women into the desert, the adoption of a solitary life outside the walls of the cities, was a thing of the future.[2]

For the inhabitants of the cities of the Roman world, especially those living in the eastern provinces, the desert was never far from mind or even from sight. In Egypt it lay only a few hundred yards from most communities, and one could stand on a small hill and gaze across the green strip that hugged the Nile to the far side of the river, where the lush fields ended abruptly and the mauve sand began. In Jerusalem, it was possible to stand on the Mount of Olives and look over a vast expanse of desert stretching to the Dead Sea shimmering in the distance. In time, the calm solitude of the desert proved irresistible to Christians.

Philo, a resident of cosmopolitan Alexandria, deemed it altogether fitting that God revealed the Law to Moses in the "depths of the desert" rather than in a city (*Decal.* 2). And Origen, also a native of Alexandria, in a happy phrase, extolled the desert as a place "open to heaven."[3] In the Scriptures the desert (or wilderness as the term is commonly translated) became an abiding symbol of intimacy between God and the people of Israel. "I will allure her, and bring her into the wilderness, and speak tenderly to her," said the Lord in an oracle of the prophet Hosea (Hos 2:14). After Elijah challenged king Ahab he retired to the desert east of the Jordan, and later it was in a cave deep in the desert of Sinai that God spoke to him "in a still small voice" (1 Kings 19). Never was Elijah closer to God than when he was alone in the desert. John the Baptizer, too, was at home in the desert, and when he preached, "all the country of Judea, and all the people of Jerusalem went out to him" (Mark 1:5). Among those who went into the desert to hear John was Jesus of Nazareth, who became his disciple, and, according to the gospels, Jesus withdrew to the desert at turning points in his life. There he found solitude and peace, said John Chrysostom, because the "desert is the mother of tranquillity."[4]

Up to this point the chief figures in our narrative, Origen, Eusebius, Jerome, Paula, Theodoret of Cyrus, were urban dwellers, men and women whose spiritual and intellectual home was the great cities of the Roman Empire. Early in the fifth century, however, a group of men and women began to settle in the desert east of Jerusalem, and it was these solitaries who first claimed the term *holy land* for Christians. In their lives and in their piety they embodied the changes that had begun to take place in Christian Palestine in the late fourth and early fifth centuries.

The Desert of Judea

The vast deserts of Egypt were the first to entice men and women out of the towns and villages to experiment with a new way of life. In the deep quiet and solemn stillness of remote caves and desolate wadis zealous men and women, unencumbered by the constraints of family life and the expectations of society, were able to seek God alone and contend with the devil firsthand. At first only a few hearkened to this new vision of the gospel's imperative, "Be ye perfect," but by the end of the fourth century, the solitary life had attracted thousands, not only in Egypt, but also in Syria, Armenia, Cappadocia, and elsewhere. Within a few generations the deserts were filled with devout Christians eagerly "hunting after God" (Theodoret of Cyrus, *hist. rel.* 13.6). Often uneducated, unable to read the Scriptures in Greek, suspicious of book learning, speaking only the language native to their regions, Coptic or Syriac, these hearty folk were untouched by the literary culture and refinement that formed the outlook of the bishops. By the simplicity of their lives and their pungent homespun wisdom they delighted and provoked the faithful and stirred them to new heights of virtue.

By the beginning of the fifth century, as the number of pilgrims to Jerusalem mounted and people from all over the Christian world became familiar with the geography of Palestine, some discovered that the Holy Land had not only shrines and memorials, but also a desert, the desert of Elijah, John the Baptizer, and of Jesus. The idea of withdrawing into this desert had not occurred to Christians in Palestine before this time. Indeed when the first monks in Palestine withdrew (the technical term for adopting the solitary monastic life) in the early fourth century they showed little interest in the Judean desert. Hilarion, whom Jerome calls the "founder and teacher of this way of life [monasticism]" in this "province," (Palestine), came from a tiny village called Thabatha five miles south of Gaza (*Vita Hil.* 14). Geographically Gaza was closer to Egypt than to Jerusalem, and Hilarion modeled his way of life on Egyptian practice, that is, on the example set by Antony.[5] On one occasion (but only one, according to Jerome) Hilarion went up to Jerusalem to venerate the holy places, but he did not choose to live in the desert of Jerusalem. "The blessed Hilarion, a Palestinian who lived in Palestine, set eyes on Jerusalem for only a single day, lest one who lived so close to the holy places appear to despise them, yet on the other hand, he did not wish to appear to confine God within prescribed limits" (*ep.* 58.3). Whether it is Jerome or Hilarion who provides the theological explanation for Hilarion's reluctance to dwell in the wilderness near Jerusalem I cannot say; but it is clear that Hilarion believed he would be as close to God in the desert near his home as he would be in Judea.

The first monk to settle in the Judean desert was Chariton, a native of Iconium in Asia Minor (present-day Konya) who came to Jerusalem as a pilgrim in the fourth century.[6] In contrast to Hilarion, he seems to have made his home in the Judean desert *because* it was close to Jerusalem.

How it came about that he actually settled in the desert was, however, due to fortune. He fell into the hands of a band of robbers who bound him and brought him to a cave located in the Judean desert. One day a viper crept into the cave and poisoned the wine jugs of Chariton's captors. When they drank the wine they all died, and Chariton, instead of returning to Jerusalem or his home in Iconium, founded a monastery near 'Ein Fara, an abundant spring northeast of Jerusalem. In time he also founded two other monastic settlements, one on the cliffs overlooking Jericho and the other south of Bethlehem.

Unlike Hilarion, Chariton had not been influenced by Egyptian monasticism, and he inaugurated a new and distinctively Palestinian monastic pattern of organization. Up to this time the two forms of monastic life were that of a single monk living by himself, the eremitic life, and that of a group of monks living in community, the cenobitic life. The pattern in Palestine was a cross between the two: the monks lived in individual cells or caves scattered about the desert, but they shared a chapel, bakery, and perhaps one or two common buildings. During the week the monks lived alone in their individual cells, and on Saturday and Sunday they gathered for worship, to collect supplies, and carry on any business. This form of monastic life went by the name *laura*, which originally may have designated the path from the cells to the chapel and common buildings.[7]

By the end of the fourth century, during the reign of emperor Theodosius (379–95), the presence of the holy places in Jerusalem and vicinity had begun to lure wealthy and well-connected men and women from the West. One famous visitor was a colorful noblewoman, Poemenia, who had come east to visit Christian hermits in Egypt. In a great display of piety she sailed up the Nile River in her own boats to visit John of Lycopolis in the Thebaid. While in Egypt she resolved "to go to the city Jerusalem to pray at the tomb of Christ as well as at Golgotha and the Anastasis." Once in the Holy Land, she gave freely of her wealth and provided funds for the building of a church on the Mount of Olives.[8]

Poemenia was one of the first of a stream of aristocratic women whose piety and largesse made the Mount of Olives a gathering place for religious men and women from the West. The most famous of these women is Melania, who renounced her husband and children to pursue an ascetic way of life in the East. Like Poemenia she first traveled to Egypt but eventually settled in Jerusalem, where she and her friend and companion Rufinus founded monasteries on the Mount of Olives. As these monasteries became well known they attracted other well-connected pilgrims from the West who knew they would not only be welcomed hospitably but could also hear the latest ecclesiastical gossip. Not to be outdone by Melania and Rufinus, Jerome and Paula founded a monastery in Bethlehem near the Church of the Nativity. The reason for their choosing Bethlehem rather than Jerusalem is unclear, but as E. D. Hunt has remarked, "There is a strong impression, fostered by the tensions of the following years, that the establishment in Bethlehem functioned (if not by design then certainly in its practical effects) as a *rival* to the Mount of Olives."[9]

The founding of these two western monastic establishments in Jerusalem and Bethlehem stands in sharp contrast to other developments that were taking place in the Judean desert at the same time. At the beginning of the fifth century, Euthymius, a monk from Armenia (later revered by Christians of the East as Euthymius the Great), made the long journey from his native land to settle permanently in the Judean desert. Unlike the urbane intellectuals from the West who came to the Holy Land to write learned books and inquire about biblical geography, Euthymius's only desire was to live and pray in the desert that was near the Holy City. His sentiment was more like that of T. S. Eliot on his visit to Little Gidding: "You are not here to verify, / Instruct yourself, or inform curiosity / Or carry report. You are here to kneel / Where prayer has been valid."[10] By his humble and rustic life and the largeness of his spirit, Euthymius drew dozens, then hundreds, and finally thousands to the desert east of Jerusalem. His coming transformed the Judean wilderness into a thriving Christian community, thereby altering the relation of Christianity to the Land of the Bible.

The desert east of Jerusalem is a relatively narrow strip of land approximately fifty miles long and ten to twelve miles wide, bounded on the west by the Judean hills and on the east by the Dead Sea and the Jordan River.[11] The terrain is marked by deep valleys and high cliffs, and the climate varies from region to region owing to the abrupt change in altitude between the Judean hills, which rise more than three thousand feet above the Dead Sea. The amount of precipitation also declines, from seven hundred millimeters in the Judean hills to fifty millimeters in the area of the Dead Sea.

The chief sources of water are springs, which can be found in the canyons of the large valleys and along the cliffs that face the Dead Sea, and seasonal rock pools that collect water on the bottom of valley beds—but catchments were built to collect the meager rainwater. The building of a cistern and the construction of a bakery were the first tasks that the monks undertook when they settled in a new place. Most of the monasteries were built on the desert margin, an even narrower strip on the eastern slope of the Judean hills. This area was close to the cities in Judea and had supported settlement for some time. It was along this narrow strip that the Romans had built fortresses to defend the eastern edge of the empire from attack. Here rain was relatively plentiful, making possible the cultivation of grains, fruit trees, and olives without irrigation. During the Byzantine period some settlers had begun to farm the region adjacent to the desert, and in the desert itself there were nomads with whom the monks had close and cordial relations.

A Historian for the Christian Holy Land

The life of Euthymius and that of his industrious disciple Sabas were written by Cyril, a native of Palestine from the city of Scythopolis a few miles south of the Sea of Galilee in the Jordan valley, and the first self-consciously Palestinian writer in Christian history. Cyril was born circa 524 C.E. in Scythopolis (present-day Beth Shean), the metropolis of Palaestina Secunda, a city probably founded in the third century B.C.E. by Ptolemaic mercenaries, though it may go back to the time of Alexander the Great.[12] Sitting astride two principal roads, the routes from Damascus to the Mediterranean Sea and from Damascus through Pella to Gerasa, it was the economic, political, and cultural center of the region. Its Hellenistic roots were deep, and during the Roman period its citizens adorned the city with the familiar marks of Greek culture: a hippodrome, an amphitheater, and a theater which seated eight thousand spectators. During the Byzantine period the city's population was predominately Christian, but Scythopolis was also home for a sizable Jewish community.[13] The famous Beth Alpha synagogue excavated earlier in this century was located in Scythopolis, and more recent excavations have uncovered several other synagogues in the city and vicinity. From Cyril, however, we learn little of Scythopolis. Though he lived in the city at the height of its prosperity and splendor, his heart, it seems, was captive to the desert.

Cyril's father was in the employ of the bishop, his mother was a devout Christian, and their home was a gathering place for monks. Cyril calls it a hostel (217.13–19), and when he was six years old he met Sabas, who was staying with his parents. According to Cyril's account, the aged monk took him in his arms and said, "From now on this child is my disciple and a son of the fathers of the desert." Sabas told the bishop to oversee his education because "I have need of him" (180, 11–14). When Cyril was eighteen years old he left Scythopolis for Jerusalem "to worship at the holy and venerable places of the life-giving wood of the holy cross" (71, 25–72, 1). Jerusalem was the port of entry to the monasteries of the Judean desert, and Cyril, in his own words, "had a deep longing to dwell in the desert" (71, 19–20).[14]

First he went to John the Hesychast, to whom his mother had commended him, but John would not receive him because he was too young. He sent him to the monastery of Euthymius, which was located closer to Jerusalem; there, novices were led through the first steps of the monastic life. For the next ten years he followed the cenobitic, or communal, way of life; only when he was thirty years old did he adopt the distinctively Palestinian style of living by himself during the week and returning to the communal house for the liturgy on the weekend. During this period he began to keep notes which he would later use as the basis for his biographical work.

Like many authors, Cyril found it easier to collect data than to compose a book, and his account of his difficulty in writing these biographies is humorous and touching. When he was living at the New Laura, founded by his hero, St. Sabas, he began to organize his notes, but according to his account he lacked the proper education to turn them into a literary work. Like an anxious and frustrated graduate student Cyril sat at his desk with a pile of note cards before him, incapable of putting pen to paper. One day, however, Euthymius and Sabas appeared to him in a vision, and he heard Sabas say to Euthymius, "Look at Cyril. He has his notes on your life in his hands and is very eager to carry out the task. Though his efforts have been great and he has labored hard, he is not able to begin composing the work." Euthymius said, "How can he begin to write the book about us when he has not received the gift of a worthy style that he might open his mouth and speak?" Sabas said, "Give him, father, that gift." Euthymius took out a box of alabaster and silver filled with honey. He touched Cyril's lips three times with the honey. It had the consistency of oil, and its taste was "much sweeter than honey to my mouth." At once Cyril began to write the preface to the work (83–84).

Cyril's *Lives* comprises seven distinct biographical studies: two long lives, those of Euthymius and Sabas, and five shorter lives of John the Hesychast, Kyriakos, Theodosius, Theognios, and Abraamios. These lives belong to the tradition of Christian hagiography that had begun with Pontus's *Life of Cyprian* in the third century and that received its distinctive character from Athanasius's *Life of Antony,* the first desert monk, in the middle of the fourth century. During the early centuries of Christian history Christians did not write biographies of holy persons, even though the practice of writing so-called lives of memorable people for instruction and edification was practiced in antiquity: for example, in

Plutarch's *Lives,* in Xenophon's account of Socrates, in various lives of Pythagoras, Porphyry's *Life of Plotinus,* in the lives of the philosophers written by Diogenes Laertius and Eunapius. By the time Cyril wrote, however, he had before him a whole series of Christian lives (in addition to the *Life of Antony*) on which to model his work: Palladius's *Lausiac History,* Theodore of Cyrus's *Religious History, Life and Miracles of St. Thecla,* and others.[15]

In the judgment of modern scholars, Cyril's works stand out among the writings of ancient hagiographers: his historical information is detailed and precise, his dating of events is accurate (based on ancient imperial indictions)—a trait that has endeared him to modern readers—and his prose is free of affectation. As Eduard Schwartz, his editor, observed, he exhibits none of the self-conscious mannerism of such other Palestinian writers of his age as Hesychius, Sophronius of Jerusalem, or the rhetoricians of Gaza.[16] He writes a crisp, lively narrative with a keen sense for details and timing. His efforts at characterization are less successful than his skill in storytelling.

Cyril is much more than a Christian hagiographer who wished to display Christian virtue in the form of a life. He is also a partisan spokesman for Palestinian Christianity, for the Christian Holy Land, if you will. The *Life of Antony,* the *Life of Pachomius,* and the *Apopthegmata Patrum* were written to extol the virtues of Egyptian monasticism, and Theodoret of Cyrus had written his religious history to celebrate the flamboyant asceticism of Syria. For Palestine, however, there was nothing comparable. "The authors from which Cyril borrows are not only his models. They are his rivals," writes Bernard Flusin.[17]

Cyril may have borrowed the idea of a regional grouping of holy men and women from Theodoret. In the preface to his work Theodoret had said that his purpose was to write about those whose lives "have shown forth in the Orient" (*hist. rel.* prol. 9), which meant Syria, not the East in general. The care which Theodoret takes in describing his heroes' lives and his fascination with the most bizarre forms of asceticism—living in the open air, inhabiting a hut too tiny to stand in and too narrow to lie in, sitting for years on the top of a pillar shunning all human intercourse—may be his way of placing Syria in competition with Egypt. If you wish to see ascetic stars, he implies, Syria is the place to visit.[18]

Cyril, however, does not simply recount the exploits of the heroes of the Judean desert, as Theodoret told the stories of the holy men and women of Syria; his book reads more like a history of Palestinian Christianity in the fifth and sixth centuries (in particular of the church of Jerusalem) than a conventional collection of holy and exemplary lives. In contrast to most ancient lives, the lives that Cyril wrote give information on the succession of bishops, the churches that were built and consecrated in the Holy City and environs, the course of religious controversies in Palestine, and the relation of the church of Jerusalem to the imperial officials in Constantinople. "Without Cyril," writes Herman Usener, "the history of the church of Jerusalem in that period would lie in darkness."[19] He also provides precious details on the spread of Christianity in Palestine and records the consecration of the first Bedouin bishop, the bishop of the camps, as he calls him, and he sets all this information in a comprehensive chronological and historical framework.

Another sign that his purpose is not simply hagiographical is evident in the structure of the work. In the life of Euthymius, Cyril recounts Euthymius's death (473 C.E.) in chapter 40, yet the life goes on for another twenty chapters after his death and recounts events during the reign of Emperor Anastasius (491–518), the succession of *higoumens* (abbots) of the monastery founded by Euthymius, and other historical details. The same pattern can be found in the *Life of Sabas*. Sabas's death is recorded in chapter 76 yet the work continues for another fourteen chapters so Cyril can narrate the events surrounding the Council of Constantinople in 553, the fifth ecumenical council, at which Sabas's followers were vindicated. The lives, then, cover the period from 400 to 550 C.E., a time when Christians living in Palestine began to realize the unique status of the church in Jerusalem.

Although Cyril of Scythopolis was a native of Palestine, all his heroes were natives of other countries. This feature of the work is no doubt deliberate. Palestinian monasticism was an international movement of men and women who left their native countries to live in the desert close to Jerusalem.[20] Euthymius and John the Hesychast came from Armenia, Sabas, Theodosius, and Theognis from Cappadocia, Kyriakos from Greece, and Abraamios from Syria. Likewise those who came to be their disciples came from abroad. The first three to join Euthymius were from Cappadocia, then three from Armenia, and three more from the Sinai. Only one of his first disciples came from Palestine. So many monks came from Armenia that at the monastery of Theodosius the Liturgy of the Word, the first part of the Eucharistic service, was conducted in Armenian (105).[21] In Egypt and Syria those who took to the desert came in the main from cities and towns in the region. Not so with Palestine. Most of the monks of Palestine came from abroad, and they adopted the Holy Land as their new home, never again to return to their native countries. Theodosius came to be called the "pride of Palestine" (235, 28) and Theognis the "great ornament of all Palestine" (241, 13).

For the monks who settled in the Judean desert, withdrawal into the desert of Judea called for a new beginning. Gerasimos had already achieved notoriety as a solitary in his native country of Lycia in Asia Minor, but when he left his "fatherland" to dwell in the Holy Land he "*began anew* the anchoritic life in the desert near the Jordan" (44, 23–24). John the Hesychast was an accomplished ascetic and bishop in Armenia, yet when he arrived in the Judean desert all his former accomplishments counted for naught. Even though he was much older than the other novices he took on himself the most menial tasks and had to learn anew the monastic way of life as it was practiced in the Judean desert. The "treasure of his virtuous deeds" was hidden from the monks of the Judean desert (205, 8–9).

Cyril's book takes its shape from *place,* the desert that was contiguous with Jerusalem the holy city. There were deserts aplenty in Egypt, in Syria, in Cappadocia, in Armenia, but only this desert was called "the desert of Jerusalem" or "the desert east of the holy city," "the desert of the holy city" or simply the "dear desert."[22]

Colonizing the Judean Desert

Cyril begins his account of the monks of the Judean desert with the arrival of Euthymius in Palestine in 405 C.E.:

> Our great father Euthymius led by the Holy Spirit came to Jerusalem in the 29th year of his life and adored the Holy Cross and the Holy Anastasis and the other holy places. He visited the God-fearing fathers who lived in the desert, and as he learned the virtue and way of life of each one, he stamped this on his own soul. Then he came to live at the Laura at Pharan six miles from the Holy City. Because he loved solitude, Euthymius remained in a hermit's cell outside of the laura possessing nothing at all of the things of this world. He learned, moreover, to make rope so that he would not be a burden to anyone, and could from his own labor give to those in need. He freed himself from all earthly responsibility so that he had only one care—how to please God in prayers and fasting. [14][23]

In Armenia Euthymius had been consecrated to God as an infant. His mother, whom Cyril likens to Hanna the mother of Samuel, presented him as a sacrifice to God when he was three years old, and, from the time he learned to read, he served as lector in the church. As he grew older and was instructed in the Scriptures and in "secular subjects," he amazed his teachers with his wisdom, and, as he learned the Scriptures, "he desired to be an imitator of those divine and virtuous men who are contained in the Scriptures." He was zealous in prayer and in attendance at the liturgy. Later he was ordained a presbyter and eventually put in charge of several monasteries; since childhood he had loved the solitary life and desired solitude and stillness so that he might serve God alone. As he grew in maturity, he initiated the practice of retreating to the desert in the period from Epiphany to Easter "imitating the philosophy of Elijah and John." When he arrived in the Judean desert, however, all this was forgotten, and Cyril depicts him as a tyro who must learn the monastic life from the ground up.

Euthymius settled first at the Laura of Pharan to begin his apprenticeship in the Judean desert. He remained there for five years, during which time he became friends with Theoctistus. Together they began the practice of withdrawing shortly after the feast of the Epiphany in early January into the "desert of Koutila," a name that Cyril uses for the more arid regions east of the monastery at Pharan.[24] They remained in this wilder, more isolated part of the desert until Palm Sunday "to commune with God in silence through prayer" (15, 1). During one of their journeys to the desert of Koutila, Euthymius and Theoctistus came to a deep, inaccessible gorge. High up on the north flank they saw a cave and managed to climb up to it. They consecrated the cave as a "church of God" and lived on plants from the area. The place was inhabited by shepherds, and as Euthymius and Theoctistus became friendly with them, the monks began to depend on the people of the local village, Lazarion (Bethany), for their necessities. In time, other monks joined them, and a cenobitic monastery was founded at this location.

Euthymius, however, again grew restless because he desired greater solitude and seclusion. In the company of a young monk from his hometown, Dometianus, he decided to go deeper into the wilderness, and he withdrew into the desert of Rouba, which lay south and east of the desert of Koutila (closer to the Dead Sea and in the direction of Masada [Mount Marda]).[25] "Traveling southward in the desert along the Dead Sea, he came to a high mountain set apart from the other mountains called Marda, and finding on it a broken-down cistern for water he rebuilt it and remained there nourished by the plants and wild berries which he found. In that place he built the first church in the area, which is preserved to this day, and he constructed an altar in it" (22, 2–8). At Masada the Christian monks were able to use cisterns and building materials left by Jews who inhabited the region during the period of the Second Temple.

Euthymius remained at Masada only for a short time, but others came after him and eventually established a monastic settlement on the mountain. One can still see the remains of a church built during this period.[26] Now Euthymius headed west into the region of Ziph, east of Hebron, because "he wanted to see the cave in which David had fled when he tried to escape Saul" (22, 9–10). Here, too, he established yet another monastery, really a hermitage. Euthymius cured the son of a local chieftain possessed by a demon, and the people of the village of Aristobulias "built a monastery for him."

Cyril's account of Euthymius's wanderings was not simply a story of the colonization of the desert of the holy city; Euthymius's adventures were also presented as a mythical tale of the restoration of a pristine state in which human beings were no longer subject to the hegemony of sin. Euthymius is a second Adam and an image of the new creation. Among his gifts, writes Cyril, was authority over wild animals and snakes, for when God "dwells or comes to rest in a certain human being all things are subject to him [or her] as they were before Adam transgressed the commandment of God." In addition to the wild beasts even the elements are subject to such a person (23, 6–9).

After traveling around the Judean desert, Euthymius returned to the vicinity of Jerusalem frustrated, it seems. No matter how deeply he withdrew into the desert he always attracted a crowd. Finally he decided to settle in a cave a few miles east of Jerusalem (present-day Mishor Adumim on the West Bank) not too far from Theoctistus's monastery. Although it was less isolated than the places he had visited, it was to become his permanent home. It may have been chosen because of its proximity to Jerusalem or simply because Euthymius was very fond of the site. "He loved this place very much because it was flat and quiet and well-aired . . . ," writes Cyril. "The whole area is pleasant and quite exceptional, due, as has already been mentioned, to its temperate climate" (23, 24–26.2). The monks were not immune to the majesty and beauty of the desert. Not only did they place their monasteries in beautiful and commanding locations, they also embellished the landscape with gardens and fruit trees.[27]

If one looks at the map of the Judean desert, one can see that Euthymius's wanderings in search of solitude took him in a grand arc around the edges of the desert. He went east from Jerusalem to the Dead Sea, from there walked parallel to the sea until he reached Masada, and from there turned back west to the desert south and east of Hebron, making his way back northward through Bethlehem to the vicinity of Jerusalem, where he had begun. In Cyril's view, Euthymius's journey had a purpose: he was sowing seed that would lead to the "colonizing" of the desert. "Today it is the gateway into the entire desert that had been colonized by his seeds" (24, 4). When the empress Eudocia came to the Judean desert, the "solitary cells sprinkled across the desert" reminded her of the passage in Numbers which drew a picture of the tribes of Israel encamped in the wilderness: "How fair are your tents, O Jacob, your encampments, O Israel" (Num 24:5) (53, 15). During Euthymius's lifetime the number of monasteries in the Judean desert increased from three to fifteen.[28]

Euthymius was responsible for the conversion of a Saracen, or Arab-speaking Bedouin, tribe to Christianity and the consecration of the first bishop to the Arabs in Palestine.[29] When Euthymius was establishing the monastery of Theoctistus he came in contact with a Bedouin tribe headed by a certain Aspebet, a Sassanid phylarch who had become an ally of the Byzantines. Aspebet's son's body was withered on his right side from head to foot. While living in Arabia the son had a vision of Euthymius, and, in a dream, the lad was directed to seek him out in his monastery east of Jerusalem. At first Theoctistus refused to allow Aspebet and his son to see Euthymius, but after Aspebet showed him the paralyzed hand of his son, he relented. When Euthymius saw the boy he made the sign of the cross over him, and he was healed at once. When Euthymius saw that the Bedouins believed, he catechized them and had them baptized in a font in a corner of a cave. Aspebet was renamed Peter. For forty days Euthymius instructed the tribe with the divine word, teaching them they were no longer Agarenes or Ishmaelites but descendants of Sarah. Peter built a cistern and a bakery for the monastery. As the number of Christians grew among the Saracens, Euthymius asked Juvenal to ordain a bishop. Euthymius proposed the name of Peter, and he was consecrated the first bishop to the Arabs in Palestine with the title bishop of the camp of tents. Euthymius's relations with the Arab-speaking tribes can perhaps be seen as a portent. Several hundred years later, when Arabic had become the lingua franca of the region, it was the monks in the monasteries established by Euthymius who would be responsible for the first translation of Christian writings into Arabic and the beginning of Christian Arabic literature.[30]

As to so many of the great spiritual leaders of Christian antiquity, it was given to Euthymius to "know the day of his death." As we have seen, it was his custom to withdraw into the outer desert after Epiphany to remain there until Palm Sunday. In 473, when he was ninety-seven years old, the monks noticed he had made no preparations for the journey. "Do you not plan to go tomorrow, honored father?" they asked. Euthymius answered, "I will remain here this week and on Saturday at night I will leave." He was, says Cyril, speaking of his death (57, 16–23). At a vigil in memory of the holy father Antony, he told the brothers that he would not keep another vigil with them in the flesh. In the morning, he called together the brothers and spoke his final words to them:

> My beloved brothers, I go the way of my fathers. If you love me, keep these commandments. Through everything hold fast to sincere love, which is the beginning and end of all doing of good and the bond of perfection. Just as it is not possible to eat bread without salt, so it is impossible to practice virtue without love. All virtue is established through love and humility by experience and time and grace. Humility, however, exalts, but love does not allow the proud to fall. The one who humbles himself will be exalted, but love never ceases, for love is better than humility. . . . Offer then to the [divine Logos] the purity of soul and the chastity of your body and sincere love with all zeal.

After saying these things he dismissed all except Dometianus, his faithful companion. Dometianus remained with him three days, and on the night of the Sabbath he fell asleep and was "gathered to his fathers an old man and full of years" (Gen 25:8) (58, 2–59, 15).[31]

Sabas the Jolly Builder

Euthymius had sown the seed in the desert of Jerusalem, but his disciple Sabas would nurture the young plants, uproot the weeds, hoe and cut and prune, and bring the garden to full bloom. Euthymius was a "lover of solitude" who desired only "to commune with God in silence through prayer."[32] Sabas, however, was a jolly builder, as the Byzantinist H. G. Beck called him. Unlike Euthymius he was no recluse. He loved the sound of the hammer and saw, the scrape of a trowel on stone. He would have been at home in the company of those nineteenth-century American bishops whose legacy of massive stone churches and sturdy red brick schools still mark some of the neighborhoods of America's large cities. Appropriately, Sabas's foundation high up over the brook Kidron east of Bethlehem, Mar Saba, even to this day stands as a working monastery.

Sabas was Euthymius's junior by almost forty years. When he arrived in Palestine as a youth of eighteen from Cappadocia, Euthymius was in his mid fifties. At first Euthymius turned him away. The monks were wary of accepting boys whose smooth skin and girlish features tempted the brothers. "My child, I do not think it right for you, being so young, to remain in the laura. For it is not good for the laura to have such a young person, nor is it proper for a young person to live in the midst of anchorites [solitary monks]. Go then, my son, to the monastery below with Abba Theoctistus and there you will profit exceedingly." Theoctistus was abbot of a cenobitic house whose regimen was less rigorous than that followed by the anchorites.

Sabas's ambitions for the desert east of the Holy City were more enterprising than those of his predecessors. Cyril presents Sabas's decision to leave Cappadocia and settle in the Judean desert as follows: "Eager to advance from glory to glory, conceiving in his heart the ascent to God, and completing ten years in his monastery, he had the god-pleasing desire to go to the Holy City and to live the solitary life in the desert surrounding it. For it was necessary through him to *colonize* it and to *fulfil* the prophecies about it of the sublime Isaiah" (90, 5–10).

In Cyril's account, Sabas's journey to the Holy Land was a fulfillment of biblical prophecy. Which prophecies he had in mind, however, are not mentioned. The term translated "colonize" means "build" or "found" a city and is seldom used in early Christian literature. It does, however, occur in Athanasius's *Life of Antony,* a work that Cyril knew. After Antony had spent twenty years alone in the desert pursuing the ascetic life by himself, he came forth from his cell and began to persuade others to follow his example. Athanasius writes, "And so, from then on, there were monasteries in the mountains, and the desert was colonized by monks who left their own people and registered themselves for the citizenship in the heavens" (*V. Ant.* 14).

Cyril of Scythopolis was no doubt thinking of Antony when he depicted Sabas as "building a city" in the Judean desert. But in the *Life of Antony* this term is not geographical. It is used rather as a metaphor for the spread of the new monastic way of life. So many followed Antony that they transformed the once-empty desert into a thriving human community. In Cyril of Scythopolis's account of Sabas, however, the idea of building a city has reference to the desert east of Jerusalem, the desert of Elijah and the prophets, of David, of John the Baptizer and Jesus, in short the desert of biblical history and hope.

Eduard Schwartz thought the reference was to Isaiah 58:12: "And your ancient deserts [waste places] shall be rebuilt; you shall raise up the foundations of many generations." But Cyril may just as well have intended other passages. "The parched wilderness shall be glad, the desert shall rejoice and blossom like a lily, and the deserted places of the Jordan shall bloom and rejoice. . . . My people shall see the glory of the Lord and the majesty of God" (Isa 35:1–2). Or the following: "The Lord will comfort you O Zion, and give courage to all its deserted, and will make her wilderness like the garden of the Lord; joy and gladness will be found in her, thanksgiving and the voice of song" (Isa 51:3).

Biblical passages such as these that speak of a renewal of the land and the rebuilding of its cities were, as I noted in chapter 7, taken by Jews to signal the restoration of Israel in the land. As Jerome observes in his commentary on Isaiah 58:12, "The Jews and friends of the 'letter that kills' [2 Cor 3:6] refer these things to the restoration of the cities of Palestine" (*Comm. in Isa.* 58:12; *CC* 73b, 672). It is doubtful that Cyril's appeal to the prophecy in Isaiah has anything to do with the Jews. He seems oblivious to the concerns that motivated Jerome's exegesis of the prophets. Yet, by introducing the theme of colonization, he implicitly sees the growth of Christianity in Palestine as a fulfillment of biblical hopes. Almost imperceptibly Christians were beginning to use the biblical language and images of Jerusalem and Judea to speak about the Christian communities living in the land. Which is to say, Christians were beginning to give the biblical promises a political or historical interpretation.

The theme of colonizing the desert of Jerusalem also appears in the founding of the great laura on the brook Kidron. When Sabas had reached the age of forty he traveled around the desert seeking an isolated place to settle. One day he arrived at a high bluff overlooking the brook Kidron, and while he passed the night in prayer God appeared in an angelic form in a shining robe and showed him a "wadi which came down from the pool of Siloam" (the brook Kidron) and said, "If you wish to *colonize this desert,* stop to the east of the wadi where you will see facing you an unspoiled cave. Enter and dwell in it and He who gives food to the beasts and nourishment to the young ravens that cry will himself care for you" (98, 2–6).[33]

When Sabas awoke he saw a wadi to the south, and to his great joy he discovered a cave high up on the side of a cliff. After he found a way to reach the cave Sabas hung a rope from its mouth so that he could go up and down. For water he had to walk to a cistern over a mile away. After some time, a small company of Saracens came to the place, and Sabas allowed them to enter the cave. When they discovered he had nothing, they left and returned some days later bringing him dry bread, cheese, and dates. Sabas lived there for five years "conversing with God in silence and purifying his spiritual vision in order to behold with unveiled face the glory of the Lord" (99, 5–9). Finally, in the forty-fifth year of his life, he was entrusted with the direction of souls, and he began to receive all those who came to him. In a short time the community included 70 monks, and Sabas provided a "small cell with a cave" for each one. Eventually the community grew to 150 monks, and Sabas found a cave on the other side of the wadi with a natural apse. He converted the cave into a church (still functioning today as the church of St. Nicholas) and built the other structures that would compose the laura. This monastery, the Great Laura of Sabas, wrote Cyril, "stands at the head of all the lauras in Palestine," and Sabas was the "founder and guardian of our city in the desert and the illuminator of all Palestine" (141, 8–11).

At the height of this monastic movement, the number of monks who lived in the Judean desert was approximately three thousand.[34] Most of these solitaries, as noted earlier, came from outside of Palestine. One biblical text that appears in several biographies of the Judean monks (though not in Cyril's book) is Genesis 12, the call of Abraham: "Now the Lord said to Abram, 'Go from your country and your kindred and your father's house to that land I will show you.'" Paul of Elousa writes of Theognis, "After he passed some time in silence living a way of life fitting for solitaries, he heard the word of Scripture God had spoken to Abraham: 'Go forth from your land and your kinsmen and go up to the land I will show you.' At once he did as he was commanded; he left his native land and went up to Jerusalem to pray at the holy places."[35] Theognis then settled in the Judean desert, never to return to his native land. This text from Genesis 12, observes Derwas Chitty, could well have appeared in every life of the holy men and women of the Judean desert.[36]

Another hagiographer gave a somewhat different twist to the same theme. When Peter the Iberian left his homeland for the Holy Land he was reminded of the words to Moses in Deuteronomy 32:1: "As an eagle watches over its nest and loves its young, spreads its wings and takes them up . . . the Lord alone will lead you." Peter, however, unlike Moses, was given the privilege of living in the Holy Land. "God led him and allowed him to dwell in the power of the Holy Land." According to his biographer John Rufus, as Peter and his company drew near "to the Holy City of Jerusalem which they loved" and saw the holy places, they cried out in the words of the prophet, "Behold, there is Zion the city of our redemption" (Isa 33:20).[37]

As the monks settled in their new home, never to return to their native lands, the desert of Jerusalem conferred on them a new identity, one that could be given by this desert alone and that in time would alter the relation of the Christian community in the holy land to the empire at large. The city of Jerusalem alone among the cities of the Roman Empire enjoyed the favor of divine solicitude. In the words of a seventh-century Palestinian Christian, "Even if our Lord, a compassionate and loving Father, punishes us on account of our sins, he will not abandon his Holy

City. His eyes watch over it and over this land through everything because it is the land of the gospels until the end of time, just as the gospel states."[38]

Dwellers of This Holy Land

As I have mentioned on several occasions, the term *Holy Land* occurs infrequently in early Christian literature. When it does appear it is interpreted as a Jewish expression signifying the land promised to Abraham and his descendants that would one day be restored to the Jewish people. For this reason, the term was rejected out-of-hand by Christian thinkers, and it is only in the course of the fifth century that it begins to appear in Christian texts. The most notable instance was the passage in Augustine's City of God where "terra sancta" designated dirt from the Holy Land with curative powers (*civ.* 22.8). On occasion Jerome used the term to refer to the land of the Bible. But it was the monks of the Judean desert who first gave it a distinctly Christian content and used it as a self-conscious designation for Christian Jerusalem and the territory surrounding it. It occurs in a letter sent by the Judean monks to the emperor Anastasius at the beginning of the sixth century.

In the fifth century, the Christian world, particularly in the eastern provinces of the Roman Empire, erupted in a great theological controversy over the definition of the divine and human nature in the person of Christ. Leading bishops of the principal sees in the East, in Egypt, Asia Minor, and Syria, including, of course, the bishop of Jerusalem, took part in the dispute. The controversy was deeply political, and several bishops seemed as interested in promoting the prestige of their sees as in resolving the theological confusion. But it was a theological problem that ignited the dispute and a theological term that led, in the end, to a permanent fissure in the church's life and polity. The question was how to use the Greek term for nature (*physis*) in speaking about the relation between the divinity and humanity of Christ. Some bishops employed the term *nature* to designate a quality, like redness, and for them Christ was said to have two natures, that is, two qualities, divine and human. Others used the term to designate a unique individual entity, hence they said that Christ had only one nature. For them nature was the equivalent of person.

At a council convened at Chalcedon in 451 C.E. in northwestern Asia Minor across the Bosporus from Constantinople, the bishops agreed to the following creed: "Following the holy fathers we all unanimously teach that our Lord Jesus Christ is to us one and the same Son, the self-same perfect in God, the self-same perfect in manhood . . . acknowledged in *two natures,* unconfusedly, unchangeably, indivisibly, inseparably." This formulation, which seemed to favor one party over another, outraged and offended many Christians in Syria, Palestine, and Egypt. Its critics, who preferred the formulation "one nature" or "out of two natures," came to be known as monophysites (from the Greek *monophysis,* "one nature"). As the decades passed their resistance to Chalcedon hardened, and, by the beginning of the sixth century, the churches of the East were divided into a Chalcedonian and a non-Chalcedonian party. Non-Chalcedonian communions would eventually be formed in Syria and Egypt.

At the time of the Council of Chalcedon most of the monks of Palestine were hostile to the decrees of Chalcedon. The bishop of Jerusalem, Juvenal, who was in attendance at the council, however, signed the council's creed. On his return to Palestine he was met by an angry crowd of monks. Only through the intervention of imperial authorities was he able to hold on to his office.[39] By the time Cyril wrote his *Lives* a century later, many monks had swung to the Chalcedonian side. Indeed one of the purposes of Cyril's *Lives,* besides exalting the monks of Palestine, was to defend the cause of Chalcedon and chronicle the triumph of the orthodox monks in the Judean desert over their foes, the Origenists. The final lines of the *Life of Sabas* celebrate the expulsion of the Origenists (who were identified with the monophysites) from the New Laura. "Let the desert rejoice and bloom like a crocus" (Isa 35:1), writes Cyril. "For God has shown mercy on his children. And I say these things to myself; 'I have seen the affliction of my people who are in Jerusalem [biblical text says Egypt], and I have heard their lamentation and I wish to deliver them'" (Exod 3:7–8) (200).

In 491 Anastasius became emperor, and though he wished to heal the breach in the East, he was identified with the non-Chalcedonian party. His actions set the stage for a conflict with the monks of the Judean desert, and in an effort to resist his attempt to impose non-Chalcedonian teachings on the church of Jerusalem, they appealed for the first time to the singular place of the Holy Land in Christian tradition. The issue was joined when the patriarch of Jerusalem, Elias (the patriarchs of Jerusalem often had Hebrew names), refused to support the emperor's political maneuvering, specifically the deposition of Chalcedonian bishops. At a local council in Constantinople in 511 C.E., the emperor, influenced by two monophysite leaders, Philoxenus of Mabbug and Severus (who was to become patriarch of Antioch in 512), deposed Macedonius, the Chalcedonian patriarch of Constantinople. Anastasius asked for the support of Elias of Jerusalem and Flavian patriarch of Antioch. Each refused and the emperor was incensed. At once he arranged for Flavian to be deposed and replaced by his own candidate, Severus.

Elias countered Anastasius's move by sending his famous monk, holy Sabas, on an embassy to Constantinople to plead the Chalcedonian cause, to appease the emperor's wrath, and also to insure, according to Cyril, that the "*mother of the churches* [Jerusalem] be protected from all disturbance" (139, 24). It was an uncommon assignment for this man of the desert. Leaving his responsibilities in Judea, he traveled to Constantinople, where he stayed the winter to press his case before the emperor. He argued that Elias was orthodox, that he followed the teaching of Cyril of Alexandria, the great luminary of the East who was particularly revered by the non-Chalcedonians. Emperor Anastasius was unmoved. In spite of his admiration and affection for Sabas, he spurned the counsel of the holy man. His sympathies lay with Severus, the leader of the monophysites. Consequently he removed the intransigent Elias from office and, over the protest of the monks, exiled him to Aila (Elath) on the Gulf of Aqaba, a garden of delight for twentieth-century sun-worshippers but to a bishop in the sixth century a miserable and inhospitable town on the edge of civilization. Elias was replaced by John, who admitted Severus of Antioch into communion. Under pressure from the Judean monks, however, John soon began to tilt toward Chalcedon.

At this point Sabas and Theodosius, the leader of the cenobitic communities in Palestine, took it upon themselves to address a petition directly to the emperor:

> Theodosius and Sabas, Archimandries, and all the other abbots and monks who dwell in the Holy City of God and all the desert around it and the vicinity of the Jordan, send this petition to the God beloved and very pious emperor, Augustus and Pantokrator by God's grace, Flavius Anastasius, friend of Christ. The king of all, God and ruler of all things, Jesus Christ, only Son of God, has entrusted to your authority, beloved of God, the scepter of rule over all things after him, to arrange, through your piety, the bond of peace for all the holy churches, but especially for the mother of the churches, Zion, where was revealed and accomplished for the salvation of the world, the great mystery of piety, which beginning with Jerusalem has caused the light of truth to shine, through the divine and evangelical preaching, in all the regions of the world. From that precious and supernatural mystery of Christ, through the victorious and precious cross and life-giving Anastasis, indeed all the

> holy and adorable places, receiving by tradition from above and from the beginning through the blessed and holy apostles, the true confession, a confession without illusion, and faith, we, the *inhabitants of this Holy Land,* have kept it invulnerable and inviolable in Christ. By the grace of God we maintain it [this faith] always without being intimidated in any way by our adversaries, according to the council of the apostle without allowing ourselves to be driven about by every wind of doctrine by the cunning of men and by the malice of those who by their fair and flattering sophisms deceive the hearts of the innocents and by their false doctrines disturb the pure limpid stream of the true faith.

The monks are astonished that the emperor, who had been nourished in the true faith, has allowed "such turmoil and trouble to be poured over the Holy City of Jerusalem, to such an extent that the *mother of all the churches,* Zion, and the Holy Anastasis of our God and Savior, a place of refuge and asylum for those who have been treated unjustly and are in need of safety, have become a public *agora* and a common place." For Jerusalem is the "eye and light of all the world," the place from which the Law and Word of the Lord (Isa 2:3) go forth into all the world and in which "we the inhabitants of Jerusalem, as it were, touch with our own hands each day the truth through these holy places in which the mystery of the incarnation of our great God and savior took place. How then, more than five hundred years after the savior's presence among us, can we Jerusalemites learn the faith anew?"[40]

The language of this petition is without precedent in Christian history. Many of its central ideas had been germinating for generations, but here for the first time they are united in a theological concept that brings together history, practice, and belief. By the middle of the fifth century, at the time of the Council of Chalcedon, some Christian leaders had recognized the theological significance of the holy places. No less a figure than Leo the Great, bishop of Rome (d. 461), had appealed to the testimony of those places "by which the whole world is taught" as evidence of the truth of the doctrine of the "two natures" formulated at the Council of Chalcedon. "The evidence of his miracles and the proofs of his sufferings proclaim that Jesus Christ is *true God and true man* in one person."[41]

There is, however, a notable difference between Leo and the monks of the Judean desert. Leo is interested only in the theological significance of the holy places; he shows no interest in the Christian community that lived in Jerusalem. Indeed in the fifth century the monks of the Judean desert were in revolt against their bishop, Juvenal, for signing the Creed of Chalcedon. For Leo, the holy places do not imply Holy Land and certainly do not confer authority on the bishop of Jerusalem. He would not have suffered himself to be instructed in matters of faith by the bishop of Jerusalem or by the monks of the Judean desert. But it is precisely this link between place and people that is central to the petition to Emperor Anastasius. It uses the formulation "inhabitants of this Holy Land," and by this means the church of Jerusalem, or, in its words, Zion, "the mother of all the churches," the seat of the bishop of Jerusalem, the priests and monks and faithful who lived in Palestine.

In this petition the earlier pilgrimage piety centered on holy places has given way to a nascent theology of a *Holy Land* embracing a territory. For the monks of the Judean desert the Holy Land was the land in which they lived, not an assemblage of shrines to visit and adore. In their conception Holy Land is irrevocably linked to the community of Christians living in Jerusalem and vicinity, which could trace its origins back to the apostles and to the time of Jesus. Only the "inhabitants of the Holy Land" had a tangible relation to the events in which God's glory was shown forth on this earth: "We the inhabitants of Jerusalem, as it were, touch with our own hands each day the truth through these holy places in which the mystery of the incarnation of our great God and savior took place." Of course, what gave the inhabitants of the Holy Land their distinctive privilege were the holy places and the relics (preeminently the holy cross) that were located in Jerusalem and other places in the land. Jerusalem is no "common place," they write. Yet the point of the petition is not that the emperor should venerate the places, but that he should show deference to the Christians living in Jerusalem. Living in Jerusalem did make a difference; the city conferred on its inhabitants a unique status. Contrast the words of Jerome 150 years earlier: "It is not being in Jerusalem, but living a good life there that is praiseworthy" (*ep.* 58.2). The monk Hilarion, it will be recalled, chose *not* to live in the vicinity of Jerusalem.

Earlier Christian leaders in Palestine, notably Cyril of Jerusalem and Hesychius of Jerusalem, had intimated that living in the land conferred privileges on the inhabitants. On several occasions Cyril had celebrated the things that had happened "among us" or "here," and on occasion he used the word "privilege" for Christians living in Jerusalem, but what he meant by that is vague and undefined. Several generations later Hesychius of Jerusalem extended the sense of Jerusalem to include the history of the Christian community in the city.[42] But it was the Judean monks who yoked the spiritual qualities of the land with the actual community of Christians living in Jerusalem and gave the city political and ecclesiastical significance. No Christian leader, not even the emperor, has authority to instruct the church of Jerusalem.

By an alluring coincidence, the first self-conscious occurrence of the term *Holy Land* in Christian literature has parallels with the first appearance of the term *Holy Land* in Greek Jewish literature. The reader will recall that the term first occurred in the book of 2 Maccabees in a letter from Jews in Jerusalem and Judea to Jews living in Egypt. This letter exhorted the Jews of Egypt to recognize the privileges of Jerusalem and the Holy Land (2 Macc 1). The term did not simply designate a territory; it signified a place with obligations and responsibilities that extended to Jews living in other parts of the world. In the same way Sabas and Theodosius exhort the emperor to acknowledge the unique status of the Holy Land and to recognize his obligations to the land. Concretely this means that he should not impose a doctrine that subverts the very thing to which the land bears witness: "the mystery of the incarnation of our great God and savior." The Wisdom of God, as Origen had written three centuries earlier, had appeared within the circumscribed limits of a man who appeared in Judea. This land is the home of Christ, the land where he was born, where he lived and taught, where he suffered and died and rose from the dead, and its stones and its soil are witnesses to this great mystery. Without the evidence of these places and the testimony of those who inhabit the land, God's gracious intervention in the person of Jesus Christ is a chimera. By imposing a false teaching on the Christian world the emperor did not keep faith with the land.

By the middle of the sixth century, then, the heavenly Jerusalem had an image on earth. In earlier Christian tradition the Jerusalem above was the "mother of believers,"[43] but for the Judean monks the church of the earthly Jerusalem is the "mother of the churches." From Zion the word of the gospel had gone out into the world, and here the faith had been transmitted inviolate since the time of the apostles. The term "mother of the churches" had begun to be used in the liturgy of the Jerusalem church a century earlier, but this petition is the first time that the theological ideas are given political content.[44] The church of Jerusalem is the "eye and light of the world."

For the monks "the terrain of sacred history stood as a spiritual entity in its own right," writes Thomas Noonan in a study of the political thought of the monks of Palestine.[45] By the sixth century the Christian presence in the Judean desert had created a new spiritual and political fact within the Christian world. The monks had a cool indifference to the stratagems and blandishments of the emperor in Constantinople. For them Jerusalem, not Rome, was the apostolic see par excellence. Since the time of the "savior's presence among us," they insisted, the inhabitants of the Holy Land have handed on the faith pure and undefiled. Had the Muslims not conquered Jerusalem in the seventh century Jerusalem might one day have challenged the authority of the church of Rome.

9 The God-Trodden Land

In 1884 the Greek Orthodox patriarch of Jerusalem, Nicodemus, received a report that a mosaic map of the Holy Land had been discovered on the floor of a Christian church at Madaba, a village east of the Jordan River not too far from Amman. In its present state, the largest fragment measures 10.5 meters by 5 meters, but the original map may have been as large as 22–24 meters by 6 meters and covered the entire width of the church (whose exterior walls were only 30 meters wide) in the area immediately in front of the apse. At first few people took notice of the find, but soon church officials, historians, and archaeologists hurried to the town to view the map and study its topographical features. As the decades passed it became the focus of learned debate among scholars and an object of curiosity for pilgrims and tourists. Except for the Tabula Peutingeriana, an ancient Roman road map of Palestine, the Madaba map is the only visual representation of the Holy Land from antiquity. The map was produced at a time when the Christian presence in the land was at its height. The mosaicist was a contemporary of Cyril of Scythopolis, and he depicts the Holy Land during the reign of the emperor Justinian (527–65 C.E.). From the Madaba mosaic we can begin to see how a picture of the Holy Land was being formed in the mind of Christians in the Byzantine period.[1]

Ephraim Where the Lord Walked

The Madaba mosaic is no ordinary map. To be sure, it includes the kind of information one would expect to find on a map: cities, rivers, deserts, valleys, lakes. But it also includes biblical sites and monuments commemorating events in the history of Israel, places mentioned in the gospels or church history, pilgrimage centers, monasteries, as well as winsome drawings of fish, plants, and animals. Palm trees grow up on the shores of the Dead Sea, and two boats of oarsmen are sailing across its briny waters. Unfortunately, the oarsmen no longer have faces; the tiles have been rearranged so that their human features have vanished. Cities, in the conventions followed by ancient mosaicists, are represented by actual buildings.

In its present state of preservation (some sections are no longer extant) the map extends to the Canobic branch of the Nile River in the south (it probably included Alexandria) and includes monasteries in the Mareotic desert in Egypt. Why Egypt? Egypt was, of course, part of the biblical history, and its ties to Palestine were deep. It was the birthplace of Christian monasticism. It was also the only land besides Palestine that had been touched by the physical presence of Christ. According to the Gospel of Matthew, Joseph, Mary, and the child Jesus fled to Egypt to escape the wrath of King Herod and remained there until Herod's death (Matt 2:13–23). In Egypt as well as in Palestine one could find the traces of God's visitation on earth.[2]

The most northern site on the extant map is Sarepta, south of the Sea of Galilee, but the original map certainly extended further north into Syria. The western boundary of the map is the Mediterranean Sea, while it extends to the east as far as Transjordan. Historically, Transjordan had been part of the biblical land, and, in the Byzantine period, its cities and towns—Philadelphia (Amman), Gerasa, Amathus, Gadara—were part of the Christian world. Mount Nebo, the traditional location from which

Moses looked over the promised land, and the presumed site of his burial, drew a steady stream of pilgrims. Like other pilgrim shrines it had a monastery attached to it, and when Egeria visited the site she was welcomed warmly.[3]

Jerusalem sits at the center of the map and over the city stands the legend The Holy City Jerusalem. So detailed is the depiction that scholars are able to identify its principal buildings and streets, its gates and towers, and even its public baths. The most prominent building is, of course, the Rotunda at Christ's tomb and the Great Martyrium with its three doors facing east. Other monasteries and churches in the city such as the basilica on Mount Zion and the New Church of the Theotokos built by Justinian also appear. The mosaicist also included the remains of the wall supporting the massive platform on which the Jewish temple stood, the Western Wall, an object of veneration by Jews then and now. Christians had not forgotten that Jerusalem was once the site of the Jewish temple. More than one Christian writer in the Byzantine period observed that the new city of the Christians was built "facing that old and deserted city."[4]

Legends on the map explain and identify many of the sites. In some cases, the sixth-century name is coupled with the biblical name, for example, "floor of Atad now Bethagla" (Gen 50:10), "Sychar which is now Sychora" (John 4:5–6). In other cases, the legend gives a short account of the event that took place at the site: "Ailamon—where stood the moon one day in the time of Joshua the son of Nun" and "the desert where the Israelites were saved by the serpent of brass" and the "desert of Zin where the manna and quails were sent down" and "Thamna where Judah sheared his sheep." Modiim, the native town of the Maccabees, and the Jewish city of Jabne (Jamnia) are also marked. The map identifies several of the tribal territories of ancient Israel, for example, the lot of Benjamin and of Judah. It identifies Beersheva as the border of Judea on the south and Dan near Paneas as the border on the north. It also includes several of the blessings of the patriarchs, for example, the blessing of Joseph: "God shall bless thee with the blessings of the deep that lie under" (Gen 49:25) and "Blessed of the Lord be his land" (Deut 33:13).

Why the mosaicist included the blessings of the patriarchs is unclear. It is possible that he wished to call attention to the ancient promise of the land. In Deuteronomy 32–33, as the Israelites reached the end of their wanderings in the desert and were preparing for the conquest of the land, God said to Moses, "Ascend this mountain of the Abarim, Mount Nebo, which is in the land of Moab, opposite Jericho, and view the land of Canaan, which I give to the people of Israel for a possession." God tells

Moses he will die on the mountain and will not enter the land, but he is allowed to look over to the land, "for you shall see the land before you but you shall not go there, into the land which I give to the people of Israel." Then, Moses blesses the tribes of Reuben, Judah, Levi, Benjamin, Joseph, Zebulun, Gad, Dan, Naphtali, and Asher. The passage quoted on the map is from the blessing of Joseph: "Blessed by the Lord be his land, with the choicest gifts of heaven above, and of the deep that couches beneath, with the choicest fruits of the sun, and the rich yield of the months, and the finest produce of the ancient mountains, and the abundance of the everlasting hills" (Deut 33:53). In the biblical text the phrase "his land" refers to the land of Joseph, but perhaps the mosaicist understood "his land" to mean the "Lord's land."[5]

Besides the chief Christian cities, Jerusalem and Bethlehem, specific places are marked: Gethsemane, Jacob's well, Aenon near Salim, where John baptized (John 3:23), Bethabara, where Jesus was baptized, Arimathea, which is the home town of Joseph who provided the tomb for Jesus' burial, the place where St. Philip baptized the Ethiopian eunuch, and "Ephraim which is Ephraea where the Lord walked." The reference here is to John 11:54, "Jesus went to the country near the wilderness, to a town called Ephraim; and there he stayed with his disciples." The gospels say nothing about Ephraim except that Jesus went there. It is not the site of a miracle or of a significant event in Jesus' life, not a place where he uttered a cryptic saying or told a parable. He seems only to have come to the town and remained there for a time with his disciples.

Nevertheless the town was celebrated in Christian tradition. Ephrem the Syrian, a fourth-century Christian writer from Nisibis in Mesopotamia, wrote two hymns on the city of Ephraim. Drawing on parallels between Jesus' "flight" to Ephraim and the Exodus of the Israelites from Egypt, Ephrem offers an "elaborate typological interpretation"[6] of the text in the Gospel of John. Yet what is of prime importance is the site itself. In the second of the two hymns Ephrem sings,

> Blessed are you, Ephraim, that in your city
> that distant one, neighbor of the desert, companion of solitude
> the Lord of cities found rest.
> Blessed are your gates, blessed by His entry,
> and your streets sanctified by His footsteps.[7]

The city of Ephraim appears on the Madaba map because Jesus once "walked in Ephraim" and the faithful could find there "traces" of God's presence.

Madaba is located only a few kilometers from Mount Nebo in Transjordan. A decade after the mosaic was discovered, the French scholar Clermont-Ganneau proposed that the map was linked with Mount Nebo. In his view the map was intended to depict the Holy Land as it was viewed by Moses from the height of Mount Nebo.[8] As tantalizing as this suggestion might first appear, Clermont-Ganneau realized it had a fatal flaw. The map is not oriented to Mount Nebo, that is, to a mountain east of the land, but to the west, as the land would be viewed from the Mediterranean Sea, indeed almost as though one is viewing it from an airplane about to land at Lod airport. Further, the country that one sees is not the promised land at the time of the Canaanites, but the land as it existed in Byzantine times.

The mosaicist likely had at hand Eusebius's *Onomasticon*, which included a map or some other depiction of sites in the land, but he seems also to have had before him a pilgrim's map, the type of map of Palestine used by professional guides and tour managers who conducted pilgrims around the country. As the number of pilgrims grew, such maps became necessary and were no doubt readily available to professional guides and wealthy travelers. These maps provided detailed information about sites, distances from one place to another, itineraries for individual trips (all beginning from Jerusalem), and historical details about the holy places.[9]

A map is a utilitarian and practical instrument, yet once what was drawn on a parchment was set in mosaic on the floor of a church, it became fixed. Like the apse mosaic of Santa Pudenziana in Rome that depicted, for the first time, the actual city of Jerusalem as a stately and majestic metropolis, so the Madaba map, by portraying the Holy Land as a country with cities, churches, roads, lakes and rivers, flora and fauna, helped create a sense of the region as a territory, a land, not simply an assemblage of holy places.

Although the city of Jerusalem dominates the map, the map does not distinguish Israelite sites from sites associated with Jesus. Indeed, the ancient sites seem to predominate, as was the case in the *Pilgrim from Bordeaux*. In some cases, Christians may have learned about the location of certain places from Jews who also venerated them, as for example Gilgal, the first encampment of the Israelites after they crossed the Jordan River into Canaanite territory. The legend on the map reads, "Galgala, also the twelve stones." Others, such as the tomb of the prophet Zechariah, may have been discovered by Christians. According to an early Christian historian, the remains of the prophet had been found intact by a poor serf who was instructed by the prophet in a dream where to dig (Sozomen, *h.e.* 9.17). Christians had built a shrine to Lot at Zoar, east of the Dead Sea, in the area where Lot had taken refuge and his wife was turned into a pillar of salt. The map marks it as "the place of St. Lot."

It is no doubt true, as Avi-Yonah wrote in his book on Madaba, that the map "contains a good deal of Jewish lore."[10] This is, however, to miss the point of the references to persons and events from the history of ancient Israel. For Christians living in the biblical land the Jewish Bible had become the Christian Old Testament, and the tales of the patriarchs and prophets as well as the saving acts of God on behalf of ancient Israel were now part of Christian history. On the map at Madaba, the topography of Israel's history and the topography of the church's history merge into a single territory whose center is Christian Jerusalem.

Archaeology and Christian Palestine

The Madaba mosaic is a map both of the past and of Palestine, Transjordan, and parts of Egypt as they existed at the time the map was produced. Not all of its sites are holy places. It marks, for example, the location of Archelais, a village mentioned on the Peutinger Table, where one could change horses and find an inn and the "hot baths of Callirhoe," a Byzantine spa. In this respect it differs from, let us say, a map in a modern Bible dictionary or a historical atlas. It gives the name of cities in the Negev desert, for example, Mampsis and Elusa, that flourished in the sixth century but did not exist in biblical times and were not part of sacred history. The Madaba map bids us look a bit more closely at the society that existed in the Holy Land at the height of the Christian era.

In the previous chapter, I discussed the writings of Cyril of Scythopolis, our most important literary source for the period. His work is of capital importance for understanding the religious outlook that gave rise to the Christian Holy Land. The *Lives* are a precious source for constructing the history of the monastic communities in the Judean desert and tracing the impact of theological and religious controversies in Palestine in this period. But like other literary sources such as the lives of the saints, theological tracts, devotional works, and sermons, its vision of the world is myopic. If it were not for archaeology, we would have a very limited picture of the cultural, social, and economic history of Byzantine Palestine.

Until a generation ago, most archaeologists were interested in the earlier history of the Holy Land, for example, the Bronze Age (Canaanite period) or the Iron Age (Israelite monarchy), and to a lesser extent the period of the Second Temple. In recent years, however, the Byzantine period has become an object of intense interest, and its material remains have begun to be examined with the same scholarly enthusiasm that was once given over to earlier epochs.

During the period extending from the fourth century through the seventh century, the population of Byzantine Palestine grew rapidly, new buildings were constructed at a dizzying pace, trade increased, the economy flourished, jobs were plentiful (especially for skilled craftsmen and artists), and agriculture and viticulture were extended to previously uncultivated areas like the Negev and Judean deserts. The density of the population increased exponentially. It is estimated that the number of inhabitants of Jerusalem rose to over fifty thousand from a previous high of ten to fifteen thousand. Other cities and towns expanded beyond their walls to hold the influx of new residents. At Caesarea on the Mediterranean coast and Gerasa in Transjordan north of Philadelphia (Amman), population density was higher than in any previous period; Scythopolis (Beth Shean) expanded to the south to accommodate its growing population. On the basis of archaeological surveys of the region, it has been estimated that there were four times as many people living in the country in the Christian period as in biblical times. If one compares the relative density of the population in different periods the ratio would be the following: Canaanite: 1; Israelite: 1.5; Byzantine [Christian]: 5–6. As Avi-Yonah wrote, "The Byzantine period . . . indubitably represents a very high point of material development attained by this country."[11]

The reasons for this growth were several. The emperors had developed trade across the desert from the Mediterranean to Aila (Eilat, Aqaba) on the Red Sea (Gulf of Aqaba). Cities located on this trade route in the Negev desert flourished. As war with the Persians tapered off the entire region enjoyed undisturbed peace for generations. Yet the most potent new factor was the influx of people and money as a result of the discovery of the holy places. Pilgrims, like tourists, were good for business. Again, Avi-Yonah: "The stream of capital which then began to flow explains better than any other factor the astonishing prosperity of Palestine in the Byzantine period."[12]

As the number of pilgrims grew, the inhabitants of the towns and cities in Palestine and Transjordan set about the happy task of providing for their material and spiritual needs. They built hostels and made their homes into inns, packaged relics for sale, made flasks to hold water from the Jordan and oil from the lamps of the Holy Sepulchre, and learned the tricks of guiding pilgrims quickly and safely to the holy places. Goldsmiths in Jerusalem thrived on the influx of pilgrims from abroad. The Holy Land had a natural monopoly on certain kinds of relics, for example, the bones of the patriarch Joseph and the prophets Samuel, Zechariah, Habakkuk, and St. Stephen, and, of course, splinters from the holy cross.

As churches and memorial shrines began to sprout up in cities and towns all over the country, the demand for skilled craftsmen, stonecutters, artists, architects, and builders seemed insatiable. Many had to be recruited from abroad, and some settled permanently in Jerusalem and other cities. During the Byzantine period, the widespread use of marble in building created a market for those who quarried, dressed, and transported the precious stone.[13] Many of the churches (and synagogues) had mosaic floors, and skilled craftsmen were needed to design the floors and cut and set the tiles; others had to obtain and transport lumber (usually from Lebanon) for the roofs of the churches. Procopius gives us a vivid firsthand description of what effort it took to build the church dedicated to the Mother of God (the New Church) in Jerusalem:

> The church is partly based upon living rock, and partly carried in the air by a great extension artificially added to the hill by the emperor's power. The stones of this substructure are not of a size such as we are acquainted with, for the builders of this work, in struggling against the nature of the terrain . . . had to abandon all familiar methods and resort to practices which were strange and altogether unknown. So they cut blocks out of unusual size from the hills which rise to the sky in the region before the city, and, after dressing them carefully, they brought them to the site in the following manner. They built wagons to match the size of the stones, placed a single block on each of them and had each wagon with its stone drawn by forty oxen which had been selected by the emperor for their strength. But since it was impossible for the roads leading to the city to accommodate these wagons, they cut into the hills for a very great distance, and made them passable for the wagons as they came along there, and thus they completed the length of the church in accordance with the emperor's wish. However, when they made the width in due proportion, they found themselves quite unable to set a roof upon the building. So they searched through all the woods and forest and every place where they heard that very tall trees grew, and found a certain dense forest which produced cedars of extraordinary height, and by means of these they put the roof upon the church, making its height in due proportion to the width and length of the building.[14]

Another source of wealth was the gifts of emperors and wealthy citizens for the construction of churches and other public buildings.[15] Jerome's friend Paula gave enough of her inheritance to build a hospice and two monasteries in Palestine. Melania the Younger, granddaughter of Melania the Elder, gave fifteen thousand gold pieces to the churches of Palestine.[16] The mother of Sabas gave money to build a hospice in Jericho, and another donor gave Sabas two hundred gold pieces to pay for a hospice in Jerusalem.[17] The empress Eudocia donated a copper cross weighing six thousand pounds to be mounted on the top of the Mount of Olives, and she endowed monasteries in the Judean desert. In Jerusalem she built the church of St. Stephen and a residence for the patriarch.[18] Not all the donations went to the building of churches and religious edifices. The New Church of the Theotokos in Jerusalem built by Justinian, reports Procopius, was more than a church: it was a hospice for "visiting strangers" and an "infirmary for poor persons suffering from diseases,"[19] a social fact that did not escape Gibbon's mischievous eye: "The pious munificence of the emperor was diffused over the Holy Land; and if reason should condemn the monasteries of both sexes which were built or restored by Justinian, yet charity must applaud the wells which he sunk and the hospitals which he founded, for the relief of the weary pilgrims."[20]

Christianity in the Negev

No region of the country gives greater evidence of the changes that were taking place in this period than the Negev desert south of Beersheva. In the words of Kenneth Gutwein, "It is a remarkable experience to visit the remaining ruins of the major Byzantine cities of Palestine III [the Roman province that embraced the Negev]. It is difficult to comprehend how such urban centers could have flourished within such a bleak environment. Yet never before in the history of the region had the total size of the population, the amount of trade, intensity of cultivation and maximization of land usage reached the proportions it did under Byzantine rule."[21]

The Negev desert, shaped like a large triangle standing upside down, was the ancient grazing land of the patriarchs.[22] Its base forms a line running from Gaza to the Dead Sea, one side running from the sea to Aila on the Gulf of Aqaba, the other running from Gaza to Aila. In this parched land the Israelites may have spent some of the years of their journey from Egypt to the promised land. Later it was inhabited by the Nabataeans, a Semitic people from the Arabian desert who had settled in the region in the fourth century B.C.E. Though the Negev is not as mountainous as the lower Sinai, nevertheless it is marked by deep ravines and small mountains. Water is scarce and the climate is severe. Only by skillful husbandry and an intricate system of catchments to channel the sparse precipitation into cisterns was it possible to support human life in the region. Yet in the Byzantine period, the inhabitants of the Negev cultivated such field crops as wheat, barley, and various legumes and grew grapes, olives, dates, and almonds. Five sophisticated winepresses were found in one city, indicating the primacy of viticulture, and it appears that the production of olive oil was the second most important industry. After the Arab conquest the cities furnished olive oil to the Arab troops.

At the height of the Christian epoch there were six cities located within a few miles of each other in the Negev: Mampsis (Kurnub), Oboda (Avdat), Elusa, Rhibah, Sobata (Shivta), and Nessana.[23] Each city had at least two Christian churches, several had three or four. In Mampsis the population increased so rapidly in the fourth century that the streets had to be narrowed, public squares used for housing, and the walls of the city extended. Nevertheless, the inhabitants found room to build three churches. Because wood was so scarce in the desert, the first buildings had roofs made of stone slabs set on large pillars, but apparently the pillars made it difficult for the worshippers to see and hear what was happening in the apse, and the later buildings adopted a more conventional plan. An intricate system of drainage carried rainwater from the roof to a reservoir in the atrium. One of the churches, dedicated to St. Nilos, housed the remains of a holy person or persons, and the visitor can still see a stone table with a hole through which one could see, and perhaps touch, the relics of the saint.

From papyri found at Nessana it is clear that in the Negev, in contrast to the Judean desert, monks lived in the midst of the cities and took an active part in the civic and commercial life of the towns. One monk was mayor of the city. The papyri are partly literary, including a Latin-Greek glossary of the *Aeneid,* passages from Vergil and the Gospel of John, but there are also items such as letters on personal and business matters. One letter was written by a certain Abraamios to the abbot of the monastery: “In the name of the holy, glorious and life-giving Trinity, Father, Son and Holy Spirit, and in the name of our exalted and blessed mother of God and eternally virgin Mary and of the holy martyrs.” After this grandiloquent introduction, one expects to read a solemn pronouncement on an ethereal point of theology, but the letter is about money, nine solidi of gold to be lent at the rate of 6 percent. Another letter in the same collection has to do with the purchase of fish! “Please receive from the bearer of this letter eighty pounds of sea fish and twenty large heads. Kindly give confirmation to my messenger, Anacles, that you have received these goods. Pray to the Lord for me."[24]

At Nessana excavators uncovered three churches, one dedicated to Saints Sergius and Bacchus at the end of the fifth century, one dedicated to St. Mary Theotokos from the end of the sixth century, and a third from the first half of the fifth century. There may also have been a fourth church in the lower city. In Sobata a church was built in the middle of the fourth century, and, about the same time, a second church was constructed outside of the city. The latter building was probably dedicated to a local saint and was attached to a large monastery. Later a third building in the basilica style with two rows of columns was built, and these three churches were still in use at the time of the Arab conquest in 634 C.E. In the apse of the first church the excavators found a well-preserved baptismal pool. Carved from a single block of stone, it was made in the shape of a cross, and, like other baptismal pools from the period, it was large enough to walk down into. Christians in antiquity did not sprinkle people for Baptism.[25]

The Negev reminds us that Byzantine Palestine was a *homeland* for Christians as well as a Holy Land, a place where men and women tilled the ground and planted orchards, built homes and raised families, bought fish and sold olives. Many if not most of the churches built in the country were modest, even small, parish churches or monastic chapels designed to serve the needs of the Christian population of the land. They had little to do with the traffic of pilgrims. A small town like Madaba had fourteen churches, and Gerasa (also on the east bank), which had one church in the fourth century, had twelve in the sixth. Even outside of the great pilgrimage centers Christians were changing the face of the country. Asher Ovadiah writes, "The picture is . . . one of a flourishing economy side by side with extensive cultural activity expressed principally in the building of a great number of churches and monasteries."[26]

Church Architecture and Holy Places

In the Roman Empire prior to the triumph of Christianity temples were a familiar feature of the urban landscape, but Rome's architectural greatness lay in theaters, hippodromes, public squares and streets, and the stoas that lined the city squares. In the Byzantine period the public space of the Greek and Roman cities gave way to the interior space of the church. All that remains today of most of these buildings are the foundations, parts of the walls, and in some felicitous cases the mosaic floors.

Only the church at the monastery of St. Catherine in the Sinai desert remains intact with its original floor plan and roof, an extraordinary monument to the skill of Justinian's builders. The Church of the Nativity in Bethlehem is still standing, but it has been altered in so many ways that it is hard to envision the original building. As for the Church of the Holy Sepulchre in Jerusalem, the changes in that structure are so profound that it is impossible for the untutored visitor to imagine its former grandeur. On a first visit even the most devout pilgrim is keenly disappointed. Only by standing in the rotunda and looking at the columns that encircle the tomb or by walking along the length of the original building on the street that runs parallel can the visitor imagine, however dimly, the impression it made on people in the fifth or sixth century. "In Palestine today," writes James Crowfoot, "we cannot find a single church which will give an idea of the quality of early Christian architecture such as one finds in Rome or Ravenna or Salonica. What would anybody make of San Vitale or the Dome of the Rock if the blazoned walls had been leveled to the ground and all that remained was a ground-plan and some handfuls of loose tesserae? That is the position on most Palestinian sites; two churches happen to be still erect, at Bethlehem and Ezra' [Transjordan]; the latter is indescribably forlorn; neither gives the faintest conception of the beauty we have lost."[27]

In 1970 Asher Ovadiah published a *Corpus of the Byzantine Churches in the Holy Land* in which he described 181 churches that had been excavated. The list did not include buildings that are mentioned in literary sources or buildings on the east bank of the Jordan. A decade later he published (with G. de Silva) a supplement to the original list, and the total number of churches constructed from the beginning of the fourth century till the early eighth century C.E. now totaled 250. The greatest period of building fell in the fifth and sixth centuries, with the number of churches tapering off in the seventh century. If we add to Ovadiah's list the buildings constructed east of the Jordan and those mentioned in literary sources, the number of churches built in the Holy Land during the Christian era is over 500.[28]

The first great builder of churches in the Holy Land was the emperor Constantine. Before his accession to the imperial throne and conversion, there may have been house churches in the region, but evidence for the early period is meager. In his *Ecclesiastical History,* Eusebius mentions a church in which one could find the "book of the divine Gospels," but that is all we hear of it (*h.e.* 6.15.4). In Eusebius's day, however, there was already a shrine at Caesarea Philippi (Panias) to commemorate Jesus' healing of the woman with an issue of blood (Matt 9:20). Visitors were shown the house of the woman, and a bronze statue of Jesus and the woman had been erected at the site of the healing, but Eusebius makes no mention of a church.[29] Constantine's first endowment in the region was a large and sumptuous church at Tyre on the Phoenician coast. Eusebius himself delivered the sermon at the dedication of the church in 314 C.E., and in his *History* he immodestly cites his sermon word for word, describing the unnamed orator as a man of "moderate parts." His elaborate description of the building was designed not only to celebrate its grandeur and beauty, but also to eulogize its benefactor, Constantine, "our most peaceful Solomon."

The church in Tyre, the "temple of God," as Eusebius calls it, had a large ceremonial entrance, an atrium open to the air with a fountain, three doors at the main entrance, the middle one with "bronze fastenings bound with iron and various embossed work," a spacious nave with clerestory windows, a marble floor, a roof of cedar wood, and a number of secondary buildings for administrative and educational purposes (*h.e.* 10.4). Tyre was a portent. As Crowfoot remarks, Eusebius's "description might serve as the description of a dozen of the grander churches in our area."[30] With the building of the church in Tyre, Christians in Palestine inaugurated a brilliant epoch in the history of religious architecture in this ancient land. Even the arrival of the Muslims in the country in the seventh century did not put an end to the building of churches. Only a few years ago two fine churches with spectacular mosaic floors were discovered in Jordan near a village called Um er-Rasas, not too far from Madaba. The later of the two is dated 785 C.E., 150 years after the Muslim conquest of the region.[31]

The fourth, fifth, and sixth centuries were a golden age in the history of church architecture all over the Mediterranean world, and in many respects the surge of building in Palestine paralleled what was happening in other parts of the Christian world. Yet the Holy Land offered a distinctive challenge: the holy places were fixed and immovable, and buildings had to be constructed not only to conform to the constraints imposed by the sacred topography, but also to serve the needs of the pilgrims. The memorial churches of Palestine were designed to display the holy places; that is, they were built not so much to accommodate a congregation of worshippers as to create space which highlighted the holy place.[32] Recall the words of Paulinus of Nola: "No other sentiment draws people to Jerusalem than the desire to *see* and *touch* the places where Christ was physically present, and to be able to say from their very own experience, 'We have gone into his tabernacle, and have worshipped in the places where his feet have stood'" (*ep.* 49.14).

Some examples can illustrate the point. The Church of the Ascension on the Mount of Olives was circular, and in the center one could see the rock from which Christ had ascended into the heavens. A church built at the site of Jacob's well in Samaria was in the shape of a cross with the well at the center of the cross. Although the remains of this building are not extant, a drawing of the ground plan of the church appears in a medieval manuscript of the pilgrim account of Adamnan, *de locis sanctis*. The drawing shows that the church was built around the well; the well is located at the very center where the two arms of the cross meet.[33]

The Church of the Nativity in Bethlehem was originally designed as a memorial shrine and later adapted to accommodate congregational worship.[34] The first building was centered on the cave where according to Christian tradition Christ had been born. Over the cave was constructed an octagonal building with a large central hole in the roof directly over the place of Jesus' birth and open to the heavens. This section was, in turn, joined to a basilica that opened on the one end to the shrine and on the other end to an atrium. The interior was divided into a central room lined by two rows of columns on either side, creating four aisles. The pilgrim entered the octagonal chapel from the basilica and was able to peer down into the cave, which was located directly below. "The shrines," writes Crowfoot, "were not built for liturgical worship but that all might *see* the places where Christ was born and buried and rose from the dead. No altar was necessary for evidential purposes and it was enough that the sacred place should be visible from above."[35]

It is apparent, however, that buildings constructed for the purpose of displaying a holy place had distinct limitations when used for congregational worship. From the floor plan of the original Church of the Nativity, it is unclear where the altar would have been located, if there was one, and where the clergy could have stood without blocking access to the shrine. No doubt this was one reason, when the church was rebuilt in Justinian's time, the apse of the main basilica was extended over the grotto. In remodeling the building, the architects treated the basilica and the shrine as two distinct spaces. Furthermore, access to the shrine was provided by *two* staircases, a down staircase for those entering the shrine and an up staircase for those who were exiting.[36] The church of the Eleona on the Mount of Olives also had up and down staircases, an arrangement that allowed pilgrims to visit the shrine without disturbing the worship in the main basilica.[37]

A smaller, less auspicious church a few miles south of Bethlehem, at Horvat Berachot, solved the architectural problems of combining a shrine and a worshipping congregation as did the church in Bethlehem, but without the octagonal room enclosing the shrine.[38] The church is built over a crypt (whose mosaic floor is well preserved) with a vaulted ceiling to support the floor of the apse, and the crypt was built over a natural cave that was a shrine. Whose memory the shrine commemorated, however, we do not know, except that it was probably a holy person venerated by Muslims as well as Christians. After the building was taken over by the Arabs it seems to have been made into a Muslim shrine. At least this is one conclusion to be drawn from a fragmentary Arabic inscription found in situ. The inscription reads, "In the name of God the merciful the compassionate; O God, grant pardon to Yusuf son of Yasin." The excavators write, "If the Early Arabic inscription really proves continued awareness of the holiness of the site in the Early Arab period, it is preferable to connect this crypt with some Old Testament tradition rather than a later Christian one. It was, in any case, a tradition of secondary importance, since it was not mentioned by any pilgrims."[39]

The church itself, built in the basilica style, is relatively small, fifty feet on the exterior and thirty-eight feet on the interior, excluding the apse. But the shrine, even if it was of secondary importance, must have been popular. The architect built two sets of stairs to the crypt to allow easy passage in and out. Furthermore, as at the shrine in the church of Bethlehem, the crypt was accessible from the side aisles of the church, allowing pilgrims to enter and leave the crypt without disturbing the worshippers in the main hall.

Burning Bush and Sacred Cliff

When Egeria visited the Sinai in the late fourth century she discovered that the burning bush—miraculously!—was still to be seen. Here was the holy place where the angel of the Lord appeared to Moses "in a flame of fire out of the midst of a bush" (Exod 3:2). When Moses turned to see "this great sight, why the bush is not burnt," God said to him, "Do not come near; put off your shoes from your feet, for the place on which you are standing is holy ground" (Exod 3:5). As early as Egeria's time, a church had been constructed at the site:

> Our way out took us to the head of this valley because there the holy men had many cells, and there is also a church there at the place of the Bush (which is still alive and sprouting). It was about four o'clock by the time we had come right down the Mount and reached the Bush. This, as I have already said, is the Burning Bush out of which the Lord spoke to Moses, and it is at the head of the valley

with the church and all the cells. The Bush itself is in front of the church in a very pretty garden which has plenty of excellent water. Nearby you are also shown the place where holy Moses was standing when God said to him, "undo the fastening of thy shoes."[40]

In the sixth century, during the reign of Justinian, a new church was built at the site, and that building is still standing intact. Unlike other holy places, the site in the Sinai had no cave or tomb, and hence no possibility of a crypt. Accordingly, the church was built contiguous to the site so that pilgrims would be able to view the bush. The apse end of the church was placed near the bush so that worshippers inside the church would face in its direction, and a small garden was planted to enclose the bush. Later a small chapel, the chapel of the bush, was constructed in the garden. The plan of the church shows that it was possible for the worshippers to pass through the side aisles of the church to reach the holy place outside of the church. The architectural plan, then, was similar to what had been developed at other holy places but adapted to the peculiar requirements of the "place of the Bush."[41]

A different kind of holy place was excavated a few years ago at Kursi on the eastern shore of the Sea of Galilee across from the city of Tiberias.[42] According to the Byzantines, Kursi was the site of the miracle recorded in Mark 5. In this region a man had been possessed by an unclean spirit. He lived among tombs and went about day and night crying out and bruising himself with stones. Often he had been bound with chains, but he broke his fetters, and "no one had the strength to subdue him." When Jesus saw him he said, "Come out of the man, you unclean spirit!" At the same time Jesus noticed a herd of swine feeding on the hillside. The demons inside the man cried out, "Send us to the swine; let us enter them." So Jesus "gave them leave," and the unclean spirits came out of the man, entered the swine, rushed down the *steep bank* into the sea, and were drowned in the sea.

Even in Origen's day the region of Kursi had been identified as the site of the miracle of the swine.[43] Its distinguishing feature, as Origen observed, was a steep bank not far from the lake. There is indeed such a bank at the site, though today it is several hundred yards from the lake, and it was from this cliff that the swine may have leaped to their deaths. Because of the distinctive topographical features of this site, the main church was constructed on the level ground below the cliff, and a small chapel was perched on the cliff itself. Though the site is seldom mentioned in pilgrim accounts, it is one of the most impressive monuments from the Christian era. At its height in the sixth century, Kursi included a large basilica, a monastery, a hostel, and a chapel on the "sacred cliff." The entire compound, excluding the chapel, was enclosed by a wall which measured 145 meters by 123 meters. Underneath the church the excavators found a crypt filled with bones. The crypt, however, does not seem to have been a shrine but rather the burial place of the monks. The floor of the church, like others from the period, is composed of geometric designs in which are placed medallions (196 in all on the side aisles) depicting exotic birds, fish, stylized flowers, plants, vegetables, fig leaves, grape clusters, and cups (or chalices).[44]

The tomb of Christ in Jerusalem offered, of course, the most challenging assignment to the Byzantine architects.[45] For this, the archetypal holy place of Christians, was not only the primary goal of all pilgrims to the Holy Land; it included not one but two distinctive places: the tomb itself and Golgotha, the place of the Crucifixion. But Jerusalem was also the seat of a bishop (later patriarch) and the dwelling place of a sizable Christian population. Besides a memorial shrine there also had to be a church large enough to serve the needs of the Christian community in Jerusalem as well as the pilgrims who often stayed in Jerusalem for a period of days or even weeks. Unlike holy places located elsewhere in Palestine, where pilgrims might have stayed for a day or two, Jerusalem was their home while in Palestine, and from there they traveled to other parts of the country, much as pilgrims do today. And at certain times of the year, particularly holy week, the city was filled with pilgrims who participated in the series of services which took place at the Anastasis, the Great Martyrium, and in other churches and shrines scattered throughout the city and it environs.

Whether all these considerations were in the mind of the architects who designed the original set of buildings at the tomb and Golgotha, we cannot say. The model they seem to have followed was that of a Roman mausoleum constructed to house the remains of an emperor, for example, the Mausoleum to Diocletian in Split in present-day Croatia or the *heroon*, a tomb to honor the founder of a city.[46] The basic plan, however, was adapted for Christian use and included a basilica designed for liturgical worship with a full apse that was set apart from the tomb and Golgotha. In contrast to Bethlehem, where the basilica opened directly into an octagonal room over the shrine, in Jerusalem the basilica was physically distinct from the shrine.

In the original plan the tomb was enclosed in a rectangular courtyard called the Anastasis in antiquity; the basilica itself was called the martyrium or the great martyrium. From archaeological evidence as well as from the account of Eusebius of Caesarea and the reports of pilgrims, we know that at first the shrine at the tomb had no roof. In Bethlehem the building over the cave had an opening to the heavens, but in Jerusalem the tomb stood in the open air. It seems to have been located at an indentation on one side of the courtyard where the faithful could gather for morning and evening prayer. It was surrounded by the Edicule (from the Latin *aedicula*, "small house"), which had a peaked roof resting on small columns, between which were metal screens. The screens allowed the faithful to look at the tomb, but also served to protect the rock from being disfigured by religious zeal. The hill of Golgotha was located across from the tomb to the south and east, but exactly how the rock of Calvary fit into the overall plan of the courtyard is still unclear. At some point a large cross was erected on the rock, but as Coüasnon observes, "The architectural arrangement of all this is difficult to envisage."[47] The basilica was located directly east of the courtyard surrounding the tomb, offset a bit from the courtyard of the Anastasis, because "the apse was contiguous to the rock of Calvary."[48] The central room was flanked by two rows of columns on either side (hence five aisles), and the outer aisles were covered with galleries. Its floor plan was similar to those of dozens of other large churches that would be built in Palestine in the fourth to seventh centuries. But in its size, in the opulence of its materials and the splendor of its decorations this basilica was without rival.

The ceremonial entrance to the basilica had three large doorways, and immediately to the east of the front of the church was an atrium surrounded by porticoes on three sides. The atrium, too, had three gateways, which can be clearly seen on the Madaba map. These opened on to the chief north-south street of Aelia, the Cardo Maximus, a street which even today is the main north-south street in the old city of Jerusalem.

Although the sumptuous splendor of the buildings at Golgotha and the tomb of Christ delighted the faithful and thrilled the pilgrims, the buildings were not simply for show. They were designed to serve the needs of the local Christian community and to accentuate the series of "saving events" that had taken place at the site. Egeria says little about the grandeur of Jerusalem's churches; her account dwells on the movement of the faithful from one part of the complex to another to celebrate the events that marked Jesus' final days. Describing the rites of holy week, the "great week" as she calls it, she says that on Sunday the faithful assemble in the "Great Church," the Martyrium, "because it is located at Golgotha behind the Cross where the Lord was put to death" (30.1). On Friday the faithful gather "before the Cross . . . in the very spacious and beautiful courtyard between the Cross and the Anastasis, and there is not even room to open a door, the place is so crammed with people. They place the bishop's chair before the Cross, and the whole time between midday and three o'clock is taken up with readings. The readings are all about the things Jesus suffered" (37.4–5). Later in the same day they "leave the Martyrium for the Anastasis where . . . they read the Gospel passage about Joseph asking Pilate for the Lord's body and placing it in a new tomb" (37.8). On Saturday evening they celebrate the Paschal Vigil in the Martyrium and then process "with singing to the Anastasis where the resurrection Gospel is read" (38.2).

The historical character of the events being celebrated was accentuated by the distinction made between the two holy places, Golgotha and the tomb, even though they were located in the same area. As the faithful moved from one place to another, they focused on the "holy mysteries," first the death and then the resurrection of Christ, and the salvific power of these events was imprinted on their minds and hearts. What Egeria "admired most" about the liturgy in Jerusalem was that the prayers and hymns and readings always conformed to the "day being observed" and "to the place where [the event] happened" (47.5). On the Madaba map the Great Martyrium and the Anastasis are the most prominent buildings, a visible sign that the city of Jerusalem was now dedicated to Christ and had become the holy city of the Christians. As the mosaicist placed the Anastasis at the center of Jerusalem, so too he set Jerusalem at the center of the land.

Land of God's Presence

"Blessings" was the name given to relics and other holy things that pilgrims carried home from the Holy Land, for example, oil from the lamps in the Anastasis, water from the Jordan River, dried flowers from the garden of Gethsemane, and stones or dirt from Golgotha.[49] After seeing and touching the places where Christ walked, pious pilgrims would take home these blessings—a "pinch of dust" or a "tiny particle from the wood of the cross"—as remembrances.[50] When the pilgrim from Piacenza arrived at the Jordan River he noticed that shipowners from Alexandria had come to the river with great jars of spices and balsam. On reaching the river they poured out the contents of the jars into the river and filled them with "holy water," and "this water they used for sprinkling their ships when they set sail."[51] A reliquary in Samaria that enclosed a stone bore the inscription, "rock from the Holy Skull [Golgotha]."[52]

As pilgrims returned from the Holy Land with these blessings, some cities were able to put together their own private collection of Holy Land relics. One such city was Amaseia in Pontus in western Asia Minor, and at the place where the relics were kept the following inscription was found: "Here are many tokens [evidences] of the 'God-trodden' land." The precise meaning of the inscription is uncertain, but Louis Robert, the distinguished French epigraphist, believed the phrase "God-trodden land" referred to Palestine, that is, to the Holy Land, and that the term "token" is synonymous with "blessing."[53] For the Christians of Amaseia as well as for Christians all over the Roman Empire and beyond, the term "God-trodden" was a fitting epithet to describe the land they loved and venerated. For what set this land apart from all others was that God had been present not once or twice, not in one age or to one person, but in many ages and to many people—to Abraham, Moses, Elijah, in the desert, on the mountains, in the towns and cities, at the time of the Exodus, in the age of the prophets, during the time of the Maccabees, and, of course, preeminently in the life and suffering of Jesus of Nazareth. In the words of a Franciscan monk who lived centuries later,

> Christ by touch drew nearer to the Holy Land than to any other part of the world. . . . It is piously believed that there is not in it a mountain, a valley, a plain, a field, a fountain, a river, a torrent, a castle, a village, not even a stone which the Savior of the world did not touch, either with his most holy feet in walking . . . or with his knees when he prayed to the Father, or in truth with his legs when fatigued from walking, or when eating he sat down, or with his hands when thirsty he drank of the water, or with his forehead when he made profound genuflections in prayer to the Father, or with his holy body when at the time of sleep, weary in body, he threw himself on the bare ground.[54]

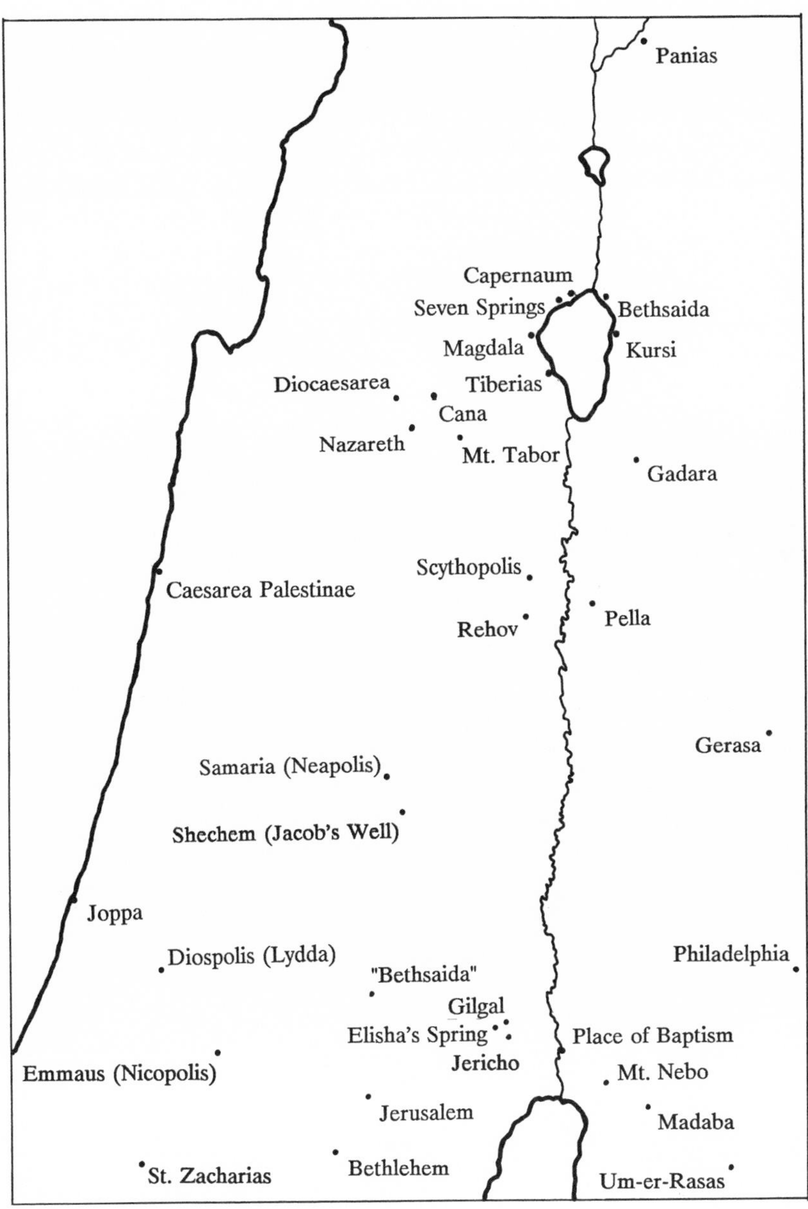

Fig 1
Byzantine Palestine (northern section)

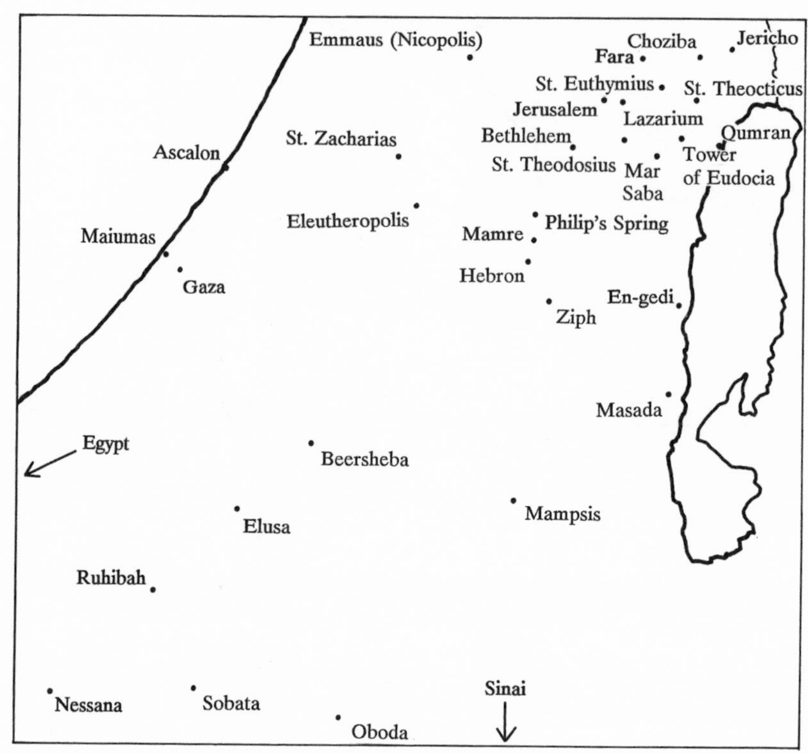

Fig 2
Byzantine Palestine (southern section)

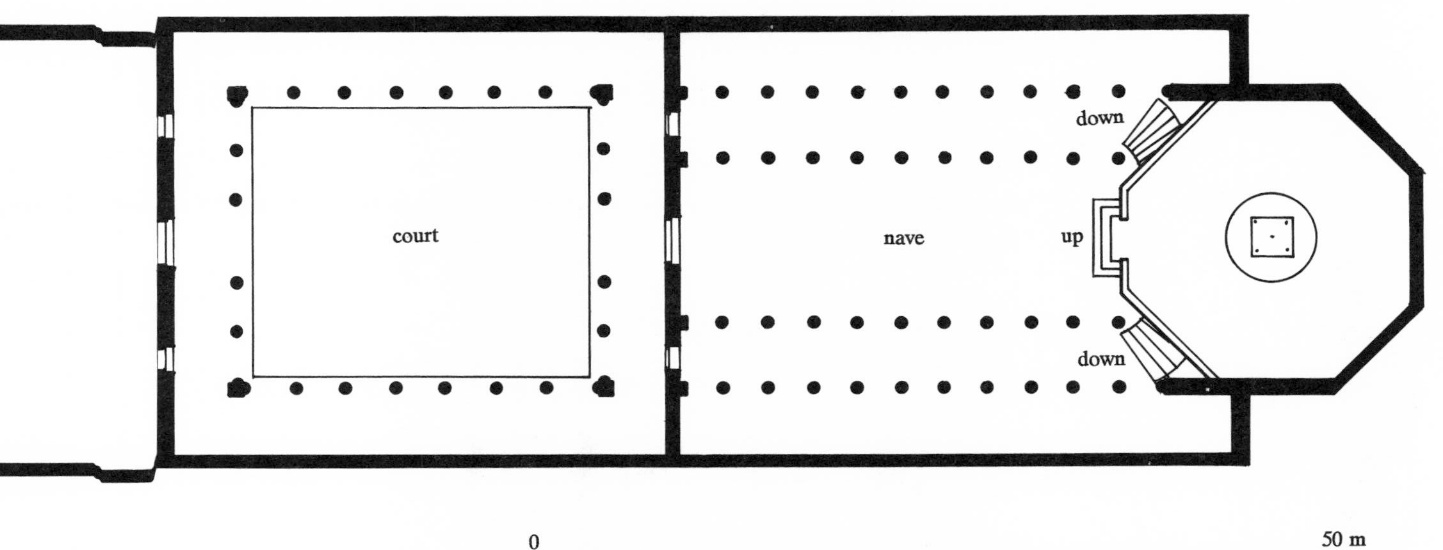

Fig 3
Floor plan of the Church of the Nativity, Bethlehem, from the time of Constantine, fourth century C.E.

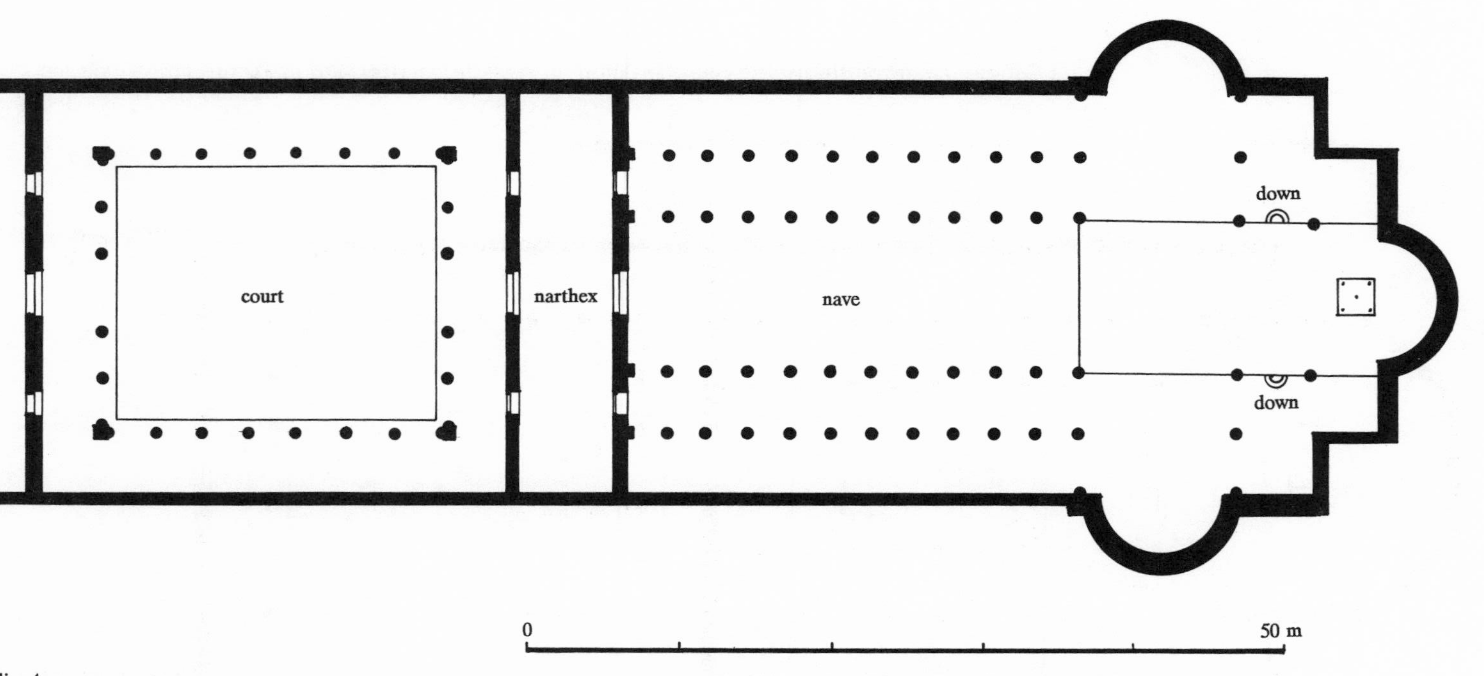

Fig 4
Floor plan of the Church of the Nativity, Bethlehem, sixth century C.E.

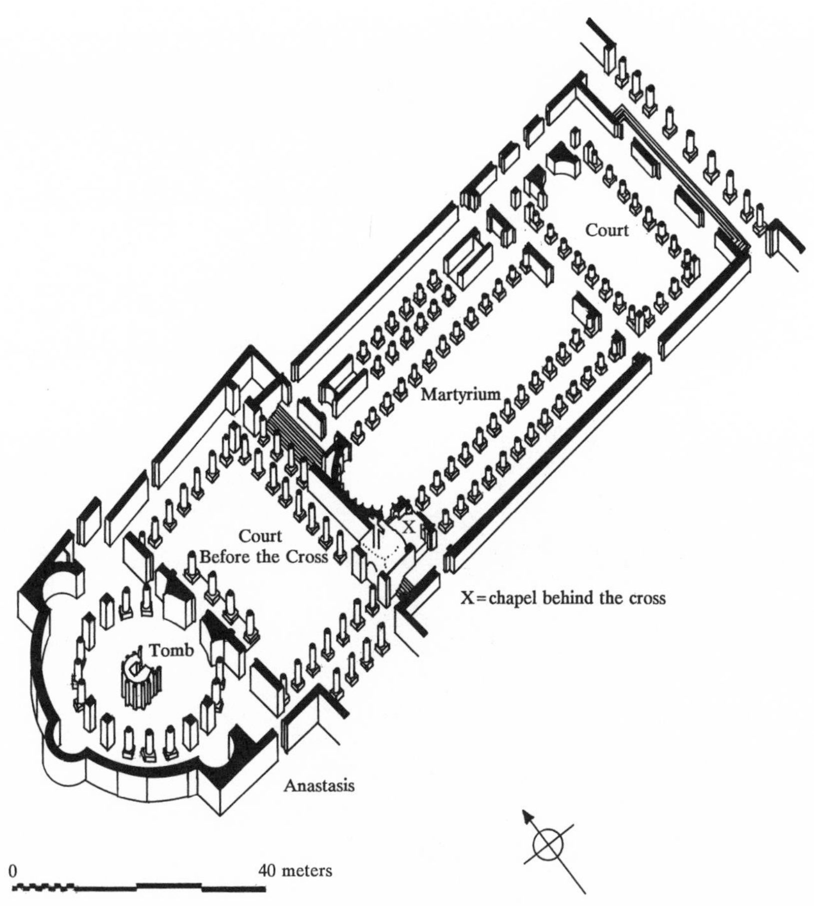

Fig 5
Basilica and shrine at Golgotha and the tomb of Jesus, during the time of Egeria, late fourth century C.E. (after Wilkinson)

Fig 6a
The Madaba map, fourth century C.E., a mosaic representation of the Holy Land (courtesy Michelle Piccirillo, Studium Biblicum Franciscanum Archive, Jerusalem)

Fig 6b
The Madaba map (detail) (courtesy Michelle Piccirillo, Studium Biblicum Franciscanum Archive, Jerusalem)

Fig 7a
Portion of northern panel of the mosaic floor at the Church of Saint Stephen, Um er-Rasas, Jordan (sixth century C.E.). Shown here are four of the eight Palestinian cities depicted in the mosaic: (*from top*) Jerusalem, Neapolis, Sebastis (Sebastia), and Caesarea (courtesy Michelle Piccirillo, Studium Biblicum Franciscanum Archive, Jerusalem)

Fig 7b
The mosaic panel of Jerusalem in the Church of Saint Stephen, Um er-Rasas, Jordan (courtesy Michelle Piccirillo, Studium Biblicum Franciscanum Archive, Jerusalem)

10 When Will the Light of Israel Be Kindled?

As Abraham was about to sacrifice his son Isaac God said to him, "Do not lay your hand on the lad or do anything to him." Then Abraham lifted his eyes and looked and "behold, *behind* him was a ram, caught in a thicket by his horns." Taking the ram, Abraham sacrificed it as a burnt offering to the Lord instead of his son (Gen 22). The Hebrew term for "behind" (*ahar*) usually means "after," and in *Genesis Rabbah,* a collection of exegetical traditions compiled in Palestine during the Byzantine period, the rabbis chose to interpret the term according to its conventional meaning. Rabbi Judah said "*Ahar* is used in the sense of 'after,' that is: after all that happened [after what God has done for Israel], Israel will nevertheless be 'caught' in sin and will be 'entangled' in misfortunes; but in the end it will be delivered by the horns of a ram, as it is written, 'And the Lord will blow the ram's horn'" (Zech 9:14). "After" in the text signifies Israel's future redemption, the great day of the Lord when the Jews will be redeemed from their sorrows by the "horns of a ram," that is, the trumpet that will sound announcing the day of deliverance.

Other rabbis gave the term "after" a more specific application to the trials of the Jews in the Land of Israel. Just as the ram "got himself out of one thicket only to be entangled in another one," so Abraham's descendants have been "entangled in one kingdom after another" subject to foreign rule in their own land, first to Babylon, then to Persia, later to Greece, and finally to Edom (Rome). "In the end, that is to say, afterwards," said some rabbis, Abraham's descendants "will be redeemed by the horns of a ram."[1]

In its earliest form God's promise to Abraham was that he and his descendants would "possess the land" God had given them. After Jerusalem was captured by the Babylonians and its people taken into exile in Babylonia, this hope came to be focused on the return of the exiles and the reestablishment of a Jewish kingdom in Jerusalem. Later, as Jews found themselves subject to the hegemony of foreign power—to the Persians, to the Greeks (first the kingdom of the Ptolemies in Egypt and then that of the Seleucids in Antioch), and finally to the Romans—the land promise took another form: deliverance from foreign bondage. In the words of the Babylonian Talmud, "There is no difference between this world and the days of the Messiah except our bondage to the heathen kingdoms" (*b. Ber* 34b). As Jacob Neusner has observed, commenting on the passage about the ram's horn in *Genesis Rabbah,* "From the perspective of the Land of Israel, the issue is not exile but the rule of foreigners."[2]

What did Jews living in Christian Palestine think about the Christian remaking of the face of Palestine? Jews could see the churches and monasteries that had been constructed in every town and city in the land, they could not ignore the steady stream of pilgrims that traveled up and down the country, they were learning to adjust to the calendar of Christian festivals and saints' days, they witnessed public liturgical processions in and around Jerusalem during holy week and they could sense that these Christians, unlike the Romans of old, were not indifferent to the spiritual qualities of the land. What did they make of the Christian presence in Eretz Israel?

The Continuity of Jewish Life

Jewish life in Palestine went on undisturbed during the Christian era—such is the testimony of archaeology. The construction of new synagogues and the remodeling of older buildings continued without interruption. With few exceptions Jews were to go about their communal affairs and practice their way of life without interference. Jews also shared in the prosperity and economic growth that permeated the country as a whole, and Jewish intellectual life, as reflected in the Jerusalem Talmud and the midrashim, flourished. Lee Levine writes,

> Heretofore it has been commonly assumed that the late Roman-Byzantine period witnessed a steady decline of Jewish life and the recession into a kind of Dark Age which was to last for centuries. Large-scale emigration, loss of political status, lapse of key communal institutions, economic hardships and religious discrimination bordering at times on persecution, were assumed to have had their cumulative effect, leaving the Jewish community in an impoverished state. This perception has been challenged on a number of fronts. The Cairo Geniza has revealed a series of literary works dating from this period, indicating the existence of a creative cultural life among Jews. This impression is the result of the now-accepted dating to late antiquity of a series of liturgical, apocalyptic, halakhic, and mystical works, previously thought to be medieval in origin. To these examples can now be added the ever increasing number of Byzantine synagogues being found throughout Israel. Moreover, other synagogues, products of a somewhat earlier age, continued to undergo extensive renovations, and were in use down to the Arab conquest of Palestine and beyond.[3]

The archaeological evidence is more abundant for the fourth and fifth centuries than for the sixth, yet at a number of sites where the architectural history of a particular building can be traced, the continuity of life over generations and centuries is apparent. The greatest disruption came not from social causes but from natural disasters such as earthquakes. To illustrate: Gush Halav (Giscala, El Jish) is located five miles northeast of Safed in northern Galilee. As early as the nineteenth century travelers noted the ruins of two synagogues in the region. Giscala (as Josephus called it) was the home of a company of Jewish zealots during the war with the Romans, and during the Roman period it retained its Jewish character. Many coins dating from the early fourth century to the early sixth century were found at the site, with the greatest concentration toward the end of the period. According to the report of archaeologists who excavated the site, the history of the principal synagogue at Gush Halav can be narrated as follows:

250 C.E.—Constructed
306—Damaged by earthquake
306—Repaired
362—Again damaged by earthquake
362—Repaired
447—Damaged by third earthquake
447—Repaired
551—Damaged by massive earthquake and site taken over by squatters[4]

In Nabratein, a neighboring village, the synagogue was spared the severe damage suffered in Gush Halav. Constructed in the early second century C.E., this synagogue underwent a second phase of building at the end of the third century and then a third early in the fourth century. It continued to be used by the community well into the sixth century, when it was thoroughly remodeled. An inscription appears on the lintel of the synagogue: "Four hundred and ninety-four years after the destruction [of the Temple], the house was built during the office of Hanina son of Lezer and Luliana son of Yudan." The synagogue continued to be used for at least another 150 years.[5]

These two synagogues were located in upper Galilee, a region that was populated largely by Jews and was slow to accept Christianity. In the course of the fourth and fifth centuries at least fifteen synagogues were constructed in the region, and many of these were no more than an hour's walk from each other.[6] In Scythopolis (Beth Shean), located in the Jordan valley south of the Sea of Galilee, the home of Cyril of Scythopolis, the Jews lived in a quite different cultural environment. Scythopolis was a cosmopolitan community with a large gentile Christian population. Yet the number of Jews living in the city was considerable, and they mixed freely with the other inhabitants, too freely, according to some rabbis.[7] Archaeological evidence shows that six synagogues were built or remodeled in the city and vicinity during the fifth and sixth centuries.

The archaeological remains in Scythopolis and vicinity allow us partial but intimate glimpses of the differing ways Jews adapted to a social and religious world that was not of their own making.[8] At times Jews modified conventional artistic representations in subtle ways to express distinctively Jewish beliefs and attitudes, but in other cases, they were content to let the icons of Hellenistic civilization stand on their own, as though they delighted in them for their own sake. On the floor of the home of a wealthy Jew named Leontis Kloubas in Scythopolis, the figure of Odysseus (from Homer's *Odyssey*) appears twice. In one scene he is pictured tied to the mast of his ship as the sirens call out to him, in the other he is sitting in his ship fighting with a sea monster.[9] Sometimes Jews displayed a resolute indifference to anything that clouded the memory or compromised the life of the community. They avoided, for example, the designation Palestine (which Christians freely used) as well as Greek and Roman names for cities and towns of Eretz Israel. In their view these names were ephemeral, without root, and, in the face of the eternity of Israel, would one day vanish.[10]

Apparent indifference to the non-Jewish world is evident in an extraordinary floor mosaic discovered in 1974 in a synagogue excavated at Rehov, a few miles south of Beth Shean on the road to Jericho. Constructed in the fourth century, the synagogue was remodeled various times over the next several hundred years. Many inscriptions were found at the site, some listing donors and others dealing with ritual matters. But the most unusual was an inscription in Hebrew and Aramaic containing 360 words, the longest in these languages discovered in Palestine. What is more, the inscription deals with halakhic matters. According to Jacob Sussman, "The inscription belongs to the last stage of the synagogue, and it is among the last of the ancient synagogues and is dated, approximately, to the seventh century either before or after the Arab conquest."[11]

The Rehov inscription deals with Jewish laws concerning the seventh year, specifically the regulations of produce grown within the boundaries of the Land of Israel.[12] According to Leviticus 25 the land must lie fallow every seventh year: "When you come into the land which I give you, the land shall keep a sabbath to the Lord. Six years you shall sow your field, and six years you shall prune your vineyard and gather in its fruits; but in the seventh year there shall be a sabbath of solemn rest for the land." The law was a reminder to the Israelites that the land was not their own but a gift from God.

In the period of the Second Temple the laws of the seventh year had been observed (2 Macc 6:49, 53), and Julius Caesar exempted the Jews from taxes during the seventh year (*Ant.* 14.202). To keep these laws, however, required uncommon devotion, for the farmer had to pay taxes on the land even though it lay fallow; yet he needed produce to feed his family. Hence the rabbis applied the verse "you mighty ones who fulfil his word" (Ps 103:20) to the "upholder of [laws] of the Seventh year" with the explanation, "This man [who observes the laws of the seventh year] sees his field untilled, his vineyard untilled, and yet he pays his taxes and does not complain."[13] This new inscription gives evidence that the laws of the seventh year continued to be observed by Jews in the Byzantine period. But because of the hardships it imposed on Jews, the rabbis had devised means to reduce the territory in which the laws applied. Hence the inscription designates specific towns and sections of towns in which it was allowed to cultivate the land during the seventh year.[14]

The inscription also includes a version of a *baraita* (authoritative tradition that goes back to an earlier generation of rabbis) on the boundaries of the land of Israel known from other sources. The text give a schematic overview of the borders of the land of Israel, beginning with Ashkelon on the coast, moving north to Acco, east to the Golan, down the Jordan valley to Petra and back westward to Ashkelon. "The intention of the *baraita*," writes Sussman, "was primarily to delineate this short border segment on the edge of the dense Jewish settlement in Galilee and to define precisely the limits of the land as denoted in *[Mishnah] Sheviit* 6. Hence what we have here is plainly a halachic *baraita* . . . rather than an early historiographical document."[15] The inscription defines those areas of the Land, particularly in Galilee, that were inhabited primarily by Jews and sets them off from "gentile" regions. Scythopolis was, of course, a gentile city, and Judah the prince, the codifier of the Mishnah, had exempted it from the laws. Nevertheless it was forbidden to grow certain fruits there, and these are enumerated in the inscription. When land that was once outside of the domain of Jewish law came into the hands of Jews, it was made subject to the law.

The authors of the inscription clearly assume the existence of a geographical entity called Eretz Israel and use the expression the "territory [or boundaries] of Eretz Israel." Eretz Israel is the land which "those who went up from Babylonia claimed" when they returned. At the same time the inscription displays a hard realism. It does not mention Jerusalem or the heart of Eretz Israel, Judea, because few Jews lived in Judea in the Byzantine period and the laws of the seventh year were inert in that region of the country. The Rehov inscription presupposes the political and social fact that Judea was no longer a Jewish territory. In Galilee, however, where there was a concentration of Jews, laws originally designed to apply to the land as a whole were observed. Where possible the Jews observed the agricultural laws as though the Land of Israel was still a Jewish land.[16]

Within the city of Scythopolis itself, the mosaic floor of the famous Beth Alpha synagogue presents us with another perspective on Jewish piety during the Byzantine period.[17] According to an Aramaic inscription in the floor, this synagogue was constructed during the reign of Justinus (either the emperor Justin I [518–27] or Justin II [565–78]), which was at the height of the Christian era. The mosaic floor is well preserved, and in its center is an image of Helios, the sun god, driving a four-horse chariot; surrounding the central medallion is a wheel with the signs of the zodiac encircling the image of Helios. At four points on the wheel appear personifications of the four seasons. Both the zodiac signs and the four seasons are identified by Hebrew legends. Above and below the central floor mosaic are two smaller panels: one depicts a Torah shrine, two large menorahs, two birds, two lions, various cultic instruments associated with the Temple, the *lulav* (a palm leaf) and *ethrog* (citrus fruit), an incense shovel, and a shofar; the second panel includes a narrative sequence depicting the binding of Isaac (Gen 22). One scene shows two servants holding Abraham's donkey, a second the ram tethered to a tree; another depicts Abraham and Isaac and in the distance an altar with a fire on it. The mosaic includes several Hebrew phrases from the biblical account of the binding of Isaac.

Because of the mixture of Jewish and Hellenistic motifs in this floor, the synagogue at Beth Alpha has been the subject of ongoing debate. Why would Jews place the figure of a pagan God, Helios, on the floor of a synagogue? Helios rides in a chariot, and some have proposed that the artist wished to depict the "chariot" representing God in the book of Ezekiel. Others have said that Helios signifies Elijah on his chariot. Yet others have concluded that the zodiac may simply be decorative and the figure of Helios represents "nothing more profound than an image of the sun, not as god, but as a symbol of the passage of night into daytime."[18]

Whatever interpretation one gives to the zodiac, the two other panels of the floor, the binding of Isaac and the Torah shrine—the one depicting sacrifice, the other displaying cultic instruments—directed the attention of the worshippers to the former Temple in Jerusalem. According to the biblical account, Abraham and Isaac had gone to an unidentified mountain in the "land of Moriah." Later tradition identified Moriah with the Temple Mount (2 Chron 3:1), and as the story of the binding of Isaac came to occupy a central place in Jewish piety, it was assumed that the sacrifice had taken place at the site of the Temple in Jerusalem. Even though the Christian name for the story of Abraham and Isaac is the "sacrifice of Isaac" and the Jewish name is the "binding [*Akedah*] of Isaac," for Jews the sacrificial features of the story are paramount. Indeed in Jewish tradition Isaac is an active participant in the act of sacrifice. One of the targums on Genesis 22 puts these words into the mouth of Isaac: "Father tie me well lest I kick you and your sacrifice be rendered useless."[19]

As the binding of Isaac came to be associated with major festivals in the life of the Jewish people, notably Pesach and Rosh Hashanah, it came to serve as a kind of paradigmatic redemptive event. At the synagogue of Dura-Europos it is the only biblical scene to appear on the Torah shrine.[20] Other biblical events are portrayed on wall paintings, but the Akedah had a position of prominence at the front of the synagogue, as it does in the panel on the floor at Beth Alpha. For the Jew, the Akedah was a symbol of God's mercy and goodness toward Israel. In prayers it was recalled to remind God of his love for Israel and to plead for mercy during times of affliction. Again, the targum on Genesis 22: "And now when his sons are in the hour of affliction, remember the Akedah of their father Isaac and listen to the voice of their supplication and hear them and deliver them from all tribulation, because the generations to arise after him shall say: On the mountain of the sanctuary of the Lord, where Abraham offered his son Isaac, on this mountain the Glory of the Shekinah of the Lord was revealed."[21]

The final lines of this prayer are a reference to the Temple in Jerusalem, and it is possible that the Temple provides the link between the panel with the Akedah and the panel with the torah shrine at Beth Alpha.[22] Besides familiar cultic objects, for example, the incense shovels and shofar, this panel also has a light suspended from the roof of the shrine that may represent the perpetual light in the Temple, and two birds which could represent the cherubim in the Temple. Another synagogue in Scythopolis from roughly the same period also has a floor panel that depicts a torah shrine flanked by a seven-branched menorah, incense shovels, and shofars. These representations of cult objects helped to keep alive the memory of the Temple in Jerusalem, thereby sowing seeds of hope. By calling attention to objects whose sole purpose was cultic, the Jews of Scythopolis may also have been pointing to the future, to the day when the Temple would be rebuilt and sacrifices would again be offered on Mount Moriah in Jerusalem.

Although the majority of the synagogues from this period are to be found in Galilee and in the northern part of the country, there have been some discoveries in other regions. A synagogue from this period was excavated at En Gedi, the oasis on the west shore of the Dead Sea.[23] The building was first constructed in the early third century and was in use until the middle of the sixth century C.E. A long, puzzling Aramaic and Hebrew inscription in the synagogue includes a genealogy from Adam to Japheth (1 Chron 1:1–4), the names of the zodiac, the months of the Jewish calendar, then the names of Abraham, Isaac, Jacob, Daniel's companions, Hannaiah, Mishael, and Azariah, followed by "Peace on Israel."

Not too far from En Gedi, in Jericho, a synagogue was discovered with its entire mosaic floor intact. It includes an Aramaic inscription with the words "May they be well remembered, may their memory be for good, all the holy community, its elders and its youth, whom the King of the World helped and who exerted themselves and made the mosaic. He who knows their names and the names of their children and the names of their households, shall write them in the book of life, together with the just. They are associates with all Israel. Peace." Besides this inscription there are two large panels in the floor, one that represents a torah shrine standing on four legs surmounted by a conch shell and a second that frames a menorah flanked by a lulav and shofar with the inscription "Peace on Israel."[24]

The phrase "Peace on Israel" occurs in several psalms, specifically in songs of ascent that may have originally been sung by pilgrims going up to Jerusalem. "Peace on Israel" occurs at the end of the well-known psalm that begins, "Those who trust in the Lord are like Mount Zion, which cannot be moved, but abides for ever. As the mountains are round about Jerusalem, so the Lord is round about his people, from this time forth and for evermore" (Ps 125:1–2). Psalm 128 uses similar phrasings: "The Lord bless you from Zion! May you see the prosperity of Jerusalem all the days of your life. . . . Peace be upon Israel." The blessing, "Peace on Israel," is set in a mosaic with cult objects, the menorah, the shofar, and the lulav.[25] The lulav was associated with Sukkoth, one of the three pilgrimage festivals to Jerusalem and a festival that has eschatological overtones. On the day of the Lord, according to the prophet Zechariah, all the nations will go up to Jerusalem "to worship the King, the Lord of hosts and to keep the feast of Sukkoth" (14:16). According to Jerome, the Jews, "in their vain hope," believe that this grand celebration of the "feast of tabernacles" will take place at the coming of the Messiah (*in Zach.* 14:16–17; *CC* 76A, 893–95).

Jews had lived in Gaza since the days of the Maccabees, and a synagogue excavated in the 1960s and 1970s indicates that there was a sizable Jewish community in the city during the Byzantine period. The main hall was thirty by twenty-six meters. The building was constructed in the style of a basilica with an external raised apse and four rows of columns that create four side aisles, which explains why it is not much longer than wide. The apse was enclosed by a marble "chancel" screen and railing. The building dates from the third century and was rebuilt in the sixth century. An inscription in the floor reads, "Menahem and Yeshua the sons of the late Isses, wood merchants, as a sign of respect for a most holy place, have donated this mosaic in the month of Loos, 569."[26]

In floor plan, in the style of its mosaic floor, and in its decorative carving this synagogue resembles others found in Palestine during this period. But one feature sets it apart from all others: in a panel on the floor in the main hall is a mosaic of the familiar figure of the Thracian singer Orpheus, holding his lyre and surrounded by wild animals. The representation of Orpheus with a lyre and wild animals is common in late antiquity, but the mosaic at Gaza is unusual. Directly alongside the head of Orpheus is a Hebrew inscription with the words KING DAVID. Orpheus usually wears a pointed hat, but the figure in the mosaic wears a crown. According to Paul Finney, "He is portrayed after his accession to the throne, 2 Sam 2:1 ff., dressed in royal garments, a long chiton made of blue and red tesserae, and a gilded overgarment which covers his mid-section to the knees. He wears a jeweled diadem and his head is nimbed."[27]

David is pictured as Orpheus because, like Orpheus, he played the lyre (or cithara) and composed songs. David came to the attention of King Saul by playing the lyre and singing. But in Jewish tradition David was not only the author of many of the psalms, but also a powerful king of Israel who united the northern and southern parts of the country into a single monarchy. David chose Jerusalem as the capital of his kingdom, and he brought the ark of the covenant to the city. In Jewish memory the name of David, more than that of any other king, was associated with Jerusalem, and one of the names for Jerusalem came to be the city of David. David's rule was more than a historical memory; David was also a symbol of hope and restoration. In Ezekiel, David is a messianic figure who will one day reestablish Jewish rule in the land and bring home the exiles: "My servant David shall be king over them. . . . They shall dwell in the land where your fathers dwelt that I gave to my servant Jacob . . . and David my servant shall be their prince forever" (Ezek 37:24–25). In the person of King David the steady strength of Jewish memory continued to guide the imagination and give the people grounds for hope. Yet it would take a world-shattering event in Jerusalem to fan the flame that had quietly burned for centuries.

Sassanid Conquest of Jerusalem

In 614 C.E. the armies of Chosroe II, king of the Sassanids, who had ruled the Persian Empire since the third century, entered Jerusalem, occupied the city, and captured the relic of the holy cross. Christians were stunned and bewildered, and the Jews were exultant. For centuries the Sassanids and Romans had fought with each other for control of the vast area extending from the Euphrates River to the Mediterranean. On several occasions the Romans had reached the Persian capital of Ctesiphon, and the Sassanids had pillaged Antioch and taken parts of eastern Asia Minor. But this was the first time the Persians had penetrated Palestine and taken, in the words of a Christian eyewitness, "that great city, the city of the Christians, Jerusalem, the city of Jesus Christ."[28]

Two generations earlier, at the end of Justinian's reign in 565 C.E., for a moment the empire, it seemed, had secured its onetime boundaries and restored its former glory. "The magnificent dream of extending the Roman Empire to its ancient limits seemed all but realized, for by the campaigns of Belisarius and Narses, Africa, Spain, and Italy had been recovered. But the triumph had crippled the conqueror; already ruinous overdrafts had anticipated the resources which might have safeguarded the fruits of victory. Rome relaxed, her grasp exhausted. Time was ringing out the old and ringing in the new."[29] In the East the Byzantines held the fortress in Petra (in present-day Jordan), and a peace treaty had been signed with the Sassanian king Chosroe I. But the payment of tribute at the rate of thirty thousand gold solidi a year was burdensome to the Romans, and Justin II, Justinian's successor, refused to pay, with impunity.

During the reign of Emperor Maurice (582 C.E.) the new Sassanian king, Chosroe II, the "victorious," appealed to the Byzantines to aid him in subduing a band of rebels who had challenged his succession. In return, Chosroe abandoned his claim to several frontier cities and to Armenia, long a source of tension between Rome and Persia. A few years later, however, Maurice was murdered and a usurper, Phocas, crowned in his place. Chosroe, supposedly to avenge Maurice's murder, invaded eastern Anatolia. The Romans were impotent to stop his advance.

For the Jews of Palestine, the disarray and weakness within the Roman Empire and the mounting strength of the Persians were seen as auspicious auguries. In the city of Sycmania[30] in Palestine it was reported that the Jews rejoiced at the murder of the emperor Maurice because his death was taken as a sign of the "decline of Roman power."[31] Even during Maurice's reign, some Jews in Tiberias in Galilee saw the threat of a Persian invasion as evidence of the imminent arrival of the messianic king. A Jew living in Tiberias announced that the time of deliverance was at hand: "In eight years the anointed one, the king of Israel, the Christ, will come . . . and he will raise up the nation of the Jews."[32]

In 610, Heraclius, a contemporary of Mohammed and the Roman prince who was destined to witness the loss of the Holy Land to the Arabs, became emperor. When he took office, the empire was occupied by Slavs in the Balkans and Persians in the East, what was left of the army was in disarray, there was no money in the treasury to recruit new soldiers, the capital was torn by dissension and divided into competing factions. Even before Heraclius could rebuild the army and replenish the treasury, the Sassanids had begun to march south toward Syria, Palestine, and Egypt. In 613, under the command of Chosroe's able general Shahrbaraz, the Persian forces captured Damascus and headed directly on to Palestine. To reach Caesarea and Jerusalem from Damascus they had to march directly through Galilee, the most densely populated Jewish area in the country. As the Sassanid forces made their way through the cities and towns of Palestine, a new wave of messianic fervor broke out among the Jews, who welcomed the invaders and offered them support. "When the Persians approached Palestine," wrote an Armenian Christian historian, "the remnant of the Hebrew people rose up against the Christians. They committed great crimes out of national zeal and did many wrongs to the Christian community."[33]

That the conquerors of the Romans came from Persia was a happy coincidence. Centuries earlier, at the time of the exile in Babylonia, the Persians had delivered the Jews from the hands of the Babylonians. The Persian king who had liberated them, Cyrus, was called the anointed—the Messiah—by Isaiah, and there was an uncanny correspondence between the name of the present Persian king, Chosroe, and Cyrus.[34] Under the Persians, the returning exiles had built the Second Temple, which the Romans destroyed in 70 C.E. How sweet that the rule of Rome might be undone by the power of Persia. As one prescient rabbi had predicted several generations earlier, "Rome will fall into the hands of the Persians."[35]

For the Jews of Palestine and Syria the genial prospect of a Persian invasion was fortuitous. In spite of the testimony of archaeology, it appears that the situation of the Jews in the Byzantine Empire was being altered in troubling ways. "Their fundamental privileges remained untouched," writes Andrew Scharf.[36] Nevertheless several of Justinian's laws indicate that imperial authorities on occasion intervened in the internal life of the Jewish community. According to Procopius, Justinian "took pains to abolish the laws which the Hebrews honor." Procopius says that Justinian decreed that in those years that the date of the Jewish Passover fell before the Christian Easter, Jews were forbidden to celebrate Passover on its appointed date.[37] Unfortunately, the text of this law is not extant, and the passage occurs in Procopius's *Secret History,* a work written to discredit and defame the emperor.

But we do have the text of another law from Justinian dealing with

Jewish ritual. In a *novella* published in 553 Justinian instructed the Jews on two matters dealing with synagogue worship. Apparently there was a dispute among Jews at the time about the use of languages other than Hebrew for the reading of the Torah (Greek was widely used in synagogues in the East), and Justinian presumed, as emperor, to legislate on the matter. His first instruction was that Jews were allowed to read the Torah in Greek, preferably in the Septuagint version, but also in the translation of Aquila. His second instruction, however, contrasts markedly with the first for in it he prohibited the reading of the Mishnah in the synagogue. His reason: The Mishnah was not one of the holy books, by which he meant it was not part of the Bible recognized by Christians.[38]

We have no way of knowing how this law was interpreted by local officials or whether it was enforced. However, the Jewish community of Palestine seems to have retained a memory of the legislation. According to Rabbi Yehudai, gaon of Sura (ca. 760 C.E.), in the years before the Arab conquest "it was decreed that the Jews of *Eretz Israel* would not be allowed the reading of the Shema and the daily prayer." Jews were allowed to gather only on Sabbath morning to recite the Shema and other prayers for the Sabbath. It has been argued, with some plausibility, that this local tradition goes back to the situation in Palestine in the years after Justinian, that is, in the period immediately prior to the Persian invasion.[39]

Any effort on the part of Byzantine authorities to insinuate themselves into the internal affairs of the Jewish community, especially on a question of religious ritual, would, of course, have created resentment, anger, and discontent. Whether such feelings resulted in open dissent or direct political action is more difficult to establish. But there are scattered bits of evidence that in some cities Jews participated in incidents that could have contributed to the weakening of Byzantine rule in the region. In 611 in Antioch Jews took part in a riot that led to the death of the Chalcedonian patriarch of the city, Anastasius II.[40] Eastern Christians, as I pointed out earlier, were bitterly divided over the decrees of the Council of Chalcedon (451 C.E.). Persecuted by imperial authorities, the non-Chalcedonians (monophysites), many of whom came from Syria, wished to rid themselves of the "tyrannical rule of the Romans," that is, the Greek emperor in Constantinople. By exploiting divisions among the Christians, Jews helped undermine what fragile unity and stability existed in the East, weakening the will of the populace to resist the invaders. "It is not surprising," writes Zvi Baras, "that the Jews in *Eretz Israel* did not hesitate to seize the singular opportunity which had been created to take part in what was happening and to join openly with the Persians and to free themselves from the Byzantine yoke."[41]

Before marching on Jerusalem the Sassanid armies made their way toward the coast, subduing the cities and towns that lay in their path, until they reached Caesarea, the capital of Palestina Prima.[42] As the inhabitants received word of the arrival of the Sassanid armies, the city capitulated without a struggle.[43] From Caesarea they turned back east to march to Jerusalem. When the armies arrived, the patriarch Zacharias, hoping to protect his flock and to save the holy places, urged the citizenry to sue for peace. But the leaders of the city and many citizens resisted. They sent a monk, Modestus, from the monastery of Theodosius, to appeal for aid to the Byzantine force camped at Jericho. However, when the Byzantine troops saw the strength of the Persians they fled, leaving the city undefended. In April or May 614 the Persian general Shahrbaraz began his siege of the city. He dug large trenches under the walls and built a wood scaffolding to support the walls. When the wood was set on fire the walls came crashing down and the Persians stormed into the city "with unbounded fury." Without mercy they massacred men, women, children, and old people, destroyed churches, profaned the holy places, and killed priests, monks, and holy women.[44] Even today archaeologists have found evidence of the Sassanid destruction in the south wall of the city.[45]

The most detailed account of the conquest was written by an eyewitness, Strategos, a monk from the monastery of Sabas in the Judean desert.[46] Like other Christian writers who describe the doleful events of 614 C.E., he has harsh words about Jewish complicity in the Persian plundering of the city: "When the hostile Jews saw that the Christians had been handed over into the hands of the Persians, they rejoiced with exceeding joy, because they hated the Christians. At that time they thought up an evil plan against the Christians, because their standing with the Persians was great. So the Jews went to the edge of a reservoir and called out to the Christians who were in the lake of Mamila: 'Who among you wishes to become Jewish come up to us that we might ransom you from the Persians.' But their evil plan did not work out, and their efforts were in vain." According to Strategos, after the Persians sacked the city and took some Christians into captivity, "the Jews began to destroy the churches."[47]

In another contemporary source, a poem entitled "On the Captivity of Jerusalem," Sophronius, later to become patriarch of Jerusalem, called the Jews ("Hebrews" in the language of the poem) "friends of the Persians."[48] Coming as these statements do from Christian writers who were outraged at Jewish collaboration in the plundering of the holy city, they no doubt exaggerate the role of the Jews in the conquest. Christian feelings were running high. Yet there is no reason to doubt that Jews took the side of the Persians. What role they played is more difficult to assess; the Persians were quite capable of defeating the Byzantines on their own. Some have claimed that the Jews made an alliance with the Persians or that they fielded a Jewish army or even that they were able to gain control of the city for a time.[49] But the ancient sources make no mention of a Jewish army or a treaty, and it is unlikely that the Jews had in place the political or military structures that would have allowed them to act as a nation.[50]

The *Book of Elijah* and the *Book of Zerubbabel*

The events leading up to the Persian conquest of the Holy Land and the city of Jerusalem gave birth to several Jewish apocalyptic works written in Hebrew in Palestine in the early seventh century. Among these the most important were the *Book of Elijah* and the *Book of Zerubbabel.* Unfortunately, these works, like other apocalyptic books, cannot be dated with certainty. Scholars have assigned the *Book of Elijah* a date from the third century to the seventh century.[51] Several different texts have come down to us, and historical and chronological details vary from one text to another, reflecting additions and alterations as the books were made to fit changing circumstances.[52] Nevertheless it is likely that the *Book of Elijah* and the *Book of Zerubbabel* were written (or rewritten) in the early seventh century at the time of the Persian conquest.

The titles of the two books are noteworthy. Each is named after a heroic figure in ancient Israel who was also a symbol of future deliverance. It was believed that Zerubbabel would reveal the time of the coming of the Messiah and that Elijah would come as a herald of the Messiah.[53] Of the two books the *Book of Elijah* is probably the earlier of the two.

As the book opens, Elijah is sleeping under a "broom tree" (1 Kings 19:5) on Mount Carmel. Michael, "the great prince of Israel," awakens him and speaks to him about the "end which is to come at the end of days." A wind carries Elijah to a high place and Michael again speaks to him: "The end is coming in the days of the king who is going to rise up at the end of days. His name will be Harmelat [or Haksera, that is, Chosroe II, the Sassanid king]" (l. 10).[54] The *Book of Elijah* cites a number of oracles that describe the triumph of Israel over its enemies and the rebirth of the people of Israel in the land. All are familiar messianic texts. "After this all the nations will come and prostrate themselves before each one of

Israel and will lick the dust of their feet, as it is written: 'Kings shall be your foster-fathers, and their queens your nursing mothers; with their faces to the ground they shall bow down to you, and lick the dust of your feet'" (Isa 49:23). This verse, indeed the whole passage from which it was taken, was one of the texts that Jerome discussed in his commentaries as evidence of the persistence of Jewish hope in the rebuilding of Jerusalem. Jews, he said, take this to mean that one day a future Jerusalem of gold and precious gems will come down from heaven. This Jerusalem, whose boundaries will be infinite, is the same Jerusalem spoken of in the final chapters of Ezekiel.[55]

Next the *Book of Elijah* describes the great eschatological battle between the Messiah and the evil hordes of the kings of Gog and Magog who have come from the north. "All the peoples of the earth will be assembled and will encircle Jerusalem for battle. The Holy One, blessed be He, will go up and fight against them. The Messiah will come and the Holy One, blessed be He, with his help will make war against them, as it is written: 'The Lord will go forth and fight against those nations'" (Zech 14:3). On that day the mountain will shake, many cities will be destroyed, the birds of the air and the beasts of the field will prey on the flesh of the dead and drink their blood. But when the battle has ended Elijah sees Abraham, Isaac, and Jacob and all the righteous in a garden enjoying the fruits of the land: "On the banks, on both sides of the river, there will grow all kinds of trees for food" (Ezek 47:12).

At the end of the book Elijah sees Jerusalem coming down from the heavens: "And Elijah, may his name be remembered for good, said: 'I see a beautiful, splendid and great city descending from heaven already built, as it is written, Jerusalem, built as a city which is bound firmly together (Ps 122:3)—built and perfected with its people dwelling in it. It sits upon 3,000 towers and between each tower is 20 stades and between each stade are 25,000 cubits of emeralds and of precious stones and of pearls, as it is written: 'I will make your pinnacles of agate [your gates of carbuncles, and all your walls of precious stone]' (Isa 54:12)."

There is little in the *Book of Elijah* that is new. Indeed much of the book is a pastiche of biblical texts strung together in a simple plot: humiliation, hope, conflict, victory, and restoration. Its themes are familiar and traditional and are well documented in Jewish and Christian sources in early centuries, but they indicate that at the time of the Sassanid conquest the ageless hope of deliverance came rushing to the surface with irrepressible force and energy. No event since the destruction of the Second Temple, except Julian's effort to rebuilt the Temple, had unleashed such fervor and enthusiasm among the Jews of Palestine.

Among medieval apocalypses the *Book of Zerubbabel* was the most widely read and the most influential.[56] In tenth-century Germany it had a "quasi official status."[57] After reading the book, the sages in the Rhineland wrote to Jews in Eretz Israel to inquire about the date of the messianic redemption. Like the *Book of Elijah*, the *Book of Zerubbabel* takes the form of a revelation, in this case to Zerubbabel, a descendant of David, who lived in the sixth century B.C.E. On him fell the responsibility of leading the exiles back to Jerusalem from Babylon and renewing life in Judah during the reign of Cyrus. According to the prophet Haggai, he was given the charge to rebuild the Temple in Jerusalem (1:1–2), a task he undertook as soon as the exiles had settled in the city (Ezra 3, 4). He had probably held an official position in the Persian administration, perhaps as governor of Yehud, but the prophets attribute to him a royal, even messianic, status (Hag 2:20ff.). As he was instrumental in building the Second Temple, it was believed he would play a role in the establishment of the Third Temple. For Jews of later times Zerubbabel was a symbol of hope, of the eventual return of the exiles and the rebuilding of Zion.

"The word which was addressed to Zerubbabel, son of Shealtiel satrap of Judah. On the 24th day of the month of Shevat the Lord showed me this sight, and the sight which I saw on the river Kedar was like a vision." So begins the *Book of Zerubbabel*. Like earlier apocalypses, for example, 2 Baruch, the vision takes place at the time of the captivity in Babylon. After this formulaic introduction the text continues: "I [Zerubbabel] was praying before the Lord and I said. 'Blessed are you O Lord, who gives life to the dead.' My heart was groaning within me saying, 'What will be the plan of the eternal Temple?'"[58] As Zerubbabel contemplates the future Temple, a Temple that would never be destroyed and would last forever, he is filled with sadness: "A great yearning came over me because my sufferings were grievous, and I arose from my grief to pray and to entreat the God of Israel" (ll. 9–10).[59]

A wind lifts up Zerubbabel and he is brought to a strange place, the "city of blood," a house of indecency, Rome, which in the seventh century meant Constantinople, the seat of the Christian emperors. There he sees a man whom he describes with the words of Isaiah as "wounded and despicable" (Isa 53:3). He does not understand what to make of this forlorn creature. Clearly he is the Messiah, but the Messiah is supposed to be mighty, warlike, and glorious. Zerubbabel asks who this is, and the person replies, "I am the Messiah of the Lord, and I am imprisoned here in this jail until the 'time of the end' (Dan 12:9)." When Zerubbabel realizes he is the "Messiah of God . . . and the light of Israel," at once the person before him appeared "like a young man, beautiful and fair." Zerubbabel asks, "When will the light of Israel be kindled?" (l. 18). As Zerubbabel is speaking a "man with wings" appears and says, "What do you ask of the Messiah of the Lord?" And Zerubbabel answers, "When will the time of deliverance come?" (l. 31).[60]

A few lines later the author introduces Hefzivah, the mother of the Messiah, the son of David. The name means "my delight is in her." In the Scripture it is used, paradoxically, for the mother of the evil king Manasseh and also as a name for Jerusalem: "You shall no more be termed Forsaken, and your land shall no more be termed Desolate; but you shall be called *My delight is in her*" (Isa 62:4). Although the figure of the Messiah's mother appears on occasion in Jewish sources, she is "a shadowy and enigmatic human figure to whom little attention was paid."[61] In some texts she remains anonymous, and her role is usually secondary to that of the main actors. In the *Book of Zerubbabel,* however, she is a central figure. To her is given the "rod of deliverance," when she goes forth a star shines before her, and with the rod she slays two kings. In the great battle the Messiah son of Joseph is killed, but Hefzivah survives and remains in the city of Jerusalem guarding the eastern gate. "Nowhere else in Jewish messianic speculation," writes Martha Himmelfarb, "is the mother of the messiah an important participant in the eschatological drama."[62]

The prominence of Hefzivah in this book may be due to the influence of Christian belief and practice, specifically, devotion to the Virgin Mary. In one of the most interesting passages in the book the author describes the idolatrous practice of the inhabitants of the land who worship a beautiful woman:

> And he [Armilius] will begin to plant on the face of the land all the *asheroth* [idols] of the *goyim* [gentiles, that is, Christians] which the Lord hates, and he will take the stone from which he was born and transport it to [the valley of Arbael], and he will build seven altars for it, and it will be the chief object of idolatry, and all the peoples will come from all places and worship this stone and offer incense to it and pour libations, and everyone who lifts up his heart to look at her will not be able to, because no man is able to look on her face because of her beauty. And Armilius angered the Lord with his evil deeds" (ll. 116–22).

In this passage, directed against Christian worship, the *Book of Zerubbabel* calls up the memory of the Canaanites to vent its rage at those who pollute the land. Asherah was a goddess whose cult was practiced by the

Canaanites, who inhabited the land before the conquest of the Israelites. After the Israelites settled in the land, she (and her consort Baal) continued to be venerated by the Canaanites. During the monarchy, this Canaanite goddess proved irresistible to many Israelites, both commoners and kings, as can be seen in the story of king Ahab and his wife Jezebel and the legendary confrontation between Elijah and the priests of Baal on Mount Carmel. The term *asheroth* in time came to refer to cultic objects associated with the worship of the goddess such as wood carvings representing the goddess that were adored and worshipped at her shrines throughout the land. When they came into the land, the Israelites were enjoined to destroy the asheroth that defaced the land: "These are the statutes and ordinances which you shall be careful to do in the land which the Lord . . . has given you to possess all the days that you live upon the earth. You shall surely destroy all the places where the *goyim* whom you shall dispossess served their gods, upon the high mountains and upon the hills and under every green tree; you shall tear down their altars, and dash in pieces their pillars, and burn their *asherim* with fire; you shall hew down the graven images of their gods, and destroy their name out of that place" (Deut 12:1–3).[63]

It has been suggested that *asheroth* in the *Book of Zerubbabel* designate Christian crosses.[64] Since the most conspicuous public buildings in Christian Palestine were Christian churches, this interpretation is plausible. Further, many churches were dedicated to the Virgin Mary, whose veneration appeared blasphemous to Jews. In a panegyric to Mary written by a disciple of the monk Euthymius, the Virgin Mary is addressed as "dispenser of life . . . the root of all goodness . . . the *stone* of the pearl surpassing all others in honor."[65] It is easy to see how the Jews could identify Mary with the Canaanite goddess Asherah and execrate the idolatrous worship of Christians.

From the perspective of the Jews of Palestine the Christians, like the ancient Canaanites, had polluted the land, and one day, perhaps soon, God would drive them out of the land and break their altars into pieces. From other sources we know that Jews in this period had begun to think of Eretz Israel as being defiled and contaminated: "The elders of Israel say, 'Flee my beloved, Lord of the universe, from this *polluted land,* and let your presence dwell in the high heavens.'" These words are taken from the targum on the Song of Songs, an Aramaic version of the Hebrew, written down in Palestine in the Byzantine period. For the author of this translation the land will not be free of pollution until the Messiah comes. On that happy day, the Messiah will sit down with Israel to study the Law, and the Jews will return to Jerusalem to offer sacrifices in the Temple.

"Look on us and regard our pains and afflictions from the high heavens, until the time when you will be pleased with us and redeem us and bring us up to the mountain of Jerusalem, and there the priests will offer up before you incense of spices."[66]

The *Book of Zerubbabel* concludes with a depiction of the return of the Israelites from exile, the descent of the Temple from heaven, and the offering of sweet-smelling sacrifices to the Lord:

> And Nehemiah ben Hoshiel and all the dead who have come to life, and Elijah the prophet with them . . . will go up to Jerusalem. And in the month of Ab in which they mourned Nehemiah, they will put the swords of Jerusalem into sheaths, and there will be great rejoicing in Israel. And they will offer sacrifices to the Lord, he will be pleased with them, and the offering of Israel will be as sweet to the Lord as it was at the time of the first Temple and as in former days. The Lord will smell the pleasant odor [of the offering] of his people Israel and he will rejoice and there will be great joy in Israel.
>
> And the Lord will bring down the Temple constructed above to the earth, and the cloud of incense which is in the Temple of the Lord will go up to the heavens. And the Messiah of the Lord will go out and all Israel after him, and they will stand before the gates of Jerusalem across from the Mount of Olives, and the Holy God will stand on the peak of the mountain and awe will come upon the heavens . . . and upon the earth . . . and upon all flesh and living things, for the Lord God is revealed to the eyes of all. And the exiles of Jerusalem will go up to the Mount of Olives, and Zion and Jerusalem will see and rejoice. Zion will say, "Who begat these for me?" and "Who are these?" And Nehemiah will go up to Jerusalem and say to her, "Behold your sons which you bore and which were exiled from you. Rejoice exceedingly, daughter of Zion, and shout, daughter of Jerusalem. Enlarge the place of your tent, and let them stretch forth the curtains of your habitations [Isa 54:2]" (ll. 145–58).

Jerusalem is pictured as a vast metropolis whose walls extend over the whole of Eretz Israel from the desert to the Lebanon and from the great river to the Mediterranean Sea. In its midst stands the Temple constructed on the peaks of five mountains. These, says the author, are the mountains on which the Lord "chose to set his 'holy place,'" echoing the promise of Deuteronomy (Deut 12:5).[67]

Though the *Book of Zerubbabel* depicts sacrifices in the Temple as a future hope, there is one puzzling passage in the book that suggests some

Jews in Jerusalem may have been able to offer a sacrifice on the Temple Mount during the Persian occupation. "Nehemiah ben Hoshiel will come and gather all Israel as one person in Jerusalem, as a man gathers the members of his family, and they will arrange themselves there. And they will offer *a sacrifice* and it will be pleasing to the Lord. And the people of Israel will be registered according to their families" (ll. 67–71). Other versions of the *Book of Zerubbabel* mention the building of booths for Sukkoth and prayer at the gates of the Temple Mount.[68] These ritual actions may have been a way Jews could make a symbolic claim on the holy city. That this passage occurs in the middle of the *Book of Zerubbabel,* rather than at the end, where the future Temple is portrayed, suggests that it may be a reference to what actually had happened during the Sassanid occupation. Further, the text says that "all Israel will gather as one person, as a man gathers the members of his family, and will secure a place there" (ll. 78–79). This passage is reminiscent of the scene described by Ezra when the exiles returned from Babylon in the sixth century: "The people gathered as one person in Jerusalem," and Zerubbabel and Jeshua "built the altar of the god of Israel to offer burnt offerings upon it as it is written in the law of Moses, the man of God" (Ezra 3:1–2). The Jews of the seventh century may have been imitating the action of Zerubbabel, who offered a sacrifice in Jerusalem before the Temple was rebuilt.[69] Even the reference to the registration of the people according to families may echo the account of the return of the exiles in Ezra 2.

Some have conjectured that the Sassanids handed over the city to the Jews and that for a brief period the Jews ruled in Jerusalem: "The Jews were thus again the rulers of Jerusalem. The form and acts of their government are shrouded in obscurity, apart from information supplied by its enemies. Clearly in Jewish eyes the new authority was legitimate and was invested with the full powers of government."[70] As intriguing as the idea of a brief period of Jewish hegemony in Jerusalem in the early seventh century may be, it lacks support in the ancient sources. The population of Jerusalem was almost wholly Christian, and it is unlikely that a small cadre of Jews would have been able to exercise authority over the city. Nevertheless, the Persians may have granted the Jews privileges that were prohibited under the rule of the Christians. By offering a sacrifice in Jerusalem and celebrating the festival of Sukkoth, Jews intended to "restore Jewish authority in the land."[71]

The Persian occupation of Jerusalem made a deep impression on the Jews. In later Jewish tradition, it overshadowed the Muslim conquest. Sassanid authority held sway in Palestine for a decade and a half, long enough, it appears, to sever the continuity of Byzantine rule in the region. Even when the emperor Heraclius regained Jerusalem in 628 and returned the holy cross, the days of Byzantine rule were numbered. By 634 the Muslim armies were threatening. In Jewish memory it was the Sassanids, not the Muslims, who rang down the curtain on Christian (that is, Roman) rule in the Land of Israel. A Hebrew poem written several hundred years later marks the end of Roman rule 550 years from the destruction of the Second Temple, approximately 613 C.E. Using the imagery of the book of Daniel, in which the kingdoms of the world are identified with beasts, the poet identifies the Roman (Christian) Empire with the fourth and final beast: "I rejoiced because the reign of the four beasts had ended."[72]

An Inheritance to Abraham and His Posterity

Though the books of Elijah and Zerubbabel speak in the timeless diction of ancient prophecy, like many apocalyptic writings they are the offspring of the moment. In the seventh century the appointed time had arrived, it seems, because of the declining fortunes of the Byzantine Empire and the military successes of the Persian king, Chosroe II. What gave Chosroe's actions uncommon symbolic potency was that he had captured Jerusalem, the holy city of the Christians. In the past Christians had demoted the earthly Jerusalem in favor of the heavenly city, but now they claimed Jerusalem as the City of Christ and the new dwelling place of God. Jews understood this well. As a medieval writer put it, "The Romans who destroyed the Temple in the days of the wicked Titus . . . made no claim that they had an inheritance in the Holy Temple or that it was a fit place of prayer for them. But when the wicked Constantine was converted they made these claims."[73]

Earlier Christians had laid claim to the Jewish Scriptures as their own (the Old Testament), adopted the heroes of ancient Israel—Abraham, Joseph, Moses, David—as Christian saints, appropriated even the name Israel by calling the church the New Israel, and now they had taken possession of the land itself, the most enduring sign of Israel's unique relation to God and of the destiny of the Jews as a people. Unlike other peoples in the ancient world, Jews continued to call their own a land over which they had had no sovereignty for centuries. By claiming that the Land of Israel was a Christian Holy Land, Christians dispossessed the Jews of their inheritance, and hence of their future.

In an earlier period of Jewish–Christian relations, when Jews realized that Christians had appropriated the books of the Torah, they insisted that gentiles had no right to study the Law. Study of the Law was a prerogative of the Jews because possession of the Law was one of the distinguishing marks of the Jewish people. Rabbi Yohanan said, "A gentile who studies the Law deserves death, for it is written, 'Moses commanded us a law for an *inheritance*.'" To which he added, "[The Law] is an inheritance for us, not for them" (*b. Sanh.* 59a). In the Byzantine period, when Jerusalem had become a Christian metropolis and the Land of Israel a Christian Holy Land, another Jew, in a debate with a Christian, plaintively asks, "Why do you take what is ours and make it your own?"[74]

In the long history of the Jewish people in the Land of Israel, the Persian conquest was a time of high expectation and fulsome hope. For a moment it appeared that the light of Israel might indeed be kindled. During the Persian occupation of Jerusalem, it was reported that a group of Jews, possibly from Persian-occupied Palestine, sent an embassy to the Byzantine emperor as the Muslim armies were gathering for their assault on the Holy Land, saying, "God has given this land as an inheritance to our father Abraham and to his posterity after him; we are the children of Abraham; you have held our country long enough; give it up peacefully, and we will not invade your territory; otherwise we will retake with interest what you have taken." Six hundred years after the destruction of the Second Temple and over a thousand years since the exile in Babylonia, Jews still dreamed of possessing the land.[75]

11 The Jerusalem Above Wept over the Jerusalem Below

To men and women of old, victory in war was a sign of divine favor and defeat proof of celestial displeasure. For the Hebrews, however, God was not a benign spirit slowly turning the wheel of fortune and gently guiding the affairs of statesmen and kings. In the rise and fall of neighboring kings and in wars, God intervened as a mighty warrior on behalf of the people of Israel. After Moses and the Israelites passed unharmed through the billowing waves of the sea of reeds and the waters rushed back over the horsemen and chariots of the Egyptians, the Israelites sang this song to God: "The Lord has triumphed gloriously; the horse and his rider he has thrown into the sea" (Exod 15:1).

If God's power was evident in victory, defeat was a sign of divine impotence, at least to Israel's foes. When misfortunes beset the ancient Israelites the nations taunted them with the scornful refrain, "Where is their God?" (Ps 79:10). Within the biblical tradition, however, in times of calamity and misfortune, God was not the sole protagonist. To the victors defeat might expose the shortcomings of Israel's God, but to the Israelites, catastrophe and loss came about because of their own wrongdoings, their shortcomings, their unfaithfulness. Misfortune was a sign not of divine weakness, but of God's displeasure and wrath at their sin. The appropriate response to a national calamity was neither doubt about God's power nor loss of faith in God's steadfast love, but communal lamentation over the sins of the people.

In the Lamentations of Jeremiah, a ritualized outpouring of grief written after the Babylonian conquest of Jerusalem, the poet sang of the taunts of the enemy: "When her [Jerusalem's] people fell into the hand of the foe, and there was none to help her, the foe gloated over her, mocking at her downfall." But then he lamented the unfaithfulness of the people of Jerusalem: "Jerusalem sinned grievously, therefore she became filthy. . . . Her uncleanness was in her skirts; she took no thought of her doom. . . . Look and see if there is any sorrow like my sorrow which was brought upon me, which the Lord inflicted on the day of his fierce anger" (Lam 1).

Nothing exemplifies better the transformation that had taken place in the Land of Israel than the obvious, yet seldom observed, fact that when Jerusalem was captured by the Persians in the seventh century of the common era, it was the Christians, not the Jews, who sang a lamentation over the Holy City. Until the Persian conquest in the seventh century, it was Jews who had lamented the city's misfortunes. Besides the Lamentations of Jeremiah, the classic texts are found in the prophets and psalms written at the time of the Babylonian captivity and in the apocalypses written in the aftermath of the destruction of Jerusalem at the hands of the Romans in 70 C.E., for example, 4 Ezra and 2 Baruch discussed in chapter 2.

Christians had little sympathy for Jews who mourned, in the derisive language of Christian polemics, the passing of a city of stone. It is "not possible to say that a city overrun by enemies and plundered by war is 'God's place,'" writes Eusebius (*Comm. in Ps.* 76.1; *PG* 23, 876).[1] Jerome ridiculed those who came to Jerusalem on the ninth of Ab to lament the city's destruction at the Western Wall (*Comm. in Soph.* 1:15–16; *CC* 76a, 673). Of course, Jerome knew that Jesus had wept over the city and acknowledges that "he would not have done so had he not loved it" (*ep.* 46.5). But in his day Christian attitudes toward the city were only beginning to be formed and were not yet marked by feelings that arise out of constant intercourse with places and things. Christian Jerusalem had been built only recently, and its history as a Christian city was brief. For most Christians Jerusalem had not yet become part of their communal experience.

By the seventh century even Christians living in other parts of the Roman Empire identified with Jerusalem and its fate. When John the Almsgiver, patriarch of Alexandria, received word that the Persians had ravaged and despoiled the city, "He sat down and made lament just as though he had been an inhabitant of the city." The final phrase is significant. Jerusalem's fall was not only a calamity for its inhabitants; its destruction reverberated across the Christian world. John the Almsgiver lamented the conquest of Jerusalem not for one or two days, not for a week or a month, but for a full year. "Wailing and groaning bitterly, he strove by his lamentations to outdo Jeremiah, who of old lamented the capture of *this same city,* Jerusalem." Like Jeremiah [by which he means the Lamentations of Jeremiah], the patriarch committed his lamentation to writing.[2] Unfortunately it no longer exists. There are extant, however, two other laments written by Christians in the wake of the Persian occupation, and from them we can see how deeply the Persian occupation affected Christians. These works are the *Capture of Jerusalem* by Strategos, the monk of the monastery of Sabas mentioned in the previous chapter, and a metrical poem entitled "On the Capture [of Jerusalem] by the Persians," by Sophronius, patriarch of Jerusalem in the short period after the Persian conquest and during the Muslim invasion.

"Who could look on Jerusalem that day without weeping?"

The biblical language of lamentation over Jerusalem was, of course, familiar to Christians from the Psalms, the prophets, and the Lamentations of Jeremiah. In early Christian tradition the book of Lamentations was understood *historically* as an outpouring of Israel's grief and sadness over the fall of Jerusalem in the sixth century B.C.E. or as a more general expression of sorrow over one's sins. "Lamentation," writes Theodoret in the preface to his brief commentary on the book, is a "sign of sympathetic affection and love." The prophet Jeremiah wrote the book of Lamentations "for the benefit of those who lived at the time [of the exile]." But he also had in mind "those who would come later . . . in order that they might learn from the Scriptures how many evil things are the result of sin."[3] Lamentation, in the sense of grief over the fall of Jerusalem, is not a major theme in early Christian thinking or piety; few Christian commentators showed interest in the book, and passages in the prophets lamenting Jerusalem's fall were inevitably turned against Jewish affection for the city of Jerusalem.

As I pointed out in the previous chapter, the *Capture of Jerusalem* is an eyewitness account of the Sassanid occupation of the city composed soon after the event. Written in Greek, the treatise survives only in several Arabic translations, in Georgian, the language of the Christian community on the eastern shore of the Black Sea, and in a few Greek fragments. The earliest translations are those in Arabic found at the monastery of St. Catherine in the Sinai Desert.[4] They are of interest not only for what they tell us about the impact of the invasion on Christians at the time, but also for what they reveal about the way the Persian occupation was remembered by Christians several hundred years later. That the text was translated several times into Arabic, the new vernacular of Palestinian Christianity, is an indication of how deep an impression the events made on later generations of Christians, long after the city had come into the hands of the Muslims.[5]

Strategos's book is presented as a historical account of the Persian invasion of Jerusalem.[6] He describes the seizure of the holy cross, the capture and deportation of the patriarch Zachariah, and the sack of the city by the Persians (with the help of the Jews). One of the most appealing features of the work is the author's delight in telling the stories of valiant Christians who stood firm in their faith in the face of adversity: the patriarch Zachariah, a deacon who saw his two daughters cut down by the Persians because they would not "worship fire" (16.3), twin boys who were separated by the Persians, and the beautiful tale of a virgin woman who, by her shrewdness, deceived her Persian captor.[7] The work also includes information about people killed during the invasion, listing the numbers of dead by location in and around Jerusalem.[8] A concluding section, probably added later, recounts the return of the holy cross to Jerusalem after the Byzantines regained control of the city under the emperor Heraclius.

Although the historical details in the book refer to the sack of Jerusalem by the Persians in the early seventh century, they are set within the framework of the Babylonian captivity in the sixth century B.C.E. Strategos does not give us an account of the sacking of an ordinary city; like the Jewish apocalypses written after the fall of Jerusalem in 70 C.E., the *Capture of Jerusalem* is a self-conscious effort to set the destruction of Jerusalem within the framework of biblical history. From the very beginning of the work, Strategos imposes on the events of his time the experience of captivity drawn from the biblical prophets. The subject of his book is the "destruction of Jerusalem" and the "*capture* of the true cross and plundering of the church's sacred vessels and the *captivity* of the flock and *capture* of Zachariah the patriarch" (1.1).[9] He draws a direct parallel between the present conquerors and the ancient Babylonians and cites psalms that were sung by the Israelites in captivity.[10]

Strategos contrasts his book with the writings of the evangelists. They proclaimed a message of great joy, but he writes with a heavy heart: "I do not write to you of gladness and joy, I do not call you to rejoice, but I call you to mourn. Grieve, oh brothers [his fellow monks at Mar Saba], grieve, because today my spirit is heavy from great weeping. . . . I do not call [my treatise] a codex, but I call it sadness; I do not call it a book, but I call it captivity; I do not call it an epistle, but I call it lamentation. . . . I do not call it joy but I call it weeping" (1.1–5).

Once Strategos has provided his reader with a historical and theological framework to interpret the calamity,[11] he proceeds to draw out other parallels between Christian and Israelite experience. Following the biblical pattern of lament, he finds cause for the disaster in the sins of Jerusalem's inhabitants, in particular certain perfidious individuals and groups.[12] His accusations are phrased in the words of the prophet Ezekiel: "'You took some of your garments and sewed for yourselves idols and you fornicated in them . . . you took your sons whom you had borne to me and you offered them as sacrifices to be devoured, and you went to extremes in the extent of your fornication; for this reason God had handed you over to the hands of your enemies,' thus says the Lord" (2.5).[13] But laying blame plays only a small part in the work. Strategos is more interested in describing the spiritual significance of the capture for Christians living in the Holy Land and elsewhere.

The account of the capture begins with the Persian advance into Palestine, the march through the center of the country and to Caesarea on the coast but moves quickly to the chief subject of the work, the occupation of "the city of the Christians, Jerusalem." The Persians had captured two monks who told them, "You labor in vain . . . for the hand of God will protect this holy city." Hearing this (according to Strategos), the Persians offered to spare the city and the patriarch Zachariah agreed. But the inhabitants resisted (19).[14] Realizing that the situation was desperate, Zachariah sent a monk named Modestus to summon aid from a Roman garrison in Jericho. But help was not forthcoming.[15]

When the Persians realized that no one would come to the aid of the city and it was theirs for the taking, "they were certain that God was angry at the Christians" (8.2). Building towers and balustrades for the siege, they breached the walls and entered the "city of God with fierce anger." They pillaged and killed women, children, and priests. "For the citizens of Jerusalem it was a fearful calamity." At this point, the author wrote the most poignant line in the work, a line that would have been inconceivable on the lips of Christians in earlier centuries: "*And the Jerusalem above wept over the Jerusalem below*" (8.9).[16] So great was the sorrow in heaven that "on that day a great darkness came over the city" which reminded people of the darkness at the time of Christ's crucifixion. As the Persians destroyed Jerusalem's churches and spit on the offerings on the altars and blood flowed in the midst of the city as a river, the Christians of Jerusalem wept as they had at Christ's death: "O my beloved, who could look at the sadness in Jerusalem on that day without weeping and his heart breaking" (8.10).

The central character in the *Capture of Jerusalem* is Zachariah, the patriarch of Jerusalem at the time of the Persian conquest. It was his unhappy lot to be taken into captivity by the Persians for fourteen years. During Zachariah's years in Persia, Modestus, a monk from the monastery of St. Theodosius, acted in his place. Zachariah resumed his duties as patriarch after he returned from captivity in 628 and was succeeded a few years later by Sophronius, who was to have the unenviable task of presiding over the church in Jerusalem at the time of the Muslim conquest a few years later.

As Strategos describes Zachariah being led out of the city, he is reminded that Christ was led *into* the city through the same gate before his death. "He [Zachariah] did not enter Zion like Christ, for Christ sat upon an ass when he entered Zion; the enemies shoved the shackled shepherd out through the gate. There were not any children there praising him, but the whole people mourned over him. . . . The multitude did not cry out "Hosanna" but walked with him weeping; they did not lay their garments on the earth, but soaked the earth with their tears; . . . O gates of Zion, how many calamities have passed through you. . . . O gates of Zion, an honored cross went out from you twice; for once the cross went out with Christ, and now the cross goes out with the patriarch and shepherd Zachariah in captivity. O Zion, how much joy and sadness and lamentation you have showed us. . . . Zachariah the patriarch went out through Zion's gate as Adam went out from paradise. Christ is led out for the salvation of the world, and Zachariah the patriarch was led out for the salvation of Jerusalem" (13.1–9).

As Zachariah left the city, the people followed him down into the Kidron valley and up the Mount of Olives, where the band of captives halted briefly. What follows might be called the people's lament over the city. Strategos writes, "They raised their eyes and beheld Jerusalem ablaze with flames and began to lament with tears. Some struck their faces, and others threw ashes over their heads, and some threw dirt in their faces, and some pulled hair from their scalps. They were not grieving over their own sins but because of the destruction of Jerusalem; and some struck their breasts, and some lifted their hands to heaven crying out and saying, 'Have mercy on us, O Lord; have mercy on your city, O Lord, have mercy on your altars. . . . O Lord, look how your enemies are rejoicing in the destruction of your city and of your altars. . . . O Lord, do not chastise us in your wrath, but in your mercy; deal with us not according to our sins but on account of your pity. . . . Let not the enemies say, "Where is their God?" Let not the enemies say, "Where is their cross?"'" (13.14–20).

When Zachariah the patriarch saw the people throwing ashes over their heads and beating their breasts, he raised his hand to calm them. Opening his mouth he addressed them for the last time. His words, really a sermon on bearing up under suffering, urged the faithful not to lose hope in this time of grief. When he finished, Zachariah realized that the time had come for him to be taken off into captivity. Before being led away, however,

> he turned to Zion, and as a husband consoles his wife, so Zachariah, comforting Zion as he wept, extended his hands, crying out and saying, "O Zion, with a sorrowful word that makes one weep I speak peace to you; peace be with you O Jerusalem, peace be with you O *Holy Land,* peace on the whole land; Christ who chose you will deliver you. . . . O Zion, what hope do I have, how many years before I will see you again?
>
> "What use is there for me, an old man, to hope? How will I see you again? I will not see your face again. I beseech you, O Zion, to remember me when Christ comes to you. O Zion, do not forget me, your servant, and may your creator not forget you. For if I forget you, O Jerusalem, let my right hand wither. Let my tongue cleave to the roof of my mouth if I do not remember you. Peace on you, O Zion, you who were my city, and now I am made a stranger to you. I adore you, O Zion, and I adore him who dwelled in you. . . . To die and to be run through with a sword is sweeter than to be separated from you, O Zion. O Lord, let this cup pass from me." (14.12–16)

After the patriarch had given his final blessing over the city the Persians tried to lead him away, but Zachariah kept turning back, and, as they were about to go down the other side of the mountain out of sight of Jerusalem, he turned again and addressed the city: "Peace to you O Jerusalem; do not forget your servant for you know how I love you and how I served you, and I beseech you to remember me and this people when it calls on Christ." From the Mount of Olives the captives made their way down through the Judean desert to Jericho and the Jordan River and on to Damascus.

This extraordinary scene is reminiscent of David's departure from Jerusalem after the revolt of Absalom. Absalom, one of David's sons, engineered a successful revolt against the powerful king. With the help of David's counselor Ahithophel, Absalom was able to put together a revolutionary band which took control of Jerusalem and forced David to leave the city. As David left the city, crossed the brook Kidron, and ascended the Mount of Olives he was followed by the people of the city. The ancient Israelite historian describes the scene in these words: "But David went up the ascent of the Mount of Olives, weeping as he went, barefoot and with his head covered; and all the people who were with him covered their heads, and they went up, weeping as they went." When David reached the summit he said goodbye to his friends, turned to the East, and headed down the other side of the mountain into the desert (2 Sam 15).

The final section of Strategos's narrative is set in Sassanid Persia. When Zachariah and the small band of Christians who had been taken captive with him had passed through the gate of the Sassanid capital, he recalled the "captivity of the children of Israel [in Egypt] and said, 'Blessed is our God, for all that which happened in the time of Moses long ago has happened in the time of the disciples of Christ in the gospel.'" The captives were placed in a large enclosure, and Zachariah asked his captors if they could be left alone. He gathered the deacons and monks and, standing in their midst, he turned to the East [!] and bowed in adoration. Zachariah asked one of the deacons to begin the prayers by singing several psalms, and he sang verses from the psalms of ascent which refer to Jerusalem. "'In my distress I cry to the Lord . . . [Ps 120:1],' and 'I was glad when they said to me, "Let us go to the house of the Lord"'[Ps 122:1]" (18.9–11).

Finally the patriarch concluded his prayers with other verses from the same psalms: "My dwelling place has been taken captive and I dwell in the tents of the sons of Kedar" (Ps 120:5). Another in the party responded with "Our feet have been standing within your gates, O Jerusalem!" Yet another said, "When the Lord turned back the captivity of Zion, our hearts were filled with great joy." Then the patriarch stood on a high place and sang "Alleluia," and the patriarch's tears caused the whole company to weep and in the midst of the alleluias they mourned and lamented. Zachariah extended his hand and pointed to the river and said, "By the river of Babylon we sat down and wept when we remembered

Zion;... If I forget you, O Zion, may my right hand be forgotten" (Ps 137). When they had finished singing the psalm, they all bowed their heads, and the patriarch beseeched Christ with weeping and groaning (18.12–16).

Occupation of Jerusalem and Sack of Rome

The only event in early Christian history comparable to the Persian conquest of Jerusalem was the sack of Rome by Alaric in 410 C.E., and it is instructive to compare Strategos's lament with the Christian response to the plundering of Rome two centuries earlier. For centuries Rome had been the dominant military and political power in the Mediterranean world. The Italian city-state had conquered all its neighbors by the might of arms, but, as it became an imperial power, it also blessed them with peace and justice. By the beginning of the fifth century, Rome was no longer the political center of the Roman world. It was, however, still a major city, the home of ancient senatorial families, and the seat of the bishop of Rome, the patriarch of the West. As the living embodiment of an ancient civilization, it had endeared itself to Christians by placing itself under the rule of Christ.

Christians as well as pagans believed Rome would endure forever. Robert Markus writes, "Jupiter's promise of unending empire to Rome in Vergil's Aeneid has become transmuted in the achievement of Theodosius. With deliberate allusion to Vergil's famous lines Prudentius affirms his belief that Rome's empire is to last, her power and glory shall know no age."[17] In the words of Prudentius himself, "The world receives you now, O Christ, the world which is held in bonds of harmony by peace and by Rome. These you have appointed to be the chief and highest powers in the world."[18]

When Rome fell into the hands of the Visigoths in 410 C.E., the news alarmed and terrified Christians across the empire. Jerome, writing not in Rome, but in Bethlehem a thousand miles to the east, was consumed with grief. "Suddenly," he writes, "I was informed of the siege of the city of Rome and the falling asleep of many brothers and sisters. I was so astonished and stunned that day and night I thought of nothing else but the deliverance of all." With the fall of the city of Rome "the head of the Roman Empire was cut off, or more accurately I would say that in one city the whole world perished."[19] Jerome's sentiments were shared by men and women in North Africa, Syria, Spain, Egypt, and other provinces of the empire. A Syriac Christian poet composed poems on the "sack of Great Rome." A monk in the desert in Egypt (Scete) whose monastery had been destroyed by a band of marauding nomads, bemoaned his double fate: "The world has lost Rome and the monks have lost Scete." Palladius, the author of a popular collection of monastic lives, wrote that the "barbarian storm" did not spare even the bronze statues in the Forum. . . . Rome, beautified for twelve hundred years, became a ruin."[20]

Like the occupation of Jerusalem in the seventh century, the fall of Rome touched the lives of men and women all over the Roman empire. As Walter Kaegi writes, "The fall of Rome [was] not [regarded] as a local event affecting only the inhabitants of the city but as a loss for all of the world."[21] The sacking of the city stunned Christians everywhere. If Rome could perish, wrote Jerome, nothing in the world was safe (*ep.* 123.6). The fall of Rome was more than a military defeat and a political catastrophe; it was also a spiritual challenge. For pagans, the city was an abiding symbol of the glory of the ancient gods, and they laid the blame for its misfortunes on the Christians, who had abandoned the gods of Rome. Had Rome not deserted the worship of its ancestors' gods and embraced the God of the Christians, Rome would have been spared. Whether one reads Augustine's massive work *The City of God,* the history *Adversus Paganos* of his disciple Orosius, or the works of eastern historians and theologians, it is evident that the sack of Rome challenged the best minds of the Christian world to account for what happened.[22]

The spiritual crisis provoked by the fall of Rome, however, had to do with general philosophical and religious questions (for example, divine providence), not with specifically Christian beliefs. Rome, in the Christian view, was not the city of God, and its fate was not a chapter in the history of salvation. It had no place within the framework of biblical history. In a famous letter about the sack of Rome Jerome wrote, "My voice chokes, and sobs interrupt me as I dictate this. The city which has taken captive the entire world is itself captive." He cites Psalm 79, "O God, the heathen have come into thy inheritance; they have defiled thy Holy Temple; they have laid Jerusalem in ruins. They have given the bodies of thy servants to the birds of the air for food, the flesh of thy saints to the beasts of the earth. They have poured out their blood like water round about Jerusalem and there was none to bury them" (Ps 79:1–3). Though Jerome uses the language of the Bible to express his grief and even mentions biblical Jerusalem, he cites the Bible as he would a verse of poetry. He is interested not in Jerusalem as such or in the words "inheritance" or "Holy Temple," but in the gory description of the bodies of the dead lying in their streets. He may have quoted this particular psalm because it reminded him of Vergil. Without interrupting his train of thought, he turns to Vergil in the next sentence: "Who can describe the havoc of that night / Or tell the deaths, or tally wounds with tears?

The ancient city falls, after dominion / Many long years. In windrows on the streets, / In homes, on solemn porches of the gods, / Dead bodies lie" (*Aeneid* 2.366–71). Once Jerome has cited the psalm and the Roman poet he resumes his account of the sacking of the city without further reflection on its spiritual significance (*ep.* 127.12).

The fall of Jerusalem was an event of another magnitude. For the Jerusalem that was captured by the Persians was the city that Christians read about in the Scriptures and whose many biblical names—Zion, city of David, Salem—were familiar from prayers and hymns, particularly the Psalms. Rome had no such place in the Christian imagination or for that matter in Christian hope. Christians did not speak of a "heavenly Rome" when they dreamed of the kingdom of God. Unlike the city of Rome, Christian Jerusalem was important for what it had *been,* for what it had *become,* as well as for what it *signified.* Its history was the history of biblical Jerusalem. The reluctance of Christians to adopt the Roman name, Aelia Capitolina, to designate the Christian city is only one small indication of how intimate were the bonds between the Jewish city of old and the new Christian city. Christian Jerusalem was the same city that David had conquered and made the capital of his kingdom, it was the city destroyed by the Assyrians and the Babylonians, the city that the exiles longed for and to which they returned at the time of Zerubbabel, the city in which Christ, descended from David according to the flesh, had suffered, died, and been raised from the dead. Only of this city could one say, "The Jerusalem above wept over the Jerusalem below." The angels in heaven did not shed tears over the sack of Rome.

The Lament of Sophronius

It is perhaps fitting that Strategos's treatise the *Capture of Jerusalem* has come down to us in Arabic, not in its Greek original. Some of the terms it uses to designate Jerusalem, the Temple, and holy things are cognates of terms used in Hebrew to refer to the same or similar things. For example, the Arabic term for Jerusalem, *bait al-muqaddis,* is similar to one of the Hebrew terms used to refer to the Temple in Jerusalem, *bet miqdash,* the holy house. Arabic is, of course, not Hebrew, but certain features of the Arabic translation of the *Capture of Jerusalem* highlight the biblical character of the work. Later, Christians in Palestine and elsewhere in the Near East who knew the Bible in Arabic and learned of the Persian conquest by reading this work would readily see the continuity between Christian Jerusalem and the biblical city.

But there was another lament over Jerusalem written during the time of the Persian conquest. Composed by Sophronius, who became patriarch of Jerusalem after the Byzantine emperor Heraclius had recaptured the city, it is written in verse and belongs to a quite different literary tradition. His poem takes the form of an *anacreonticon,* a showy and pretentious genre of poetry favored by rhetors in this period, for example, by the orators at Gaza.[23] These poems were usually written in acrostic with a fixed meter and employed old and rare words, unusual spelling (for the sake of meter), and neologisms. Some scholars consider Sophronius's anacreontica (he wrote approximately twenty) outstanding examples of the genre; others think them risible. Photius, a Byzantine literary historian who lived in the ninth century and had read Sophronius's poems, said that in them Sophronius "kicked up his heels like a young colt."[24]

Sophronius was born in Damascus in Syria, and like many leading Christian bishops of antiquity he had received a superb rhetorical education at the hand of private tutors.[25] As a young man he taught rhetoric in Damascus, but like other able and intelligent men of his day he was attracted to the monastic life. He lived for a time in Egypt, then at a monastery near the Jordan River, and finally settled at the monastery of Theodosius (Deir Dosi) near Bethlehem. There he met John Moschus, the author of *Spiritual Meadow,* one of the most popular spiritual writings in the Christian East, a work that recounted the tales of the holy men and women in the desert east of Jerusalem.[26] The two men spent a number of years traveling together around the eastern Mediterranean to visit monastic communities, observing the deeds of holy men and women and listening to their sayings. Sophronius was also a gifted orator and prominent theologian.

The date of the poem, "On the Capture [of Jerusalem] by the Persians," is uncertain, but it was probably written shortly after the siege of the city in 614 C.E.[27] Even though the language is ostentatious and affected, the poem has an immediacy to it. That is not to say that it is a simple historical account of what happened. As Clermont-Ganneau observed, somewhat myopically, almost a century ago, the poem is a "tearful lamentation" which is "more credit to Sophronius' feelings than his talents as a historian."[28] But that is precisely the point; what is most interesting about the poem is not the bits of information it provides about the occupation, but what it tells us about Sophronius's affection for the city. Like Strategos's *Capture of Jerusalem,* it is a lament over the fall of Jerusalem.

The poem begins:

Holy City of God
Home of the most valiant saints

Great Jerusalem
What kind of lament should I offer you?
Children of the blessed Christians
Come to mourn high crested Jerusalem

In the face of such tragedy
The flow of my tears is too brief
The dirge of my heart
Too measured before such suffering

Nevertheless, I shall sound forth a lament
Weaving my garment of groans for you
Because you have suffered such brigandage
Concealing the rushing forth of my tears. [14.1–14]

As can be seen in these opening lines Sophronius's lament is no less fervid than that of Strategos, but it is expressed in a wholly different idiom.[29] Later in the lament when he mentions the captivity of Jerusalem, he does not use the Greek term for *captivity* used in the Septuagint to designate the captivity of the Jews in Babylon. Indeed the poem makes no allusion to the destruction of Jerusalem in the sixth century B.C.E. Nevertheless his thinking is similar to Strategos's in other respects. Why should one mourn the loss of Jerusalem? Because it is the "Holy City of God," "great Jerusalem," the home of Christians. In another poem, a hymn to Jerusalem, Sophronius begins with a similar ascription:

Holy City of God
How I long to stand
Even now at your gates
And go in rejoicing.

Like Strategos, Sophronius views Jerusalem as a political as well as a religious center. In Strategos's threnody it was the "great city of the Christians," and in Sophronius's poem it is the "great Jerusalem" and the city of the "children of the blessed Christians." In the war between the Roman and Sassanid empires, Jerusalem was the emblem of the Christian empire. The capital of the empire may have been located at Constantinople, but its spiritual shield and buckler was Jerusalem. In the poem "On the Captivity of Jerusalem" Sophronius presents the occupation of Jerusalem as an attack on Rome:

Deceitfully the Mede
Came from terrible Persia
Pillaging cities and villages
Waging war against the ruler of Edom [Rome]

Advancing on the Holy Land
The malevolent one came
To destroy the city of God, Jerusalem.

Cry out in grief you tribes of blessed Christians
Holy Jerusalem is laid waste

With fearful wrath a demon has arisen
With the terrible envy of a warrior
To sack God-blessed cities and towns
With murderous daggers.

In Christian Jerusalem piety and politics meet, and its inhabitants call on Christ to take up arms on their behalf:

All together
They raised on high their holy hands
Beseeching the Lord Christ
To fight on behalf of their city.

And they implore Christ to rain fire from heaven on their enemies:

May you grant O Christ that
We will see Persia in flames
Instead of the holy places.

As early as the second century a Christian bishop had sensed that the destiny of Christianity and that of the Roman Empire would be inextricably bound together.[30] At the time of Constantine in the early fourth century Eusebius championed the view that their destiny was identical, though Augustine a century later made a valiant effort to keep them distinct. But for many Christians of the East, these debates were academic; the fate of Jerusalem and the Holy Land were dependent on the strength and valor of the emperor's legions. If Roman hegemony collapsed, the holy places would be profaned, the holy cross desecrated and taken out of the city, the patriarch taken into captivity, Christians murdered and tortured, and the links with the Christian past severed.

In Sophronius's poems the heavenly city of Jerusalem merges with the historical city. At one point in the poem he actually uses the phrase "heavenly city" to designate the Jerusalem ravaged by the Persians. The prayers of the faithful seem to have come to naught, he writes, "because the *heavenly city* has suffered such a mournful fate" (l. 55). In other places he delights in other biblical terms for Jerusalem, for example, Salem, a biblical name for Jerusalem as well as the Hebrew word for peace (Psalm 76). In its Greek form, *Jerusalem* was sometimes written

Hierosolyma, which could be understood to signify *ieros* (holy) *solyma* (salem, that is, peace):

> A divine longing for Holy Solyma [Hierosolyma, Jerusalem]
> presses on me fervently.

This passage is taken from one of two poems Sophronius wrote on the city of Jerusalem. John Wilkinson has speculated that they may have been written when Sophronius was absent from Jerusalem and the Holy Land, and that may give them their warmth and poignancy. These poems are without parallel in early Christian poetry.[31] In the accounts of pilgrims to the Holy City and in comments of others who visited the Holy Land one can find descriptions of the holy places, but no one, at least since Egeria, had written about the city with such tenderness and feeling, and no Christian writer had brought the literary sophistication and skill that are evident in Sophronius's poems.

> Let me walk your pavements
> And go inside the Anastasis
> Where the King of all rose again
> Trampling down the power of death
> And as I venerate that worthy Tomb,
> Surrounded by its conches
> And columns surmounted by golden lilies,
> I shall be overcome with joy.
>
> Prostrate I will kiss the navel point of the earth, that divine Rock
> In which was fixed the wood
> Which undid the curse of the tree
>
> How great your glory, noble Rock, in which was fixed
> The Cross, the Redemption of mankind.

By Sophronius's time the idea that Jerusalem was the navel of the earth, the *axis mundi,* was commonplace. As we have seen, it occurs first in the book of Ezekiel (Ezek 5:5; 38:12, speaking of the land of Israel) as well as in later Jewish texts, for example, Jubilees in the period of the Second Temple ("Mount Zion was in the midst of the navel of the earth" [Jubilees 8:19]), and in rabbinical literature. In time it was appropriated by Christians. Cyril of Jerusalem wrote that Christ stretched out his hands on the cross to embrace "the ends of the world, for this Golgotha is the very center of the earth" (*cat.* 13.28).

Sophronius's poems on Jerusalem have a ritual character which makes it appear as though the poet were moving in procession along the path taken by the pilgrim: "Let me *walk* your pavements," I will "*enter* that worthy tomb," "*go*" to the tomb," or "*run* to bend the knee." Like other accounts of the ritual acts of pilgrims, the dominant metaphors of the poems are visual: "May I *behold* that floor where the paralytic went." Seeing, however, is not enough; the pilgrim must touch, even kiss, the object of devotion. Sophronius mentions "kissing the sweet floor" of the Anastasis and "kissing the rock" of Golgotha. When the poem reaches the place of Christ's birth in Bethlehem, Sophronius sings:

The shining slab which received the infant God
I will touch,
With my eyes, my mouth, my forehead,
To gain its blessing.

For Sophronius, as for other Christians of his time, the holy places were alive, filled with light and life and grace, for in these places "God who alone is holy, has rested," as John of Damascus would express it a few generations later.[32] Stones were not simply stones, but images of the divine, and the earthly Jerusalem had taken on the qualities of the celestial city. "Zion," in Sophronius's words, was "the radiant sun of the universe," and its holy places were sources of light and life. "O Light-bearing Tomb—You are truly an ocean of eternal life!" (*Anac.* 20, ll. 27–28).

The laments over Jerusalem of Strategos and Sophronius are the culmination of beliefs and attitudes that had been developing for centuries. No other writers in Christian antiquity spoke of the city of Jerusalem with such intensity and with such passion. On occasion earlier authors—Jerome, Theodoret of Cyrus, and Cyril of Scythopolis—gave us a glimpse of ideas that foreshadow the language of these works, but none of these earlier writers was faced with the alarming and inexplicable fact of the conquest of the Holy City by a foreign and hostile foe. That "holy Jerusalem" would be "laid waste" was beyond belief, and feelings that few Christians fully understood came rushing to the surface for the first time.

The Sassanid occupation of Jerusalem was a temporary interruption of Christian rule in the city and the land. The Byzantine emperor, Heraclius, was not ready to concede Jerusalem and the Christian East to the Sassanids. Shrewdly realizing that he could not best the Persian armies in face-to-face combat in Syria and Palestine, he launched an unexpected counteroffensive through Armenia and northern Syria directed at Persia itself. Fortune was on his side. When he reached the Persian capital, Ctesiphon, he received word that his foe, Chosroe II, had died, and, in this moment of disarray and weakness, the Sassanids sued for peace. By spring of 629 Heraclius had reached Palestine, bringing with him the most sacred relic in Christianity, the holy cross, and in March of that year he entered Jerusalem in triumph. Yet the victory, though real, was short-lived. In less than a decade the Muslim armies would be at the gates of the city, and there would be no valiant emperor to drive out the infidel.

12 The Desolate Amalek Rose Up to Smite Us

When the Muslim armies streamed into Palestine in the summer of 634 C.E., they struck first in the vicinity of Gaza on the Mediterranean coast. This dazzling and luxurious city, with its resplendent domed church dedicated to St. Sergius and its renowned school of Christian rhetors, lay directly on the route to the southeast, exposed to armies arriving from Arabia. The initial aim of the invaders, however, was neither to capture the major cities nor to seize the prime agricultural areas, but to establish control over the Arabic-speaking tribesmen living in the deserts near the cities.[1]

The task proved easy. The local Arabs had been accustomed to receiving a subsidy from the Byzantines for guarding the mouths of the desert, the wadis, or dry river beds. But during the previous twenty years, when the Sassanids occupied the region, Byzantine support had ceased. The bedouins, nettled by the loss of their customary bribes, welcomed the new invaders and "showed them the route to the land of Gaza, which is in the mouth of the desert of Mt. Sinai and is very rich."[2] Once the Muslims had won the loyalty of these tribesmen they began the task of laying siege to the cities.

With the arrival of commander Khalid b. al-Wahid, who had marched with his troops across the desert from Iraq, the order had gone out to move on the cities. The first to fall was Bostra, east of the Jordan River, the capital of the Roman province of Arabia. After a brief siege its people, mindful of the perils that awaited them, submitted to the invaders. On the condition that they pay an annual tax, the citizens of Bostra were able to secure an agreement that the city and its inhabitants be spared. With Bostra securely in their control, the army turned westward toward Palestine, where they joined another division of soldiers that was facing a large corp of Byzantine troops.

On hearing the news of the advance of the Arab armies, the beleaguered Byzantine emperor Heraclius had dispatched his brother Theodore at the head of a company of troops from the province of Syria to meet the foe. But at Ajnadayn, twenty-five kilometers southwest of Jerusalem, at the end of July 634, he fell in battle, and the Byzantine armies met their first defeat at the hands of the Arabs. The victory did not, however, come easily, and to this day Muslim tradition remembers the valor of the soldiers who died as martyrs in battle that day.

Retreating in disarray, the Christians fled to the town of Pella (Fihl) east of the Jordan across from Scythopolis, where a Byzantine garrison was quartered. There the Muslims won their second victory. Again the Byzantines were forced to retreat, this time to Damascus. A plea for reinforcements went out hastily to the emperor, but the column of soldiers that was to bring aid was defeated before it reached the city. Scythopolis held out for several months only to fall in August or September 635.

As the dolorous news of Byzantine losses reached Heraclius in Antioch, he realized that it was only a matter of time before the invaders reached the major cities of Palestine, principally Caesarea and Jerusalem. He made a heroic and, as it turned out, final effort to halt the advance. Marshaling all the resources he could muster, he assembled a fresh army composed of men from cities in Syria, for example, Antioch and Berea (Aleppo), as well as a contingent of Armenians and a company of Arab tribesmen loyal to Constantinople commanded by the Ghassanid chief Jabala b. al-Ayham. On hearing of their approach, the Muslims abandoned Damascus and retreated to a position on the Yarmuk River, a small tributary that runs into the Jordan south of the Sea of Galilee. There in the summer of 636 was fought, as a Muslim chronicler put it, "the battle between the Muslims and the Romans."[3] Though the Byzantines outnumbered the Muslim forces by as much as four to one, the armies of the New Rome were no match for these fervent warriors from the desert. As much by the lassitude of the Christians as by the valor of the Muslims, the emperor's legions were soon routed. The date was August/September 636 C.E. The way now lay open to Jerusalem and Caesarea, the two great cities of Palestine. A Christian chronicler writing in the next century wrote, "The desolate Amalek rose up to smite us, Christ's people."[4]

It had long been the custom (and still is today) for the bishop, monks, and faithful of Jerusalem to celebrate the Feast of the Nativity with a solemn procession from Jerusalem to Bethlehem to offer the Christmas liturgy at the place of Jesus' birth. In a sermon preached on the Feast of the Nativity in 638, with the invaders camped outside the walls of Jerusalem, the aged Sophronius bitterly lamented that soldiers impeded the procession: "Let the inspired magi and God-filled shepherds travel to Bethlehem, the city that welcomed God. Let them follow the star of their fellow runner and traveler. Let them behold the wonder beyond wonder. . . . The roads are barred to us and against our will we are constrained to remain in our homes, bound together not by tethers, but by fear of the Saracens. . . . The savage and barbarous sword of the Saracen . . . makes us exiles from the vision of blessedness [Bethlehem] and forces us to stay home."[5] Compelled to remain in Jerusalem, that year the faithful celebrated the festival huddled behind the walls of the city.

Only two decades after his predecessor Zachariah was taken captive by the Sassanids, Sophronius watched helplessly as invaders again swept across the Holy Land. To him was assigned the unhappy task of negotiating a treaty with Caliph Umar, the Muslim conqueror of Jerusalem. The meeting between the representative of the Christian Roman civilization and the general of the new religion from the desert of Arabia was so filled with drama and historical significance that several detailed accounts have come down to us. One, composed by a Christian chronicler, Ibn Batriq, who wrote in Arabic in Egypt in the tenth century, tells us how Christians of the East under Muslim rule remembered the meeting several centuries later. The narrative begins as the victorious caliph stands outside the walls of Jerusalem. Addressing the Christians, he assures them he means no harm and gives them a letter guaranteeing their safety:[6]

In the name of God, the Compassionate the Merciful. This is the letter from Umar ibn al-Chattab to the inhabitants of the city of Aelia. Their lives, possessions, and churches will be kept secure and the churches will neither be destroyed nor made into dwellings. [Umar] arranged for witnesses to be present to bear witness to these things. The gate of the city was opened before him and Umar and his companions entered the city and sat in the courtyard of the Church of the Resurrection. When it came time for prayer he said to Sophronius the patriarch, "I wish to pray." And the patriarch said to him, "Pray in the place where you are." Umar said to him, "I will not pray here." Then the patriarch led him into the church of Constantine and laid down a mat for him in the middle of the church. But Umar said to him, "Nor can I pray here." Then Umar went out to the steps of the eastern entrance of the Church of Mar [Saint] Constantine and prayed alone on the steps. Then he sat down and said to Sophronius the patriarch, "Do you understand, O patriarch, why I did not pray within the church?" The patriarch said to him, "The prince of believers [Umar] understands the reason why." Umar said to him, "If I had prayed in the church it would be ruined for you. For it would be taken from your hands and after I am gone the Muslims would seize it saying, 'Umar prayed here.' For that reason bring me paper on which I might write a document for you." Then Umar wrote a document stating that none of the Muslims should pray individually on the steps, nor should they gather together for communal prayer in the church, nor be called to prayer on the steps. He gave the document to the patriarch.

Then Umar said to him, "There is however one duty and obligation on your part. You must show me a place where I might build a mosque." The patriarch said, "I will give you a place where you can build a mosque, a place where the emperors of Rome would not allow anything to be built. At this place can be found the rock where God spoke to Jacob and which Jacob called the gate of heaven.[7] Jews called it the holy of holies and it is in the middle of the earth. The temple of the Jews once stood there and Jews venerated it. Wherever they were when they prayed they turned their faces to it. I will show you this place on the condition that you write a document that only this one mosque will be built in Jerusalem." And Umar ibn al-Chattab wrote a document to this effect and handed it to him.

Now when the Romans converted to Christianity, Helen, the mother of Constantine, built churches in Jerusalem. At that time the place of the rock and the area around it had become covered with dirt and it was left deserted. They had thrown dirt on the rock until a large dungheap had arisen over it. The Romans left it this way because they did not venerate it as did the Jews. They did not build a church on it because of what our Lord Christ said in his holy Gospel. "Behold your house is forsaken and desolate" (Matt 23:38) and "There will not be left here one stone upon another that will not be thrown down" (Matt 24:2). For that reason they left it in ruins and did not build any church on it.

Then Sophronius the patriarch took Umar ibn al-Chattab by the hand and led him directly over the dungheap. Umar took hold of the edge of his garment filled it with dirt and threw it into the valley of Gehenna. When the Muslims saw Umar ibn al-Chattab carrying dirt in his lap, each one hurried to carry dirt in their laps and in their cloaks and shields, as well as in baskets and jars, until the place was cleared and cleansed and the rock was visible. Then someone said, "Let us build the mosque and let the rock serve as the *qibla* [direction of prayer] facing south." But Umar said, "No. We will build a mosque and put the rock at the end of the mosque." And Umar built the mosque with the rock at the end of the mosque.

This account is filled with legendary details. Sophronius, who calls the Muslims "godless Saracens" in his sermons, would hardly have addressed the caliph as "prince of believers." The language of this passage reflects a setting sometime after the conquest of Jerusalem, when Christians and Muslims had worked out a modus vivendi in cities where the Christians were the majority of the population and the Muslims were their rulers. As Robert Schick writes, "The covenant [between Umar and the Christian inhabitants of Jerusalem] presupposes a period of urban social contact between Muslims and Christians."[8] Ibn Batriq wished to establish that, from the beginning of Muslim hegemony, Christians had been granted privileges: their homes would not be destroyed, their families spared harm, and their churches would not be coopted as dwellings for the new rulers. In fact, this is what happened in Jerusalem and in many other cities. The archaeological record provides little evidence of Muslim destruction of Christian buildings during the conquest and its aftermath.[9] At the time that Ibn Batriq wrote his chronicle, the Church of the Resurrection in Jerusalem had not been touched by the Muslims and retained its original majesty and grandeur.

The Muslim accounts of Caliph Umar's entry into Jerusalem serve quite a different purpose. As in the Christian chronicles, the Temple Mount is pictured as being covered with a dungheap, and Umar expresses a desire to build a mosque in the city; but he does not engage in an aimless quest for the proper site to build the mosque. He knows exactly where he wanted the building to stand—on the site of the temple of Solomon, which had been destroyed by Bukhnassar, the biblical Nebuchadnezzar.[10] Accordingly, when Umar meets with the patriarch, after signing the "treaty of capitulation," he says to him, "Take us to the sanctuary of David." The patriarch took Umar to the church, which is called Dung Heap [a play on the Arabic term for resurrection],[11] and said, "This is David's sanctuary." Umar looks at the place, ponders it for a moment, and says, "You are lying, for the Messenger [Muhammad] described to me the Sanctuary of David and this is not it." Then the patriarch took him to the Church of Zion and said, "This is the Sanctuary of David." But again the caliph said, "You are lying." Finally the patriarch took him to the "noble sanctuary" of the Holy City:

> Now the dung which was then all about the noble sanctuary had settled on the steps of this gate so that it even came out into the street in which the gate opened, and it had accumulated so greatly on the steps as to reach almost up to the ceiling of the gateway. The patriarch said to Umar, "It is impossible to go on further and enter, except crawling on one's hands and knees." So the patriarch went down on hands and knees, preceding Umar, and all crawled after him until he had brought us out in the court of the noble sanctuary of the Holy City. Then we arose from our knees and stood upright. Umar looked around him, pondering for a long time. Then he said, "By him in whose hands is my soul, this is the place described to us by the Apostle [Muhammad] of God."[12]

This account, too, includes legendary features. The gate to the noble sanctuary, for example, is called the Gate of Muhammad, clearly an impossibility at the time of the conquest. Even if some details are embellished, it nevertheless embodies early Muslim ideas about Jerusalem. Muslims, as this version of the conquest makes clear, had a religious interest in Jerusalem. Jerusalem, it will be recalled, had been the site of the first *qibla,* the place to which the faithful turned in prayer. It was venerated as the city of Abraham, Jesus, and other prophets mentioned in the Quran, and the site of the temple of Solomon. It was the place where Muhammad had traveled on his famous night journey on the mare Buraq with the angel Gabriel and from which he ascended into the heavens to converse with the prophets and angels.[13]

The Arab conquerors of the Holy Land were not simply belligerents, they were the vanguard of a new religion that made a spiritual as well as a political claim on Jerusalem. The commanders of their armies were disciples and heralds of the Prophet as well as soldiers, harbingers of a new civilization that would displace the language, transform the institutions, remake the architecture, convert much of the population, and in time create a new civilization in a region that had been dominated for a thousand years by the culture of Israel, Greece, Rome, and Christianity. But to the Christians they were simply "godless Saracens."[14] In his Christmas sermon Sophronius does not even mention Muhammad. To him, the Saracens were a temporary scourge, a harsh but just punishment for the sins of Jerusalem's Christians. He had no inkling that the Muslims had come to stay and that the unity of the Mediterranean world had been shattered forever. Once the Mediterranean had been a western lake joining the deserts of Egypt with the cities of Italy, but with the coming of the Muslims it would become an immense moat dividing East and West. In two hundred years the Christians of Palestine would be speaking Arabic, and the country would be ruled by Muslims from Ramlah (in Palestine) and Baghdad, not by Christians from Caesarea and Constantinople.

Sophronius, who had witnessed the expulsion of the Persians from Palestine by Heraclius after fifteen years of occupation, was confident the Saracens would fall prey to a similar fate. If we repent of our sins, he tells the faithful, "we will laugh at the demise of our enemies the Saracens and *in a short time* see their destruction and complete ruin. For their bloody swords will pierce their hearts, their bows will be splintered, their arrows will be left sticking in them, and they will open the way [to Bethlehem] for us . . . that without anguish or dread . . . we might embrace the God-endowed cave and worship the holy manger."[15] A century and a half later the Byzantine chronicler Theophanes would have a much clearer sense of what Muhammad meant for Christians. He begins his account with the lapidary notice, "I think it necessary to discuss his ancestry in full."[16]

The End of Time

Unlike the Persian occupation of Jerusalem, Islam's conquest of Christian Palestine was not a temporary scourge that would soon pass, leaving the Byzantines in control of Jerusalem and the Holy Land. With the arrival of Muhammad's armies and the swift establishment of Arab hegemony in the region, Christian rule in Jerusalem came to an end, decisively and definitively. There would be no Roman emperor to turn back the foe and regain the holy city. Heraclius had expended all his energy and the resources of the empire to defeat the Persians and restore the holy cross to Jerusalem. In the battles with the Persians he could be seen astride his horse personally leading his troops into the fray, but now, broken in spirit and sick in body, he remained distant and aloof, delegating authority to his brother and his generals. He died in 641 as an Arab commander was advancing toward Alexandria in Egypt. Any hope of halting the advance or, miraculously, driving back the invaders was illusory. The Christian East was now in the hands of the infidel.

For centuries Jerusalem had served as a symbol of a higher, transcendent, heavenly reality. But with the building of Christian Palestine, the earthly city had been clothed in heavenly glory; once scorned as the city of the Jews, Jerusalem was now the holy city of Christ, the great city, the city of the Christians, even the city of God. When it was set ablaze by the Persians, the Christian world was stunned. The City of God and the Holy Temple at the mercy of idolatrous fire-worshippers from the East! In the treatise of Strategos and the poem of Sophronius we glimpsed the bewilderment and pathos of that moment. So completely were they overcome by the troubles of the present that they could not look ahead. Yet they believed Jerusalem would remain a Christian city. At the close of his letter to the Christians in Jerusalem (written from exile), Zachariah prays that God would be merciful and "lead us out of our torment back to Jerusalem" (Expug. 22.29). That Jerusalem would be held long by infidels was beyond belief.

The Muslim conquest allowed no such sanguine view of the future. If the unthinkable happens once, perhaps it is explicable, but twice within a generation? The infidels were beginning to build their own political institutions and to construct a new society. If mosques were being built in the holy city, there must be darker forces at work. The coming of the Muslims was of far greater historical significance than the short-lived triumph of the Persians. Sophronius saw none of this; in his Christmas sermon he cast the events of 638 in the same terms that Christians had used to interpret the Persian conquest. The Arabs were God's instruments to chastise Christians for their sins, and in time they would be driven from the holy land.

Within a few decades, Christians in the East viewed the Arab victories with much less equanimity. A great evil had been let loose on earth. The Ishmaelites were more than another marauding foe from the East; their presence in the Christian lands was a portent of the coming of the Antichrist (Maximus, *ep.* 14; *PG* 91, 540b) and the end of the world. Lamentation gave way to apocalyptic visions of supernatural deliverance by divine intervention. Some searched the Scriptures in hopes of discerning the signs of the times. If the "Roman empire . . . is being torn asunder and shattered" as one Christian put it, then Daniel's predictions about the fall of the fourth kingdom were now being fulfilled (Daniel 7).[17] Like the Jews, some Christians began to hope for a Messiah-like deliverer who would drive out the Saracens and restore the "kingdom of the Christians" to Jerusalem. His coming would inaugurate a great age of peace and prosperity in Palestine and prepare the way for the final triumph over evil and the reign of Christ. Then the kingdom would be handed over to God the Father, and God would be all in all.

This eschatological scenario is found in a relatively obscure, but very popular text written in Syriac that goes under the name Pseudo-Methodius.[18] In the manuscript of the book the author is identified as Methodius of Olympus, a bishop in the third century, but the work clearly comes from a much later period. The text of Pseudo-Methodius had long been available in Greek and Latin versions, but a Syriac text was discovered in the Vatican library in the 1930s. It is now reasonably certain that the original version was written in northern Syria at the end of the seventh century, less than two generations after the Arab conquest of the Middle East.[19]

Pseudo-Methodius departs from traditional Christian eschatology, at least in its more familiar version. His views are much closer to Christian chiliasm and to Jewish apocalypticism (as reflected in the books of Elijah and Zerubbabel) than they are to the eschatology of Eusebius, Jerome, or Theodoret of Cyrus. He draws chiefly on traditions that were current in the Christian East, particularly among Syriac-speaking Christians.[20] Yet, what gives the work its unusual importance for the theme of this book is that the eschatological drama is set in the Holy Land, or the promised land as he calls it, by which he means Christian Palestine.[21] Had the Arabs taken Damascus or Alexandria, not Jerusalem, it is unlikely that Christian apocalypticism would have burst forth with such intensity.

His book begins as follows: "By the help of God, Lord of all, we are going to write down the treatise composed by Blessed Mar [Saint] Methodius, bishop and martyr, about the succession of the kings, and about the *end of time*." The phrase "end of time" or "last days" is a biblical expression that occurs with minor variations at several places in the Septuagint and in the Christian New Testament. In its original setting within the Hebrew prophets it referred to the day when the "mountain of the house of the Lord shall be established as the highest of the mountains" (Isa 2:2), that is, the return of the exiles to Jerusalem and the rebuilding of the city and the temple, events associated in Jewish tradition with the coming of the Messiah. The earliest Christians identified the messianic age with the coming of Christ, the Messiah, and used the phrase "end of the age" or "last days" to designate the "new age" that began with Christ's saving work and continued in the life of the church.[22]

But the phrase "end of the age" could also refer to the day of judgment at the end of history and the catastrophic events that would lead up to it. In the so-called little apocalypse in the gospels Jesus spoke to his disciples about the signs that would take place at the "close of the age" (Matt 24:3). At this time, nation will rise against nation, kingdom against kingdom, Christians will be delivered up to tribulation and put to death, and many will fall away and betray one another. "When you see Jerusalem surrounded by armies," Jesus said, "then know that its desolation has come near. Then let those who are in Judea flee to the mountains, and let those who are inside the city depart, and let not those who are out in the country enter it; for these are days of vengeance to fulfill all that is written" (Luke 21:20–21).

When this prophecy of Jesus (as well as the later chapters of the book of Daniel) was read in light of the Muslim conquest in the seventh century, it appeared that the end of the age had indeed arrived. Using the future tense as befits apocalyptic convention, Pseudo-Methodius describes the desolation and social upheaval that followed the invasion: the "spoiler . . . will behave haughtily in his rage and in his boastfulness, even to the point of exacting tribute from the dead who lie in the ground. He will take a poll tax from the orphans and the widows, and even from the holy men. . . . They will ridicule the wise, deride the legislators and mock the knowledgeable." As the armies advance, "old men and women, rich and poor . . . will hunger and thirst and suffer with heavy chains to the point that they will bless the dead."[23] Some of the details echo the words of Jesus' prophecy. Jesus said, "Alas for those who are with child and for those who give suck in those days" (Matt 24:19). Pseudo-Methodius wrote, "At the time of their coming forth from the desert [they will tear open pregnant women] and they will take babies by force from their mothers' arms and dash them against the rocks like unclean animals."[24] But most of the horrors described by Pseudo-Methodius are based on the actual experiences of Christians in the Christian East in the seventh century. "They will sacrifice the minister within the temple, and then they will sleep with their wives and with the captive women inside the temple. They will make the sacred garments into clothing for themselves and their sons. They will tether their cattle in the shrines of the martyrs and in the burial places of the saints. They are insolent and murderous, shedders of blood and spoilers; they are a furnace of trial for all Christians."[25]

For Pseudo-Methodius these trials were not ordinary afflictions, the sorrow and misery that inevitably accompany war; they were signs of a cosmic ordeal that foreshadowed the arrival of the prince of evil, the Antichrist himself. In the midst of his description of the sufferings of Christians he says, "This is the chastisement about which the apostle spoke."[26] He is referring to the famous passage in 2 Thessalonians in which Paul describes the appearance of the Antichrist at the end of the age: "Let no one deceive you in any way; for *that day* will not come, unless the rebellion comes first, and the man of lawlessness is revealed, the son of perdition, who opposes and exalts himself against every so-called god or object of worship, so that he takes his seat in the temple of God, proclaiming himself to be God" (2 Thess 2:4). In Christian tradition the Antichrist had been identified at times with the Roman emperor, at other times with the evil deeds of heretics, and at still others with the false Messiah of the Jews.[27] But one feature of the tradition that remained constant was that the Antichrist would not come until the last days. Cyril of Jerusalem had written, "The . . . Antichrist is to come when the times of the Roman empire shall have been fulfilled, and the end of the world is drawing near."[28]

As important as the Antichrist is in the apocalypse of Pseudo-Methodius, he is secondary to another player in the eschatological drama. When the Antichrist appears, says Pseudo-Methodius, the "king of the Greeks" will arise from sleep and "will come out against them [the Arabs] with great anger." The king of the Greeks, like the Messiah of the Jews, is a mighty and valiant warrior. His task is to throw off the yoke of the Arabs and return to the Christians the land that belongs to them. His armies "will seize the regions of the desert and will finish by the sword any survivor left among them in the *promised land*. They, their wives and their sons, their leaders and all their camps, the whole land of the desert of their fathers will be delivered into the power of the king of the Greeks." After the victory over the enemy, the land will enjoy a great peace, "the like of which there had not been before."[29] In describing this peace, which will be found on earth, not in the heavens, Pseudo-Methodius sounds very much like the Christian chiliasts of an earlier time as well as the Jewish apocalypses of his own time: "Humankind will live at rest; they will eat and drink; they will rejoice with merry hearts; men will take wives and women will be given to men; they will build buildings and plant vines."[30]

For Pseudo-Methodius the victory over the Arabs will not be complete until Jerusalem is restored to the Christians and the most holy relic in Christendom venerated in the holy city. "As soon as the Son of Perdition is revealed, the king of the Greeks will go up and stand on Golgotha, and the Holy Cross will be put in that place where it had been erected when it bore Christ. And the king of the Greeks will put his crown on the top of the Holy Cross and stretch out his two hands to heaven. And he will hand over the kingdom to God the Father. The Holy Cross on which the Christ was crucified will be taken up to heaven, and the royal crown with it. . . . As soon as the Holy Cross is taken up to heaven, the king of the Greeks will deliver his soul to his Creator, and then all sovereignty, authority and power will be abolished."[31]

Although Pseudo-Methodius employs apocalyptic language to set forth his vision of the future, his book is as much oriented to this world as it is to the world to come. His final paragraph speaks of the "heavenly kingdom," where the faithful "will offer up glory, honor, worship and praise now and for all times, and forever and ever." But before the final coming of Christ he dreams of the day the Arabs will be defeated, and he yearns for the restoration of "the kingdom of the Christians."[32] His hopes are territorial and political.

The Restoration of Jerusalem

The apocalypse of Pseudo-Methodius is a book about the recovery of Christian Jerusalem from the infidel. Although there are many antecedents to the work, both Jewish and Christian, the author has molded traditional Christian ideas to conform to the religious and political fact that Jerusalem is the premier Christian city. His question, like that of Zerubbabel in the *Book of Zerubbabel,* is, "When will come the time of deliverance?"[33] Paradoxically, as Islam muscled its way into the politics of the eastern Mediterranean Jewish and Christian hopes converged, at least for a moment, as can be seen in the adaptation of Ezekiel's prophecy about the invasion of Gog and Magog, the evil kingdoms from the north who would plunder the Land of Israel in the "latter days" (Ezek 38).

In a Hebrew poem written shortly after the Arab invasion of the Holy Land—that is, contemporary with Pseudo-Methodius—the evil hordes from Gog and Magog descend on the Land of Israel to terrorize and massacre the population:

> On that day when the Messiah, son of David, will come
> to a downtrodden people,

These signs will be seen in the world,
and will be brought forth:
Earth and heaven will wither,
and the sun and the moon will be blemished,
And the dwellers in the Land will be struck silent.

Describing the arrival of the Arab armies, the poet writes,

And a king will go forth from the land of Yoqtan
And his armies will seize the Land. . . .
Gog and Magog will incite one another
and kindle fear in the hearts of the Gentiles.[34]

Pseudo-Methodius uses similar language to depict the Muslim conquest: "At the end of the ages, it will be in accordance with the word of Ezekiel, the prophet, who prophesied about them [the unclean nations], 'At the *end of time,* from the ends of the world, they will come from the house of Gog and Magog to the land of Israel'" (Ezek 38:14–18).[35] When he narrates the actual invasion of the Arab armies, he again uses words taken from Ezekiel's description of the end of time: "During that period of peace the Gates of the North will be opened and those hosts of nations will come forth who were imprisoned there, and the earth will shake before them."[36]

In other ways the Jewish poem and Pseudo-Methodius envision a similar scenario. The poet looks forward to the return of the exiles and the rebuilding of Jerusalem:

Let us go up to the mountain of the Lord.
An eternal temple will be built,
And it will be established on the highest peak.[37]

In Pseudo-Methodius the final battle is followed by the appearance of the Antichrist and the restoration of the holy cross in Jerusalem.[38]

At a very early stage in Christian history many, if not most, Christians believed that at the end of time Christ's kingdom would be established, at least for a time, in Jerusalem. Yet over the course of centuries mainstream Christian tradition became restive with these beliefs and forged an eschatology that was centered on a heavenly kingdom. The ancient promise to Abraham that his descendants would possess the land was divorced from the fate of the earthly city of Jerusalem. Yet even as these ideas were being elaborated, Christians could not escape the intractable fact that Jesus had suffered, died, and had been raised from the dead in Jerusalem. *Where* God had entered human history came to be as important as *when*. And if the *time* of his coming marked the beginning of the last days, as the writer of Hebrews said (Heb 1:1), then what can be the meaning of the desecration of the *place* of Christ's victory? It must signify that the final consummation of God's purposes was at hand. There is a great irony here. In the wake of the Arab conquest of Jerusalem, Christians began to imagine, like the Jews before them, a Christian version of the restoration of Jerusalem. To be sure, there are large differences between Pseudo-Methodius's vision of deliverance and that of the Jews. For Pseudo-Methodius the deliverer is not the Messiah, but a Messiah-like figure, a valorous and heroic emperor called the king of the Greeks. Moreover, this anonymous Syriac-speaking Christian had not abandoned Christian belief in a celestial kingdom. After the coming of the Antichrist and the restoration of the holy cross, Christ would return to gather all the saints in a heavenly kingdom.[39] Yet, though the soul of Pseudo-Methodius was destined for the Jerusalem above, his heart was fixed on the Jerusalem below.

Pseudo-Methodius, as well as many other Christians in the East, dreamed of a day when foreigners would be driven out of the Holy Land and Christian rule restored to Jerusalem. His yearning for restoration was no less urgent because it was voiced by a Christian rather than by a Jew. However, like the Jews, the Christians who dreamed this dream would have to learn to live with disappointment. God would not drive out the infidel, and the cross of Christ would not be raised aloft in the holy city.

The idea of a Christian Holy Land, however, did not perish. If it is true that apocalypticism is born out of disappointment, its hopes are no less real than the dreams of those who raise armies and lead troops in battle. Under other conditions and in other places, ideas that may seem quixotic give birth to unexpected offspring. In the generations immediately after the Muslim conquest seeds were already germinating, seeds that would sprout four hundred years later in the Christian soil of Europe.

Epilogue

The intrepid pilgrim who makes his way to the monastery of Mar Saba in the Judean desert and waits patiently outside its high walls until one of the monks answers his knock will be shown the diminutive body of St. Sabas in a small chapel in one of the courtyards. If the pilgrim is persistent, he may be shown a room that appears, on first sight, to resemble a museum. Its glass cases, however, contain human skulls, not gold crosses or ancient manuscripts. The monks living in the monastery today say that these are the remains of monks who were killed by the Persian invaders centuries ago.

As I recall, there are dozens of skulls in these cases, and even if all do not go back to the seventh century, they nevertheless bear silent witness to the human cost of the

Sassanid conquest of Jerusalem. Although some of those who were massacred in Jerusalem were no doubt pilgrims and tourists, the people who suffered most grievously during the invasion were those who called the city and the region their home. Strategos's *Capture of Jerusalem* ends with a list of those who died in the conquest. This section of the document may not have been written by the original author, but it was penned by someone who shared his profound grief over what had happened to the people of the Holy City.

According to this account, a man named Thomas made it his business to compile a record of how many people had been killed in Jerusalem and to determine where they had been buried. At the monastery of St. George he found 7 corpses, in a government building he found 28, in cisterns 275, before the gate of Holy Zion 2,250, at the altar of the New Church 290, in the church of St. Sophia 369, in the monastery of the Holy Anastasis 212, in the marketplace 38, at the gate of Probatike 2,107, at the spring of Siloam 2,318, on the Mount of Olives 1,207, on the steps of the Anastasis 83, in front of Holy Golgotha 80. The total number by his reckoning was 66,555.[1]

As this doleful catalogue reminds us, the blood of Christians now mingled with the soil of the Holy Land. The Persian occupation had produced a new generation of martyrs who were buried in the same earth that held Abraham and Sarah and Joseph and David and Zachariah and the Maccabean martyrs and Stephen and James the brother of the Lord and the "martyrs of Palestine," Eusebius's epithet for those who died during the Diocletianic persecution in the early fourth century. As Christians suffered in and with the land and buried their dead in the land, the Holy Land became irrevocably part of the Christian experience.

"In order for land to be my land," writes the historian of religions Jonathan Z. Smith, "one must live together with it. It is . . . living in relationship with [one's] land that transforms uninhabited wasteland into homeland, that transforms the land into the land of Israel. It is that one has cultivated the land, died on the land, that one's ancestors are buried in the land, that rituals have been performed in the land, that one's deity has been encountered there in the land, that renders the land as a homeland, a land for man, a holy land. It is briefly, history, that makes a land mine. . . . [It] is the shared history of generations that converts the land into the land of the Fathers."[2] Of course, the land that the ancient Israelites occupied was not uninhabited, and Palestine was not empty when Christians began to build churches and monasteries in its cities and towns. The Israelites had first to subdue the Canaanites, and Christians had to win over the inhabitants to the new religion. Yet

Smith's point is well taken. Affection for a land comes from living in the land. Land is not a simple gift of nature. It was only as Christians raised families and built churches, told stories of heroic men and women, and laid their dead to rest in its earth that they came to call the land holy.

To be sure, it was the inhabitants of Jerusalem and the region that identified most closely with the land. As we have seen, the idea of a Christian Holy Land was largely the work of those who resided in Palestine. The first writer to use the term *Holy Land* as a designation for Christian Jerusalem was Cyril, a native of Scythopolis. Yet the patriarch of Alexandria lamented the Persian conquest of Jerusalem as though it were his own city. During the Arab conquest, Maximus the Confessor grieved that the Arabs had "overrun a foreign land as though it were their own."[3] Maximus's words are reminiscent of the speech of the Jewish high priest Simon after the Hasmoneans had defeated the Seleucids and restored Jewish rule in the Land of Israel. "We have not taken foreign land," he writes, but the inheritance "which at one time had been unjustly taken by our enemies" (1 Macc 15:33).

The arrival of the Muslims did not mean the displacement of the Christians any more than the coming of Seleucid or Romans rule meant the end of Jewish life in the land. Most of the Christians in Palestine and greater Syria were indigenous to the region and had no place to flee. Furthermore it appears that the destruction during the conquest was relatively minor, and in many places life went on without interruption. Battles took place in the countryside, and most cities surrendered peacefully. Gaza, for example, was not captured in the initial battle near the city; it surrendered peacefully several years later. Caesarea, however, was captured only after a long siege and, it was reported, many "horrors."[4] In some towns there is evidence that churches were built and dedicated during the years of the conquest, and, in the decades following the invasion, Christians built new churches and repaired old ones. Even in cases of deliberate desecration of mosaic floors (because of images which were offensive to the Muslims), the damage was carefully repaired. Stones were removed so that the faces were no longer discernible.

Five years ago, in the summer of 1986, a team of Italian archaeologists excavated several Christian churches in Jordan at Um er-Rasas, a site not too far from Madaba (where the sixth-century map of the Holy Land had been found).[5] In the nineteenth century Johann Burchardt, the Swiss adventurer, had visited the site, and in the 1940s several archaeologists made preliminary soundings. But no one was prepared for what was found below the sands in 1986. The excavators uncovered two churches. One was dedicated to Bishop Sergius of Medaba in 587 C.E. Its mosaic floor was badly damaged, but part was still visible because the altar base had been placed on top of it.

The second church, however, dedicated to St. Stephen, revealed the most extraordinary floor mosaic of any church in the region. Set in the floor were depictions of twenty-four cities in Palestine, Jordan, and Egypt. Among them were Jerusalem, called the Holy City, Neapolis (Nablus), Sebastia, Caesarea, Diosopolis (Lod), Eleutheropolis (Beth-Guvrin), Ascalon, Gaza, Philadelphia (Amaan), Madaba, and Alexandria. But the church is important for another reason. It includes two dated mosaics. The one was dedicated in 756 C.E. at the time of Bishop Job. The second, in the nave, was dedicated in 785 C.E. The latter date is 150 years *after* the Muslim conquest of Jerusalem and well into the period of Abassid rule, the line of caliphs who succeeded the first Umayads and moved the capital from Damascus to Baghdad. The date of the former inscription is 36 years later than any known inscription from the area. As a scholar of the archaeology of Christian buildings in the years after the Muslim conquest observed, "The . . . Church of St. Stephen is of revolutionary importance."[6] At the end of the eighth century Christians were able to build a *new* church and had the wherewithal and artistic skill to design and construct a complex, sophisticated mosaic floor.

In the early eighth century the Muslim caliph Al-Walid called Syria (which included Palestine) the "country of the Christians," a place where one could find "beautiful churches whose adornments were a temptation and whose fame was widespread, as for example, the church of the Resurrection and the churches of Lod (Lydda) and Edessa; [Al-Walid] therefore undertook to construct for the Muslims a mosque [in Damascus] which would attract them away from these churches, and he made it one of the wonders of the world." Similarly the Dome of the Rock on the Temple Mount in Jerusalem was intended to rival the great domed churches of the Christians.[7] Two centuries later during a visit to Jerusalem another Muslim observed that "learned men are few and the Christians are numerous." Significantly he also noted the presence of Jews in the city: "Everywhere the Christians and the Jews are in the majority; and the mosque is empty of the faithful and of scholars."[8]

It is apparent that Christianity was not a passing phenomenon in the history of the Holy Land. Accordingly it is of some historical interest that in Palestine Christians first began to adopt Arabic, the language of the conquerors, as a language for Christian worship and scholarship. Of course the language of the Christians native to the area was Syriac (Aramaic), a Semitic tongue, and this made the transition into Arabic easier for them than for Christians who spoke Greek or Coptic, like those in Egypt. As early as the end of the eighth century the "scholarly activity" of the monks at the monasteries of Mar Sabas and Mar Chariton "was beginning to be conducted in Arabic."[9]

The monastery of Mar Sabas produced the first Christian thinker to write theological works in Arabic, Theodore Abu Qurra. So skilled was he in Arabic, the Saracen language as it was called by Christians, that he was an "object of wonder to the simple folk."[10] According to one source he was asked to write in Arabic by patriarch Thomas of Jerusalem.[11] A fascinating glimpse of the transition from Greek to Arabic can be seen in a fragment of an Arabic version of Psalm 78 written in *Greek* characters dated from the eighth century. By this time Christians had begun to make translations of the Scriptures, liturgical books, and devotional works, and apparently some knew how to speak Arabic but could not read the Arabic characters.[12] From the next century there are extant manuscripts of the works of Stephen of Ramlah, a Christian monk who translated a small library of earlier Christian writings into Arabic. A native of Ramlah, the Islamic capital of the province that included Jerusalem, he was associated with the monastery of Mar Chariton, founded in the fourth century, another center of the new Christian scholarship in the Judean desert. In the colophon (the "signature") of one of his books he identified himself as "Stephen . . . son of Hakam, known as ar-Ramli, [who] wrote it in the laura of Mar Chariton, for his teacher . . . Anba (Father) Basil."[13]

Among Stephen's works was a translation of the gospels into Arabic. This manuscript, presently at St. Catherine in the Sinai, "is the oldest dated manuscript of the Gospel in Arabic known to modern scholars," and in all probability its text "represents the earliest project anywhere systematically to translate the Gospel into Arabic."[14] Though used as a lectionary, it was not in the format of a lectionary. It was designed to serve both liturgical and scholarly purposes. Besides biblical texts, Stephen translated devotional works and seems to have written a kind of catechism of Christian teaching in Arabic. As Sidney Griffith, a scholar of Arabic-speaking Christianity wrote, "He played a major role in the Church's successful campaign to come to terms with life within dar al-islam, and he seems to have been in the forefront of the programme to publish the Christian kerygma in Arabic. His name and works deserve to take their place in the history of the Christian church in the Holy Land."[15]

The Christians in the Holy Land, then, were looking to the future. The apocalyptic visions of Pseudo-Methodius had faded, and the Christian communities had begun to make the slow transition to a new language, a new culture, a new society shaped by the religion of Muhammad. Christians (and Jews) always look to the future with eyes focused by the past, and as Palestinian Christians were beginning to build for the future, a monk living in Palestine wrote a little work to remind Christians what had given the Holy Land its singular place in Christian devotion and memory.[16]

This treatise, which might be entitled the "Traces of Christ," is a catalogue of places that bear witness to God's presence on earth: "Wherever there is a place that God glorified and hallowed by the appearance in it of his Christ and the presence of his Holy Spirit, whether it be a plain or a mountain, wherever there is a place in which God spoke to any of his prophets earlier or in which his wonders were seen, he has set all these places in the hands of those who believe in Christ, to pass on as an inheritance from parents to children forever, until He brings them the kingdom of heaven which does not perish."[17]

The description of each place begins with a formulaic phrase borrowed from the Muslim Creed,[18] the "Shahadah":

> the church of Nazareth in Galilee of the Jordan *bears witness* to the annunciation of Mary by the archangel Gabriel . . . ; the church at Bethlehem . . . *bears witness* to the birth of Christ in a cave from the Virgin . . . ; the church of the river Jordan . . . *bears witness* to the baptism of Christ in the river at the hands of John . . . ; the church of Kursi, east of the sea of Tiberias, *bears witness* that he healed the man possessed who was called Legion . . . the church of Jericho in the river valley *bears witness* that, as Christ was going to Jerusalem by that road, two blind men were sitting beside the road begging.[19]

In the early eighth century, several generations after the Muslim conquest, John of Damascus, a monk from Mar Saba, had begun to reflect on the significance of the holy places in Christian life and memory. John was writing against those who opposed the veneration of icons (images painted on wood), and in defending their use in Christian worship he observed that there were other kinds of material images. Among these were "places in which God had accomplished our salvation." By means of such images, he said, "things which have taken place in the past are remembered." Specifically he mentions Mount Sinai, Nazareth, the cave at Bethlehem, the mountain of Golgotha, the tomb which is the "fountain of our Resurrection," the stone which sealed the sepulchre,

Mount Zion, the Mount of Olives, the pool of Bethsaida, the garden of Gethsemane, and "all other similar places."[20]

For John of Damascus these holy places were "receptacles of divine energy." By this he means that they were not simply historical sites that mark the place where something had happened long ago, but palpable signs of God's continuing presence on earth.[20] The anonymous monk calls them an inheritance filled with blessing and promise. "Christ has given us . . . *traces* of himself and *holy places* in this world as an *inheritance* and a *pledge* of the kingdom of heaven . . . which he promised to us." Through these places Christ has given "blessing, sanctification, access to him, pardon for sins . . . , spiritual joy . . . and witnesses that confirm what is written in the book of the Gospel."[21]

From this catalogue of the places marked by the "traces" of Christ's presence it is possible to construct the entire story of the Christian gospel. The church at Nazareth bears witness to the Annunciation, the church at Bethlehem to the Nativity, the church at the river Jordan to the baptism of Christ, the one at Cana to the miracle of turning water into wine, the one at Banyas (Caesarea Philippi) to the healing of the women with the issue of blood, that at Nain to the raising of the only son of a widow woman, that at Mount Tabor to the Transfiguration, that at Mount Zion to the institution of the Eucharist, that called the Church of the Resurrection and Calvary "in the middle of the world and at its navel" to the crucifixion and the Resurrection, and that at Emmaus to Christ's appearance to Cleopas and Luke.

This telling of the Christian story, however, differs in one noteworthy feature from the accounts of Christ's life written in the gospels and read throughout the Christian world. The anonymous monk inserts the little word "there" (in Arabic, "in that place") when he names the site: "The church of Cana in Galilee also bears witness to the presence of Christ at the marriage *there* . . . ; the church of Capernaum near the sea of Tiberias bears witness that Christ healed a man with a withered hand *there* . . . ; the church of Nain in the Fuljah bears witness that Christ raised a dead man *there*." The story of Christ's life can be told and retold in many places all over the world, but no verbal testimony can ever replace the witness of the places themselves. Christian memory is inescapably bound to place.

Stones, however, do not speak, as this wise monk knew well. His little treatise is not simply a list of places, it is a catalogue of *churches*. "The *church* at Bethlehem bears witness to the birth of Christ . . . ; the *church* at the river Jordan bears witness to the baptism of Christ . . . ; the *church* at Magdala bears witness that Christ expelled seven devils from Mary

Magdalene . . . ; the *church* of the village of al-Azar (Lazarus) bears witness that Christ raised Lazarus there." This is not the language of a medieval *Guide Bleu* describing ancient archaeological sites or a handbook on Byzantine architecture; it is a testimony to the perseverance of Christian life in the Holy Land. In these buildings of stone and wood "people come together to celebrate festivals"[22] at the places marked by the traces of Christ's presence. As the monk remembers the past and meditates on the present, his face is resolutely set toward the future.

For Christians the Holy Land is not simply an illustrious chapter in the Christian past. As Jerome wrote to his friend Paula in Rome urging her to come and live in the Holy Land, "The whole mystery of our faith is *native* to this country and city."[23] Nothing else in Christian experience can make this claim; nothing has such fixity. No matter how many centuries have passed, no matter where the Christian religion has set down roots, Christians are wedded to the land that gave birth to Christ and the Christian religion.

Land, alas, is immovable; like mountains and seas it is stationary. If it should happen that the only Christians to survive in the Holy Land were caretakers of the holy places, Christianity would forfeit a precious part of its inheritance. Like Judaism and Islam, Christianity, as I noted at the beginning of this book, is not a European religion. Its homeland is in the Middle East, and continuity with its past is dependent on the Christians who continue to live in that land in which the faith is native. Were the holy places turned into museums or archaeological curiosities, as they have been in Turkey and Tunisia, the tangible links that stretch back through history to the apostles and to God's revelation in Christ would be severed. Without the presence of living Christian communities, the witness of the Holy Land can only be equivocal. The martyrs and teachers, the monks and bishops, the faithful who lived in Bethlehem and Beit Jala and Nazareth and Jerusalem would no longer be signs of a living faith, but forgotten names from a distant past. Bethlehem would become a shrine, and Christian Jerusalem a city of ancient renown. Only people, not stones and earth and marble, can bear an authentic witness.

Abbreviations

ANRW Aufstieg und Niedergang der roemischen Welt

BA Biblical Archaeologist

BASOR Bulletin of the American School of Oriental Research

BZ Byzantinische Zeitschrift

BZAW Beihefte zur Zeitschrift für die altestamentliche Wissenschaft

CBQ Catholic Bible Quarterly

CC Corpus Christianorum

CCG Corpus Christianorum Series Graeca

CH Church History

CR Classical Review

CSCO Corpus Scriptorum Orientalium Christianorum

CSEL Corpus Scriptorum Ecclesiasticorum Latinorum

DACL Dictionnaire d'Archéologie Chrétienne et Liturgie

DJD Discoveries in the Judaean Desert

DOP Dumbarton Oaks Papers

DPV Deutscher Palaestina-Vereins

ET Expository Times

HR History of Religions

HTR Harvard Theological Review

HUCA Hebrew Union College Annual

IEJ Israel Exploration Journal

IOSOT International Organization for the Study of the Old Testament

JAC Jahrbuch für Antike und Christentum

JAOS Journal of the American Oriental Society

JbAC Jahrbuch für Antike und Christentum

JBL Journal of Biblical Literature

JEH Journal of Ecclesiastical History

JES Journal of Ecumenical Studies

JQR Jewish Quarterly Review

JRS Journal of Roman Studies

JTS Journal of Theological Studies

OGIS Orientis Graeci Inscriptionis Selectae

PEQ Palestine Exploration Quarterly

PG Patrologia Graeca

PL Patrologia Latina

QDAP Quarterly of the Department of Antiquities in Palestine

RAC Reallexikon für Antike und Christentum

RB Revue Biblique

REG Revue des études Grecques

REJ Revue des études Juives

RHR Revue de l'histoire des religions

ROC Revue de l'Orient Chrétien

SC Sources Chrétiennes

SJT Scottish Journal of Theology

TLZ Theologische Literaturzeitung

TRE Theologische Realenzyklopädie

TS Theological Studies

TU Texte und Untersuchungen

VC Vigiliae Christianae

ZAW Zeitschrift für die altestamentliche Wissenschaft

ZDPV Zeitschrift des deutschen Palaestina-Vereins

ZNW Zeitschrift für die neutestamentliche Wissenschaft

Notes

Preface

1 David Vital, *The Origins of Zionism* (Oxford: 1975), 151.

2 George Eliot, *Daniel Deronda,* ed. with an introduction by Graham Handley (New York: 1988), 454.

3 "Jerusalem the Golden" (Urbs Sion Aurea), hymn written by Bernard of Cluny c. 1145; trans. John M. Neale *(The Handbook to the Lutheran Hymnal,* ed. W. G. Polack [Saint Louis: 1942], 437) 41–42.

4 Roland A. Browne, *The Holy Jerusalem Voyage of Ogier VIII, Seigneur d'Anglure* (Gainesville: 1975) 41–42.

5 Edward E. Robinson, *Biblical Researches in Palestine, Mount Sinai and Arabia Petraea* (New York: 1977) 1:329.

Chapter 1
To Possess The Land

1 "The movement from beginning to end is the key to the historical importance of the Exodus story. The strength of the narrative is given by the end." Michael Walzer, *Exodus and Revolution* (New York: 1985), 11.

2 "O Zion, will you not ask how your captives are—the exiles who seek your welfare, who are the remnant of your flocks? From west and east, north and south, from every side, accept the greetings of those near and far, and the blessings of this *captive of desire,* who sheds his tears like the dew of Hermon and longs to have them fall upon your hills. I am like a jackal when I weep for your affliction; but when I dream of your exiles' return, I am a lute for your songs." Judah Halevi, "Ode to Zion," *Penguin Book of Hebrew Verse,* ed. T. Carmi (New York: 1981), 347. According to the medieval Jewish commentator Nachmanides, the land would remain desolate until the exiles returned. The verse "I will devastate the land, so that your enemies who settle in it shall be astonished at it" (Lev 26:32) was interpreted as follows: "And so what is said here 'and your enemies shall be astonished' was good news, announced to all in exile, that our land does not receive our enemies. This is a great proof and promise to us: no land among all the settled parts of the world will be found which was good and broad and which had been settled of old and is [now] desolate like this one. For from the time we left it, it has not received any people or tongue, and all who attempted to settle in it are not able to do so" (*Pirushei ha-Torah,* ed. Chaim Rav Chavel (Jerusalem: 1967), 2:190, at Leviticus 26:16ff.).

3 For these and other illustrations, see Zev Vilnay, *The Holy Land in Old Prints and Maps* (Jerusalem: 1965), 82ff.

4 On the promise of the land in the Hebrew Bible, see Claus Westermann, *The Promises to the Fathers: Studies on the Patriarchal Narratives* (Philadelphia: 1980); Ronald Clements, *Abraham and David: Genesis XV and Its Meaning for Israelite Tradition* (London: 1967). Clements writes, "Thus the basic theme of the Yahwist's history is given in Gen 12:1–3 which forms his introduction to the patriarchal period . . . the land, which belonged to the very foundation of the whole patriarchal tradition" (57). See also the fundamental study of W. D. Davies, *The Gospel and the Land* (Berkeley: 1974), and the essays edited by Georg Strecker, *Das Land Israel in biblishcher Zeit* (Göttingen: 1983).

5 The phrase is used in the title of Joan Peters's controversial book about Arabs and Jews in Palestine, *From Time Immemorial: The Origins of the Arab-Jewish Conflict over Palestine* (New York: 1984). It is, however, a common translation of the Hebrew *me'olam.*

6 Miriam Lichtheim, *Ancient Egyptian Literature; A Book of Readings* (Berkeley: 1975), 1:226.

7 Emmanuel Anati, *Palestine before the Hebrews: A History from the Earliest Arrival of Man to the Conquest of Canaan* (New York: 1963); Yohanan Aharoni, *The Archaeology of the Land of Israel: From the Prehistoric Beginnings to the End of the First Temple Period* (Philadelphia: 1982). On Canaanite art, see *Treasures of the Israeli Museum* (Jerusalem: 1985).

8 Conquest is the biblical way of depicting Israelite occupation of the land. Among historians and archaeologists it is generally agreed that the Israelites settled in Palestine around 1200 B.C.E., but how they came into possession of the land is disputed. Some believe they acquired the land by invasion, others think the Israelites were nomads who gradually infiltrated the region, and still others believe they gained control of the land through a social reorganization among the Canaanite cities. For a recent discussion of the archaeological data (with bibliography), see Volkmar Fritz, "Conquest or Settlement? The Early Iron Age in Palestine," BA 50 (1987): 84–100.

9 Some texts justify the driving out of the inhabitants because they were idolaters: "For these nations, which you are about to dispossess, give heed to soothsayers and to diviners; but as for you, the Lord your God has not allowed you so to do" (Deut 18:14). See also Psalm 44:1–3. The same theme occurs much later in the Wisdom of Solomon in one of the few texts that uses the term *holy land*: "Those who dwelt of old in the holy land, you hated for their detestable practices (Wisdom 12:3–4).

10 On this point, see chap. 3, pp. 30–33. But the apologetic motif occurs even in the Bible, as the citation from Deuteronomy 18 in n. 9 above shows. On this point, see Davies (1974), 25–28. Even the book of Jubilees, where this apologetic tradition is found, occasionally uses the phrase "land of Canaan" (34:5).

11 John Van Seters believes the tradition *originated* at the time of the exile. *Abraham in History and Tradition* (New Haven, 1975), 271–72.

12 The Talmud observes at one point that Ezra brought some of the exiles up from Babylon to Eretz Israel "against their will" (*b. Qidd.* 69b).

13 On the exilic origin of certain sections of Deuteronomy, see H. W. Wolff, "Das Kerygma des deuternomistischen Geschichtswerks," *ZAW* 73 (1961): 171–86; Frank Cross, *Canaanite Myth and Hebrew Epic* (Cambridge: 1973), 274ff; Jon Levenson, "Who Inserted the Book of the Torah?" *HTR* 68 (1975): 203–33.

14 Origen, *hom.* 5 *in Ps.* 36 [37]. 4 (*PG* 12, 1362).

15 In some places the phrase carried distinctly bellicose overtones of conquering the land and displacing its inhabitants: "Take possession of the good land which the Lord swore to give to your fathers by thrusting out your enemies from before you as the Lord has promised" (Deut 6:16). Joshua 13:1ff. uses the term "possess" in the very concrete sense of territory that belongs to others peoples that has not yet been conquered: "You are old [God says to Joshua] and advanced in years, and there remains yet very much land to be *possessed*. This is the land that yet remains; all the regions of the Philistines, and all those of the Geshurites (from the Shihor, which is east of Egypt, northward to the boundary of Ekron, it is reckoned as Canaanite." Elsewhere "possess the land" has the sense of living in the land and multiplying one's descendants (Deut 8:1), of shunning evil and bequeathing the land to one's offspring in righteousness (1 Chron 28:8, Ps 25:13; Ps 37:29), of faithfully observing the commandments and the statutes there (Deut 5:31–63), of acting justly in the land (Deut 16:20), and keeping the land free of idolatry (Deut 16:21). In some texts "to possess the land" signifies a time when the people will serve God in purity and holiness, when their hearts will be circumcised and they will love God with their hearts and souls (Deut 30:6). And at a much later date, "possess the land" will serve as an epigram to designate the mes-

sianic age (see the fragment of a commentary on Psalm 37 found at Qumran, 4QpPs37).

16 In some texts Transjordan is considered unclean (Josh 22:19). In other texts Transjordan (and beyond) is included in the land, and the account of the settling of Transjordan is similar to Greek accounts of the colonization of a new territory. Cf. Joshua 18:1–10 and Plato, *Laws* 745b-c. On this point, M. Weinfeld, "The Extent of the Promised Land—The Status of Transjordan," in Strecker (1983), 59–75. One midrash says that the Land was given by God, but "the land beyond the Jordan you took by yourself" (*Sifrei Deuteronomy,* sec. 299 [ed. Finkelstein, 318]). Unlike the land west of the Jordan, Transjordan was "not flowing with milk and honey," according to Rabbi Jose the Galilean (*Sifrei Deuteronomy,* sec. 301, ll. 16–17). On the borders of the land, see Zecharia Kallai, "The Reality of the Land and the Bible," in Strecker (1983), 76–90.

17 W. D. Davies' apt title for his other book on the land, *The Territorial Dimension of Judaism* (Berkeley: 1982), strikes exactly the right note.

18 Note the description of the land in 1 Maccabees 14:8ff. after the victories of the Hasmoneans: "They tilled their land in peace, the land yielded its increase and the trees of the plains their fruit. Old men sat in the streets, all of them talking about the good old times, while youth donned the glory and apparel of war. . . . Everyone sat under his own vine and fig tree, with no one to make them afraid. No one was left in the land to fight them."

19 On the Deuteronomic conception of the "holiness of the people," see Moshe Weinfeld, *Deuteronomy and the Deuteronomic School* (Oxford:1972), 225–32. He distinguishes this idea from that of the Priestly document in which the territory is sacred, and all who dwell within it, resident alien and Israelite, are subject to a "sacral code." In Deuteronomy the Law applied only to true Israelites (229).

20 There exist letters from the Canaanite king of Jerusalem in the fourteenth century B.C.E., long before it had become an Israelite city. James B. Pritchard, *Ancient Near Eastern Texts Relating to the Old Testament* (Princeton: 1969), 483–90.

21 F. W. Cross writes, "David's endeavor to draw to himself and his city the cultic traditions of the league . . . was fabulously successful" F. M. Cross, *Canaanite Myth and Hebrew Epic* (Cambridge, 1973), 230–31.

22 Diana Eck, *Banaras, City of Light* (New York: 1982), 5.

23 Jon D. Levenson, *Theology of the Program of Restoration of Ezekiel 40*–48 (Missoula, Mont.: 1976), 8.

24 Ezekiel is a composite work whose oracles are closely associated with the prophet himself. On Ezekiel, see esp. Walther Zimmerli, *A Commentary on the Book of the Prophet Ezekiel. Chapters 1–24* (Philadelphia: 1979), and *A Commentary on the Book of the Prophet Ezekiel. Chapters 25*–48 (Philadelphia: 1983) as well as the work by Levenson cited above. On the exilic prophets, see Peter R. Ackroyd, *Exile and Restoration: A Study of Hebrew Thought in the Sixth Century B.C.* (Philadelphia: 1975).

25 Jonathan Z. Smith, *To Take Place* (Chicago: 1987), 48.

26 As scholars have long recognized, Ezekiel's images of a cosmic mountain, of a river that flows from the mountain to refresh and give life to the earth, of the land as the "navel of the earth" are not unique to ancient Israel. They are well docu-

mented in the Far East as well as in the ancient civilizations of the Middle East. The closest parallels come from the Canaanites, who depicted the mountain of El as a source of a lifegiving river that watered the earth. Other Canaanite myths spoke of the god Baal dwelling on a mountain with the name Zaphon, a word meaning "north" that was used as a title for Mount Zion in the Hebrew Bible (Ps 48). The Canaanite text reads,

> Come, and I will see it,
> In the midst of my mountain, divine Zaphon
> In the holy place, the mountain of my *heritage*
> In the chosen spot, on the hill of victory. [Clifford, 68]

Ezekiel was not the first to appropriate these traditions, but he forged them into a coherent whole. Richard J. Clifford, *The Cosmic Mountain in Canaan and the Old Testament* (Cambridge: 1972); Jon D. Levenson, *Sinai and Zion* (Minneapolis: 1985), 111ff. The parallels in other cultures are numerous. Here is one from the Tibetan Buddhist *Life of Milarepa*:

> "I dreamed that in the vast North of the world
> A majestic snow-clad mountain arose,
> Its white peak touching the sky.
> Around it turned the sun and moon,
> Its light filled the whole of space,
> And its base covered the entire Earth.
> Rivers descended in the four cardinal directions,
> Quenching the thirst of all sentient beings,
> And all these waters rushed into the sea.
> A myriad of flowers sparkled."

The Life of Milarepa, trans. Lobsang P. Lhalungpa (Boston: 1984), 83. On the topic of sacred space as the center of the world, see Mircea Eliade, *Patterns in Comparative Religion* (1958), and G. van der Leeuw, *Religion in Essence and Manifestation* (1967); also Shigeru Matsumoto, "The Meaning of Sacred Places as Phenomenologists of Religion Understand It," *Tenri Journal of Religion,* 10 (October 1969): 46–56. Jerusalem, it should be noted, was not the most prominent mountain in the area. It was overshadowed by the Mount of Olives immediately to the east, from which one could look down on the city. Historians of religion speak of holy places (mountains or rivers or trees) that are sacred "by nature" and are simply "discovered" by human beings. There are, however, places that are "selected," and Jerusalem falls in this category; it became sacred by virtue of its history and associations.

27 Smith (1987), 56.

28 Ezekiel's temple is modeled on the kind of cultic community he came to know in Babylonia that included territory and a resident population. "These temples were not just places of sacrifice and prayer; they served as administrative centers with their own bureaucracies, issued loans, controlled and collected revenues from real estate, supported colleges of scholars and scribes, not to mention hordes of temple servants including butchers, bakers, and keepers of sacrificial herds, and the

like." Joseph Blenkinsopp, *A History of Prophecy in Israel* (Philadelphia: 1983), 227–28.

29 In the one place in which Ezekiel actually uses the phrase "navel of the earth" (38:14) he has reference not to Mount Zion, or to the "holy mountain," or to the temple or Jerusalem, but to the land as a whole.

30 Levenson (1976), 112.

31 Zimmerli (1983), 527.

32 Ibid., 198. In answer to the charge that they had no claim to the land, the returning exiles, speaking through Ezekiel, reply that those who remained in Judea had polluted the land by worshipping false gods. "You eat flesh with the blood, and lift up your eyes to your idols, and shed blood; shall you then *possess* the land?" (33:25) Their hope to reclaim the land rested on the same promise to which the "natives" appealed. Ezekiel writes, "When I gather the house of Israel from the people among whom they are scattered, and manifest my holiness in them in the sight of the nations, then they shall dwell in their own land which I gave to my servant Jacob. And they shall dwell securely in it, and they shall build houses and plant vineyards" (Ezek 28:25–26).

33 Moshe Weinfeld, "Inheritance of the Land—Privilege versus Obligation: The Concept of the Promise of the Land in the Sources of the First and Second Temple Periods," *Tsiyon* 49 (1984): 126 (in Hebrew).

34 On Second Isaiah, Dieter Baltzer, *Ezechiel und Deuterojesaja. Berührungen in der Heilserwartung der beiden grossen Exilspropheten* (*BZAW* 121; Berlin: 1971), 162–75.

35 Levenson, *HTR* 68 (1975): 229, "Deuteronomy never mentions the Temple or Jerusalem by name and never links monarchy with sacrifice."

36 See Joshua 11:23, where the term is "inherit" (*nahalah).*

37 Blenkinsopp (1983), 247.

38 George Steiner, *After Babel* (London: 1975), 23.

39 On Haggai and Zechariah, Carol L. Meyers and Eric M. Meyers, *Haggai, Zechariah 1–8*. A New Translation with Introduction and Commentary (Garden City: 1987), and W. Rudolph, *Haggai: Sacharja 1–8; Sacharja 9–14; Maleachai* (Gütersloh: 1976).

40 See, for example, 4 Ezra 4:33, "How long and when will these things be?" and the Book of Zerubbabel, l. 29, "When will the light of Israel be kindled?"

41 In Zechariah's phrase the term used is "ground" or "soil" (in Hebrew, *adamah*), not "land" (*aretz*). The term *adamah* designates what one can rub between the fingers and is often rendered "ground"—for example in the phrase "everything that creeps upon the ground" (Gen 2:25). It signifies undefined and undifferentiated earth (Joshua 7:6). On occasion *adamah* will refer to an area defined by a particular people's life and culture (Gen. 7:40), but it does not bear political connotations and is seldom used to designate a territory under a specific rule. (*Theological Dictionary of the Old Testament* [Grand Rapids: 1974], 1:88–98, 388–405). *Aretz* is the conventional term to refer to a distinct territory or political entity, as in the phrase the "land of the Philistines" (Gen 21:32), "land of the Chaldeans" (Isa 23:13), "land of Egypt" (Gen 13:10). But it can have the more general sense of "earth" as distinguished from heaven, as in the phrase "the God of the heavens

and the earth" (Gen 24:3) or in the opening sentence of the book of Genesis, "In the beginning God created the heavens and the earth."

In the conventional biblical expression "land of Canaan" or "land of Israel" the usual term is *aretz,* and in the phrase "possess the land" or "inherit the land" the term is also *aretz,* meaning of course "land of Israel." "Land" is used similarly in the phrase "land flowing with milk and honey." Indeed so fixed was this formula that in one passage in which "ground" appears in place of "land," some manuscripts insert the term "land" (Deut 31:20). It may be significant that Zechariah uses not "land" but "ground," yet the book of Ezekiel uses the terms if not interchangeably at least without any consistent pattern. Ezekiel is as likely to say "ground of Israel" as "land of Israel": Ezek 7:2 (*adamah*), 11:17 (*adamah*), 13:9 (*adamah*); 14:17, 19 (*aretz*). In 11:14–17 and 20:38 both terms are used without apparent differentiation. The phrase *eretz Israel* is pre-exilic (1 Sam 13:19), but it may not have gained wide acceptance by Ezekiel's time. Jeremiah also uses *adamah* where one would expect *aretz*: 16:15, 23:8. Ezekiel's practice of using both terms did not gain acceptance by later generations. *Eretz Israel,* not *admat Israel,* became the traditional term to designate the land promised to Abraham and his descendants. Zimmerli, however, thinks that Ezekiel's characteristic term for the Land of Israel is *admat Israel.* See his "Das 'Land' bei den vorexilischen und fruehexilischen Schriftpropheten," in Strecker (1983), 39.

When the Hebrew Bible was translated into other languages, Zechariah's "holy ground" came out "holy land," and any differentiation, however subtle, between "land" and "ground" was lost. But for the Hebrew reader, the linguistic fact remains: the Bible never uses the phrase "holy land" or "land of holiness." It uses only "holy ground." "Holy" is an appropriate epithet for "ground" because *adamah* is undifferentiated soil, land that receives definition and character from context. But *aretz* was never undifferentiated. Its character was determined by the historic associations of the term; unlike ground it did not need further definition or qualification. When the word was *aretz* or *ha-aretz* (the land) the term "holy" was redundant. It was sufficient simply to say: "the Land" or "Land of Israel." Paradoxically, the epithet "holy" profaned the traditional designation for the land.

42 Commentators have noted apparent parallels between the passage in Zechariah and the account of Moses before the burning bush in the book of Exodus (3:5): "When the Lord saw that he turned aside to see, God called to him out of the bush, 'Moses, Moses!' And he said, 'here am I.' Then he said, 'Do not come near; put off your shoes from your feet, for the place on which you are standing is holy ground." As in the passage from Zechariah, the term "holy ground" refers here to a zone surrounding a sacred object, but in Zechariah the sacred object is the temple and the holy mount is Zion. Zechariah's holy land is a place with history and memory, whereas in Exodus, "holy ground" has no such features. What makes the place holy is the theophany at the burning bush, and the bush could be located anywhere or, more accurately, whenever God appeared. The particular place is inconsequential. In the same chapter of Exodus the term "land" occurs in its conventional sense to refer to the land promised to the Israelites, "a good and broad land, a land flowing with milk and honey" (Exod 3:8). There is no relation between the

"holy ground" or "holy zone" around the burning bush and the promised land spoken of elsewhere in Exodus.

43 Whether the holiness of the temple extended to the entire city in which people lived or only to the "temple city", i.e., a smaller area immediately contiguous to the temple, is debated by scholars of the Temple Scroll. See Baruch Levine's criticisms of Yadin's views in "The Temple Scroll: Aspects of Its Historical Provenance and Literary Character," *BASOR* 232 (1978): 5–23.

Chapter 2
Within My Holy Borders

1 On chapters 44–50 of Sirach, see Helge Stadelmann, *Ben Sira als Schriftgelehrter* (Tübingen: 1980), 177–217; E. Jacob, "L'histoire d'Israël vue par Ben Sira," *Mélanges bibliques rédigés en l'honneur de A. Robert* (Paris: 1957), 288–94.

2 In the catalogue of heroes, inheritance or possession of the land is also mentioned at 44:21 (Abraham), 44:23 (Jacob), and it is said a second time of Joshua (46:1). Contrast the way the heroes of Israel are presented in the Christian book of Hebrews, chapter 11, or in 1 Clement 9.3–12.3.

3 On religion among diaspora communities, see Jonathan Z. Smith, "Native Cults in the Hellenistic Period," *HR* 11 (1971): 236–49; also his chapter "Earth and Gods," in *Map Is Not Territory* (Leiden: 1978), esp. 119ff. The most important parallel to the Jews is the Samaritans. Recently discovered inscriptions from the Greek island of Delos show that the Samaritans were not confined to Palestine but had also established communities in a diaspora. They thought of themselves as Israelites whose loyalty was directed to Mount Gerizim. One inscription reads, "The Israelites on Delos who make offerings to hallowed *Argarizein* [*Har Gerizim*, i.e., Mount Gerizim] crown with a gold crown Sarapion, son of Jason, of Knossos, for his benefactions toward them." The inscriptions have been edited by Bruneau, "Les Israélites de Délos et la juiverie délienne," *Bulletin des Correspondances Hellénique* 106 (1982): 465–504. For discussion, see A. T. Kraabel, "*Synagoga Caeca*: Systematic Distortion in Gentile Interpretations of Evidence for Judaism in the Early Christian Period," in *To See Ourselves as Others See Us*, ed. Jacob Neusner and Ernest S. Frerichs (Chico, Calif.: 1985), 219–46.

4 On pilgrimage, Shmuel Safrai, *Die Wallfahrt im Zeitalter des Zweiten Temples* (Neukirchen: 1981). A poignant testimony to the devotion to the land of those living in exile can be found in 1 Kings 8:48: "If they repent with all their heart in the land of their enemies . . . and pray to thee toward their land . . . then hear . . . and forgive thy people."

5 Elias Bickerman, *From Ezra to the Last of the Maccabees* (New York: 1962), 3.

6 See Doran Mendels, *The Land of Israel as a Political Concept in Hasmonean Literature* (Tübingen: 1987), 9–17.

7 James Kugel in Kugel and Greer, *Early Biblical Interpretation* (Philadelphia: 1986), 37.

8 Gershom Scholem, *The Messianic Idea in Judaism* (New York: 1971), 1–2.

9 The poem is by Yose ben Yose (ed. Aharon Mirsky, *The Poems of Yose ben Yose* [Jerusalem: 1977], 92 [in Hebrew]) and will be discussed in chapter 7.

10 *Temple Scroll* 56:12–15, echoing the words of Deuteronomy 17:14. The first coins minted by the Hasmonean rulers, during the reign of Alexander Jannaeus, bear the legend YEHONATHAN THE KING—KING ALEXANDER. Yigal Ronen believes the coins come from Aristobulus I, who preceded Alexander Jannaeus. See his "The First Hasmonean Coins," *BA* 50 (1987): 105–08.

11 "Much of post-biblical Jewish theology and literature was influenced and sometimes governed by a hope for a Davidic heir to throw off the shackles of foreign domination and restore Israel's sovereignty; the gathering of one people around a new and glorified Temple." George Nickelsburg, *Jewish Literature between the Bible and the Mishnah* (Philadelphia: 1981), 18.

12 For some writers, the period was an "age of wrath," as Jonathan Goldstein observes: "The first centuries of the postexilic period could only have been puzzling for faithful believers: the glorious prophecies of restoration uttered by the true prophets were not being fulfilled. Yet a believer could hardly conclude that those inspired utterances were false. Fulfillment would come, but later. . . . Despite the joyous proclamations of the postexilic prophets, despite the return of many exiles to the promised Land, despite the completion of the Second Temple, it was clear to believing Israelites that they were still living in the 'Age of (God's) Wrath'" ("How the Authors of 1 and 2 Maccabees Treated the 'Messianic' Promises," in *Judaisms and Their Messiahs at the Turn of the Christian Era,* ed. Jacob Neusner, William Green, and Ernest Frerichs [Cambridge: 1987], 70).

13 Jewish hope was not univocal. Tobit, for example, makes no mention of a king, nor do other writings from the period, e.g., Jesus ben Sirach, 1 and 2 Maccabees, or Daniel. Belief in the restoration of a *Davidic* monarch appears only in a few of the extant texts, e.g., Psalms of Solomon 17.4. At Qumran the future Priest seems to have been as important as a future king, and Josephus reports that at the time of Hyracanus and Aristobulus the "nation . . . asked not to be ruled by a king, saying that it was the custom of their country to obey the priests of the God who was venerated by them" (*AJ* 14.41). On the many forms of Jewish hope in this period, see the essays in Neusner-Green-Frerichs (1987); for a survey of messianic conceptions, see Emil Schürer, *The History of the Jewish People in the Time of Jesus Christ* (New York: 1972), 2:488–543, and Joseph Klausner, *The Messianic Idea in Israel* (New York: 1955).

14 For the importance of the idea of "possession of the land" in this period, see Moshe Weinfeld, "Possession of the Land—Privilege or Obligation. The Conception of the Promised Land in the Sources from the Period of the First and Second Temple," *Tsiyon* 49 (1984): esp. 129–35 (in Hebrew).

15 On the paucity of evidence for the influence of Persian material culture in Palestine, see Ephrain Stern, "The Archaeology of Persian Palestine," in *Cambridge History of Judaism* (Cambridge: 1984), 1:112–13.

16 Jonathan Goldstein, *II Maccabees. A New Translation with Introduction and Commentary* (New York: 1983), 3.

17 On Hellenism among the Jews, see Schürer (1973), 1:145–46. For a subtle and nuanced discussion of the reception of Hellenism among Jews of this period, see the provocative essay of Jonathan Goldstein, "Jewish Acceptance and Rejection of

Hellenism," in *Jewish and Christian Self-Definition,* ed. E. P. Sanders (Philadelphia: 1981), 2:64–87.

18 Schürer (1973), 1:139.

19 The letter, however, was not composed by the author of 2 Maccabees. In fact, the section in which the term occurs belongs to a second letter within the first letter. The first letter was written in 124 B.C.E, and the second, cited by the author of the first letter, was written a generation earlier, in 143 B.C.E. On the letter's authenticity, see E. Bickerman, "Ein jüdischer Festbrief vom Jahre 124 v. Christus," *ZNW* 32 (1933): 233–54. For a rich and detailed discussion, see Jonathan A. Goldstein's commentary on 2 Maccabees, 137–53. On 2 Maccabees, see, besides Goldstein's commentary, Robert Doran, *Temple Propaganda: The Purpose and Character of 2 Maccabees,* (*Catholic Biblical Quarterly Monograph Series* 12 [Washington: 1981]).

20 Translation by Goldstein, 137.

21 Ibid., 148.

22 Ibid., 148–50. His argument rests on the archaeological work of Paul Lapp at 'Arâq el-Emîr, "The Second and Third Campaigns at 'Arâq el-Emîr," *BASOR* 171 (1963): 24, 26, 38–39, but he is careful to qualify his comments with the proviso, "If Lapp is right." Recent excavations at the site have suggested another reading of the evidence, as Goldstein recognizes. Whether or not Jason served at a temple in Transjordan, the letter is nevertheless a defense of the prerogatives of Jerusalem.

23 In the letter to the Jews of Egypt the Greek term in the phrase "land of Judea" is *chora*; in the phrase "holy land" it is *ge*. The terms could, however, be interchanged. Philo uses both *ge* and *chora* to designate the "holy land" (*Spec.* 4.215, *chora*; *Her.* 293, *ge*). First Maccabees uses *ge* to designate the "land of Judah" (1 Macc 5:45,53); the Gospel of Mark uses *chora* for "country of Judea" (Mark 1:5). In the LXX *ge* is the normal word to translate the Hebrew *aretz* in the sense of "the land" or the phrase "the land of Israel" whatever the original Hebrew term; Ezekiel 37:12 (*adamah*), 40:2 (*eretz Israel*), 20:28 (*ha-aretz*). The LXX translates Zach 2:15 ("holy ground") as *agia ge*.

24 I borrow this phrase from the Qumranic text *Community Rule,* 1QS VIII,3, though it is not used there of Jason.

25 Philo, *Legat.* 202; see also 205. The Hasmoneans also expelled non-Jews from the land. See Goldstein, "Jewish Acceptance of Hellenism," 82, and the evidence cited in his fns. 112–13.

26 On occasion the term "motherland" (*metris*) is used; Plato, *R.* 575d; Plutarch 2.792e. In the Hebrew Bible no term bears the overtones of the Hellenistic *patris* (homeland). The term *moledeth* (usually translated as "homeland" in modern Hebrew literature) does occur but it simply means place of origin. In Genesis it is used of the land *from which* Abraham migrated and in the RSV is translated as kinsmen (the term is based on the Hebrew root for "give birth"). After Sarah's death Abraham, who is very old, asks his servant to swear that he will not take a wife for Abraham's son from among the Canaanites, but will go "to my country and to my kindred [where I was born, *moledeth*] and take a wife for my son Isaac" (Gen 24:4; also 24:7). In Ezekiel it is used of the Land of Israel. God tells Ezekiel to

speak to Jerusalem: "Your origin and your place of birth (*moledeth*) are of the land of the Canaanites" (Ezek 16:3). Here the term bears overtones of the later usage, but the very formulation betrays its ambiguity. The land in which the Israelites lived was an adopted land, the land of the Canaanites. Perhaps for this reason the rabbinical tradition (i.e., Jewish tradition in Hebrew and Aramaic in contract to Greek) did not adopt the term. Hebrew-speaking Jews preferred *Eretz Israel*. Only in modern times does "homeland" (*moledeth*) gain currency in Hebrew, and its meaning is sometimes uncritically projected back into the biblical sources. See Eliezer Schweid, *The Land of Israel: National Home or Land of Destiny* (Cranbury, N.J.: 1985), 211; Arnold M. Eisen, *Galut: Modern Jewish Reflection on Homelessness and Homecoming* (1986); Shalom Rosenberg, "The Link to the Land of Israel in Jewish Thought: A Clash of Perspectives," in L. Hoffman, *The Land of Israel* (1986), 141ff.

27 Other references to fatherland: 2 Macc 4:1; 5:6; 13:3; 13:10; 13:14; 4 Macc 1:11; 4:20. Third Maccabees speaks of Jews as a "foreign people" living in a "foreign land." The term does not occur in 1 Maccabees, though traditional formulations, when rendered in Greek, carry Hellenistic overtones, as for example 1 Macc 15:33. Josephus distinguishes Jewish devotion to the law from loyalty to the fatherland. It is meritorious for human beings to care "more for the observance of their laws and piety toward God than for their well-being (*soteria*) and their fatherland" (*Ap.* 1.212).

28 See also Sirach 48:15, "their land." Josephus: "Ours is not a maritime country" (*Ap.* 1.60); "our country" (*Ap.* 1.74). Of course the extent of "our country" expanded as the borders of the Hasmonean kingdom were extended. Describing the extent of Jewish territory under Alexander Jannaeus, Josephus wrote of Pella (Fihl) on the east bank: "This last city Alexander's men demolished because the inhabitants would not agree to adopt the national customs (*patria*) of the Jews" (*AJ* 13.15.4).

29 Philo, *Legat.* 277–78.

30 J. Heinemann, "The Relation between the People and Their Land in Hellenistic Judaism," *Tsiyon* 13/14 (1948–49): 6 (in Hebrew).

31 See also Jubilees 1:19; 8:10, 17; 12:22–13, 21; 14:7, 18; 15:10, and passim. I have used the translations of Jubilees by O. S. Wintermute in *The Old Testament Pseudepigrapha,* ed. James H. Charlesworth (New York: 1985), 2:35–142, and James C. Vanderkam, *The Book of Jubilees* in CSCO 511 (Louvain: 1989).

32 *M. Kelim* 1.6a; *Midrash Tanhuma, Kedoshim* 10.

33 Jubilees 12:28; 13:1; 14:7; 15:10; 34:4; 49:18.

34 The account begins at Jubilees 7:7 and runs through 10:34.

35 David Winston, *The Wisdom of Solomon. A New Translation with Introduction and Commentary* (New York: 1979), 238. See in this connection the following passages in the Torah: Lev 17:24 and Num 35:33.

36 "The land most precious of all to thee" is one of several designations of the land in this period. See also Jubilees 13:2, 6, "a land pleasant to your eyes"; "the glorious land" (Dan 11:16); "pleasant and glorious land" (1 Enoch 89.40); "extensive and beautiful" (*Ep. Arist.* l. 107); "holy soil" (*Sib. Or.* 3.267); "pleasant land" (Ps

106:24); "holy land of the pious" (*Sib. Or.* 5:281). In Psalm 78:54 the phrase "holy border" is used and the RSV translates it "holy land."

37 See also *T. Lev.* 7:1.

38 Another fascinating text from this period that depicts Jewish claims to the land is the *Genesis Apocryphon* found at Qumran. In a dream Abraham is told to go to the highest peak in Judea to view the entire region, the Jordan valley, Transjordan, Jeruslem, and the hill country of Judea. In the dream God speaks to Abraham: "To your descendants I shall give all this land; they will possess it forever." After Abraham has beheld the extent of the land, God tells hims: "Rise, walk about, and go to see how great is its length and how great is its width." Then Abraham, like a prosperous heir, walks the length and breadth of his land, surveying his new possession. What is most remarkable is that Abraham's walk takes him east to the Euphrates River, south to the Red Sea, north into Lebanon, and west to the Mediterranean, i.e., the *Genesis Apocryphon* assumes the most expansive boundaries of the promised land to be found in the biblical tradition. Furthermore the text gives the impression that Abraham is surveying an estate that is uninhabited. Text and translation in Joseph A. Fitzmyer, *The Genesis Apocryphon of Qumran Cave I. A Commentary* (Rome: 1971), 68–69.

39 The Temple Scroll shows no embarrassment: possession of the land requires that the Amorites, Canaanites, Hittites, and other peoples be "driven out" (col. 1; col. 51). When the Israelites enter the land, according to the Temple Scroll, they will occupy the cities and destroy the people living in them. In wars with peoples living outside of the land the Israelites are to take spoils, but "in the cities of the peoples that I give you for an *inheritance,* you shall not leave alive any living thing, but you shall utterly destroy the Hittites and the Amorites and the Canaanites" (62.13).

The scroll is a book about the life of the people "holy to the Lord" when they will one day "possess" the land given to them as an "inheritance" (64.12; cf. 48.11). As the title of the work suggests, however, the land is dominated by the temple. This is, of course, anachronistic because in the Torah, from which most of the laws in the scroll are taken, only a movable tabernacle is mentioned, not a temple located in Jerusalem. The author of the scroll had to amplify and modify what he read in the Torah to fit a permanent sanctuary located in one place. In the scroll the land acquires its unique character from the presence in it of the "house in which I cause my name to dwell" (29.3; 46.12). As we have seen, Ezekiel had made the temple the center of the land, and the book of Jubilees located the sanctuary "in the midst of the land" (1.10,17). Though the scroll does not use this language, its description of the temple's architecture, a rectangular main building surrounded by three concentric courtyards, portrays a central axis around which everything in the city of Jerusalem and the land is oriented. Proximity to the temple determines the degree of sanctity of everything in the land: "You shall not slaughter a clean ox or sheep or goat in all your towns, near to my temple within a distance of three-day's journey. . . . And every clean animal which has a blemish you shall eat it within your towns, far from my temple, thirty stadia around it" (col. 42.13–18).

The "cities of Israel" share in the holiness that extends out from the holy of holies, but they belong to a lesser grade of sanctity: "You shall not consider any of your cities to be as pure as my city. . . . If you slaughter . . . in my temple, it shall be adequately pure for my temple; but if you slaughter . . . in your cities it shall be pure enough for your cities" (col. 47).

The *Letter of Aristeas* also says the temple was at the center of the land (of Judea), but its description is topographical and realistic, not mythical and cosmic, as in the Temple Scroll: "When we approached near the site, we saw the city built in the midst of the whole land of the Jews, upon a hill which extended to a great height. On the top of the hill the Temple had been constructed, towering above all" (83–84).

As in the books of the Torah on which it is modeled, the Temple Scroll depicts an actual land, not a spiritual haven. Its king will be a human figure whose kingdom will be firmly fixed on the earth, like that of the "nations" that surround Israel. The temple is a place where animals are tethered and birds caged to be prepared for sacrifice, where priests roast animals and eat their flesh. "The temple portrayed in the Scroll was meant as a real temple, to be built by the Jews in accordance with God's instructions. It was to stand in Jerusalem until the time when God himself would replace it with his own future temple." See Baruch Levine, "The Temple Scroll: Aspects of Its Historical Provenance and Literary Character," *BASOR* 232 (1978): 23. The Temple Scroll also mentions a future temple to be constructed by God: "And I will consecrate my temple by my glory, the temple on which I will settle my glory, until the day of blessing on which I will create my temple and establish it for myself for all times according to the covenant which I have made with Jacob at Bethel" (29.8–10). There is a parallel passage in the book of Jubilees 1:16. For a discussion of the two temples, see Yadin (1983), 1:182–87. There is also a fragment from Qumran (5Q15) describing the dimensions of a rebuilt Jerusalem. See *DJD* III (1962): 184–93 for text, translation, and commentary, and Jacob Licht, "An Ideal Town Plan from Qumran and the Description of the New Jerusalem," *IEJ* 29 (1979): 45–49. See also 1 Enoch's depiction of an eschatological temple: 1 Enoch 90:28–36; 91:13; 93:7.

For the author of the Temple Scroll there could be no talk of "possessing the land" that did not include the temple in Jerusalem. At the beginning of the scroll, immediately after the opening lines that speak about driving out the former inhabitants of the land and tearing down their altars, the scroll turns at once to the first task of the Israelites when they enter the land—to build a sanctuary, a "house to put my name on it" (2.4). Without the temple there could be no holy community, no holy city, and no holy land. For the text of the scroll, see Yigael Yadin, ed., *The Temple Scroll,* 2 vols. (Jerusalem, 1983). See also Hartmut Stegemann, "Das 'Land' in der Tempelrolle und in anderen Texten aus den Qumranfunden," in Strecker (1983), 154–71.

40 Moshe Weinfeld (1984), 130. The term "uninhabited" occurs in Judith 5:19.

41 Text of Hecateus in Diodorus Siculus, *Bibliotheca Historica* 40.3. See Menahem Stern, *Greek and Latin Authors on Jews and Judaism,* (Jerusalem: 1976), 1:26–27.

42 Doron Mendels, "Hecataeus of Abdera and a Jewish '*patrios politeia*' of the Per-

sian Period (Diodorus Siculus XL, 3)," *ZAW* 95 (1983): 96–110. On Hecataeus and the expulsion for Egypt, see also Y. Guttman, "Hecataeus of Abdera," *Jews and Judaism in the Eyes of the Hellenistic World* (Jerusalem: 1974), 55–57 (in Hebrew).

43 *Lev. Rab.* 17.6. Joshua offered three possibilities to the Canaanites, one of which was to make peace. The other two were to leave or to do battle. See also *j. Sheb.* 6.5, 36c.

44 *Lev. Rab.* 17.5.

45 *Mekilta,* Parashah 18, ed. Horowitz (Jerusalem: 1970), 69–70.

46 For a discussion of this topic, see the fascinating article by J. H. Lewy, *Studies in Jewish Hellenism* (Jerusalem: 1969), 60–78 (in Hebrew); also Mendels, *The Land of Israel,* 65–66; Weinfeld (1984), 130–33; V. Aptowitzer, "Les premier possesseurs de Canaan," *REJ* 82 (1926): 273–86. On the Canaanites as a theological problem in the Hebrew Bible, see the suggestive article by Jon Levenson, "Is There a Counterpart in the Hebrew Bible to New Testament Antisemitism?" *JES* 22 (1985): 242–60.

47 Josephus, *AJ* 14.64–68; Dio Cassius 37.16.1–3.

48 As mentioned earlier, Jewish hope took many forms during this period, and belief in a Davidic Messiah, as in Psalm of Solomon 17, may not have been typical. In other works, e.g., 1 and 2 Maccabees, the history of Jason of Cyrene, Daniel, Ben Sirach, there is no mention of a Davidic line. First Enoch 90:37–38 may be Davidic, drawing on Ezekiel 34. On this point, see Jonathan Goldstein in Neusner-Green-Frerichs (1987), 72–73, 90–91, and Collins's criticism of his views, "Messianism in the Maccabean period," ibid., 100–01. Goldstein, in my view, has the better of the argument. The Davidic Messiah also appears in the Qumran texts. For example, here is a comment on the blessing of Jacob in Gen 49:10: "As long as Israel rules, there will not fail to be a descendant from the house of David on the throne" (4QPatr). On Qumran, see Collins, ibid., 104–05, and S. Talmon, "Waiting for the Messiah at Qumran," ibid., 111–31. In later Jewish texts the hope of restoring the Davidic line is more prominent. Of the blessing "He who rebuilds Jerusalem" in the Tefilah, it was said, "Whoever does not say the kingdom of the house of David when speaking the blessing 'He who rebuilds Jerusalem' has not fulfilled his obligations" (*b. Ber.* 49a). On the Davidic Messiah in the later period, see Jacob Neusner, *Messiah in Context* (Philadelphia: 1984), 168–78, and on messianism in general, Peter Schäfer, "Die messianischen Hoffnung des rabbinischen Judentums, zwischen Naherwartung und religiosem Pragmatismus," in *Studien zur Geschichte und Theologie des rabbinischen Judentums* (Brill: 1978).

49 For the attitude toward homeland, *Deus* 17.

50 Samuel Sandmel, *Philo's Place in Judaism* (New York: 1971), 116. Also Betsy Halpern Amaru, "Land Theology in Philo and Josephus" (in Strecker [1983], 172–87). This article, which evaluates Philo according to a crude biblicism, is wholly lacking in subtlety (it uses, for example, the vulgar phrase "piece of real estate" to designate the Land).

51 See also *QG* 3.1–2 (Gen 15:7–8), where the land is understood as "fruitful wisdom."

52 For a different and more convincing reading of Philo, see Berndt Schaller, "Philo von Alexandreia und das 'Heilige Land'" in Strecker (1983), 172–87; David Winston, *Logos and Mystical Theology in Philo of Alexandria* (Cincinnati: 1985), 55–58; and J. Amir, "Philo's Version of the Pilgrimage to Jerusalem," in *Jerusalem in the Second Temple Period*, Abraham Schalit Memorial Volume, ed. A. Oppenheimer et al. (Jerusalem: 1980), 154–65 (in Hebrew).

53 On Jerusalem as the "mother city" of the Jews, see the speech of Agrippa (*Legat.* 278) cited earlier and the discussion of A. Kasher, "Jerusalem as a 'Metropolis' in Philo's National Consciousness," *Cathedra* 11 (1979): 45–56 (in Hebrew); also Heinemann (1948–49), 8–9, and A. J. Werblowsky, "Jerusalem—The metropolis of all the countries," in *Jerusalem Through the Ages* (Jerusalem: 1968), ed. Aviram, 172–78 (in Hebrew).

54 In his treatise on providence he speaks of his pilgrimage "to our ancestral temple to offer up prayers and sacrifices." Parenthetically, in that same treatise he says that he passed through Ascalon on the seacoast of *Syria*. Apparently the coastal region was not part of the holy land (*Prov.* 2.64).

55 Personal correspondence with David Winston, Jan. 6, 1987.

56 For a discussion of the halachic problems of pilgrimage after the destruction and the emergence of nonhalachic forms of pilgrimage, see Shmuel Safrai (1980).

57 Gedaliah Alon, *The Jews in Their Land in the Talmudic Age* (Jerusalem: 1980) 55. Alon's remarks are directed against the facile assumption that emergence of a new piety minimized the loss of the sanctuary. As support for this view scholars often cite the words of Rabbi Johanan ben Zakkai in *Aboth de Rabbi Nathan* 4.5: "Be not grieved; we have another atonement as effective as this. And what is it? It is acts of loving-kindness, as it is said; For I desire mercy and not sacrifice" (Hos 6:6). This view, argues Alon, is one-sided and does not recognize "how deep was the void which the Destruction of the Temple created in the life of the people; how intense was the faith and the longing for its restoration 'speedily'; and what efforts were made to maintain the observance of certain commandments connected with the sanctuary" (50, 55).

58 Josephus the Jewish historian realized that the Roman victory meant the end of Jewish territorial claims to the Land of Israel, and in his account of Jewish history he downplayed the land tradition. He uses the expression "country of the Jews" (*BJ* 1.21), and he calls the country "fatherland" (1.10; also 1.34), but he makes no necessary link between people and land. In the Antiquities, a work written late in life long after the conquest, he ignores the covenant (which always included the land) and deletes all mention of the promise of the land in the story of Abraham's call to "go up to the land." He suppresses the promises made to David and in general detaches the history of the people from its territorial moorings. Josephus did not want the hope of restoration to become the basis for a new outbreak of zealotry or another abortive revolt. Our people, he writes, "care more for the observance of their way of life and for their form of piety than for their own lives and their country's fate" (*Ap.* 12.2). Josephus, however, was irresolute. Balaam's prophecy about the future of the Israelites (Num 23–24) was taken to mean that God will bless this people and lavish on them such goodness that they will become the happiest of all peoples under the sun. "And that land to which he

himself sent you, you will occupy and it will be subject forever to your children" (*AJ* 4.115). In the passage in Numbers on which this discussion is based, there is no mention of the land, no reference to occupying the land, and nothing about it being subject to the Israelites *forever*. See also his discussion of the promise to Jacob and his offspring (Gen 28:13–15) in *AJ* 1.282. Josephus was unable to launder out all scriptural references to Jewish sovereignty in the land. But as long as the Romans occupied the land it was an idle dream to hope that Jerusalem would be rebuilt as a Jewish city. On Josephus, see Marianus de Jonge, "Josephus und die Zukunftserwartungen seines Volkes," *Josephus-Studien* (Göttingen: 1974), 205–19; Harold W. Attridge, *The Interpretation of Biblical History in the Antiquitates Judaicae of Flavius Josephus* (Missoula, Mont.: 1976). Also Betsy Halpern Amaru, "Land Theology in Josephus' Jewish Antiquities," *JQR* 72 (1981): 201–29, and the article by her on Josephus and Philo cited in n. 50. A quite different perspective is Azriel Schochat, "The Views of Josephus on the Future of Israel and Its Land," in *Yerushalayim,* ed. Michael Ish Shalom (Jerusalem: 1953), 48–49 (in Hebrew). Some of Schochat's statements are shaped by modern Zionist ideas. Josephus, says Schochat, knows that "only with the establishment of the Jews as a free [autonomous] people in their land can they live in a situation of equality also in the diaspora" (48). Nevertheless, he does point to several passages in Josephus that serve as a corrective to the conventional interpretation. On the ideological questions in relation to the study of Josephus, see Daniel R. Schwarz, "On Abraham Schalit, Herod, Josephus, the Holocaust, Horst Möhring, and the Study of Ancient Jewish History," *Jewish History* 2 (1987): 9–28.

59 Delbert R. Hillers, *Lamentations* (New York: 1972), xv. On lamentation over the destruction of a city in the ancient Near East, see Jerrold Cooper, *The Curse of Agade* (Baltimore: 1983).

60 On Fourth Ezra, see Michael Edward Stone, *Fourth Ezra. A Commentary on the Book of Fourth Ezra* (Minneapolis: 1990); on 2 Baruch, P. Bogaert, *Apocalypse de Baruch,* Sources Chrétiennes 144 & 145 (Paris: 1969).

61 In the Apocalypse of Abraham, another work written in the generation after the destruction in 70 C.E., Abraham is shown a vision of sacrifices being offered in the temple. Then he is told, "Go to your inheritance!" (*Apoc. Abr.* 29:21).

62 "Holy land" also occurs in 2 Baruch 63:10 and 84:8. Other references to the Land in 2 Baruch are 3:5; 12:1; 29:2; 61:7; 66:2, 5; 77:9; 85:2 ("our land").

63 Baruch's use of the term "holy land" contrasts with that of another work of the same period, the Testament of Job, in which "holy land" designates a celestial land: "My throne is in the upper world, and its splendor and majesty come from the right hand of the father. The whole world shall pass away and its splendor shall fade. . . . But my throne is in the *holy land* and its splendor is in the world of the changeless one" (*T. Job* 33:3–5). A gnostic parallel to this usage can be found in Codex Brucianus 34: "Each Ennead has a Monad in it, and in each Monad there is a space called 'Incorruptible', that is to say, Holy Land" (Charlotte A. Baynes, *A Coptic Gnostic Treatise Contained in the Codex Brucianus* [Cambridge: 1933], 112). See also Odes of Solomon 11:18: "Blessed are those . . . who are planted in your land, and who have a place in paradise" (also 11:21). On the metaphorical use of land in later Jewish tradition, see Moshe Idel, "The Land of Israel in Medieval

Kabbalah," in Hoffman (1986), 170–87. A more typical understanding can be found in the Biblical Antiquities of Pseudo-Philo, which uses the term "holy land" (*terra sancta*) in its description of Moses' death. Moses prays that God would have pity on his "chosen race" and be merciful to them that "your heritage may be established." Then, the text continues, the Lord "showed [Moses] the land and said: 'This is the land that I will give to my people.'" He showed him the place where the clouds draw up moisture to water the earth and the "place in the firmament from which only the *holy land* drinks" (*Bib. Ant.* 19). Here "holy land" refers to the actual territory, the terrain of biblical history.

64 Frederick J. Murphy, *The Structure and Meaning of Second Baruch* (Chico, Calif.: 1985), argues that Baruch wished to discourage any hope of restoration (71ff.). Also John J. Collins, *The Apocalyptic Imagination* (New York: 1984), 170–79.

65 Syriac text of 2 Baruch in S. Dedering, *Apocalypse of Baruch*, in ed. S. Dedering, *Vetus Testamentum Syriace* (Leiden: 1973). The Syriac term for "prepared" is *m'td.* Fourth Ezra 10:44 also uses the term "established" or "constructed" city (*civitatem aedificatem)*. See A. F. Klijn, *Der lateinische Text der Apocalypse des Esra* (Berlin: 1983), 72. *Mekilta of Rabbi Ishmael,* Jethro, Parshah 9 (ed. Horowitz [Jerusalem: 1970]), 236. Rev 21 depicts Jerusalem as a city prepared in heaven, "adorned as a bride," which will come down from above.

66 The passage from Isaiah 49 about the city "graven on the palms of [God's] hands" is cited by the early Christian chiliast Irenaeus of Lyon, at the end of the second century C.E. The future Jerusalem, says Irenaeus, will be located on earth, "under heaven," not "in the heavens." Furthermore, the new Jerusalem will be "rebuilt" according to the model of the Jerusalem above: "That is what Isaiah was speaking about when he wrote: 'I have engraved your walls on the palms of my hands.'" Irenaeus seems familiar with Jewish exegetical tradition that took this passage from Isaiah to mean that the future Jerusalem will be built according to the "pattern of the Jerusalem above." In this view the Jerusalem above and the Jerusalem below are complementary. The existence of a Jerusalem that is "ready" and in God's safekeeping is a warrant that one day a new Jerusalem would be built on earth. Irenaeus also cites, as a prophecy of Jeremiah, a passage from Baruch (not 2 Baruch) 4:36–5:9. He singles out 5:3, "God will show your splendor to the whole earth which is *under heaven,*" to show that Jerusalem will be rebuilt on the earth (haer. 5.35.2). This same text from Isaiah 49 also appears in Jewish tradition from a later period: "Because of the great love God had for the Jerusalem below he made another one, the Jerusalem above, as it is written, 'I have engraved them on the palms of my hands'" (Isa 49). The midrash cites Psalm 122, "Jerusalem is built as a city that is compact together" and interprets the phrase "compact together" to mean that "the Jerusalem above is united with the city on earth as though it were one." For this reason, the midrash continues, "the Shekinah vowed that it would never enter into the city above until the city below is built" (*Midrash Tanhuma,* Pikudei Aleph, printed edition [Jerusalem, 1962], 132a). On the idea of the "Jerusalem above" in Jewish literature, see A. Aptowitzer, "The Temple above in the Agada," *Tarbiz* 2 (1931): 257–87 (in Hebrew), esp. 266–72. He cites a number of texts, the most important of which are the passage from *Midrash Tanhuma, b. Ta'an.* 5a, Baruch 4, 4 Ezra 10:29–34,

Bereshith Rabbati, Wayyeze at Gen 28:17, Gal 4:26, Heb 12:22, and Rev 21. For other texts as well as a discussion of the relation between Jewish and Christian ideas of "Jerusalem above," see Ephrain Urbach, *Jerusalem Through the Ages* (Jerusalem 1968), 158–64 (in Hebrew).

67 *b. Ta'an.* 5a.

68 Second Enoch 55:22 is often read in this way, but it could be interpreted otherwise. With the destruction of Jerusalem, Jewish eschatology exploited the mythical language already present within the tradition. Fourth Ezra contrasts the "present" and "corruptible world" with the "immoral age to come" (4 Ezra 7:112). It contrasts the suffering of this age with the "age to come," when paradise will be opened, the tree of life planted, and all sorrow will pass away (4 Ezra 8:52–53). Ezra looks for a more enduring city whose foundations were made by God (4 Ezra 10:54). On 4 Ezra's eschatology, see Michael Stone, "Coherence and Inconsistency in the Apocalypses: The Case of the 'End' in 4 Ezra," *JBL* 102 (1982): 229–43; also Peter Schäfer, "Die Lehre von den zwei Welten im 4. Buch Esra und in der tanaaitischen Literatur," in *Studien zur Geschichte und Theologie des Judentums* (Leiden: 1978), 244–91.

69 See, for example, the midrash on 2 Sam 7 about a future temple not built by human beings (4QFlor on 2 Sam 7). Extensive commentary in George J. Brooke, *Exegesis at Qumran* (1985), but on the key point of the meaning of the phrase *miqdash adam* (184ff.), I find D. Flusser more convincing. The phrase seems to mean a "sanctuary among human beings in which will be sacrificed deeds of law, i.e. sacrifices." See his "Two Notes on the Midrash on 2 Sam. 7," in *IEJ* 9 (1959): 99–104.

70 *Midrash Vayosha* in A. Jellinek, *Bet ha-Midrasch* (Jerusalem: 1967), 1:55.

71 G. W. Bowersock, "A Roman Perspective on the Bar Kochba War," in *Approaches to Ancient Judaism,* ed. William Green (Chico, Calif.: 1980), 2:131.

72 Peter Schäfer, "Rabbi Aqiva and Bar Kochba," in Green, *Approaches*, 131. Also Schäfer, *Der Bar Kochba Aufstand* (Tübingen, 1981).

73 On the messianic character of the term *Nasi* and its relation to *melek* (king), see Jon D. Levenson (1976), 88–95.

74 Leo Midlenberg, "Bar Kokhba Coins and Documents," *Harvard Studies in Classical Philology* 84 (1986): 311–55.

75 "The rebels proclaimed on their coinage, from the start, their ambition to take Jerusalem, but we have no reason to think they succeeded." Midlenberg (1986), 90.

76 John Wilkinson, *Jerusalem As Jesus Knew It: Archaeology as Evidence* (Jerusalem: 1978), 178–79.

77 J. Heinemann, "The Blessing, He Who [Re]builds Jerusalem, and Its Transformations," Hayyim Schirmann *Jubilee* volume (Jerusalem: 1970), 73–101 (in Hebrew).

78 "The Rabbinic literature in general looks forward to a restored Jerusalem under earthly conditions. The new city is described in detail in terms which are often fantastic, but the welter of imagination bestowed upon the subject does not alter the fact that what the rabbis hoped for, and described as 'the Jerusalem of the age to come,' was essentially the material capital of a material state" C. K. Barrett,

"The Eschatology of the Epistle to the Hebrews," in *The Background of the New Testament and Its Eschatology,* ed. W. D. Davies and D. Daube (Cambridge: 1956), 374.

79 Hippolytus, *haer.* 9.30. In the words of Rabbi Samuel (third century): "The only difference between this world and the days of the Messiah is that on that day we will not be subject to foreign rule" (*b. Ber.* 34b).

Chapter 3
Blessed Are the Meek for They Shall Possess the Land

1 Matt 27:53. See also Rev 11:2; Tob 13:9; 1 Macc 2:7; 2 Macc 3:1. Irenaeus says that Jewish Christians honored Jerusalem as if it were the "house of God" (*haer.* 1.26.2).

2 This was noted by early Christian writers. See Jerome, *ep.* 46.5.2.

3 See also Matthew 19:28: "Truly, I say to you, in the new world, when the Son of man shall sit on his glorious throne, you who have followed me will also sit on twelve thrones, judging the twelve tribes of Israel." Jerusalem is not mentioned, but "twelve tribes" implies "restoration" and restoration would take place in Jerusalem. On the motif of gathering the twelve tribes, see the discussion of E. P. Sanders, *Jesus and Judaism* (Philadelphia: 1985), 95–98. The "memory of the twelve tribes," says Sanders, "remained so acute that 'twelve' would necessarily mean restoration" (98).

4 Admittedly the texts do not make this explicit, but the language is instructive. Note the phrasing in the passage just cited from Matthew 23, "You [Jerusalem] will not *see* me until you say, 'Blessed is he who comes in the name of the Lord.'" Or Acts 3:21 in a sermon of Peter, preached in Jerusalem, "Repent . . . that he may send the Messiah appointed for *you,* whom heaven must receive until the time of establishing all that God spoke by the mouth of his holy prophets of old" (Acts 3:19–21).

5 T. Francis Glasson, "Schweitzer's Influence—Blessing or Bane?" *JTS* 28 (1977): 289–302.

6 The new *Harper's Bible Dictionary* (San Francisco: 1985) has no article s.v. "land."

7 "That the expression is metaphorical in Matt 5:5 there can be no doubt" G. H. Dalman, *The Words of Jesus* (Edinburgh: 1962), 1:126. Also G. Strecker, "Das Land Israel in frühchristlicher Zeit," in Strecker (1983), 193. For a full discussion of the "land" in the New Testament, see W. D. Davis, *The Gospel and the Land* (Berkeley: 1974), 161–376; and R. J. Vair, "The Old Testament Promise of the Land as Reinterpreted in First- and Second-Century Christianity" (Ph.D. diss., Graduate Theological Union, Berkeley, 1979).

8 No matter how one translates the phrase, its meaning is elusive. For one thing this beatitude is found only in Matthew, not in the parallel set of sayings in Luke. For another, it seems to be a citation of Psalm 37. Further, its location in the ancient manuscripts shifts. In some manuscripts it appears in second place, in others in third place. This uncertainty as to where it belongs may be a sign that it was an interpolation. Finally, it appears (to some interpreters) to duplicate the

sentiment expressed in the first beatitude: "Blessed are the poor in spirit for theirs is the kingdom of heaven." No doubt the passage in the Gospel of John has influenced Christian interpretation; "In my Father's house are many rooms; if it were not so, would I have told you that I go to prepare a place for you? And when I go and prepare a place for you, I will come again and will take you to myself, that where I am you may be also" (John 14:2–3). Also Phil 3:20: "But our commonwealth is in heaven." On the beatitude, see Davies (1974), 359–62. The Didache cites the beatitude (3.7), and one early Latin manuscript translates "land" as "holy land." The Latin text reads "quia mansueti possidebunt sanctam terram." The Latin version may reflect the original text of that section of the Didache, the "Two Ways" which had its origin among the Jews. Jean Audet, *La Didachè, Instructions des Apôtres* (Paris: 1958), 132–33.

9 Of course Paul set a precedent: "The promise to Abraham and his descendants, that they should *inherit the world,* did not come through the law but through the righteousness of faith" (Rom 4:13). For *aretz* as "earth" at Qumran, see 1QSb 5.24, 1QpHab 3.1; 13.4.

10 In a brief midrash on Psalm 37 found at Qumran the phrase "possess the land" was interpreted to refer to the "congregation of [God's] elect who do His will." Here "possess the land" seems to have become a metaphor for a good and holy life. Elsewhere in the commentary "land" is taken to mean the entire earth. But then the midrash becomes very concrete; "They shall possess the High Mountain of Israel [forever] and shall enjoy [everlasting delights] in His Sanctuary." See 4QpPs 37.2 and 3. Also *CD* 1.7–8; 3.7,10; 13.21 for *eretz* as the Land of Israel. See also *War Scroll,* 1QM 19.4–5, "Fill your land with glory and your inheritance with blessing." The next line reads, "Rejoice greatly O Zion, O Jerusalem show yourself with jubilation. Rejoice, all you cities of Judah."

11 Günther Bornkam, *Jesus of Nazareth* (New York: 1960), 158.

12 Sanders (1985), 62–65.

13 "Thus we conclude that Jesus publicly predicted or threatened the destruction of the temple, that the statement was shaped by his expectation of the arrival of the eschaton, that he probably also expected a new temple to be given by God from heaven, and that he made a demonstration which prophetically symbolized the coming event" (Sanders [1985], 75).

14 It is, however, interesting to compare Jesus with the seventeenth-century Jewish messianic figure, Sabbatai Sevi. See Gershen Scholem, *Sabbatai Sevi, The Mystical Messiah* (Princeton: 1973), 159ff.

15 4QFlor. See D. Flusser, "Two Notes on the Midrash on 2 Sam. vii," *IEJ* 9 (1959): 99–109.

16 Flusser (1959), 102. A noteworthy difference between Jesus, as interpreted by Sanders and Flusser, and Justin and Irenaeus is that second-century Christian writers (including the Apocalypse) did not think the destruction of the old temple implied the expectation of a new temple. No doubt one of the reasons for this was that Justin and Irenaeus lived long after the temple had been destroyed, and Christian thought and exegesis saw theological significance in the demise of the temple. Some think it was possible to imagine a restored Jerusalem without a temple. See Lloyd Gaston, *No Stone on Another* (Leiden: 1970). But that seems

unlikely. See R. J. McKelvey, *The New Temple: The Church in the New Testament* (Oxford: 1969), and Sanders (1985), 76ff.

17 G. B. Caird (1965) 5.

18 Sanders (1985), 118–19.

19 I am grateful to Harold Attridge for answering my several queries about the epistle. See his *The Epistle to the Hebrews: A Commentary on the Epistle to the Hebrews* (Philadelphia: 1989). I have learned much from George Wesley Buchanan's insightful commentary on Hebrews in the *Anchor Bible* (Garden City: 1972).

20 Besides the passage from Justin Martyr cited earlier, this is one of the few places where Joshua in mentioned in early Christian literature. When Joshua is mentioned, it is usually to draw a parallel with the Greek form of the name (*Iesous*): *Barn.* 12:8; Clement of Alexandria, *paed.* 1.7.60; Origen, *Jo.* 6.44.228–29; Eusebius, *d.e.* 4.17.

21 On the meaning of the term "rest," see *Sifre on Deuteronomy,* Piska 2. Commenting on a passage from Numbers, the "ark of the covenant . . . went before them three days' journey to seek out a 'rest' [or resting place] for them," R. Judah says, "'Rest' always refers to the land of Israel, as it is said, 'For you are not as yet come to rest and the inheritance which the Lord your God gives you.'"

22 Hans Windisch, *Der Hebräerbrief* (Tübingen: 1931), 34.

23 C. Spicq, *L'Épitre aux Hébreux* (Paris: 1953), 2:82.

24 The terminology of Hebrews 11 suggests a contrast not between earthly/heavenly but between impermanent/secure. At one point its phrase "strangers and exiles on the earth [land]" (11:13) seems to echo the words of 1 Chr 29:15, "For we are strangers and sojurners before you, as all our fathers were; our days on the earth are like a shadow, and there is no abiding." For the Chronicler, the Israelites were hoping for a more certain and stable kingdom in Jerusalem, as David's prayer makes plain (1 Chr 26:10–19).

25 R. Williamson, *Philo and the Epistle to the Hebrews* (Leiden: 1970), 491. For other commentators, see Buchanan (1972), 189.

26 Whether Jerusalem was still standing when Hebrews was written is debated by scholars. Hebrews' majestic prose and balanced periods belong to a rhetorical tradition that eschewed allusions to actual persons and events. As we have seen, other Jews could envision a new and more abiding city even while Jerusalem was standing.

27 I take chapter 13 to be integral to the epistle as a whole. See Attridge's commentary.

28 On Revelation, see G. B. Caird, *A Commentary on the Revelation of St. John the Divine* (London: 1966); also Josephine Ford's commentary in the *Anchor Bible* (Garden City: 1975); for the interpretation of Revelation in the early church, see Georg Kretschmar, *Die Offenbarung des Johannes. Die Geschichte ihrer Auslegung im 1. Jahrtausend* (Stuttgart: 1985). Revelation's idea of a temporary millennium, as distinct from a period of messianic rule, has few parallels in Jewish sources. One of the earliest commentators on Revelation, Victorinus, linked the eschatological vision of the Apocalypse with the land promise to Abraham. See his *Commentarius in Apocalypsin 20–21* (ed. Haussleiter [Vienna: 1916]), 138ff.

29 For an overview of chiliasm in early Christianity, see Hans Bietenhard, "The Millennial Hope in the Early Church," *Scottish Journal of Theology* 6 (1953): 12–30; W. Bauer, "Chiliasmus" in *RAC* 2 (1954) 1073–78; Léon Gry, *Le Millénarisme dans ses Origines et son Développement* (Paris: 1904); Hill (1992).

30 Justin mentions the thousand-year reign, but there is no way he could fit it comfortably into his scheme. In the book of Revelation the reign of a thousand years belongs to one epoch (20:4–6) and the descent of Jerusalem to another (chap. 21). Justin makes no such distinction. In Justin's scene, the city of Jerusalem will appear at the beginning of the period of restoration when those who "seek the good of Jerusalem" will be gathered together in the holy city (*dial.* 24.2). There is no suggestion (as there is in the Apocalypse) that there will be a "transitory state, to be replaced by something totally different" (Oskar Skarsaune, *The Proof from Prophecy* [Leiden, 1987], 403). Irenaeus does not mention the Apocalypse until the very end of his discussion, and only after he has provided ample biblical support for his views. He does not cite Revelation 20 about the thousand-year reign; he mentions only the passage in chapter 21 about a new Jerusalem descending to earth. In Irenaeus's view Christ's reign on earth is eternal, not for a thousand years. On this point, see Friedrich Loofs, *Theophilus von Antiochien adversus Marcionem und die anderen theologischen Quellen bei Irenaeus* (TU 46; Leipzig: 1930), 337. Also W. Schoedel, *The Apostolic Fathers* (Camden, N.J., 1967), 5:96. Richard Landes observes that though millenarianism "implies a thousand year kingdom, the crucial element lies not in whether the kingdom to come will last 100, 400, or 1,000 years, but that at the beginning of this period a total transformation in the nature of terrestrial power relations takes place ('The meek will inherit the Land')." See his "Lest the Millennium Be Fulfilled: Apocalyptic Expectations and the Pattern of Western Chronography, 100–800 CE," in *The Use and Abuse of Eschatology in the Middle Ages,* ed. W. Verbeke, D. Verhelst, and A. Welkenhuysen (Leuven: 1988), 206.

31 On the *Dialogue*, see A. L. Williams, *Justin Martyr: The Dialogue with Trypho; Translation, Introduction, and Notes* (London: 1930); L. W. Barnard, "Justin Martyr's Eschatology," *VC* 19 (1965): 86–98; and Skarsaune.

32 Another right-minded Christian was Papias, whose writings Eusebius places at the time of Ignatius and Polycarp, i.e., during the reign of Trajan (*h.e.* 3.36.1–2). According to Eusebius, Papias believed in a "thousand year period after the Resurrection from the dead when Christ's kingdom would be established physically upon this earth of ours" (*Frg.* 2c; *h.e.* 3.39.11–13). On Papias, see Schoedel, 94–96; also U. H. J. Kortner, *Papias von Hierapolis: ein Beitrag zur Geschichte des frühen Christentums* (Göttingen: 1983).

33 Skarsaune, 337–38.

34 Whether this means that Christians, like Justin, had begun to call this better land the "holy land" is uncertain, but a passage in the True Word, a book written by the philosopher Celsus against Christianity in mid second century, prompted Origen to discuss the meaning of the term "holy land" for Christians (Cels. 7.28). The idea of a heavenly city can be found in sources contemporary with Celsus. See Lucian of Samosata, *VH* 2.11–13. On this topic, see Hans Dieter Betz, *Lukian von Samosata und das neue Testament* (*TU* 76; Berlin: 1961), 92–96.

35 On Irenaeus's eschatology and its place in his theological program, see Gustaf Wingren, *Man and the Incarnation* (Philadelphia: 1959), 180–92; O'Rourke Boyle, "Irenaeus' Millennial Hope: A Polemical Weapon," *Recherches de Théologie ancienne et médiévale* 36 (1969): 5–16.

36 Irenaeus's "comprehensive view of the renewal of nature in the *regnum* [kingdom] is in complete harmony with what is central to [his] theology" Wingren, 185. The term *kingdom* in the Syriac Christian tradition preserved its sense of a messianic reign of Christ. See Robert Murray, *Symbols of Church and Kingdom: A Study in Early Syriac Tradition* (Cambridge: 1975), 239–46, 282–84.

37 The idea that the new kingdom will extend to all the earth is thoroughly Jewish. See Zech 14:9, *Sib. Or.* 3:698–726, *2 Bar.* 29, Jubilees 32:18–19. Later Jewish texts speak of the Land of Israel expanding "like a fig that is narrow below and broadens upwards" and Jerusalem extending as far as Damascus (*Sifre Deut.* Piska 1).

38 *Temple Scroll,* col. 59.

39 For example, in the *Book of Elijah,* discussed in chapter 10.

40 See, for example, Codex Brucianus 34, cited in n. 63 in previous chapter. Also *Odes Sol.* 11:18,21, Epistle of Barnabas 6.10–13.

41 Melito of Sardis (late second century) had a different view. In his *Paschal Homily,* he wrote, "The Jerusalem below was precious, but it is worthless now because of the Jerusalem above" (45).

42 For Paul "kingdom" usually designates a future "inheritance" (1 Cor. 6.9–10; 15.50; Gal 5.21; Eph 5.5), a time after Christ's resurrection when all enemies will be overcome and all things will be subject to God. "Then comes the end, when he [Christ] delivers the kingdom to God the Father after destroying every rule and every authority and power" (1 Cor 15:20, 23–28). This is one of the texts deployed by Irenaeus in defense of an earthly kingdom (*haer.* 5.36.2). The one place where Paul discusses "inheritance" (Hans Dieter Betz, *Galatians; A Commentary on Paul's Letter to the Churches in Galatia* [Philadelphia: 1979], 159) in any detail is in the passage in Galatians that begins with a discussion of Abraham's seed (chap. 3) and concludes with a citation from Isaiah 54 on the restoration of Jerusalem and the rebuilding of the cities of Judea. Isaiah 54 is cited as a restorationist text in Tobit 14 and in later Jewish apocalypses it was interpreted to mean that the "Jerusalem above" would one day descend to earth so that the exiles could return to her with rejoicing. Jerome mentions it as one of the passages cited by Jews and judaizing Christians on the rebuilding of Jerusalem and the establishment of an earthly kingdom (*Comm. in Esa* 54.1; *CC* 73a, 601), and Irenaeus cites vs. ll-14 in the catena of passages that promise a rebuilding of Jerusalem (Irenaeus, *haer.* 5.34.4); Betz, 246 gives some references, but see the *Sefer Zerubbabel,* to be discussed in chapter 10. If Paul is speaking eschatologically,—and the citation from Isaiah makes this likely,—the distinction he draws between the two cities may not be between a "heavenly city" (a term he does not use) and an "earthly city" (which he also does not use), but between Jerusalem as it is at present (in Greek, Jerusalem as it is *now*) and a future Jerusalem. The difference between the two cities is temporal, not metaphysical, between what exists at the present and is imperfect and flawed and what will one day take its place, a glorious new

city not made by human hands but graven on the palms of God. In this view "Jerusalem above" does not designate a transcendent reality to which one aspires but a model of what was yet to be. When Paul is read in the context of Jewish restorationist hopes, one can see how 1 Corinthians 15 and Galatians 4 provided biblical support for Irenaeus's belief in a future Jerusalem on earth. It is of course also easy to see how it could be taken metaphorically.

43 Like the book of Revelation, Irenaeus has no place for the temple in the new Jerusalem. No doubt one of the reasons for this is that by the time Irenaeus lived the destruction of the temple not only was an indisputable fact of history, it was also seen as the fulfillment of a prophecy of Jesus (Matt 24:1–2).

44 Alain Le Boulluec, *La notion d'hérésie dans la littérature grecque IIe-IIIe siécles* (Paris: 1985), 110.

45 Melito of Sardis, *Paschal Homily* 93. See A. E. Harvey, "Melito and Jerusalem," *JTS* 17 (1966): 401–04.

46 Justin, *dial.* 78 and *Prot. Jas.* 18 (ed. deStrycker, *Subsidia Hagiographica* 33 [1961], 146).

47 The phrase "among us" is from a sermon on Stephen the martyr preached by Hesychius of Jerusalem. See chapter 6, n. 87.

Chapter 4
Heavenly Jerusalem, the Mother of Us All

1 As can be seen in *Marc.* 3.24, Tertullian's belief in the establishment of an earthly kingdom, like that of Irenaeus and Justin, is a Christian version of the Jewish hope of restoration. Drawing on Ezekiel and the Apocalypse, he says that the new Jerusalem will be a heavenly city that comes down to earth. Recently, he reports, the city was sighted "suspended in the sky" over Judea. For forty days the city appeared in the morning and gradually disappeared as the day advanced. Tertullian also adds, like Irenaeus, a theological explanation for his belief about the future earthly Jerusalem: "For it is both just, and worthy of God, that his servants should also have joy in that place where they have suffered affliction in his name." Commenting on this passage, G. Scholem (1973) wrote, "It is this same feeling which made the medieval rabbis quote Psalm 90:15, 'Make us glad according to the days wherein thou hast afflicted us, and the years wherein we have seen evil,' and argue that the messianic era ought to be equal in length to the period of suffering and exile" (98).

2 Chiliasm, however, did not die. See the preface to book 18 of Jerome's *Commentary on Isaiah* (*CC* 73a, 741). Some of the noteworthy figures after Origen are Victorinus of Petau, Lactantius, Apollinaris of Laodicea, Tyconius, and even the young Augustine (*civ.* 20.7, 9). See Walter Bauer, "Chiliasmus" in *RAC* 2, 1073–78.

3 "Every heresy and division in the Church of the patristic period in both dogma and spiritual teaching and practice can be traced to the writings and personal influence of Origen." Thomas Hopko in the preface to Robert Payne, *The Holy Fire: The Story of the Fathers of the Eastern Church* (Crestwood, N.Y.: 1980), ix.

4 For a critical analysis of the sources for Origen's life, see Pierre Nautin, *Origène: sa vie et son oeuvre* (Paris: 1977). For accounts of his life and teaching in English, see Joseph Wilson Trigg, *Origen: The Bible and Philosophy in the Third-Century Church* (Atlanta: 1983), and Henri Crouzel, *Origen* (San Francisco: 1989).

5 On Caesarea in this period, see Lee I. Levine, *Caesarea under Roman Rule* (Leiden: 1975), and the catalogue of the recent exhibition at the Smithsonian edited by Kenneth Holum, Robert L. Hohlfelder et al., *King Herod's Dream: Caesarea on the Sea* (New York: 1988).

6 Gregory Thaumatugus, *Pan. Or.* 9.123,126. On Origen as teacher, see Robert L. Wilken, "Alexandria: A School for Training in Virtue," in *Schools of Thought in the Christian Tradition,* ed. Patrick Henry (Philadelphia: 1984), 15–30.

7 How much Hebrew Origen knew is debated. It seems unlikely he spoke the language, but with the help of Jewish scholars he was able to consult the Hebrew text of the Scriptures. Nicholas de Lange, *Origen and the Jews: Studies in Jewish-Christian Relations in Third-Century Palestine* (Cambridge: 1976), 21–23.

8 See David J. Halperin, "Origen, Ezekiel's Merkabah, and the Ascension of Moses," *CH* 50 (1981): 261–75, and Reuven Kimelman, "Rabbi Yohanan and Origen on the Song of Songs: A Third Century Jewish–Christian Disputation," *HTR* 73 (1980): 567–95. On the general question of Origen's relation with Jews in Caesarea, see de Lange and Hans Bietenhard, *Caesarea, Origenes und die Juden* (Stuttgart: 1974).

9 The commentary, as a literary form for the interpretation of a text, had been developed by the grammarians of Alexandria, e.g., Aristarchus, who had written line-by-line expositions on the writings of Homer, Hesiod, Pindar, et al. Origen was the first Christian interpreter to adapt the commentary to the interpretation of the Scriptures. Its distinguishing feature was that it required of the interpreter a line-by-line exposition of the text, so that "nothing remained undiscussed" (Origen, *hom. 14.1 in Num.*). In a sermon Origen was limited by the demands of time and the expectations of his hearers, but it is still remarkable how scrupulously his homilies follow the text verse by verse. On this point, see E. Klostermann, "Formen der exegetischen Arbeiten des Origenes," *TLZ* (1947): 203–08.

10 The term "Jewish Scriptures" is Origen's: *ep.* 1.5.

11 Levine (1975) 70.

12 For a recent discussion of the literature on Origen's principles of interpretation, e.g., the works of Daniélou, Hanson, deLubac, see Karen J. Torjesen, *Hermeneutical Procedure and Theological Method in Origen's Exegesis* (Berlin: 1986), 1–12.

13 See in particular his commentaries on Leviticus, Numbers, and Joshua. A good example of the difficulties Origen faced can be seen in his commentary on Leviticus 12, the laws concerning purification of a woman after childbirth (*hom. 8 in Lev.*); also his interpretation of the conquest of Ai in Joshua 7 (*hom. 8 in Jos.*).

14 Greek here is *holon ton noun* (*princ.* 4.3.5).

15 Tertullian says that according to the Jews the mission of the Messiah is directed "only to the Jewish people" (*Marc.* 3.21).

16 The term "promises" has a very specific referent. Dionysius, bishop of Alexandria (d. 264), wrote a treatise in two books entitled "On Promises" in which he dis-

cussed the biblical promises about the future of Jerusalem. The book was directed against the views of Nepos, a bishop in Egypt who had taken the promises in a "more Jewish fashion" (*h.e.* 7.24.1ff.). Tertullian's work "On the hope of the faithful" may belong to the same genre (*Marc.* 3.24).

17 Irenaeus, *haer.* 5.35.2; Tertullian, *Marc.* 3.24.

18 Origen gives a similar interpretation of Gal 4:21ff in *Cant.* 2.3 (1:6b); see also his discussion of Gal 4:26 in *hom. 5.13 in Jer.*

19 Kimelman, 567–95.

20 See also *Exod. Rab.* 23.10.

21 On Jerusalem as metropolis, see R. J. Zwi Werblowsky, "Metropolis of All Countries," in *Jerusalem Through All Generations* (Jerusalem: 1968), 172 (in Hebrew). Psalm 87:5, "And of Zion it shall be said, 'This one and that one were born in her,'" was understood to mean that Zion was the mother of Israel (Werblowsky, 173). In the LXX Zion became "mother Zion." On Zion as mother, see Isaiah 49:14–21; 50:1; 51:18; 54:1; 60:4.

22 Origen *cant. 2* (ed. Baehrens, *GCS,* 119).

23 See the saying of R. Yohanan in *b. Ta'an.* 5a discussed in chapter 2. For a similar idea in later Syriac Christianity, namely, that the earthly city images the heavenly city (and hence the importance of pilgrimage to Jerusalem), see J. M. Fiey, "Le pélerinage des Nestoriens et Jacobites à Jérusalem," in *Cahiers de Civilisation médiévale* 12 (1969): 113–26.

24 See also *hom. 5.13 in Jer.* on Jer 4:2–3. Commenting on the designation "holy city" in Matt 27:53, Origen says that it is more blessed to see the earth moved and tombs opened and to ascend to higher mysteries than to see a corporeal city (*ser.in Mt.* at Matt 27:51). Hippolytus said that the Jerusalem above is "the mother of the living" (*haer.* 5.7.37), and Clement of Alexandria wrote, "We have no country on earth" (*paed.* 3.8.41). On church as "mother," see C. Plumpe, *Mater Ecclesiae: An Inquiry into the Concept of the Church as Mother in Early Christianity* (Washington: 1943).

25 In this passage (*Cels.* 7.28) Origen gives a "spiritual" interpretation of the "return to Jerusalem" and the "restoration of what is called the place and city of God." Earlier in the same work he uses the term "restoration" to designate a political event. After the destruction of Jerusalem the Jewish people were overthrown, their laws made void, and "they will not be restored again" (*Cels.* 4.22).

26 See Israel L. Levine, "The Age of Rabbi Judah the Prince," in *Eretz Israel from the Destruction of the Second Temple to the Muslim Conquest,* ed. Zvi Baras et al., 94–118 (in Hebrew); D. Sperber, *Roman Palestine 200–400: The Land* (Ramat-Gan: 1978); S. Lieberman, "Palestine in the Third and Fourth Centuries," *JQR* 36 (1946): 329–70; Joshua Schwartz, "Aliya from Babylonia during the Amoraid Period 200–500 C.E.," in *The Jerusalem Cathedra,* ed. J. Levine (1983), 3:58–69. See Eric M. Meyers, "Early Judaism and Christianity in the Light of Archaeology," *BA* 51 (1988): 69–79, and Dennis Groh, "Jews and Christians in Late Roman Palestine: Towards a New Chronology," *BA* 51 (1988): 80–98, both articles with extensive bibliography.

27 On the change of attitudes, see John Gager, "The Dialogue of paganism with Judaism: Bar Kochba to Julian," *HUCA* 44 (1973) 89–118.

28 On the patriarchate, see Lee I. Levine, "The Jewish Patriarch (*Nasi*) in Third Century Palestine," *Aufstieg und Niedergang der römischen Welt* 19.2 (Berlin: 1979): 649–88.

29 "We have seen how the re-establishment of a central Jewish authority provided the focus for rebuilding national life in the Land of Israel after the Destruction. This central authority consisted of two elements: the High Court and the Patriarchate. . . . These two institutions . . . are a principal factor—perhaps even the determining factor—in the history of the several centuries after the destruction" (Alon [1980], 1:185).

30 Origen, *ep.* 1.14. For the Jewish view of the patriarch as a king, see *Tosefta Sabb.* 7(8).18 (ed. Zuckermandel, 119), where it is said that one may make a funeral pyre for kings and for patriarchs but not for ordinary citizens.

31 Israel Levi, "L'Origine Davidique de Hillel," *Revue des Études Juives* 31 (1895): 202–11.

32 On the title *Nasi,* H. Mantel, *Studies in the History of the Sanhedrin* (Cambridge, Mass.: 1961), chap. 1; also Jon Levenson, *Theology of the Program of Restoration of Ezekiel, 40–48* (Missoula, Mont.: 1976), 57ff.

33 In the LXX the final clause reads: "And he will be the expectation of the Gentiles." Earlier Christian interpretations of this text do not relate it to the patriarchate. See Justin, *dial.* 120 and *1 apol.* 32; 54. Origen's interpretation of Gen 49:10 seems set directly against Jewish interpretations of the text: "'The scepter shall not depart from Judah.' This refers to the head of the diaspora (the exilarch) in Babylonia who rules Israel with a scepter. 'The staff from between his feet.' This refers to the descendants of Hillel who teach Torah to the people" (*b. Sanh.* 5a).

34 Ownership of the Land of Israel is debated in Jewish sources from this period. It was permissible to sell felled trees to Gentiles, but not those that are still standing (because that meant selling the ground). Similarly it was forbidden to lease "houses" or fields in the "Land of Israel" to Gentiles (*m. 'Abod. Zar.* 1.8). "The underlying motivation for all these prohibitions was the desire to forestall the permanent settlement of foreigners in the Land of Israel, by preventing them for acquiring land and other economically important property" (Alon [1980], 1:286).

35 "Their land" also in Tertullian, *Jud.* 12; *res.* 30, *Marc.* 3.23.

36 Shmuel Safrai, "Pilgrimage to Jerusalem after the Destruction of the Second Temple," *Jerusalem in the Second Temple Period,* Abraham Schalit Memorial Volume, ed. A. Oppenheimer et al. (Jerusalem: 1980), 376–93 (in Hebrew).

37 The most famous passage is Jerome, *Soph.* 1.15–16 (*CC* 76a, 673). For Jewish practice, see *Lam. Rab.* 1.52: "In the past I used to go up with songs and psalms before the Holy One, blessed be he, as it is written 'with the voice of joy and praise' (Ps 42:4). Now I go up with weeping and come down with weeping." In time pilgrimage to the ruins of the temple became a yearly ritual on 9 Ab with its own distinctive features.

38 As in other discussions of the Jewish hope of restoration of Jerusalem, Origen's arguments in the *Homilies on Joshua* are historical as well as theological: "If then, O Jew, when you come to Jerusalem the earthly city, you find it overthrown and reduced to ashes and cinders, do not weep as you do now in the fashion of children; do not lament, but seek the heavenly city in place of the earthly. Raise

your eyes and look and you will find the 'heavenly Jerusalem which is the mother of all.'" Jews had not abandoned the hope they would one day obtain their inheritance, i.e. "possess the land." "If you see the altar abandoned," says Origen, "do not be sorrowful; if you do not find a priest, do not despair. There is an altar in heaven. . . . Therefore it is through the goodness and mercy of God that you have been deprived of your earthly inheritance that you might seek an inheritance in heaven" (*hom. 17.1 in Jos.*).

39 See the discussion by Annie Jaubert in *Origène. Homélies sur Josué. Texte Latin, Introduction et Notes* (*SC* 71, Paris: 1960), 17–58. On the general theme, E. Lamirande, "Jerusalem Celeste," in *Dictionnaire de spiritualité* 8 (1974): 944–58: K. L. Schmidt, "Jerusalem als Urbild und Abbild," *Eranos Jahrbuch* 18 (1950): 207–48; and Norbert Brox, "Das 'Irdische Jerusalem' in der altchristlichen Theologie," *Kairos* 28 (1986): 152–73.

Cf. *2 Enoch* 55:2, "For tomorrow I shall go up to heaven, to the uppermost Jerusalem to my eternal inheritance." For Origen the reconstruction of the temple in Jerusalem was seen as the reconstituting of the soul after the Fall into sin, the building of the church, and the restoration of souls. See Ives Marie Duval, "Vers le commentaire sur Aggée d'Origene," in *Origeniana Quarta,* ed. Lothar Lies ("Innsbrucker theologische Studien," Bd. 19; Innsbruck: 1987), 7–15.

40 Matt 5:5 is interpreted as the "good land in the heavens" in *princ.* 2.3.7. Also *hom. 9.3 in Jer.* On occasion Origen, like Justin before him and Jerome later, can use the term "holy land" simply as a designation of the biblical Palestine (*Hom. 1.1 in Ezech*).

41 The Jews have a point, documented by the New Testament. When John's disciples were sent to inquire whether Jesus was the one to come, i.e., the Messiah, Jesus says, "Go and tell John what you hear and see: the blind receive their sight and the lame walk, lepers are cleansed and the deaf hear." These are the signs of the Messiah according to Isaiah 29:18–19; 35:5–6; 61:1. See also Luke 7:18–22 and Luke 4:17–21. This is also the argument of contemporary millennialists: "If the prophecies of the Old Testament concerning the promises of the future made to Abraham and David are to be fulfilled then there must be a future period, the millennium, in which they can be fulfilled, for the church is not now fulfilling them in any literal sense" Charles Caldwell Ryrie, *Dispensationalism Today* (Chicago: 1965), 158.

42 These exchanges between Jews and Christians in *First Principles* (as presented by Origen) confirm Gershom Scholem's observation: "They [the Jews] saw no spiritual progress in a messianic conception that admittedly abdicated from the sphere of history and denied that redemption was a public act, manifest on this earth in soul *and* body. They prided themselves on their refusal to betray their idea, and distrusted a spirituality whose redemption was not realized on earth as in heaven." Scholem (1973), 94.

43 For chiliasm in the West, see Victorinus's commentary on the Apocalypse 21:1–2; also Lactantius: "[There will come a time when] the holy city will be planted in the middle of the earth in which God himself the builder may dwell together with the righteous" (*div. inst.* 7.24). On Lactantius, see Valentin Fabrega, "Die chiliastische Lehre des Laktanz," in *JAC* 17 (1975): 126–46.

44 There is other evidence of chiliastic beliefs in Egypt at this time. Fragments of the *Apocalypse of Paul* speak of the "land of inheritance" (citing Mt 5.5) as the scene of an earthly kingdom (E. A. W. Budge, *Miscellaneous Coptic Texts* [London: 1915], 1049). Another fragment speaks of the "thousand years of thine inheritance" (*Frg.* 1.19). See Hugh G. Evelyn White, *The Monasteries of the Wadi Natrun* (New York: 1926), 1:19.

45 Some later chiliasts, e.g., Apollinaris, envisioned a temple in the restored city. He wrote a work in two books against Dionysius of Alexandria (Jerome, *Comm. in Esa.*, book 18 preface [*CC* 73a, 741, ll. 28–30])

46 Robert L. Wilken, "Early Christian Chiliasm, Jewish Messianism, and the Idea of the Holy Land," *HTR* 79 (1986): 298–307.

47 Elsewhere Origen argues that the power of Jesus is proved through the historical fact that he has brought about moral reformation in many people (*Cels.* 1.26, 31, 43, 46–47).

48 On Eusebius's writings, see Timothy D. Barnes, *Constantine and Eusebius* (Cambridge: 1981), 81–190.

49 On Eusebius's interpretation of Isaiah, see Michael Hollerich, "The Godly Polity the Light of Prophecy: A Study of Eusebius of Caesarea's Commentary on Isaiah" (Ph.D. diss., University of Chicago, 1987). I cite by page and line from the edition of Joseph Ziegler in *GCS, Eusebius Werke,* Neunter Band. *Der Jesajakommentar* (Berlin: 1975). On Eusebius's shifting attitudes toward Jerusalem and the holy places, see P. W. L. Walker, *Holy City, Holy Places?* (Oxford: 1990).

50 See, for example, Eusebius's comments on the following texts: Isa 1:19, "eat the good of the land" (10); 4:2–3, "fruit of the land shall be the pride . . . of Israel" (27); 8:18, "Lord of hosts who dwells on Mt. Zion" (60); 18:7, "a nation mighty and conquering whose land the rivers divide" (123); 24:23, "the Lord of hosts will reign on Mt. Zion and in Jerusalem" (161); 40:9, "cities of Judah" (252); 51:11, "and the ransomed of the Lord shall return and come to Zion with singing" (324); 57:13, "he who takes refuge in me shall possess the land, and shall inherit my holy mountain" (354). In these passages (as well as others) Eusebius cites Hebrews 12, "You have come to Mt. Zion . . . the heavenly Jerusalem" to support his interpretation of the words of Isaiah.

51 Elsewhere Eusebius calls Judea "their own land" (*d.e.* 6:18; 284c).

52 In this passage Eusebius appeals to Galatians 4, not Hebrews 12. In some passages he relies on the third beatitude to support a "spiritual" reading of the text. At Isaiah 1:9, "You shall eat the good of the land," he says that the prophecy refers to a "heavenly land" not, as the Jews understand, a "somatic promise." For the savior taught, "blessed are the meek for they shall possess the land" (10, 1–11). A similar argument appears at Isaiah 4:2, "the fruit of the land shall be the pride and glory of the survivors of Israel." This text, says Eusebius, speaks of the "entire earth and the whole world." The "survivors" who will be called "holy" (4:3) are those who are worthy to "be recorded for life eternal in the 'heavenly Jerusalem' (Heb 12:22)" (26.36–27.5).

53 See his *Psalm Commentary* at Psalm 87:1 (86:1), "on the holy mount stands the city he founded." Eusebius contrasts the "divine commonwealth" founded by Christ with the earthbound city envisioned by the Jews. It is impious to think the

text applies to the metropolis in Palestine founded by the Jews. "Their hope is entirely inclined below and they anticipate a city on earth" (*PG* 23: 1044–45). See also his commentary on the phrase "possess the land" in Psalm 37: "If a good land is promised to the saints, those who wait on the Lord will inherit it. With the other good things that are enumerated, this same inheritance will be given to them. If the heavenly Mt. Zion of God, Jerusalem, is in the heavens, the land promised to the worthy saints must also be considered to be in heaven" (*PG* 23.328a).

54 The words in Genesis 49, "there shall not cease a prince from Judah," mean "that when there is a cessation of their [Jewish] rulers, the one prophesied will come." Judah, Eusebius notes, does not refer to the tribe of Judah but to the "whole race of the Jews." If so, the prophecy can be applied to the condition of the Jewish people today among whom there exists no "kingdom" (*d.e.* 96a). With the coming of the one prophesied, the Messiah, "there were no longer any rulers styled kings in Judah or governors in Israel" (*d.e.* 369b). In the *Evangelical Demonstration,* a biblical defense of Christianity to the Jews, the first topic that he addresses concerns the promise of the land to Abraham and his descendants. "And the Lord said to Abram, 'Go up from your country and your kindred and your father's house to the land that I will show you.'" This passage was the ultimate warrant for the claims Jews made about the land of Israel. Eusebius, however, deliberately ignores the "ethnic" features of the text (the land was promised to the descendants of Abraham) and accents the phrase "in you *all* the tribes of the earth will be blessed." The promise to Abraham, Eusebius continues, referred to all the nations of the earth, not just to his descendants according to the flesh. The laws of Moses were given to a particular people, but Abraham, who preceded Moses and represents an older way of life, was the father of primordial religion destined for all people. As evidence for this claim, observes Eusebius, the laws of Moses were intended only for the Jews; they have had no application outside of Judea. Certain laws could be fulfilled only in the land by people living in proximity to Jerusalem, for example, pilgrimage festivals, obligation to present a newly born child at the temple in Jerusalem, or laws of purification and pollution that required priests living in Jerusalem. Eusebius was, of course, aware that not all the laws of Moses were restricted to Judea, and not all required the temple. After the destruction of the temple, Jews continued to observe many of the laws, for example, the laws about the keeping of the Sabbath, circumcision, and food laws. But many could not be observed and some required that one did not live "far from Judea" (*d.e.* 18). He concludes, then, that the law of Moses was applicable only to the "inhabitants of Judea." Who were the inhabitants of Judea in Eusebius's day? The center of the Jewish community in Palestine was now located in Galilee. There *were* Jews in Jerusalem, and there seems to have been at least one synagogue, but the bulk of the Jewish population lived in Galilee, in Caesarea, and in the diaspora. Jerusalem, now called Aelia Capitolina, was a pagan city made up of "Greeks, foreigners and idolaters" (*PG* 23, 1044–45). Hence Eusebius is able to buttress his claim about the demise of Jewish institutions by pointing to the absence of Jewish life and institutions in Jerusalem. "Their once famous Mount Zion, instead of being, as once it was, the center of study and education . . . is a Roman farm like the rest of the country. Indeed with my own eyes I have seen bulls plowing there and the

holy place sown with seed" (*d.e.* 406b-c). Also *d.e.* 273d: "If our own observation has any value, we have seen in our own time Sion once so famous plowed with yokes of oxen by the Romans and utterly devastated, and Jerusalem, as the oracle says, deserted like a lodge." (trans.) On Jerusalem, see A. H. M. Jones, "The Urbanization of Palestine," *JRS* 21 (1931): 77–85.

55 In Bethlehem, says Eusebius, "a cave is shown by the inhabitants to those who come from abroad to see it" (*d.e.* 3.2; 97b). Also *d.e.* 7.2; 343b-c.

56 See *Acts of Pionius* on the land as a place of judgment. "I saw the land which to this day bears witness to the wrath of God" (4.18).

Chapter 5
A New Jerusalem Facing the Renowned City of Old

1 For a description of the traditional ceremony, see Servius's commentary on Vergil's *Aeneid* 5.755–56. He is commenting on the following passage: "Meanwhile Aeneas / Marked with a plow the limits of the town / And gave home sites by lot." On the Roman colony, see H. Vincent and F. M. Abel, *Jérusalem: Recherches de Topographie, d'archéologie et d'histoire*. Vol. 2: *Jérusalem Nouvelle* (Paris: 1914), 1–39.

2 The name, spelled Helya Capitolina, occurs in the Peutinger Table, a "map" or guide to the Roman world (and beyond) from the fourth century. K. Miller, *Itineraria Romana* (Rome: 1916), 833.

3 "Nothing was overlooked which could signify a total rupture with the past" (F. M. Abel, *Histoire de la Palestine depuis la conquête d'Alexandre jusqu'à l'invasion arabe* [Paris: 1952], 2:97).

4 *Chronicon Paschale* 119 (*PG* 92, 613).

5 F. C. Conybeare, ed., *The Dialogues of Athanasius and Zacchaeus and of Timothy and Aquila* (Oxford: 1898), 98 (Folio 130r of the Dialogue of Timothy and Aquila).

6 "From the time of Hadrian to the reign of Constantine—a period of approximately 180 years—the place of the Resurrection was occupied by a statue of Jupiter; on the rock where the cross had stood, a marble statue of Venus, set up by the pagans, was an object of worship" (Jerome, *ep.* 58.3). There is, however, dispute about what was actually on the site. See John Wilkinson, *Egeria's Travels*, 36ff., and Georg Kretschmar, "Festkalendar und Memorialstätten Jerusalem in altkirchlicher Zeit," in *Jerusalemer Heiligtumstraditionen in altkirchlicher und frühislamischer Zeit,* ed. H. Busse and G. Kretschmar (Wiesbaden: 1987), 62ff.

7 For the coins, see L. Kadman, *The Coins of Aelia Capitolina* (Jerusalem: 1956), 36–44.

8 The story can be found in Eusebius, *Martyrs of Palestine,* 2.9–13.

9 "Jerusalem was destroyed to make place for a city with a completely different character, established with its own rituals and organized according to the demands of an absolutely different civilization." Abel-Vincent, *Jerusalem* (1914), 2:1.

10 Eutychius, *Chronicles* (*CSCO* 471, 58; 472, 49). Eusebius identifies the home of a martyred deacon as Aelia (*mart. pal.* 11.5). This term occurs only intermittently in Christian writers.

11 H. Windisch, "Die ältesten christlichen Palaestinapilger," *Zeitschrift des deutschen Palästina-Vereins* 48 (1925): 145–58. More recently, E. D. Hunt, *Holy Land Pilgrimage in the Later Roman Empire AD 312–460* (Oxford: 1982), and Pierre Maraval, *Lieux saints et pèlerinages d'Orient. Histoire et géographie. Des origines à la conquête arabe* (Paris: 1985). Pilgrimage to Palestine will be discussed in the following chapter.

12 *Itinerarium Burdigalense* (*The Pilgrim of Bordeaux*) edited by P. Geyer and O. Cuntz in *CC*, vol. 175. Translation in Wilkinson, *Egeria's Travels.*

13 "It is a remarkable fact," writes S. G. F. Brandon "that the Mother Church of Christianity is known to us through no writing which can unhesitatingly be accepted as one of its own production." *The Fall of Jerusalem and the Christian Church* (London: 1957), 31.

14 Ibid., 167–84; Gerd Lüdemann, "The Successors of Pre-70 Jerusalem Christianity: A Critical Evaluation of the Pella-Tradition," in *Jewish and Christian Self-Definition,* ed. E. P. Sanders (Philadelphia: 1980), 1:161–73.

15 Hugh Jackson Lawlor and John Ernest Leonard Oulton, *Eusebius. Bishop of Caesarea. The Ecclesiastical History and The Martyrs of Palestine* (London: 1954), 2:167–70

16 "There is no ground for supposing that the Church of Aelia in 135 was a mere chance collection of Levantine Greeks looking up to the Church of Caesarea rather than back to the historic Church of Zion." William Telfer, *Cyril of Jerusalem and Nemesius of Emesa* (Philadelphia: 1955), 59.

17 *Martyrs of Palestine,* passim. Joseph Geiger, "The Spread of Christianity in *Eretz Israel* from the beginning until the time of Julian," in *Eretz Israel: From the Destruction of the Second Temple until the Muslim Conquest* (Jerusalem: 1982), 1:223–25 (in Hebrew). The largest Christian community was in Caesarea.

18 Günter Stemberger, *Juden und Christen im Heiligen Land. Palästina unter Konstantin und Theodosius* (Munich: 1987), 49–51; also Geiger (1982), 225–26. List of bishops in H. Gelzer, H. Hilgenfeld, and O. Cuntz, *Patrum Nicaenorum nomina* (Leipzig: 1898).

19 There can be little doubt that Christians lived in Galilee, but their numbers were few. One was the so-called Count Joseph, a native of Tiberias, who, according to Epiphanius (*Panarion* 30.4.1–12.8), was charged by Constantine to build churches "in the cities of the Jews," i.e., Tiberias, Diocaesarea (Sepphoris), Capernaum. Archaeological excavations give some evidence of churches in the region—e.g., in Capernaum, Sepphoris, and Nazareth—but the evidence is fragmentary and its significance is disputed. For discussion of the story of Count Joseph and the archaeological evidence, see Stemberger, 66–75.

20 On Constantine, see Timothy D. Barnes, *Constantine and Eusebius* (Cambridge: 1981), 28ff., and Robin Lane Fox, *Pagans and Christians* (New York: 1987), 609ff. "Constantine publicly declared himself a Christian before battle. It seems natural to conclude that he was converted to Christianity before the Battle of the Milvian Bridge. . . . In the ultimate reckoning, however, the precise details of Constantine's conversion matter little. After 28 October 312 the emperor consistently thought of himself as God's servant, entrusted with a divine mission to convert the Roman Empire to Christianity." Barnes, 43.

21 Text of *Res Gestae Divi Augusti* (*Monumentum Ancyranum*), in V. Ehrenburg and A. H. M. Jones, *Documents Illustrating the Reigns of Augustus and Tiberius* (Oxford: 1976), 1–31. See esp. paragraph 20.

22 "This deluge of Christian publicity exceeded any other programme in precious stone which was realized by a ruler in antiquity." Fox, 623. On Constantine's building program, Joseph Vogt wrote, "Constantine's church buildings are indisputable signs of his Christian outlook." "Bemerkungen zum Gang der Constantinforschung," *Mullus: Festschrift Th. Klauser* (*JbAC,* supp., vol. 1 [Münster, 1964], 378).

23 Drake, *In Praise of Constantine* (Berkeley: 1976), 173, n. 9.

24 Richard Krautheimer, *Three Christian Capitals: Topography and Politics* (Berkeley: 1983), 23. For the legal basis for Constantine's building program, see Ludwig Voelkl, *Die Kirchenstiftungen des Kaisers Konstantin im Lichte des römischen Sakralrechts* (*Arbeitsgemeinschaft für Forschung des Landes Nordrhein-Westfalen Geisteswissenschaften,* Heft 117 [Köln: 1964]).

25 "Instead of the usual figures and scenes from Greek mythology, there were statues of the Good Shepherd, of Daniel in the lion's den, and other biblical characters, often in gilded bronze—and a cross of precious stones hanging in midair dominated the principal hall of the imperial palace." Barnes (1981), 22.

26 K. L. Schmidt, "Jerusalem als Urbild und Abbild," *Eranos Jahrbuch* 18 (1950): 107–248.

27 The recent study of P. W. L. Walker, *Holy City, Holy Places?* (Oxford: 1990), argues that Eusebius was not able to accommodate his thinking to the new developments taking place in Jerusalem. He is correct in exposing the ambivalence of Eusebius's view of Jerusalem and the "holy land" and shows in detail the factors that went into Eusebius's thinking: rivalry between Caesarea, the metropolitan see, and Jerusaem, Eusebius's theological views, particularly his understanding of Christ's Resurrection as a "theophany," his anti-Jewish polemic, his Origenism, et al. He is also correct in highlighting the differences between Eusebius and Cyril, the bishop of Jerusalem in the middle of the fourth century. Yet in his efforts to defend the theological consistency of Eusebius's views, he misses, in my view, the subtle ways Eusebius's thinking shifted as he took account of the new things happening in Jerusalem. By drawing so heavily on *Theophania* and *Demon. Evang.,* Walker minimizes the significance of the unprecedented language for the holy places (and the land) in the *Vita Constantini* and the *de laudibus Constantini.* His argument that "Jerusalem" in *v.C* 3.33 (p. 399) refers to the heavenly city is ingenious but unconvincing. In the context I do not see how terms such as "build" or "over against" can refer to anything but the actual place. Eusebius's embryonic theology of Jerusalem fits comfortably with the realized eschatology exhibited in his depicition of Constantine's reign in book 10 of the *Ecclesiastical History.*

28 Jonathan Z. Smith, *To Take Place* (Chicago: 1988), 80.

29 A cave near Corycus in Asia Minor is called "venerable and very holy . . . worthy to be a dwelling place for the gods and believed to be" (Pomponius Mela, *Chorographia* 1.13.75, ed. A. Silberman [Paris: 1899], 22). See Walter Burkert, *Greek Religion* (Cambridge: 1985), 24.

30 H. A. Drake, "Eusebius on the True Cross," *JEH* 36 (1985): 1–21. In an unpublished paper, "Constantine, Macarius, and the Tomb of the Lord," Kenneth Holum (dept. of history, University of Maryland) argues that the present site was chosen *because* a pagan temple stood on it. By destroying the temple and building a church, Christians showed the power of their god to vanquish idols. He draws a parallel between the building of the Anastasis and the construction of a church on the site of a pagan temple in Gaza (cf. Mark the Deacon, *Life of Porphyry*). Also Kretschmar (1987), in Busse-Kretschmar, 33ff.

31 Also *l. C.* (Sepulchre of Christ), 18. On Eusebius's treatise "on the sepulchre of Christ," included in his *de laudibus Constantini,* see Drake (1976). Gregory of Nyssa said that in Jerusalem one could see the "signs" of the Lord's sojourn in the flesh (*PG* 46, 960).

32 Maurice Halbwachs, *The Collective Memory* (New York: 1980), 154, 156. See also his *La Topographie légendaire des évangiles en terre sainte* (Paris: 1971). "The past becomes part of the present; one touches it, one is in direct contact with it" (1).

33 Asterius of Amasea, *hom.* 9.2 (ed. Datema, 116–17).

34 For Eusebius the holy places served more as proofs of the truth of Christianity than objects of devotion. A. Lassus, "L'Empereur Constantin, Eusebe et les lieux saints," *Revue de l'histoire des Religions* 171 (1967): 142; also Wilkinson (1971), 20.

35 On time, see Hebrews 1:1: "In many and various ways God spoke *of old* to our fathers by the prophets; but *in these last days* he has spoken to us by a Son." Or Gal 4:4: "When the *time* had fully come, God sent forth his Son born of woman." On place, see Acts 7:48: the "Most High does not dwell in houses made with hands," citing Isaiah 66:1–2. These passages should not be overworked, at least in their original setting. John 4 may be less a reproach of the temple than a censure of impure offerings. G. Klinzing, *Die Umdeutung des Kultus in der Qumrangemeinde und im Neuen Testament* (Göttingen: 1971), 93ff.

36 "The God of the Christians is not confined by place; being unseen he fills heaven and earth and is worshipped and glorified by the faithful everywhere" (*Acts of Justin* 3.1). There is "no place of (God's) resting" (Theophilus, *Autol.* 1.4). Justin, *dial.* 127.2. Theophilus, *Autol.* 2.3; Athenagoras, *leg.* 10.1. "Every place is suitable for prayer if a person prays well" (Origen, *orat.* 31.4). Minucius Felix: "Templum quod ei extruam, cum totus hic mundus eius opere fabricatus *eum capere non possit?*" (*Octavius* 32). Also Eusebius, *demon. evang.* 1.6.40–42 (18b-19d); 2.3 (61b). In his *Leviathan* Thomas Hobbes wrote, "Holy implies no new quality in that place . . . but only a new relation by appropriation to God." Sabine MacCormack, "The Organization of Sacred Topography," in *The Blessings of Pilgrimage,* ed. R. Ousterhout (Urbana: 1990), 9.

37 Eusebius follows Origen's interpretation of the "holy city" as the "heavenly city." See d.e. 4.12,166d; 10.8,501c; and also *Comm. in Ps.* 87(88).11–13; *PG,* 23, 10641-b.

38 See the provocative article by Paul Crosby Finney, "Topos Hieros und christlicher Sakralbau in vorkonstantinischer Überlieferung," *Boreas, Münsterische Beitraege zur Archaeologie* 7 (1984): 193–225. Finney shows that there is greater continuity between early Christian veneration of particular places (the house

church at Dura, early Christian martyria) and the fourth-century veneration of holy places than many historians, influenced particularly by nineteenth-century Protestant historiography, will allow. *The Martyrdom of Polycarp,* written in mid–second century, gives evidence of worship at the site of the martyr's tomb. After his death, "we deposited his bones in a suitable place . . . and we will come together with joy and gladness to celebrate the birthday of his martyrdom" (18.2–3).

39 The literature on the martyria is extensive. For a general account, see Richard Krautheimer, *Early Christian and Byzantine Architecture* (New York: 1979), 30–37; André Grabar, *Martyrium. Recherches sur le culte des reliques et l'art chrétien antique* (Paris: 1943, 1946), 1:47ff. Klaus Staehler, "Grabbau," in *RAC* 14 (1982): 423–27; Graydon F. Snyder, *Ante Pacem: Archaeological Evidence of Church Life before Constantine* (Macon, Ga.: 1985), 87–114.

40 Excavations in Rome have uncovered a fragment of an inscription that may belong to Peter's martyrium. The inscription reads PETR ENI, which may mean PETER IN PEACE or PETER IS HERE. Another inscription found under St. Peter's (at the mausoleum di Valerii) mentions Christians being buried "near your [Peter's] body." M. Guarducci, *Pietro in Vaticano* (Rome: 1983), 65–68, 74–77.

41 On Salona, Ejnar Dyggve, *History of Salonitan Christianity* (Cambridge, Mass.: 1951). On Bonn, T. Kempf, "Frühchristliche Funde und Forschungen in Deutschland," *Atti del congresso internazionale di archeologia cristiana* 5 (1967): 61–72.

42 D. W. Rordorf, "Was wissen wir über die christlichen Gottesdienstraüme," *ZNW* 55 (1964): 110–28. Christians were sometimes buried near the holy place. See Dyggve (1951), 71ff. on burial near graves of martyrs: "iuxta loca sanctissima or martyribus adscita." See R. Egger, *Forschungen in Salona* 2 (Vienna: 1926), inscriptions # 106 and 110 (p. 82). The burial places of the apostles were called "sacred tabernacles," and their remains the "trophies of the apostles" (*h.e.* 2.25.7). Eusebius provides details of another kind of devotion to place, a monument at Panias (Caesarea Philippi) in Galilee that commemorated the woman who had suffered from a hemorrhage for twelve years and who was healed by Jesus (Matt 9:19–26). In Eusebius's day her house was pointed out to visitors. At the site were "memorials" to her healing, two bronze statues in relief, one of a woman bending her knee and stretching forth her hands in supplication, and opposite her a man clothed in a double cloak extending his hand in blessing. A curative herb grew at the base of the monument. The statue, which Eusebius had seen "with his own eyes," bore the likeness of Jesus (*h.e.* 7.18).

43 *Hom. in Ps.* 109.5 (110.5); *PG,* 55, 274a.

44 *Paradise Lost* 3.476–77.

45 Of course there were relics, chiefly fragments from the holy cross. From the end of the fourth century, veneration of these relics was part of every pilgrim's journey to Jerusalem (*Itin. Eger.* 37). Collection of earliest references to the true cross in Anatole Frolow, *La Relique de la vraie croix: Recherches sur le développement d'un culte* (Paris: 1961).

46 Mamre was a pagan and Jewish shrine before it became a Christian holy place, and even after a church had been built there, incorporating a former pagan building, the site was still venerated by Jews and pagans. See E. Mader, *Mambre*

(Freiburg im Breisgau: 1957), and G. Kretschmar, "Mambre: von der 'Basilika' zum 'Martyrium,'" *Mélanges liturgiques offerts au R. P. dom Bernard Botte* (Louvain: 1972), 272–93.

47 Constantine was called a "new Bezalel or Zerubbabel who builds blessed temples to Christ" (Antiochus Monachos, *ep. ad Eustath, PG* 89, 142a).

48 See Drake (1976), 171, n. 24, and 173, n. 6.

49 The term *temple* (*naos*) was used of other churches as well (*v.C.* 3.45). For *templum* as a term in Latin writers for the Anastasis, see Ambrosiaster, *Liber. quest.* 127.16 (*CSEL* 50. 405–06).

50 Also *Midrash Tanhuma, Kedoshim* 10.

51 Charles Coüasnon, *The Church of the Holy Sepulchre in Jerusalem* (London: 1974), 36. Also H. A. Drake, "A Coptic Version of the Discovery of the Holy Sepulchre," *Greek, Roman and Byzantine Studies* 20 (1979): 383–85; Kretschmar, *Jerusalemer Heiligstumstraditionen,* 33ff.

52 Ambrose, *exp. Luc.* 10.114.

53 Cyril of Jerusalem cat. 13.28; Didymus, *de trin.* 1.1. (*PG* 39, 324); Sophronius, *Anacreon.* 20.29. See W. H. Roscher, "*Omphalos*" in *Abhandlungen der Phil., hist. Klasse der Koenig. Saechs. Ges. der Wissenschaft* 29.9 (1913). A. Piganiol, "L'hemisphairion et l'omphalos des lieux saints," *Cahiers archaéologigues* 1 (1945): 11; also Grabar, *Martyrium,* 1:234ff. Of course the term *navel* (*omphalos*) of the world had been used earlier for Greek shrines, notably Delphi (Aeschylus, *Seven against Thebes,* 747).

54 In his commentary on Ezekiel, Theodoret of Cyrus interpreted Ezekiel 11:23 in light of the destruction of the Second Temple (*PG* 81, 901).

55 The editors of the Life of Constantine assume Eusebius is referring to the passage about the new Jerusalem in Revelation 21. But considering Eusebius's reservations about the Apocalypse (R. M. Grant, *Eusebius as Church Historian* [Oxford: 1980], 126–27, 130ff.) and his abhorrence of chiliasm, it is possible he is thinking of the prophecies of Isaiah and Ezekiel. The term *new* or *second* Jerusalem does not appear, but Isaiah speaks of a "new heaven and a new earth" (Isa 65:17) and of a city whose foundations will be laid "with sapphires" and whose walls will be made of "precious stones" (Isa 54:11–12), language similar to Eusebius's description of the new church at the site. Ezekiel envisioned a city with a new temple out of which flows a river of life whose name would be the Lord's name (Ezek 48:35, LXX).

56 In the Syriac version of the *Martyrs of Palestine,* Eusebius says that the Savior arose "like a life-giving fountain in the middle of *our* land" (*m.P.,* pref.). The pronoun "our" is striking, because elsewhere he refers to Palestine as the land of the Jews, "their land," and "their own land" (*d.e.* 6.18, 284d). "Our" probably means the land where Eusebius was born and lived, not a Christian land.

57 Jerome applies the image of the river in Ezekiel to the heavenly Jerusalem (*ep.* 129.2).

58 *JQR* 50 (1959): 97–123.

59 Dedication of the Anastasis (Encaenia) was thought to replace the Jewish feast of Sukkoth, which commemorated the dedication of Solomon's temple. "No longer does one speak of the transitory festival of Tabernacles but of the festival of the

dedication of the great temple erected for the Holy Resurrection" (G. Bayan, *Synaxaire arménien de Ter Israel* (Patrologia Orientalis [Turnhout: 1971], 6.2, 215-16). Egeria says the day was celebrated "cum summo honore" and people came from all over the East, from Mesopotamia, Syria, Egypt for the celebration. Encaenia (renewal) was the day that Solomon consecrated the temple, as recorded in 2 Chr 6.12 (*Itin.* 48–49). Some saw Encaenia as a parallel to Hannukah. See M. Black, "The Festival of the Encaenia Ecclesiae in the Ancient Church with Special Reference to Palestine and Syria," *JEH* 5 (1954): 78–86.

60 It should be observed that as late as 327 Constantine also supported pilgrimage to pagan shrines. In an inscription found at the tomb of the kings in Egypt a priest from Eleusis thanks Constantine for underwriting the trip (*OGIS* 2721). See F. Millar, "P. Herennius Dexippus: The Greek World and the Third Century Invasions," *JRS* 59 (1969): 17.

61 Hunt, 28. Constantine himself did not go to Jerusalem on pilgrimage. For a discussion of possible reasons, see Joseph T. Rivers, "Pattern and Process in Early Christian Pilgrimage" (Ph.D. diss., Duke University, 1983), 235ff.

62 See the discussion of Helen in Hunt, 29–49, and Drijvers (1992). Ambrose of Milan (d. 397) was the first to mention Helen's discovery of the cross (*in ob. Theod.* 46). See Wilkinson (1971), 240–41; also Drake (1985). For a discussion of the different ways eastern and western writers remembered the discovery of the tomb and the cross, see H. A. Drake (1979), 381–92. Ze'ev Rubin believes that Eusebius deliberately suppressed information about the discovery of the cross for political reasons, namely, he wished to guard the prerogatives of his own city, the metropolitan see in the region. This seems unlikely, but tension there was between the two cities. "The Church of the Holy Sepulchre and the Conflict between the Sees of Caesarea and Jerusalem," *The Jerusalem Cathedra* 2 (1982): 79–99.

63 Stephen Runciman, *A History of the Crusades* (Cambridge: 1951), 1:39. Eusebius, however, says nothing about the "invention" of the cross in his account of the uncovering of the tomb of Christ. This omission is puzzling. However, if the story of the discovery of the true cross did not begin to circulate until later in the fourth century (as seems likely), Eusebius can hardly be faulted for omitting it from his account. Later, however, the "invention of the cross" was made part of the Celebration of the Dedication celebrated on September 14, and Helen was accorded equal honor with her son in the "rebuilding of Jerusalem" (Socrates, *h.e.* 1.17). On Helen, see also Stefan Heid, "Der Ursprung der Helenalegenda im Pilgerbetrieb Jeruslems," JbAC 32 (1989): 40–71.

64 For Eusebius's emphasis on Palestine as a whole, see Walker, (1990), 108. I am, however, not convinced that Eusebius exalted Palestine at the expense of Jerusalem.

65 Text ed. E. Klostermann, *Das Onomastikon der biblischen Ortsnamen, GCS* (Berlin: 1904). In regard to the date, see Barnes (1981), 106–11 as well as his article "The Composition of Eusebius' Onomasticon," *JTS* 26 (1975): 412–15.

66 For analysis of the text, see Peter Thomsen, "Palästina nach dem Onomasticon des Eusebius," *ZDPV* 26 (1903): 97–188; also E. Z. Melamed, "The Onomasticon of Eusebius," *Tarbiz* 3 (1932): 314–27 (in Hebrew).

67 Dennis Groh, "The Onomastikon of Eusebius and the Rise of Christian Palestine," *Studia Patristica* 18 (1983): 29.
68 Anaia, Jetheria (266), near Eleutheropolis, and Kariatha (239).

Chapter 6
At the Very Spot

1 Jerome cites Ps 132.7 as a command to go to Jerusalem on pilgrimage. "The psalmist *commands* that we worship [Christ] in the place where his feet stood" (*ep*. 46.7).
2 "There is no great religion in the world which has not laid the gravest insistence on the sacredness of certain specified localities and enjoined on their followers the primary necessity to visit them at stated seasons and to perform with scrupulous attention the rites prescribed by tradition." H. N. Wetherd, *The Four Paths of Pilgrimage* (London: 1947), 10.
3 The literature on Christian pilgrimage is large. Besides the works on pilgrims in Christian antiquity—Kötting, Hunt, Maraval—see also the volume of essays by M. Philonenko and M. Simon, *Les Pèlerinages de l'antiquité biblique et classique à l'occident médiéval* (Université de Science Humaines de Strasbourg, Centre de Recherches d'Histoire des Religions; *Études d'histoire des Religions,* no. 1 [Paris: 1973]). For an anthropological perspective, see Victor and Edith Turner, *Image and Pilgrimage in Christian Culture* (Columbia: 1978). The Turners, whose theoretical model is widely cited, did not use evidence from early Christianity in formulating their theories. See also V. Turner, "The Center Out There," *HR* 12 (1973): 191–230.
4 Hugeburc, *Life of St. Willibald,* 94, ed. O. Holder-Egger, *Monumenta Germaniae Historiae* 15 (1) (Leipzig: 1887) 94, l. 20; trans. John Wilkinson, *Jerusalem Pilgrims before the Crusades* (Jerusalem: 1977), 126.
5 See the discussion in chapter 5.
6 Stephen Graham, *With the Russian Pilgrims to Jerusalem* (London: 1914). A beautiful book on Christian devotion to Jerusalem!
7 *Institutes* 4.13.7. For similar sentiments, see Sabine MacCormack "*Loca Sancta,*" in R. Ousterhout, ed., *Blessings of Pilgrimage* (Urbana: 1990), 9ff.
8 Samuel Johnson, *Rasselas,* chap. 11.
9 On pilgrimage in the Greco-Roman world, see Kötting, *Peregrinatio Religiosa* (Münster, 1950), 33–53, and Siebert in Philonenko and Simon (1973), 33–53. Useful material in Ramsay MacMullen, *Paganism in the Roman Empire* (New Haven: 1981), 27ff., 41ff.
10 Kötting, 25; "Healings of Apollo and Asclepius," 64, ed. R. Herzog, *Die Wunderheilungen von Epidauros, Ein Beitrag zur Geschichte der Medizin und der Religion,* in Philologus, Supplementband 22 (Leipzig: 1931), 32.
11 MacMullen (1981), 155–56, nn. 52, 53.
12 I follow Attridge's translation of *De Dea Syria* slightly revised. *The Syrian Goddess (De Dea Syria) Attributed to Lucian,* Harold W. Attridge and Robert A. Oden (*Texts and Translations* 9, Society of Biblical Literature [Missoula, Mont.: 1976]), 57. For discussion of the author of this work, see R. A. Oden, Jr., *Studies in*

Lucian's De Syria Dea (Harvard Semitic Monographs, no. 15 [Missoula, Mont.: 1977]).

13 Burkert (1985), 84.

14 "All Greek sacred architecture explores and praises the character of a god or a group of gods in a specific place. That place is itself holy and, before the temple was built upon it, embodied the whole of the deity as recognized actual force" (V. Scully, *The Earth, the Temple and the Gods* [New Haven: 1979], 1). Also R. A. Tomlinson, *Greek Sanctuaries* (London: 1976). "As for this place, it is clearly a holy one" (Sophocles, *Oedipus at Colonus,* l. 16). On the distinction between *chosen* and *discovered,* see Mircea Eliade, *Patterns in Comparative Religion* (New York: 1974), 369, and the useful article by Shigeru Matsumoto, "The Meaning of Sacred Places, as Phenomenologists of Religion Understand It," *Tenri Journal of Religion* 10 (1969): 46–56.

15 The Greeks used the term *temenos* to designate the sacred zone or precinct dedicated to a God. The term occurs in Eusebius, *l.C.* 17.4, for the "precincts" in which Constantine built churches. In later Christian writers it designates a church building. See Procopius, *aed.* 1.13.12, Germanos of Constantinople, *hist. myst.* 1; also in fifth-century funerary inscription from Tanagra in Boetia (W. M. Calder, "An Early Christian Monument from Tanagra," *CR* 62 (1948): 8–11.

16 Tadeusz Zawadzki, "Quelques remarques sur l'entendue et l'accroissement des domaines des grands temples en Asia Mineure," *Eos* 46 (1953–54): 83–96. In Japan the territory around the residence of the divinity came to be viewed as a sacred area; in time this was extended to the nation as a whole. Allan G. Grapard, "Flying Mountains and Walkers of Emptiness: Toward a Definition of Sacred Space in Japanese Religions," *HR* 21 (1982): 195–221.

17 Pausanias 1.13.8; 1.31.5; 1.35.8; 1.41.2, et al., and Lucian *Syr. D.* 55; MacMullen (1981), 156, n. 54. On collective memory in Greco-Roman religions, see Jean Rudhardt, "Mnémosyne et les Muses," in *La Mémoire des religions*, ed. Philippe Borgeaud (Geneva: 1988), 37–62.

18 Philo, *Spec.* 1.69. Some of the hymns sung by pilgrims are preserved in the pilgrim songs, or "songs of ascent," in the book of Psalms (Pss. 24, 84, 118, 120–34). On Jewish pilgrimage during the period of the Second Temple, see Shmuel Safrai, *Die Wallfahrt im Zeitalter des Zweiten Tempels* (Neukirchen-Vluyn: 1981); also "Relations between the Diaspora and the Land of Israel," in *The Jewish People in the First Century,* ed. S. Safrai and M. Stern (Philadelphia: 1974), 1:184–215.

19 Turner (1978) 7.

20 *Corpus Inscriptionum Iudaicarum* 2, no. 1404. On this inscription, see M. Schwabe in *Sefer Yerushalayim* 1 (1956): 362–65 (in Hebrew).

21 S. Safrai, "Pilgrimage to Jerusalem after the Destruction of the Second Temple," in *Jerusalem in the Second Temple Period*, Abraham Schalit Memorial Volume, ed. A. Oppenheimer et al. (Jerusalem: 1980), 376–94 (in Hebrew).

22 "Congregatur turba miserorum . . . plangere ruinas templi sui populum miserum . . . et miles mercedem postulat, ut illis flere plus liceat" (*Soph.* 1.14–16 (*CC* 76a, 673). Also *Pilgrim of Bordeaux,* 591. According to an edict of Hadrian, Jews were forbidden to enter or stay within the territory of Aelia Capitolina. Though never

rescinded it came to be "evaded in practice" (Avi Yonah, *Gazetteer of Roman Palestine* [Jerusalem: 1976], 50ff.). Jerome says that Jews bribed Roman soldiers to be permitted to get within site of the ruins of the temple. On the exclusion of Jews from Jerusalem in the fourth century, see Walker (1990), 8, and G. Stroumsa, "'Vetus Israel: Les juifs dans la littérature hiérosolymitaine d'époque byzantine," RHR 205 (1988): 119.

23 Safrai (1980), 381. Text in M. Margolioth, *Halakhoth on the Land of Israel from the Genizah* (Jerusalem: 1974), 139–40 (in Hebrew). Compare this description of a Jewish pilgrim to Jerusalem with the sixth-century account of a Christian pilgrim sighting the holy city for the first time: "When they had reached the outskirts of the holy city of Jerusalem which they loved, they saw from a high place five stades away the lofty roof of the Holy Church of the Resurrection, shining like the morning sun, and cried aloud: 'See that is Sion, the city of our deliverance!' They fell down upon their faces, and from there onwards they crept upon their knees, frequently kissing the soil with their lips and eyes, until they were within the holy walls and had embraced the site of the sacred Cross on Golgotha." *Life of Peter the Iberian*, in *Lives and Legends of the Georgian Saints,* ed. David Marshall Lang (Crestwood, N.Y.: 1956), 64; Syriac text ed. Richard Raabe, *Petrus der Iberer* (Leipzig: 1895), 26–27. For rituals associated with pilgrimage to Jerusalem among Syriac-speaking Christians, see Fiey (1969), 117ff.

24 *B. Baba Batra* 75b. For further texts see Safrai (1980), 382ff.

25 *Comm. in Is.* 58:12, ll. 15–22 (*CC* 73a, 673). *Comm. in Ezech.* 29:17–21, ll. 982–84 (*CC* 75, 416). See Robert L. Wilken, "The Restoration of Israel in Biblical Prophecy: Christian and Jewish Responses in the Early Byzantine Period," in *"To See Ourselves as Others See Us": Christians, Jews, "Others" in Late Antiquity,* ed. Jacob Neusner, Ernest S. Frerichs, and Caroline McCracken-Flesher (Chico, Calif.: 1985), 443–72.

26 The Christian pilgrim from Bordeaux, whose itinerary may have been determined in part by Jewish information or guides, visited the tombs of the patriarchs and their wives, the tombs of Joseph, of Rachel, of Hezekiah, of Ezekiel and others (*Pilgrim of Bordeaux,* 588, 595, 598–99). He also visited the place where David killed Goliath, the spring of the prophet Elisha, the house of Rahab the harlot, the place where Joshua circumcised the Israelites and buried their foreskins, the place where Elijah was taken up to heaven. It has been claimed (cf. Matt 23.29) that Jews venerated tombs of the prophets in Palestine from at least the first century. See most recently John Wilkinson, "Jewish Holy Places and the Origins of Christian Pilgrimage," in Ousterhout (1990), 41–53, and J. Jeremias, *Heiligengräber in Jesu Umwelt (Mt 23,29; Lk 11,47). Eine Untersuchung zur Volksreligion der Zeit Jesu* (Göttingen: 1958). But the primary source to document the practice is an early Byzantine work, the *Lives of the Prophets*. For criticism of the views of Jeremias and Wilkinson, see the forthcoming work of David Satran on the Lives of the Prophets.

27 "Then Joshua called the twelve men from the people of Israel, whom he had appointed, a man from each tribe; and Joshua said to them, 'Pass on before the ark of the Lord your God into the midst of the Jordan, and take up each of you a stone upon his shoulder, according to the number of the tribes of the people of Israel,

that this may be a sign among you when your children ask in time to come, "What do these stones mean to you?" . . . So these stones shall be to the people of Israel a memorial for ever'" (Joshua 4.4–7).

28 A. Goldberg, "Die Heiligkeit des Ortes in der frühen rabbinischen Theologie," *Frankfurter Judaistische Beiträge* (Frankfurt: 1976), 4: 26–31. On the tombs of the patriarchs: "Rabbi Pinchas used to say, 'If the patriarchs had asked that their resting place be located in the world above, they could have had things that way. However, they came to be called "holy ones" only after their death and the heavy stone was put in place'" (*Midrash Tehilim* 16:2 [ed. Buber, 120]). Galgala, the place of twelve stones, was venerated by Jews in the second century (*T. Sota* 8.6).

29 Marcel Proust, *Remembrance of Things Past* (New York: 1934), 1:34.

30 *Jo.* 1.28 (6.204–07; *SC* 157, 284ff.). In the same passage he mentions Gergasa, a site on the far side of the Sea of Galilee. Here "was shown" the place where the miracle of the swine who were driven over the cliff into the sea was supposed to have taken place. Also *Jo.* 1.28 (6.208–11); *SC,* 288–90). Later a hostel, church, and monastery were constructed there, and the site, called Kursi, was recently excavated and can be visited.

31 *Frg.* 3 (Eusebius, *h.e.* 4.26.3–4); see A. E. Harvey, "Melito and Jerusalem," *JTS* n.s. 17 (1966): 401–04.

32 For a listing of places of pilgrimage prior to 320 C.E., see H. Leclercq, "Pèlerinages aux lieux saints," *DACL* 14.1, cols 68–70. For the later period, see Maraval (1985), 249–310.

33 Text of *Itinerarium Burdigalense,* ed. P. Geyer and O. Cuntz in *CC* 175. Translation in John Wilkinson, *Egeria's Travels to the Holy Land* (Jerusalem: 1981), 153–63. For discussion, see H. Windisch, "Die ältesten christlichen Palästinapilger," *ZDPV* 48 (1925): 145–48.

34 *Pilgrim of Bordeaux,* 585, 588.

35 Ibid., 595–99.

36 Job's dungheap was in Arabia. John Chrysostom writes, "Many undertake the long and arduous journey traveling from the ends of the earth to Arabia to see that dungheap, and when they behold it they kiss the earth which recevied that wrestling place of that victor" (*stat.* 5.1; *PG* 49.69a). Only two waterpots remained at Cana according to the Piacenza Pilgrim, 161 (Wilkinson [1977], 79).

37 Cynthia Ozick, "Toward a New Yiddish," *Art and Ardor* (New York: 1983), 154.

38 *Pilgrim of Bordeaux,* 595.

39 S. Klein, "The Travelogue *Itinerarium Burdigalense* to the Land of Israel," *Tsiyon* 6 (1934): 1–3 (in Hebrew).

40 Richard Hartmann, "Die Palästina-Route des Itinerarium Burdigalense," *ZDPV* 33 (1910): 169–88.

41 On this point, see Wilkinson in Ousterhout (1990), 44–45.

42 Some Jewish *piyyutim* identify the site as Jezreel; Klein, "Travelogue," 3.

43 E. D. Hunt, *Holy Land Pilgrimage* (1982), 85, speaks of the "total prominence of the Bible" in the *Pilgrim of Bordeaux.*

44 Text ed. Pierre Maraval in *SC* 296 (Paris: 1982); trans. into English by John Wilkinson (1981). For recent discussion of the identity of Egeria, see Hagith Sivan, "Who Was Egeria? Piety and Pilgrimage in the Age of Gratian," *HTR* 81 (1988): 59–72.

45 Egeria expresses gratitude to the monks at Sinai "who took me round all the Biblical sites *I kept asking to see*" (5.12).

46 *Itin.* 2.2,7; 3.7; 5.1,5,8,9, passim. The impact of actually seeing the holy places is vividly described by Asterius, bishop of Amasea, a city in Cappadocia, in the late fourth century. Asterius is comparing the experience of visiting the tomb of a martyr (Phocas) in his native country to visiting the oak of Mamre in Hebron, the shrine of the patriarchs. "When one comes into the precious tomb of this one [Phocas] and touches the holy tomb of the body, the place fills me with a remembrance of all the stories that were told of him here." In Hebron the "sight of the holy places" renews the "image" so that one "sees in one's mind the faithful patriarch" and becomes a "spectator of their whole history" (*hom.* 9.2; Datema 116–17). See Jerome, *ep.* 46.13, and Gregory of Nyssa, *ep.* 2.2. On this point, see Maraval (1985) 138–39.

47 Wilkinson (1981), 94.

48 The literature is vast. The best place to begin is the recent monograph by John Baldovin, *The Urban Character of Christian Worship: The Origins, Development, and Meaning of Stational Liturgy* (Rome: 1987). See pp. 45–104 for Jerusalem.

49 Ibid., 36.

50 "Now the very spots hallowed by tradition are made available to the community—along with the money to construct on them. In fact, they have become showplaces of the imperial triumph. Hence, in Jerusalem it is natural that there should be a system of worship organized around the holy places" (Ibid., 104).

51 Jonathan Z. Smith (1987), 92.

52 M. Halbwachs, *La Topographie légendaire des évangiles en terre sainte* (Paris: 1971), 126.

53 When the faithful came to receive the wine in the Eucharist Cyril of Jerusalem urged them to touch their fingers to their lips while they are still wet with wine and then touch the brow and eyes and other organs of sense (*myst. catech.* 5.22). See also John Chrysostom, *ecl.* (*PG* 63, 898a).

54 The text is found in a pseudonymous homily among the writings of Basil, *hom. Ps.* 115.4 (*PG* 30. 112c). Relics were divided up and transported to other regions to serve as "protection" against evil: Basil, *hom. 40 mart.* 8 (*PG* 31, 521); Gregory of Nyssa, *hom. in 40 mart.* (*PG* 46, 784b). John Chrysostom, *hom. Phil. pref* (*PG* 62, 702–03). On this point, see Delehaye (1933), 61–62.

55 Jerome, *ep.* 114; *Vigil.* 4. On the *praesentia* of the saint at the tombs, see P. Brown, *The Cult of the Saints* (Chicago: 1981), 109. On veneration of the tombs of the faithful departed martyrs, see Delehaye (1933), Brown, and H. J. W. Drijvers, "Spätantike Parallelen zur altchristlichen Heiligenverehrung unter besonderer Berücksichtigung des syrischen Styliten-Kultes," *Erkentnisse und Meinungen* 2 (1978): 77–113.

56 The phrase "worship by the fingertips" comes from Ramsay MacMullen's (1981) translation of Lactantius's Latin: "retum ad solos digitos pertinentem" (*div. inst.* 5.19.29), 63.

57 John Moschus, *prat.* 91 (*PG* 87, 2949a).

58 Gary Vikan, *Byzantine Pilgrimage Art* (Washington: 1982), 13; also the essays in Ousterhout (1990).

59 *Itin.* 37 (Wilkinson [1981], 137).

60 *Hist. Relig.* 9.2. Inscription at the tomb of St. Martin of Tours reads, "Here lies Martin the bishop, of holy memory, whose soul is in the hand of god; but he is *fully here,* present and made plain in miracles of every kind." E. Le Blant, *Les inscriptions chrétiennes de la Gaule* (Paris: 1856), 1:240. Seeing is a form of touching. Augustine: "Quia radios qui per eos emicant et quidquid *cernimus tangunt*" (*trin.* 9.3.3; also 9.6.11). On this point, see Margaret Miles, "Vision: The Eye of the Body and the Eye of the Mind in Saint Augustine's *De trinitate* and *Confessions,*" *Journal of Religion* 63 (1983), 127.

61 See Origen, *Jo.* 4:54 (13.452); *Comm. in Rom.* 4:2 (*PG* 14, 968).

62 Jerome, *ep.* 109.1.

63 *Vita Macrinae,* pref. (*PG* 46, 960a); *ep.* 3 (ed. Pasquali, 20).

64 *Eun.,* 3.9.54–60 (ed. Jaeger, 2:284–88).

65 *Ep.* 3.4 (Pasquali, 21).

66 The image is from Gregory's *Commentary on Canticles* 1:3, Or. 1 (ed. Langerbeck, 36–37).

67 In the Pasquali edition the argument about whether pilgrimage is commanded occurs in pars. 3–4 (14), about place in pars. 8–9 (15–16) and 16 (18), about morals 6–8 (15). On Gregory's letter, see P. Maraval's edition in *SC* 363 and his article "Une querelle sur les pèlerinages autour d'un texte patristique (Grégoire de Nysse, Lettre 2)," *RHPR* 66 (1986): 131–46; also E. Pietrella, "I pellegrinaggi ai Luoghi Santi e il culto dei martiri in Gregorio di Nissa," *Augustinianum* 21 (1981): 135–51. Basil also discouraged travel by monks (*reg. fus.* 39). Similar sentiments appear in a letter attributed to Athanasius (preserved in Syriac) written to a group of nuns who had gone to Jerusalem on pilgrimage. The letter commends them for their devotion but goes on to spiritualize the holy places: "You have seen the place at the Nativity; let your souls be reborn. You have seen the place of the Cross: let the world be crucified to you and you to the world" (J. Lebon, "Athanasiana Syriaca II; une lettre attribuée à Saint Athanase d'Alexandrie," *Le Museon* 41 (1927): 174. On this point, see Joseph T. Rivers, "Pattern and Process in Early Christian Pilgrimage" (Ph.D. diss., Duke University, 1983). Vigilantius objected to the veneration of the tombs of the martyrs (*Contra Vigil.* 1). For criticism of pilgrimage among Syriac-speaking Christians, see Fiey (1969), 115–17.

68 Pierre du Moulin, *De euntibus Iersolyma* (Paris: 1551).

69 Jacob Gretser, *De sacris et religiosis peregrinationibus libri quatuor* (Ingolstadt: 1606).

70 Johann Heinrich Heidegger, *Dissertatio de peregrinationibus religiosis* (Schaufelbert: 1620).

71 Chrysanthus Notaras, *History and Description of the Holy Land* (Vienna: 1728) (in Greek).
72 *Hom. 7 in Ecclesiasten* (ed. McDonough and Alexander, 414).
73 *Or. catech.* 11.
74 Chrysanthus, *History,* 141.
75 John of Damascus, *imag.* 3.34.
76 On amphora to carry oil from lamps that lit the church of the Anastasis or boxes to carry soil, see Vikan (1982), E. Kitzinger, *Age of Spirituality,* 152ff, Ousterhout, and Bagatti (1949). An ampula in the British Museum has the inscription, "blessing of the Lord from the holy places." John Chrysostom encouraged the faithful to take oil or other objects home from the tombs of martyrs (*hom. in martyres, PG* 50. 664). Also K. Weitzmann, "*Loca Sancta* and the Representational Arts of Palestine," *DOP* 28 (1974): 31–55.
77 When Athanasius was welcomed back to Alexandria after his exile he rode into the city on an ass, the people spread branches and clothes with flowers consciously imitating the entrace of Jesus into Jerusalem (Gregory Nazianzus, *Or.* 21.29). But as Hunt (1982) observes, Alexandria was not Jerusalem and "the biblical echoes were mere presumption" (127).
78 See also *catech.* 4.14; *myst. catech.* 2.4 "from the cross to the tomb which is before our eyes."
79 On Golgotha as the center of the earth, see also Grabar, *Martyrium,* 1: 238ff.
80 Cyril also mentions Egypt along with the sites in Palestine. According to the gospel of Matthew, when the life of the infant Jesus was endangered Mary and Joseph took him to Egypt, where they "remained until the death of Herod" (Matt 2:15). For Christians living in Egypt this was a geographical detail of great spiritual import; their land too had been honored by Christ's presence. On this matter, see Otto F. A. Meinardus, *The Holy Family in Egypt* (Cairo: 1986).
81 *Pref. to Chronicles* (*PL* 29, 401a); Jerome says people come to Jerusalem because their devotion and knowledge would be incomplete "unless they adored Christ in the very spot where the gospel first flashed from the gibbet" (*ep.* 46.9).
82 J. N. D. Kelly, *Jerome* (New York: 1975), 120.
83 *Piacenza Pilgrim* 30 (Wilkinson [1977], 85).
84 Baldovin (1987), 48.
85 *Itin. Eger.* 6.12 (Wilkinson [1981], 98); also *Itin. Eger.* 3.1; 4.4; 5.12.
86 *Piacenza Pilgrim* 37 (Wilkinson [1977], 87).
87 *Cat.* 17.13; also 3.7 and 16.4.
88 Michael Aubineau, *Les Homélies Festales d'Hésychius de Jérusalem* (*Subsidia Hagiographica,* no. 59 (Brussels: 1978), 1:244.
89 *Ep.* 123 (*Acta Conciliorum Oecumenicorum* 2.4.66). In another letter (*ep.* 123.3) he complains of Palestinian monks who cut themselves off from the "truth of the Lord's incarnation" in spite of their "associations with the holy places." And to the patriarch Juvenal he wrote that he had no choice but to embrace the orthodox teaching on the Incarnation because of the "indisputable evidences" of the holy places, Bethlehem, the cross, the tomb, the Mount of Olives (*ep.* 139; *ACO* 2.4.91ff.). Leo's point is that sight is master of intellect.

90 *Ep.* 22.1; 71.2; 125.20. But see *ep.* 108.32.

91 In his commentary on the final chapter of Ezekiel, Jerusalem, however, he refers to the "heavenly city," the "mother of us all" (*Comm. in Ezech.* 45.1; *CC* 75, 653ff.). See the following chapter for discussion of this topic. *Comm. Ser. in mt.* 27:53 (139).

92 Walter Oakeshott, *The Mosaics of Rome* (London: 1967), 66. On the mosaic, see also Guglielmo Matthiae, *Mosaici Medioevali della Chiese di Roma* (Rome: 1967), 1:55–76, and Christa Ihm, *Die Programme der christlichen Apsismalerei vom vierten Jahrhundert bis zur Mitte des achten Jahrhunderts* (Wiesbaden: 1960), 130–02, and more recently Geir Hellemo, *Adventus Domini: Eschatological Thought in Fourth-Century Apses and Catecheses* (Leiden: 1989).

93 The term occurs in Cyril of Alexandria, *Comm. in Esa.* 13.2, as a designation of biblical Judea. As bishop of a rival see, Cyril may have been jealous of the growing authority of Jerusalem and hence had no reason to invest Palestine with spiritual power. He is one of the few Christian authors who uses the name Aelia to refer to Jerusalem. See F. M. Abel, "St. Cyrille d'Alexandrie dans ses rapports avec la Palestine," *Kyrilliana* (Cairo: 1974): 203–30.

94 *Zach.* 2:10–13 (*CC* 76a, 768, ll. 210–12); "holy land" is used to designate the church.

95 A somewhat different use of dust from the Holy Land is attested in the Sephardic Jewish practice of putting soil from Eretz Israel in a coffin. "Before the funeral, the body, prepared by the *lavadores,* is robed in a simple shroud of pure white linen and placed with some *Terra Sancta* (dust from the soil of Palestine) in the coffin, which is then closed." *Book of Prayer: According to the Custom of the Spanish and Portugese Jews,* ed. and trans. David de Sola Pool (New York: 1941), 460. A similar practice can be found among Ashkenazi Jews (see *Schulchan Aruch, Yoreah Deah* 363.1, note of the sixteenth-century R. Moses Isserles [Rema] ad locum, basing his opinion on *Tanhuma* [1:214–15, re Deut 32.43, ed. Solomon Buber (Vilna: 1885)], that those buried in Eretz Israel are resurrected first. The earliest source of this notion is *J. Kil* 9.4; 32c [below, chap. 7, n. 10]). This idea is extended to those having any connection to the soil of Eretz Israel, however minimal. Deut 32.45 "and cleanse the land of his people" is interpreted as "and his land atones for his people" (see also Sifre Deuteronomy, no. 333, ed. Finkelstein, p. 383). Isserles in the sixteenth century saw the first halakhic warrant of this practice in the thirteenth-entury work *Or Zarua* by R. Isaac ben Moses of Vienna (Hilkhot Avelut, sec. 419, end). However. R. Isaac (on the basis of *J. Kil* 9.4; 32c and especially *Tanhuma* Vayehi) questions whether anything less than actual burial in Eretz Israel is sufficient. I am grateful to my colleague David Novak for assistance on this matter.

96 *Ser.* 45 on Isa 57:13; *PL* 38, 262ff. God does not limit his possession to a small part of the earth, writes Augustine in *mor. eccl.* 10.6. Yet, Augustine recognized that God had "appointed some places rather than others to be the scene for miracles," e.g., at the tombs of martyrs (*ep.* 78.3). In another passage Augustine uses the term "terra" to designate the Holy Land. The Donatists, he says, "venerate" the land from which the gospel came to Africa, but they show no respect for Christians living there. If someone would come from there they would insist on rebaptizing him (*ep.* 52.2).

Chapter 7
Your Ancient Ruins Shall Be Rebuilt

1 Text in Socrates Scholasticus, *Historia Ecclesiastica* 7.38.

2 *Is.* 33:17 (ed. Ziegler, 217).

3 *Is.* 11:15 (ed. Ziegler, 90). See also Eusebius *d.e.* 8:1.

4 *Ep.* 129. *Ep.* 187 of Augustine is addressed to the same Dardanus.

5 Jerome also yokes these two texts, Ps 26:13 and Matt 5:5, in his commentary on Amos 9:11–15 ("I will plant them upon their land and they shall never again be plucked up out of the land which I have given them"). This passage, he says, refers to Christ's "land" about which it is said, "blessed are those who will see . . . the land of the living" and "blessed are those who will possess the land" (*Am.* 9:13–15; *CC* 76, 348). See also *Is.* 57:13–14 (*CC* 73a, 652.19–21). Diodore of Tarsus (d. 390) said that when Jews sing the refrain "Those who wait for the Lord shall possess the land" (Ps 37:9) they say the psalmist is referring "to Palestine alone" (*Ps.* 36:9b; ed. Jean-Marie Oliver; *CCG* 6, 218).

6 Nevertheless, in a rhetorical aside at one point, Jerome says: this land "has now become for us a *promised land* because of the passion and resurrection of Christ" (*ep.* 129.4).

7 Mark Twain, *The Innocents Abroad,* chap. 19. (*The Unabridged Mark Twain,* ed. Lawrence Teacher [Philadelphia: 1976], 283).

8 On Jewish views of the borders of the land in this period, see S. Klein, "Das tannaitische Grenzverzeichnis Palästinas," *HUCA* 5 (1928): 174–259; also A. Neubauer, *La Géographie du Talmud* (Hildesheim: 1967). See esp. *Sifre* Deut 51 and *t. Shevitt* 4.11.

9 *Gen. Rab.* 74.1 and *Pesikta Rabbati* 1.4.

10 *J. Kil.* 9.4; 32c.

11 On reburial in the Land of Israel, Isaiah Gafni, "Reinterment in the Land of Israel: Notes on the Origin and Development of the Custom," *The Jerusalem Cathedra* 1 (Jerusalem: 1981): 96–104, and Eric Meyers, *Jewish Ossuaries—Reburial and Rebirth* (Rome: 1971); also S. Safrai, *Die Wallfahrt in Zeitalter des Zweiten Tempels* (Neukirchen: 1981), 16–17.

12 The head of a family could force his family members to go up to the Land (from another country) against their will, but no one could coerce members of one's family to leave the Land. "Our rabbis taught: if a husband desires to go up, and if she does not consent she may be divorced without a marriage settlement. If *she* desires to go up and he refuses, he must be compelled to go up, and if he does not consent, he must divorce her and pay her a marriage settlement" (*b. Ketub.* 110b). This principle, as the Talmud observes, applied equally to men as well as to women. In practice this law was difficult of application; it could, for example, be manipulated in unhappy marriages. (See Marc Saperstein, "The Land of Israel in Pre-Modern Jewish Thought: A History of Two Rabbinic Statements," in *The Land of Israel: Jewish Perspectives,* ed. Lawrence A. Hoffman [Center for the Study of Judaism and Christianity in Antiquity, no. 6; Notre Dame: 1986], 190–95.) But the principle is instructive; the obligation to live in the Land of Israel took precedence over other claims of the Law. Jewish tradition encouraged settlement

in the Land of Israel and discouraged emigration. Other laws prohibited selling anything to Gentiles that was attached to the Land, e.g., trees or houses, lest non-Jews "acquire proprietary rights in the Land of Israel" (Richard S. Sarason, "The Significance of the Land of Israel in the Mishnah," in Hoffman [1986], 124–25). In some texts from this period it is apparent that the need to defend the legitimacy of Jewish claims to the land was still present. One Midrash observes that three places—the grave of Sarah, the temple site, and the grave of Joseph—were lawfully purchased, i.e., they were not acquired by conquest (*Gen. Rab.* 79.7). For discussion of Jewish attitudes to the Land in this period, see, besides Hoffman, I. M. H. Guttmann, *Eretz Israel in Midrash und Talmud (Festschrift zum 75-jährigen Bestehen des jüdischen-theologischen Seminars,* Fränckel'scher Stiftung [Breslau: 1921], 9–148); Clemens Thoma, "Das Land Israel in der rabbinischen Tradition," in *Jüdisches Volk-Gelobtes Land,* ed. W. P. Eckert, N. P. Levinson, and M. Stöhr (Munich: 1970), 37–51, and Günther Stemberger, "Die Bedeutung des 'Landes Israel' in der rabbinischen Tradition," *Kairos* 25 (1983): 176–99.

13 *Sifrei Devarim* 80. See also *Sifrei Devarim* 333: Citing the verse "'the land makes expiation for its people,' Rabbi Meir said: All who dwell in the Land of Israel, and repeat the Shema morning and evening and speak in the sacred tongue, are worthy of the world to come."

14 See Kelly, *Jerome* (New York: 1975), 153–67.

15 *PL* 28, 772.

16 For studies of Jerome's commentaries, see Jay Braverman, *Jerome's Commentary on Daniel: A Study of Comparative Jewish and Christian Interpretations of the Hebrew Bible* (CBQ Monograph Series 7; Washington, D.C.: 1978); P. Jay, *L'éxègese de saint Jérôme d'apres son "Commentaire sur Isaïe"* (Paris: 1985). Ives-Marie Duval, "Jérôme et les prophètes: Histoire, prophétie, actualité, et actualisation dans les Commentaires de Nahum, Michée, Abdias et Joël," in IOSOT XI Congress, Supplement to *Vetus Testamentum,* no. 36 (Leiden: 1985), 108–31.

17 Irenaeus, *haer.* 5.15.1.

18 In the twelfth century Richard of Victor, a Christian scholar living in Paris who was well acquainted with Jewish exegesis, wrote (in his commentary on Ezek 37:25) that Jews continued to hope they would return to the Land of Israel. "The Jews . . . believe that they will recover by means of their savior the land which once was theirs, and that nothing will ever be lacking for them again" (*Expositio in Hiezech.* 37:27, in *CC, Cont. Medievalis,* 53). See also Michael Signer, "The Land of Israel in Medieval Jewish Literature," in Hoffman (1986), 212.

19 Restoration of sacrifices, servitude of the gentiles, and beautiful women (*Is.* 35:3–10; *CC* 73, 427.104–06); thousand-year rule, rebuilding of a golden and jeweled Jerusalem, circumcision, reconstruction of the temple and offering of bulls, observance of the sabbath (*Ezech.* 36:1–15; *CC* 75, 499–500.633–35, 655–57); restoration of Jerusalem and the cities of Judea to their original condition (*Is.* 65:21–22; *CC* 73, 763.9–11); messianic reign in land of Judea (*Jer.* 31:37–40; *CC* 74, 323); building of Jerusalem and temple "in ultimo tempore" and prophecies fulfilled "carnaliter" (*Am.* 9:11–12, *CC* 76, 346.380–84); in this section Jerome cites Ps 26:13 and Matt 5:5 (p. 348) as noted in l. 5; king in line of David (*Ezech.*

37:1–28; *CC* 75, 520–22). In some passages Jerome identifies Jewish hopes with the establishment of a thousand-year reign in Jerusalem (*CC* 75, 400). The thousand-year reign (millennium) was of course a Christian idea drawn from the book of Revelation, and when Jerome mentions this detail he notes that some Christians held similar views. These Christians he variously calls "half-Jews," judaizers, Ebionites, or "friends of the letter" ("Iudaei et nostri semiiudaei" [*Is.* 60:1–3; *CC* 73a, 692.17]; "Iudaei et nostri iudaizantes" [*Is.* 49:14–18; *CC* 73a, 543.55]; "Haec Iudaei et amici tantum occidentis litterae" [*Is.* 48:12; *CC* 73a, 672–73.15–16]; "Iudaei et Iudaici erroris heredes Ebionitae" [*Is.* 66:20; *CC* 73a, 792.96–97]. He names a number of distinguished Christian thinkers who shared these ideas, among them Irenaeus, Tertullian, Victorinius, Lactantius, and in his own day, Apollinaris (*Is. prol.* book 18, *CC* 73a, 740–41). He has in mind, of course, Christian chiliasts, who anticipated a time Christ would return to earth and establish a thousand-years' reign in Jerusalem. As we saw in chapter 3, the chiliasts believed that the saints would "actually and really inhabit the city of God" and would "rule in the same world in which they endured slavery" (Irenaeus, *haer.* 5.35.2). Chiliasm still claimed adherents in the fifth century. Augustine was a chiliast for a time, though he later repudiated his earlier views. See *civ.* 20.7.1ff. See G. Folliet, "La typologie du sabbat chez saint Augustin: son interpretation millénariste entre 388 et 400," *Rev. Étud. Aug.* 2 (1956): 371–90.

There is, however, something perplexing about the way Jerome conflates Jewish messianism and Christian chiliasm. There is no doubt that Christian chiliasm had its origins in Jewish messianism, but the two traditions are not identical, and by the fifth century it would seem they had gone their separate ways. It is unlikely, for example, that the Jews would have appealed to the book of Revelation to support their hopes for restoration. Although some chiliasts, e.g., Nepos in the third century, mentioned the observance of festivals and sacrifices (and hence a temple) in the new Jerusalem, these features are not mentioned in the Apocalypse, and they appear only infrequently in the main trunk of Christian chiliasm. Nor can many of the other details, e.g., the practice of circumcision and observance of the Sabbath, the inclusion of the cities of Judea in the future kingdom, the return of the exiles, all characteristics of the Jewish hope as described by Jerome, be learned from the writings of Christian chiliasts. What Jerome reports is not only more extensive than what we learn from the chiliasts, it is more thoroughly Jewish. At one point he speaks of the one to come as "*their* Messiah," meaning of course the Messiah of the Jews as distinct from Christ, the Christian Messiah (*Comm. in Ezech.* 16:55; *CC* 75, 210.805–06; *Comm. in Ezech* 40:5–13; *CC* 75, 557.165). In these passages Jerome uses the term "Christus," the Latinized form of the Greek Christos. Greek-speaking Jews, however, preferred to use the term *eleimmenos* (from the Greek *aleiphein*; *christos* is from *chriein*; both mean "anoint"). This term was introduced by Aquila in his translation of the Hebrew Scriptures, because of the Christian appropriation of Christos. It occurs in Jerome at *Is.* 27:13; *CC* 73, 353.9. For other references and discussion, see E. Schürer, *The History of the Jewish People in the Age of Jesus Christ,* ed. G. Vermes, F. Millar, and M. Black (Edinburgh: 1973), 2:517–18, and Cecile Blanc, *Origène Commentaire sur Saint Jean* (*SC,* 222), 294–95. Though

Irenaeus was a chiliast he would hardly have agreed that the Messiah was *yet* to come.

Unless the chiliasts had completely abandoned belief in Jesus of Nazareth (in which case Jerome could hardly call them "our Judaizers") it is difficult to see how they could embrace a thoroughgoing Jewish interpretation of the restorationist passages in the prophets. It may be that by the fifth century chiliasm had taken a decidedly more Jewish form. Whatever the explanation for the anomalies in Jerome's account, as Jerome struggled to maintain an orthodox interpretation of the prophets, Jews and judaizing Christians (and chiliasts) appeared as common foes. In Syria and in Palestine judaizing forms of Christianity flourished in close social and religious proximity to Jewish communities (see Robert L. Wilken, *John Chrysostom and the Jews* [Berkeley: 1983], 66).

20 Jewish sources confirm Jerome's claim that certain texts from the prophets were interpreted to refer to the restoration of Jerusalem. At Isaiah 54:1–3, "Sing O barren one . . . for . . . your descendants . . . will people the desolate cities," Jerome says that the Jews believe this refers to the time of restoration of Jerusalem when the city which was once inhabited, then deserted, will be inhabited again with more people than previously (*Is.* 54:1–3; *CC* 73a, 601.68–71). In *Pesikta Rabbati,* a homiletic midrash, the same text is used as the basis for a homily on the rebuilding of Jerusalem (Piska 32). The targum on Ezekiel translates Ezekiel 36:8 as follows: "*My redemption* is soon to come. For, behold *I am about to reveal Myself to you,* and I will turn *by My Memra* [word], *to do you good,* and you shall be tilled and sown" (Samson H. Levey, *The Targum of Ezekiel* [Wilmington, Del.: 1987], 100; Aramaic text [ed. Sperber], 3:352).

21 For the second century, see Oskar Skarsaune, *The Proof from Prophecy* (Leiden: 1987).

22 For example, Jerome says that the words of Ezekiel 36:1–15 were not fulfilled at the time of Zerubbabel because the text says that God will "give greater good things to you than you had previously." Under Zerubbabel, Ezra, and Nehemiah only a "few of the people returned," and those who did were subject to the Medes and Persians, then the Macedonians and the Egyptians, then the Romans, and today are still subject to the rule of others (*Comm. in Ezech.* 36:1–15; *CC* 75, 499–500, ll. 636–64).

23 Jews noted the "forever" (*l'olam* in Hebrew; "in perpetuum" in Jerome's Latin translation) in Ezekiel 37:27: "Their children and their children's children shall dwell there forever" (*Comm. in Ezech.* 37:15–28; *CC* 75, 520, ll. 1310–15). The term also occurs in the Psalms and is discussed by other Christians writers in the same connection. On Psalm 132:14, "This [Zion] is my resting place *forever,*" Didymus the Blind, a contemporary of Jerome, wrote, "If the psalm is taken to refer to the earthly Zion, how can it be God's resting place forever?" (E. Muhlenberg, *Psalmenkommentare* [Berlin: 1977], 2:314).

24 Speaking of the second century B.C.E., Jonathan Goldstein writes, "Those unfulfilled prophecies each promised one or more of the following: the permanent liberation of the Jews from exile, from foreign rule, and from all mishap; the erection at Jerusalem of a temple more magnificent than Solomon's, which God Himself would choose as His own place, glorifying it and making it secure from

desecration and destruction; the rule over the Jews of a great and just king from the dynasty of David; their exaltation to imperial primacy among the nations; the conversion of the gentiles to follow the ways of the true God; the coming of a permanent era of peace; the resurrection of the righteous dead; and the punishment of all the wicked, past and present" (J. Goldstein, "How the Authors of 1 and 2 Maccabees Treated the Messianic Promises," in *Judaisms and Their Messiahs at the Turn of the Christian Era,* ed. J. Neusner, W. Green, and E. Frerichs [1987], 69).

25 Theodoret of Cyrus makes a similar observation: "New heart" in Ezek. 36:26 was taken to refer only to the Jews (*PG* 81.1185).

26 Solomon Schechter, "Genizah Specimens," *JQR* 10 (1898): 56–57, and Joseph Heinemann, *Prayer in the Talmud* (Berlin: 1977), 28–29. On this blessing, see also J. Heinemann, "The Blessing 'Who Rebuilds Jerusalem' and Its Metamorphoses," *Hayyim Schirmann Jubilee Volume* (Jerusalem: 1970), 93–101 (in Hebrew).

27 Heinemann, 49; A. Buechler, "The Blessing 'He who rebuilds Jerusalem' in the Liturgy," *JQR* 20 (1908): 798–811.

28 B. Mazar, *The Excavations in the Old City of Jerusalem near the Temple Mount* (Preliminary Report 1969–70. Institute of Archaeology, Hebrew University. Jerusalem: 1971), 72. See also Tsafrir, "Jerusalem" in *Reallexikon zur byzantinischen Kunst* 3:544–52.

29 H. Lewy, "Emperor Julian and the Building of the Temple," *Tsiyon* 6 (1940–41): 1–32 (in Hebrew); also Wilken (1983), 138–45. It has been argued by some scholars that the revolt against Gallus Caesar in 351 C.E. was in part motivated by messianic hopes. But the evidence is slim and inconclusive. For discussion, see Stemberger (1987), 132–50, and Barbara Nathanson, "The Fourth-Century Jewish 'Revolt' during the Reign of Gallus" (Ph.D. diss., Duke University, 1981).

30 David Levenson, "A Source and Tradition Critical Study of the Stories of Julian's Attempt to Rebuild the Jerusalem Temple" (Ph.D. diss., Harvard University, 1979).

31 Sebastian P. Brock, "The Rebuilding of the Temple under Julian: A New Source," *PEQ* 108 (1976): 103–07; and "A Letter Attributed to Cyril of Jerusalem on the Rebuilding of the Temple," *Bulletin of the School of Oriental and African Studies* 40 (1977): 267–86. For defense of the authenticity of the letter, see Philip Wainwright, "The Authenticity of the Recently Discovered Letter Attributed to Cyril of Jerusalem," *VC* 40 (1986): 286–93.

32 By computing the time elapsed since the destruction of the Second Temple, some rabbis dated the arrival of the Messiah in the fifth century: *b. Sanh.* 99a (365 years after destruction); *b. 'Abod. Zar.* 9b (400 years after destruction); *b. Sanh.* 97b (85 jubilees, between 440 and 490).

33 For the text of the supposed letter (dated 438 C.E.), see F. Nau, "Deux episodes de l'historie juive sous Theodose II (423–438) d'après la vie de Barsauma le Syrien," *REJ* (1927): 184–206. On Christian reaction, instigated by the monk Barsuma, see 197–201. On Eudocia and this incident, see Kenneth G. Holum, *Theodosian Empresses, Women and Imperial Dominion in Late Antiquity* (Berkeley: 1982), esp. 217ff.

34 Aharon Mirsky, *The Poems of Jose ben Jose* (Jerusalem, 1977) (in Hebrew).
35 Heinemann (1977), 273.
36 Text in Mirsky (1977), 92.
37 Text in Mirsky (1977), 94.
38 Ibid., 16–17.
39 Recall the words of Wisdom of Solomon 12 cited in chapter 2: "Those who dwelt of old in your *holy land*, thou didst hate for their detestable practices, their works of sorcery and unholy rites."
40 Jerome said that those who live "in this province are able to see and give proof of the things that were written" namely, that the temple was destroyed (*Soph.* 1:15–16; *CC* 76a, 673.658–63). John Chrysostom said that anyone who visits Jerusalem today will no longer see the splendor of the temple but destruction, utter ruin, desolation, and devastation (*pan. Bab.* 2.1; *PG* 48.834). The few stones that remained (and are still to be seen today at the Western Wall) did, however, trouble some Christians. For Jesus had said "*no* stone would remain on another," and some were still in place. In his commentary on Mark 13:1–3 (Jesus' prophecy) Victor of Antioch observed, "If some say a complete destruction has not taken place, and a part of these things is preserved, this does not mean the prediction is mistaken." The prophecy is true, he says, because sacrifices are no longer offered in the temple and everything except the foundations have been destroyed (*Catena in Evangelia S. Matthaei et S. Marci,* ed. J. A. Cramer [Oxford: 1840], 407).
41 *Graecarum affectionum curatio* 11.70–71 (ed. Canivet, 414–15); also *Is.* 1:8 (ed. Guinot, 1:158).
42 G. W. Ashby, *Theodoret of Cyrrhus as Exegete of the Old Testament* (Grahamstown, South Africa: 1972). On Theodoret and Jewish exegesis, see C. Thomas McCollough, "A Christianity for an Age of Crisis: Theodoret of Cyrus' *Commentary on Daniel,*" in *Religious Writings and Religious Systems,* ed. J. Neusner, E. Frerichs, and A. J. Levine (Atlanta: 1989), 2:157–74.
43 In his commentary on Hebrews 11:13–16 he says that the Jerusalem spoken of there is "the commonwealth located in the heavens" (*PG* 82, 764a). See also *Comm. in Heb.* 12:22–24, *PG* 82, 777a-b.
44 Cyril, *catech.* 12.7; Jerome, *tract. psal.* 88:1.
45 *Eran.* (ed. Ettlinger, 169–70).
46 See also his commentary on Psalm 88:30 (89:30, *PG* 80, 1589a): "Let the Jews show that the royal throne of David, which God promised to preserve, has endured until this day. And let them also show that his descendants have been honored with the monarchy." I am grateful to Angela Christman for calling my attention to this text. See also *Comm. in Micah* 4:6–7 (*PG* 81, 1764a).
47 As Theodoret worked his way through Ezekiel he inevitably came to the famous passage on Gog and Magog. According to Ezekiel, before God brings the exiles home to their own land, there will be a titanic struggle with a mysterious foe from the north, Gog, the king of Magog (chap. 38), who holds the people of Israel in bondage. Once Gog is vanquished God's glory will be displayed among the nations. The section ends with these words: "Then they shall know that I am the Lord their God because I sent them into exile among the nations, and then gathered them

into their own land. *I will leave none of them remaining among the nations any more"* (Ezek 39:28).

Theodoret belonged to an exegetical school that took seriously the historical setting of the prophets. Against the excesses of Christian interpreters who indiscriminately applied the prophecies to Christ, he believed that the words of the prophets had to be read in the context of their times. Sound exegesis must begin with history. In this passage Ezekiel was speaking about the return of the Jews from exile in Babylonia to live again in their land. The prophet spoke about things that "took place after the captivity [in Babylonia]" (*PG* 81, 1204). Hence Theodoret is impatient of an interpretation he had heard from Jews and certain Christians that the prophecy had not yet been fulfilled.: "I am amazed not only at the folly of the Jews but of others who have the name Christian yet hold fast to Jewish myths. They say that the invasion of Gog and Magog has not taken place and they are waiting for it to happen. They ought to understand that this prophecy is linked to the return from Babylon" (*PG* 81, 1117). The key words in this passage are "has not taken place" and "waiting for it to happen." This sounds very much like what we have heard from Jerome: Jews understood Ezekiel to be speaking about a promise that has not yet been fulfilled. In his commentary on Haggai 2:24 Theodoret reiterates the same point, but now he identifies these views with a Christian thinker, Apollinaris.: "I am astonished at the madness of Apollinaris who, without understanding, attempted to bring forth a contrary interpretation, saying that the campaign of Gog and Magog had not yet occurred" (*PG* 81, 1871). See J.-N. Guinot, "La cristallisatiọn d'un différend: Zorobabel dans l'exégèse de Théodoret de Mopsueste et de Théodoret de Cyr," *Augustinianum* 24 (1984): 527–48; idem, "Présence d'Apollinaire dans l'oeuvre exégètique de Théodoret," *Studia Patristica* 19, ed. Elizabeth Livingstone (Leuven, 1989), 168–72.

There was, however, another side of Apollinaris, one that was no less palatable to his fellow bishops. According to Jerome he wrote two books in answer to the work of Dionysius of Alexandria on promises written in the third century to refute the views of chiliasts in Egypt. His contemporaries charge that he holds judaizing opinions. Gregory Nazianzus says his followers introduced a "second Judaism and second circumcision and a second sacrifice." Unlike other "judaizers" who advocated the observance of the Jewish Law in the present, Apollinaris seems only to have said that the Jewish Law would be practiced in the future age. Even his critics do not claim he urged Christians to adopt these practices in the present. On Apollinaris's eschatology, see Gregory Nazianzus, *ep.* 101 (*PG* 37.189) and *ep.* 102 (*PG* 37, 197); Gregory of Nyssa, *ep.* 3.24; Basil, *ep.* 263 and 265. Epiphanius, however, is uncertain whether Apollinaris held these views (*haer.* 77.36). Apollinaris believed that one day Jerusalem would be built from "stones of a more brilliant material," that the temple would be restored, and animal sacrifices would again be offered in Jerusalem. All this would take place, according to Apollinaris, after the coming of Elijah, the precursor of the messianic age. The idea that the coming of Elijah will precede the advent of the Messiah is found in the New Testament in Mark 9:9–13 (Matt 17:9–13). According to Malachi 4:5–6 Elijah will come before the "day of the Lord." The tradition is documented in other Jewish sources. For discussion, see J. L. Martin, "We Have Found Elijah," in *Jews,*

Greeks and Christians: Religious Culture in Late Antiquity (Leiden: 1976), 181–219, and M. M. Faierstein, "Why Do the Scribes Say that Elijah Must Come First?" *JBL* 100 (1981): 75–96. For full discussion of the Jewish sources, see C. Milikowsky, "Seder Olam: A Rabbinic Chronography" (Ph.D. diss., Yale University, 1981), and his article "Elijah and the Messiah," in *Jerusalem Studies in Jewish Thought* (Hebrew University, Department of Jewish Studies, 1983), 2:491–96 (in Hebrew). Also P. Marie-Joseph Stiassny, "Le Prophète Elie dans le Judaisme," in *Elie le prophète* (Desclée de Brouwer) 2:199–255.

48 Theodoret's comments on the final verse of the book can be found in his *Comm. in Ezech.* 48:35; *PG* 81, 1248–56.

49 *The Targum of Ezekiel,* ed. Levey, 129; Aramaic text (ed. Sperber), 3:384.

50 Wilken (1983), 66–94.

51 Yet he can say, "Up to this time and even today we see other nations dwelling in *their* cities and occupying *their* land" (*Is.* 1:7 [Guinot, 1:156]).

52 *Is.* 60:4 (ed. Guinot, 3:244). See also *Is.* 49:22 (Guinot, 3:94).

Chapter 8
The Land that I Will Show You

1 Richard Walzer, *Galen on Jews and Christians* (London: 1949), 15. For the pervasiveness of asceticism in early Christianity, see Peter Brown, *The Body and Society: Men, Women, and Sexual Renunciation in Early Christianity* (New York: 1988).

2 On this point, see E. A. Judge, "The Early Use of Monachos for Monk: The Origins of Monasticism," *JAC* 20 (1977): 72–89.

3 Origen, *hom. in Luc.* 11.4 (*SC* 87, 192). Jerome echoed a similar sentiment, "O eremus familiarius Deo gaudens" (*ep.* 14.10).

4 John Chrysostom, *hom. 50 in Mt.* 14:23; *PG* 58, 503–04.

5 Jerome's *Life of Hilarion* is the chief source. On Hilarion's ties to Egypt, see *Vita Hilarionis* 3. Narcissus, bishop of Jerusalem in the third century, was said to have spent "many years in the deserts and in deserted areas" (Eusebius, *h.e.* 6.9.6), but we do not know which desert Eusebius had in mind. Narcissus took to the desert to escape his troubles in Jerusalem.

6 *La Vie prémétaphrastique de S. Chariton,* ed. Garitte, *Bulletin de l'institute historique Belge de Rome* (1941), 5–50.

7 On *laura*, see D. Chitty, *The Desert A City* (Crestwood, N.Y.: 1966), 14–16; and Yizhar Hirschfeld, *The Judean Desert Monasteries in the Byzantine Period* (New Haven: 1992), 10–11.

8 On Poemenia, see Hunt (1982), 76–78, 160–63.

9 Ibid., 174.

10 The passage is from "Little Gidding" in the "Four Quartets" in *The Complete Poems and Plays 1909–1950,* T. S. Eliot (New York: 1930), 139.

11 On the Judean desert, see Hirschfeld, 6.

12 On Scythopolis, see B. Lifschitz, "Scythopolis: L'histoire, les institutions et les cultes de la ville à l'époque hellénistique et impériale," *ANRW* 2.8 (1977): 262–94. Also Gideon Fuks, *Scythopolis—A Greek City in Eretz Israel* (Jerusalem: 1983) (in Hebrew).

13 On the Jewish community in Scythopolis during this period, see Lifschitz (1977), 147–56.

14 The text of Cyril's *Lives* has been edited by E. Schwartz, *Kyrillos von Skythopolis* (*Texte und Untersuchungen* 49.2; Leipzig: 1936). French translation with notes by A. J. Festugière, *Les moines d'Orient,* vol. 3 (Paris: 1962–66); English translation by R. M. Price, *Cyril of Scythopolis: The Lives of the Monks of Palestine* (Kalamazoo: 1991). Excellent recent study of the work by Bernard Flusin, *Miracle et histoire dans l'oeuvre de Cyrille de Scythopolis* (Études Augustiniennes; Paris: 1983). I cite by page number and line of Schwartz's edition.

15 For a comparison of Cyril's works with those of other hagiographers, see Flusin, 41–86.

16 Schwartz (1936), 413.

17 Flusin, 85–86. Theodore of Petra's *Life of Theodosius* (whose life Cyril also wrote) had ignored Cyril's great heroes Euthymius and Sabas. Perhaps like Festugiere, Cyril found Theodore's style pompous and pretentious. Festugiere referred to Theodore's *Life of Theodosius* as "cet insipide morceau de rhetorique." He offered a translation only to draw a contrast with Cyril: "Il m'a semblé utile de donner un exemple d'une sorte de littérature qui encombre l'hagiographie ancienne et qui fait mieux apprécier, par contraste, la candeur et la précision du récit de Cyrille" (vol. 3:83).

18 On the ascetic stars of Syria, see Peter R. L. Brown, "The Rise and Function of the Holy Man in Late Antiquity," *JRS* 61 (1971) 80–101. Text of Theodoret of Cyrus's *Religious History,* ed. P. Canivet and Alice Leryo-Molinghen, in *SC* vols. 234 and 257.

19 Herman Usener, *Der Heilige Theodosios* (Leipzig: 1890), xx.

20 On the international character of Palestinian monasticism, see Schwartz (1936) 359. Also Thomas Noonan, "Political Thought in Greek Palestinian Hagiography (ca. 526–ca. 630)" (Ph.D. diss., University of Chicago, 1975), 143, and L. Perrone, *La chiesa di Palestina e le controversie christologiche* (Brescia: 1980), 37.

21 Use of Armenian for parts of the liturgy (*Life of Sabas* 10; Schwartz [1936], 105). The Armenians were frequent pilgrims to the Holy Land (M. E. Stone, "Holy Land Pilgrimage of Armenians before the Arab Conquest," *RB* 93 [1986]: 93–110).

22 Schwartz (1936), 90, 7; Procopius, *aed.* 5.9.7; Moschus, *Prat.* 92 (*PG* 87, 2949); Sophronius, *carm.* 5.1–4.

23 On Euthymius, see Chitty (1966), 82ff; Hirschfeld, passim.

24 Hirschfeld, 117.

25 Ibid., 49.

26 Hirschfeld, "Masada in the Byzantine Period—The Marda Monastery," *Eretz Israel: Studies Investigating the Land and its Antiquities. Festschrift for Yigael Yadin* (Jerusalem: 1989), 262–74 (in Hebrew).

27 Hirschfeld (1992), 106–07.

28 At the height of monastic life in the Judean desert there were approximately sixty-five monasteries, Hirschfeld (1992), 12. Also Hirschfeld, "List of the Byzantine Monasteries in the Judaean Desert," in *Christian Archaeology in the Holy Land* (1990): 1–90.

29 Schwartz (1936), 18ff. On this incident as well as other early efforts to convert Arab-speaking tribes, see Francoise Thelamon, *Païens et chrétiens au IVe Siècle: l'apport de l'histoire ecclésiastique de Rufin d'Aquilée* (Études Augustiniennes; Paris: 1981), 123–43. On beginning of Arab-speaking Christianity, see J. Spencer Trillingham, *Christianity among the Arabs in Pre-Islamic Times* (London: 1979), and Irfan Shahid, *Byzantium and the Arabs in the Fourth Century* (Washington: 1984).

30 Sidney Griffith, "Stephen of Ramlah and the Christian Kerygma in Arabic in Ninth-Century Palestine," *JEH* 36 (1985): 23–45.

31 After the death of his dear friend John Moschus, Sophronius took his body "imitating Joseph who brought Israel and his brothers from Egypt and buried him among his fathers" in the Holy Land (Anonymous Prologue to John Moschus's Spiritual Meadow; French translation in Schönborn [1972], 244, text in H. Usener, *Der heilige Tychon* [Leipzig: 1907], 93).

32 On Sabas, see Chitty (1966), 94ff.

33 Later when Sabas founded another monastery in the desert Cyril uses the same motif: "This holy Sabas, then, having already shown himself triumphant over the evil spirits at the Castellion [a deserted Herodian fortress thought to be haunted by demons], showed his eagerness to colonize the desert by establishing another abode of piety with the assistance of the Holy Spirit" (126). Theodoret of Cyrus uses the term "colonize" in reference to the establishment of a "heavenly city on earth," by which he means the new spiritual religion of Christianity that does not offer animal sacrifices (*Ps.* 50:21; *PG* 80, 1252d).

34 Hirschfeld (1992), 79. Tsafrir gives the much higher figure of twenty thousand in *Eretz Israel from the Time of the Destruction of the Second Temple to the Arab Conquest* (Jerusalem: 1984), 2:265 (in Hebrew).

35 "Acta Sancti Theognii," in *Analecta Bollandiana* 10 (1891): 82–83; *Life of Theodosius* by Theodore of Petra in Usener (1890), 8.

36 Chitty (1966), 14. Even in Jerome's day Genesis 12 may have been cited by those who settled in the Holy Land. Jerome wrote, "It is not without reason that I seem to have followed the example of Abraham and left my kinsfolk and fatherland." Yet, he continues, this does not mean that "[I presume] to circumscribe God's power to a narrow strip of land" (*ep.* 58.2). For a spiritual interpretation of the text, see Gregory of Nyssa, *Eun.* 2.84ff.

37 John Rufus, *Life of Peter the Iberian*, ed. Raabe, *Petrus der Iberer* (Leipzig: 1895), trans. p. 31–32; Syriac text, pp. 26–27. On the desire to settle in Holy Land, see the *Life of Susan* by John of Ephesus: "This virtuous girl [Susan] decided that she would go and worhsip in the holy places where our salvation took place, and she implored her parents. But they laughed at her, a mere child, and said, 'You haven't even learned to understand the Scriptures, and yet you want to go to Jerusalem.'" Determined to make the trip, the girl set out and met a caravan traveling to Jerusalem. Dancing for joy, she said: "Blessed am I that the Lord wishes for my salvation, and as I asked He answered me! God forbid that I should return to the world and family and parents, and so die." After arriving in Jerusalem she refused to return "to her own country." Eventually she settled in a convent between Ascalon and Gaza. See Sebastian P. Brock and Susan Ashbrook Harvey, *Holy*

Women of the Syrian Orient (Berkeley: 1987), 134. Also Daniel the Stylite from Mesopotamia: "Daniel went forth wishing to travel to the holy places and to worship in the church of the Holy Resurrection and afterwards to retire to the inner desert" (*Life of Daniel* 9; text edited by Hippolyte Delehaye, *Les Saints stylites, Subsidia Hagiographica,* vol. 14 [Société des Bollandistes; Brussels: 1923], 10). When Daniel was not able to go to Jerusalem he settled for Constantinople, which his biographer called a "second Jerusalem" (chap. 10).

38 *Life of George Choziba* 34 (in *Analecta Bollandiana* 7 [1888]: 133-18–134.4).

39 On Juvenal, see E. Honigmann, "Juvenal of Jerusalem," in *DOP* 5 (1950): 209–79; also Perrone (1980), 89–115.

40 Text of petition in Schwartz (1936), 152–57. The latter half of the petition also occurs in Theodore's *Life of Theodosius,* ed. Usener (1890), 56–60. On the petition, see Perrone (1980), 169–73; von Schönborn (1972) 36–41.

41 Leo, *ep.* 113; *ep.* 109; *ep.* 123. "The veneration of Jerusalem was potentially a uniquely influential weapon in ecclesiastical politics" (Hunt [1982], 246).

42 For Cyril of Jerusalem and Hesychius, see chapter 6.

43 On heavenly Jerusalem as mother of believers, see Origen Pref., *Song of Song Commentary*; Augustine, *Serm.* 374 (*PL* 39, 1525); Jerome, *ep.* 58.2.

44 *St. James Liturgy,* ed. Mercier, *Patrologia Orientalis* 26 (1946): 206.

45 Noonan (1975), 49, 79.

Chapter 9
The God-Trodden Land

1 It should be stated that the Madaba mosaic does not identify itself as a map of the Holy Land; it is a depiction of biblical and Christian sites in the region. Detailed commentary on the map in Michael Avi-Yonah, *The Madaba Mosaic Map With Introduction and Commentary* (Jerusalem: 1954). For photographs of the mosaic, see H. Donner and H. Cüppers, *Die Mosaikkarte von Madaba,* 1: Tafelband (Wiesbaden: 1977). The second volume, a comprehensive study of the mosaic, has yet to appear. On maps, see Catherine Delano Smith, "Geography or Christianity? Maps of the Holy Land before A.D.," *JThS* 42 (1991): 142–52, and Kenneth Nebeuzahl, *Maps of the Holy Land: Images of Terra Sancta through Two Millennia* (New York: 1986).

2 Otto F. A. Meinardus, *The Holy Family in Egypt* (Cairo: 1986).

3 S. Saller, *The Memorial of Moses on Mount Nebo* (Jerusalem: 1941); S. Saller and B. Bagatti, *The Town of Nebo* (Jerusalem: 1949). Also Michele Piccirillo, *I Mosaici di Giordania* (Rome: 1986), 61–73.

4 Socrates, *h.e.* 1.17; Theodoret of Cyrus, *Is.* 51:3 (*SC* 315:117). And of course Eusebius *v.C.* 3.33.

5 Jews took the blessing to refer to Joseph's land (*Sifre Devarim* 353).

6 Kathleen E. McVey, *Ephraem the Syrian: Hymns* (New York: 1989), 345.

7 *Hymns on Virginity and Symbols of the Lord* 21.1. The first hymn begins, "Blessed are you . . . Ephraim, the city in which the Lord of Cities is hidden" (20.1). Text ed. E. Beck in *CSCO* 223:67, 71; translation by McVey, *Ephrem the Syrian: Hymns,* 346, 350–51.

8 Ch. Clermont-Ganneau, *Palestine Exploration Fund Quarterly Statement* (1901): 243–46.
9 Yoram Tsafrir, "The Maps Used by Theodosius: On the Pilgrim Maps of the Holy Land and Jerusalem in the Sixth Century C.E." *DOP* 40 (1986): 129–45. Sozomen, *h.e.* 9.17.
10 Avi-Yonah (1954), 33.
11 M. Avi-Yonah, "The Economics of Byzantine Palestine," *IEJ* 8 (1958): 40. By the end of the fourth century Christians were probably still a minority in Palestine. The time of greatest growth was the fifth and sixth centuries. See Rubin Zeev, "Spread of Christianity in the Land of Israel from the Time of Julian to the Age of Justinian," in Baras et al. (1982), 1:234–51 (in Hebrew). For recent survey of archaeological discoveries in the holy land from the Christian era, see *Christian Archaeology,* ed. Bottini, DiSegni, Alliata (1990).
12 Avi-Yonah (1958), 41.
13 Yoram Tsafrir, *Eretz Israel from the Destruction of the Second Temple to the Muslim Conquest* (Jerusalem: 1984), 2:394 (in Hebrew).
14 Procopius, *aed.* 5.6.8–15.
15 Eudocia, Avi-Yonah (1958), 42.
16 Palladius, *h. Laus.*, chap. 61.
17 Cyril of Scythopolis, *Life of Sabas* (Schwartz [1936], 109).
18 Cyril of Scythopolis, *Life of Euthymius* (Schwartz, 53–54).
19 Procopius, *aed.* 5.6.26.
20 Edward Gibbon, *Decline and Fall of the Roman Empire* (New York: 1905), chap. 40, 4:90.
21 Kenneth C. Gutwein, *Third Palestine: A Regional Study in Byzantine Urbanization* (Washington: 1981), 1–2.
22 Michael Evenari, Leslie Shanan, and Napthali Tadmor, *The Negev: The Challenge of a Desert* (Cambridge, Mass.: 1982).
23 On the cities of the Negev during the Christian era (and earlier), see Avraham Negev, *Tempel, Kirchen und Zisternen* (Stuttgart: 1983). On Christianity in Beersheva during this period, see Pau Figueras, *Byzantine Inscriptions from Beer Sheva and the Negev* (Beersheva: 1985) (in Hebrew), and idem, "Beersheva in the Roman-Byzantine Period," in *Boletín de la Asociación Española de Orientalistas* (Madrid: 1980), 135–62.
24 Negev (1983), 220–21. For other inscriptions from the Negev, see A. Negev, *The Greek Inscriptions from the Negev* (Jerusalem, 1981).
25 Ibid., 202–03.
26 Asher Ovadiah, *Corpus of the Byzantine Churches in the Holy Land* (Bonn: 1970), 218.
27 J. W. Crowfoot, *Early Churches in Palestine* (College Park, Md.: 1971), 157.
28 See note 26 and A. Ovadiah and Carla Gomez de Silva, "Supplementum to the Corpus of the Byzantine Churches in the Holy Land," part 1, *Levant* 13 (1981): 200–61; part 2 in *Levant* 14 (1982): 122–70. Churches in Trans-Jordan: see Robert Schick, "The Fate of the Christians in Palestine during the Byzantine-Umayyad Transition, A.D. 600–750" (Ph.D. diss., University of Chicago, 1987); M. Piccirillo, "Um er-Rasas Kastron Mefaa," Supplement to *La Terra Sancta* (November-

December 1986); M. Piccirillo, *Chiese et Mosaici della Giordania Settentrionale* (*Studium Biblicum Franciscanum, Collection Minor,* no. 30 (Jerusalem: 1981); Sylvester J. Saller and Bellarmino Bagatti, *The Town of Nebo (Khirbet El-Mekhayyat) with a Brief Survey of Other Ancient Christian Monuments in Transjordan* (Jerusalem: 1949). For discussion with photographs of the mosaics of several of the major churches in Jordan, see Piccirillo (1986).

29 On Panias, see P. Maraval, *Lieux saints,* 334–35.

30 Crowfoot (1971), 7.

31 Michele Piccirillo, "The Mosaics at Um er-Rasas in Jordan," *BA* 51 (1988): 208–31. See also the article by Piccirillo referred to in n. 28.

32 Tsafrir (1984), 2:260–62. Also J. Wilkinson, "Architectural Procedures in Byzantine Palestine," *Levant* 13 (1981): 156–72.

33 See D. Meehan, *Adamnan's De Locis Sanctis* (Dublin: 1958).

34 On the Church of the Nativity, see E. T. Richmond, "Basilica of the Nativity. Discovery of the Remains of an Earlier Church," *QDAP* 5 (1936): 75–81; idem, "The Church of the Nativity, The Plan of the Constantinian Church," *QDAP* 6 (1936): 63–66; in the same volume, see also "Alterations Carried Out by Justinian," 67–72; and Bagatti, *Gli antichi edifici sacri di Betlemme* (Jerusalem: 1951).

35 Crowfoot (1971), 28.

36 Tsafrir (1984), 2:236–41.

37 On church of Eleona (Mount of Olives), see H. Vincent and F. M. Abel, *Jerusalem Nouvelle* 2 (Paris: 1914): 337–60.

38 Y. Tsafrir and Y. Hirschfeld, "The Church and Mosaics at Horvat Berachot, Israel," *DOP* 33 (1979): 293–326.

39 Tsafrir and Hirschfeld (1979), 316.

40 *Itin. Eger.* 4.6–8 (Wilkinson [1981], 96).

41 G. H. Forsyth and K. Weitzmann with I. Sevcenko and F. Anderegg, *The Monastery of Saint Catherine at Mount Sinai—The Church and Fortress of Justinian I* (Ann Arbor: 1970).

42 Vasilios Tzaferis, *The Excavations of Kursi-Gergasa, Atiqot* 16 [English series] (Jerusalem: 1983).

43 *Jo.* 6.208–11 (*SC,* 157, 288–90).

44 For a similar combination of pilgrimage site and monastery, see Saller and Bagatti, *The Town of Nebo* (Jerusalem, 1949).

45 On the history of the church, see Charles Coüasnon, *The Church of the Holy Sepulchre in Jerusalem* (London: 1974); V. C. Corbo, *Il Santo Sepolcro di Gerusalemme: Aspetti archeologici dalle origini al periodo crociato.* Vol. 1, text (*Studium Biblicum Franciscanum,* coll. maior 29; Jerusalem: 1982); vol. 2 *Tavole* (1981); vol. 3, *Documentazione fotografico* (1981).

46 André Grabar, *Martyrium: recherches sur le culte des reliques et l'art chrétien antique* (London: 1972), 1: 257ff.

47 Coüasnon (1974), 39.

48 On the other buildings at the site, the baptistry, the church of Golgotha off the courtyard of the Anastasis, see Coüasnon (1974), 46ff.

49 B. Bagatti, "Eulogie Palestinese," in *Orientalia Christiana Periodica* 15 (1949): 126–66; Gary Vikan (1982). See also L. Y. Rahman, "The Adoration of the Magi on Two Sixth-Century C.E. Eulogia Tokens," *IEJ* 29 (1979): 34–36; and most recently the essays in *The Blessings of Pilgrimage* in Ousterhout (1990). Eulogiae came in two forms, *ampullae,* small bottles containing water or flasks of oil from lamps that burned in the shrines, and tokens made of clay or earth taken from the sites. Most were stamped with scenes from the life of Christ appropriate to the place. The tokens were intended to be ground up, dissolved in water, and swallowed for miraculous properties. Commenting on Isaiah 49:23 ("lick the dust of your feet"), Theodoret of Cyrus wrote that this prophecy was fulfilled in Jerusalem where people "seize the earth as a heavenly gift and they lavish it with kisses and regard it as a remedy of soul and body" (*Comm in Isa.* 49:23; *SC* 315, 96).

50 Paulinus of Nola, *ep.* 49.14.

51 *Piacenza Pilgrim* 11 (Wilkinson [1977] 82).

52 *Supplementum Epigraphicum Graecum* 8, no. 134; Louis Robert, "Bulletin Epigraphique," in *REG* 68 (1955): 275, and A. M. Schneider, *ZDPV* 68 (1951): 229–31.

53 Text in *Supplementum Epigraphicum Graecum* 13, no. 538; Louis Robert, "Bulletin Epigraphique," in *REG* 71 (1958): 329–30.

54 Fra Francesco Suriano, *Treatise on the Holy Land,* trans. Theophilus Bellorini and E. Hoade, with preface by B. Bagatti (Jerusalem: 1949), 28. "This blessed land above all parts of the world had the greatest contact with him, and therefore it is full of divine virtues and it has become a most holy habitation" (29). The treatise was written in the fifteenth century.

Chapter 10
When Will the Light of Israel Be Kindled?

1 *Gen. Rab.* 56.9. For a discussion of the verse in Genesis, see Marvin Pope, "The Timing of the Snagging of the Ram, Genesis 22:13," *BA* 49 (1986): 114–17.

2 Jacob Neusner, *Judaism and Christianity in the Age of Constantine* (Chicago: 1987), 51. In this book Neusner has collected texts from the Christian period to show how Jewish writings subtly respond to the Christianization of the land of Israel. See, for example, p. 27.

3 Lee I. Levine, *Ancient Synagogues Revealed* (Detroit: 1982), 9–10; also Eric M. Meyers, A. Thomas Kraabel, and James F. Strange, *Synagogue Excavations at Khirbet Shema, Upper Galilee, Israel,* 1970–72 (*Annual of the American Schools of Oriental Research,* 42; Durham, N.C.: 1975), 167–69; Eric M. Meyers and Stephen Goranson, "Early Judaism and Christianity in the Light of Archaeology," *BA* 51 (1988): 69–79; and Dennis E. Groh, "Jews and Christians in Late Roman Palestine: Towards a New Chronology," *BA* 51 (1988): 80–96.

4 Marilyn Joyce Segal Chiat, *Handbook of Synagogue Architecture* (Chico, Calif.: 1982), 21–27.

5 Ibid., 41–45.

6 Günter Stemberger, *Juden und Christen im Heiligen Land: Palestina unter Konstantin und Theodosius* (Munich: 1987), 112.

7 On the Jewish community in Beth Shean, see Gideon Fuks, *Scythopolis—A Greek City in Eretz Israel* (Jerusalem: 1983), 147–56 (in Hebrew). In some areas, e.g., the Golan, however, there may have been a sharp line between Jewish and Christian settlements. See Claudine Dauphine, "Jewish and Christian Communities in the Roman and Byzantine Gaualnitis: A Study of Evidence from Archaeological Surveys," *PEQ* 114 (1982): 129–82, and response of Zvi U. Ma'oz, "Comments on Jewish and Christian Communities in Byzantine Palestine," *PEQ* 117 (1985): 58–62. Robert Gregg's forthcoming study of inscriptions from the Golan raises questions about Ma'oz's claim that a section of the Golan was exclusively Jewish.

8 An interesting detail of the synagogues in this period is the appearance of an apse, an architectural feature that was characteristic of churches. The chief activities in the synagogue were the reading of the Scriptures, instruction, and prayer, hence synagogues, in contrast to churches, were closer in shape to a square (broadhouse plan) than to the rectangle of the basilica. There was no altar and hence no need for an apse. In the Byzantine period, however, the basilica plan (with two rows of columns) became common, and the buildings were oriented to the apse. In many ways the floor plan resembled the plan of a church. Yoram Tsafrir writes of the synagogue of Beth Alpha in Scythopolis, "It had a forecourt or atrium in front of its facade, with a cistern in the middle. Between this courtyard and the prayer hall was an entrance corridor the width of the facade, called the narthex. The hall proper was divided by two rows of columns into a nave and two flanking aisles, above which, apparently there were balconies possibly serving as the women's galleries. Even the wooden-beam construction of the roof was typical of the churches. At the southern end of the prayer hall, the end facing Jerusalem, there was a raised *bima* and an apse containing the Holy Ark." Yoram Tsafrir, "The Byzantine Setting and Its Influence on Ancient Synagogues," in Lee I. Levine, *The Synagogue in Late Antiquity* (Philadelphia: 1987), 151. See also his discussion in Tsafrir (1984), 2:285–96, and the synagogue at Ma'oz Hayyim, V. Tzaferis, "The Ancient Synagogue at Ma'oz Hayyim," *IEJ* 32 (1982): 215–44.

9 M. J. Chiat, "Synagogues and Churches in Byzantine Beit She'an," *Journal of Jewish Art* 8 (1980): 6–24.

10 Tsafrir in Baras et al. (1982), 1:381.

11 For text of the inscription and thorough discussion, see Yaacov Sussmann, "A Halakhic Inscription from the Beth-Shean Valley," *Tarbits* 43 (1973): 88–158 (in Hebrew). English translation of the inscription and summary of the previous article in J. Sussman, "The Inscription in the Synagogue at Rehob," in Levine (1982), 146–53.

12 Laws concerning the seventh year can be found in the Mishnaic Tractate *Sheviit* and *Tosefta Sheviit*.

13 *Lev. Rab.* 1.1 (ed. Mordecai Margulies [Jerusalem: 1953], 4–5).

14 Translation in Levine (1982), 152–53.

15 Sussman (1973), 149.

16 Neusner (1987), 27: "Israel remained Israel, wholly subject to its own law, entirely in control of its own destiny, fully possessed of its own land."

17 On Beth Alpha, see E. L. Sukenik, *The Ancient Synagogue of Beth Alpha* (Oxford: 1932).

18 Chiat (1980), 15. For bibliography on other interpretations of the synagogue, see ibid.

19 A. Diez Macho, *Neophyti I: Targum Palestinense Ms. de la Biblioteca Vaticana 2* (Madrid: 1968), 551–52. On the interpretation of the Akedah in Jewish tradition, see Shalom Spiegel, *The Last Trial* (New York: 1967).

20 Carl Kraeling, *The Excavations at Dura-Europos: The Synagogue* (New Haven: 1979), 56–69.

21 Diez Macho (1968), 551–52. For Christian efforts to give the story a distinctively Christian interpretation, see Robert L. Wilken, "Melito, the Jewish Community at Sardis and the Sacrifice of Isaac," *TS* 37 (1976): 53–69.

22 On the link between the Beth Alpha mosaics and the temple, see John Wilkinson, "The Beit Alpha Synagogue Mosaic: Towards an Interpretation," *Journal of Jewish Art* 5 (1978): 16–28. On possible messianic overtones, see C. H. Kraeling, *The Synagogue* (1979), 214ff., 361ff.; Rachel Wischnitzer, *The Messianic Theme in the Paintings of the Dura Synagogue* (Chicago: 1948).

23 Chiat (1982), 219–24; D. Barag, Y. Porat, and E. Netzer, "The Synagogue at 'En Gedi,'" in Levine (1982), 116–19.

24 Chiat (1982), 255.

25 Levine (1987), 184.

26 Chiat (1982), 183–86.

27 Paul C. Finney, "Orpheus-David: A Connection in Iconography between Greco-Roman Judaism and Early Christianity," *Journal of Jewish Art* 5 (1978): 6.

28 *Expugnatio Hierosolymae A.D. 614* 3.5 (Arabic version A), ed. Gerardo Garitte (Louvain: 1973), *CSCO* 340:6. In the Georgian version of this text, Jerusalem is called "that city which was a refuge for all Christians and a bulwark of their empire" (*Expug.* 8.4; trans. G. Garitte [Louvain: 1960], *CSCO* 203:13).

29 Norman Baynes, "The Successors of Justinian," in *The Cambridge Medieval History* (New York: 1964), 2:263.

30 Sycmania was a Jewish city in the vicinity of modern-day Haifa (*Piacenza Pilgrim* 3). For references to the city, see S. Klein, Sefer Yishuv, *Places of Settlement from the Time of the Destruction of the Second Temple to the Conquest of Eretz Israel by the Arabs* (Jerusalem: 1978), 155–56 (in Hebrew). Sycmania is mentioned several times in the *Doctrina Jacobi* (Bonwetsch, 53, 15; 63, 27, 86, 14–17). For *Doctrina Jacobi*, see following note.

31 The document on which this information is based is a Christian account of a dispute between a Jew named Jacob, who had been converted forcibly to Christianity, and a company of Jews from Palestine. The dispute is supposed to have taken place during the reign of Phocas (602–10 C.E.) The central question of debate was whether the "time of the Messiah, the king of Israel" had arrived. The Jews claimed that the Messiah would come soon. Christians, however, claimed that the Messiah was Jesus Christ, who had already come centuries ago. For centuries Christians and Jews had debated this topic; what makes the debate in the early seventh century so interesting is that it centers on the "signs of the times," social and political events in Palestine and in the Roman Empire. As Jews learned of the murder of the Roman emperor by a usurper and heard tales of the success of the Persians within the borders of the empire, some began to hope that

the days of the Messiah were at hand and that Roman Christian rule in the Land of Israel would soon come to an end. The text has come down in several Greek versions as well as in Ethiopic, Syriac, Arabic, Old Slavonic, and even in a partial Hebrew version. The longer Greek text was published by N. Bonwetsch, *Doctrina Jacobi Nuper Baptizati* (Abhandlungen der Koeniglichen Gesellschaft der Wissenschaften zu Goettingen, philosophisch-historische Klasse, n.s. 12, 3; Berlin: 1990), and a shorter version by F. Nau, *La Didascalie de Jacob* (*Patrologia Orientalis* 8, 5; Paris: 1912; repr. Turnhout, Belgium: 1971). The Ethiopic text (with French translation) was published by Sylvain Grebaut, *Sargis D'Aberga* (*Controverse judéo-chrétienne, Patrologia Orientalis* 3, 4: 556–643; Paris: 1909 and 13, 1: 5–95; Paris: 1916; repr. Turnout, Belgium: 1971–74). New edition and discussion by V. Déroche and G. Dagron, *Travaux et Mémoires* 11 (Centre de Recherche d'Histoire et Civilisation de Byzance, Paris: 1991): 17–273. See also A. Sharf, "Byzantine Jewry in the Seventh Century," *BZ* 48 (1955): 103–16.

32 *Doctrina Jacobi Nuper Baptizati* 4.1 (ed. Bonwetsch, 63, ll. 17–18; ed. Grebaut, 51) and 5.6 (Bonwetsch, 77, ll. 8–9, Grebaut, 76).

33 F. Macler, *Histoire d'Héraclius par l'évêque Sebêos* (Paris: 1904), 68. Sebeos also mentions a Jewish revolt in Edessa after the Persian invasion.

34 *Book of Elijah*, ll. 10–13 (ed. Even Shmuel, 42).

35 *B. Yoma* 10a.

36 Andrew Scharf, *Byzantine Jewry* (New York: 1971), 35. Also Joshua Starr, "Byzantine Jewry on the Eve of the Arab Conquest (565–638)," *Journal of the Palestine Oriental Society* 15 (1935): 280–93. Petrus Brow S.I., "Die Judengesetzgebung Justinians," *Analecta Gregoriana* 8 (1935): 109–46. On earlier efforts to restrict rights of the Jews, see Amnon Linder, "Roman Power and the Jews in the Age of Constantine," *Tarbiz* 44 (1975): 95–143 (in Hebrew).

37 *Anecdota* 28.16.

38 Text in A. Linder, *Jews in Roman Imperial Legislation* (Jerusalem: 1987), 405–07.

39 Jacob Mann, "Changes in the Divine Service of the Synagogue due to Religious Persecutions," *HUCA* 4 (1927): 241–310.

40 On this event, see Theophanes, *Chronographia*, 296 (ed. C. de Boor [Leipzig: 1883]); *Chronicle of Michael the Syrian* (ed. J. B. Chabot, *Chronique de Michel le Syrien* [Paris: 1901]), 2:379. See Joseph Dan, "Two Jewish Merchants in the Seventh Century," *Tsiyon* 36 (1971): 1–26 (in Hebrew). Also Zvi Baras, "The Persian Conquest and the End of Byzantine Rule," in Baras et al. (1982), 1:325. J. B. Chabot, "Trois épisodes concernant les Juifs," *REJ* 28 (1894): 290–94. One late source mentions forced conversion of Jews under Phocas. This is the *Chronicle of Dionysius of Tell Mahr*, ed. J. B. Chabot, *Chronique de Denys de Tellmáhré* (Paris: 1895), 4. Dionysius places the episode in Jerusalem. For discussion of the reliability of the account, see also Baras (1982), 1:306–07. He concludes that except for this one late source, "there is no information about religious persecution of the Jews during [Phocas's] reign" (323). The *Doctrina Jacobi* also mentions forced conversion of Jews, but under Heraclius (Bonwetsch, 1–2; Grebaut, 555–56). On Jews using towns near Jericho and Beit Ramla as bases for "raiding," see *PG* 89, 1692b.

41 Baras (1982), 323.

42 For a critical discussion of the sources for the Persian invasion and the events leading up to it, see Baras (1982), 300–13. Avi-Yonah, *The Jews of Palestine* (New York: 1976), 157ff., is useful in that he narrates the chief events and cites the relevant texts, but his handling of the sources is uncritical.

43 *Expugnatio Hierosolymae* 3.1–4 (Arabic text A).

44 Ibid., 8.8–16 (Arabic text A).

45 M. Ben-Dov, "The Area South of the Temple Mount in the Early Islamic Period," *Jerusalem Revealed,* ed. Y. Yadin (Jerusalem: 1975), 97–101.

46 The Arabic and Georgian texts of this work, which goes by the name *Capture of Jerusalem* (*Expugnatio Hierosolymae A.D. 614*), have been edited by G. Garitte (see note 28). Latin translation in *CSCO,* vol. 341 (Louvain: 1973). For a partial English translation of the Georgian version, see F. Conybeare, "Antiochus Strategos' Account of the Sack of Jerusalem in 614 A.D.," *The English Historical Review* 25 (1910): 502–16.

47 *Expugnatio Hierosolymae* 10.1–2 (Arabic text A).

48 *Anacreontica 14,* "On the Captivity of Jerusalem," l. 62 (ed. M. Gigante, *Sophronii Anacreontica* [Rome: 1957]), 105.

49 Avi-Yonah (1976), 263.

50 Baras (1982), 2:326. Jews, however, did serve in the Persian army; extent of their participation cannot be determined (Baras [1982], 2:327).

51 Text of the *Book of Elijah* is in Even Shmuel, *Midreshei Geulah* (Jerusalem and Tel Aviv: 1954), 41–48. Besides the edition of Even Shmuel the *Book of Elijah* was also edited by A. Jellinek, *Bet ha-Midrasch,* 3d ed. (Jerusalem: 1967), 3:65–68, and M. Buttenwieser, *Die hebraische Elias-Apokalypse* (Leipzig: 1897), 15–26. My translation is based on Shmuel's text, but I have been aided by a translation and notes of David Levenson. Discussion of dating in *Midreshei Geulah,* 38–40.

52 On the difficulties of using apocalyptic works as historical sources, see Paul J. Alexander, "Medieval Apocalypse as Historical Source," *American Historical Review* 73 (1968): 997–1018. For the specific works associated with the Persian and Arab conquests, see Joseph Yahalom, "On the Value of Literary Works as Historical Sources," *Cathedra* 11 (1979): 125–33 (in Hebrew).

53 On Elijah and the Messiah, see Chaim Milikovsky, "Elijah and the Messiah," Institute for Jewish Studies, the Hebrew University (Jerusalem: 1983), 2:491–96 (in Hebrew), and M. M. Faierstein, "Why Do the Scribes Say that Elijah Must Come First?" *JBL* 100 (1981): 75–86. On Zerubbabel and the Messiah, see Louis Ginzberg, *The Legends of the Jews* (Philadelphia: 1913), 4:352ff.

54 It is easy to see how a book such as this could be adapted to different historical circumstances. In one version the name Haksharat occurs and that is probably Artaxerxes, the founder of the Sassanid dynasty in the third century C.E. But at some point the name Haksera (*Hksr'* [Chosroe]) was placed in the text, suggesting that the book was either written in the seventh century or rewritten to fit the historical situation at that time. This king, the "last king of Persia" according to the text, "will go up against Rome for three successive years until he occupies it for twelve months. Three mighty men of war will come up from the sea to meet him, and they will be delivered into his hands" (ll. 14–16). Here the author seems

to be speaking about a war between Rome, i.e., the Byzantine Roman Empire, whose capital was at Constantinople and whose armies come from across the Mediterranean Sea, and Persia. At several points the text alludes to the mistreatment of Jews by the Romans: "He [a Roman emperor, perhaps Heraclius] will stretch out his arm against the faithful people [or 'Israel' according to another text]" (l. 21). See also ll. 59–62.

55 Jerome, *Is.* 49:14–21; *CC* 73a:543. The *Book of Elijah* cites Ezek 36:38, the prophet's vision of the rebuilding of waste places and the inhabitation of the cities by the exiles and the putting forth of new shoots in the land: "But you, O mountains of Israel, shall shoot forth your branches and yield your fruit to my people Israel; for they will soon come home." Later the author quotes a passage from the vision of the dry bones in Ezekiel 37, "And as I looked there were sinews on them [and flesh had come upon them]."

56 Text of the *Sefer Zerubbabel* in *Midreshei Geulah,* 71–88. Besides the text of Even Shmuel (n. 51) the *Book of Zerubbabel* has been edited by Adolf Jellinek, *Bet ha-Midrasch,* 3d ed. (Jerusalem: 1967), 2:54–57, and Israel Levi, "Apocalypse de Zorababel et le Roi de Perse Siroes," *REJ* 68 (1914): 129–60; *REJ* 69 (1919): 108–28); *REJ* 70 (1920): 57–65. Levi dates the work to the early seventh century, *REJ* 69, 112. My translation is based on text of Even Schmuel. For discussion and English translation, see now Martha Himmelfarb, "Sefer Zerubbabel," in *Rabbinic Fantasies: Imaginative Literature from Classical Hebrew Literature,* ed. David Stern and Mark J. Mirsky (Philadelphia: 1990), 67–90.

57 Gerson D. Cohen, *Messianic Postures of Ashkenazim and Sephardim* (Leo Baeck Institute; New York: 1967), 12. In this essay Cohen observes that apocalyptic books such as the *Book of Zerubbabel* need not imply popular uprisings or political or military action. Instead of postponing comfort to a distant future, the apocalyptic works placed it in the imminent future. In this sense even the "ostensibly explosive literature of Palestinian . . . apocalypticism" could lead to a channeling of emotions into visionary fantasy rather than inciting people to act (30–31). Zvi Baras (1982) also makes a sharp distinciton between those who wished to "force the end" and apocalypticism in which the attitude might have been "sit still and don't do anything" (325). The distinction is necessary; it is not possible to say that those Jews who aided the Persians were the same who authored the books of Elijah and Zerubbabel. Yet in the context of the seventh century the two seem to converge.

58 See *Tosefta Zebakhim* 13. The "eternal temple" is a rabbinical phrase used to designate a temple that will never be destroyed, as, for example, the temple depicted in the final chapter of Ezekiel. See also Even Shmuel (1954), 70.

59 The prayer mentioned here is not simply a general outpouring of grief, but a prescribed prayer, the Tefilah, the traditional prayer of eighteen benedictions said each day by devout Jews. The phrase "Blessed are you, O Lord, who gives life to the dead" cited by the *Book of Zerubbabel* comes from the Tefilah. This prayer includes a petition for the rebuilding of Jerusalem. Zerubbabel's petition is, however, more specific. He asks what the plan will be for the "eternal temple."

60 Zerubbabel is told that an angel of the Lord who fought the battles with the kings of Canaan and led Abraham into the land will fight alongside of the Messiah against Armilius, the son of Satan who was born of the image of a stone. In Jewish tradition Armilius was a "figure of menacing terror," a satanic ruler, king of Edom, who appears at the end of time to destroy Israel. Zerubbabel asks what the name of the Messiah is and what he is doing in this place. Zerubbabel had already been introduced to a messianic figure, but because of his uncomely appearance, he did not recognize him. By the time this book was written there was a tradition of two Messiahs, one from the tribe of Ephraim, Messiah son of Joseph, and the second the son of David. In the eschatological drama the Messiah son of Joseph appears first but falls in battle; after his death the Messiah son of David appears and is victorious. In answer to Zerubbabel's persistent questioning Metatron (or Michael) reveals the name of the second Messiah: "This is the Messiah, the son of David, and his name is Menachem ben Amiel, and he was born king of Israel of the house of David. . . . And I will lift him up by the spirit [or wind] of the Lord and hide him in this place until the time of the end" (ll. 46–69). See David Berger, "Three Typological Themes in Early Jewish Messianism: Messiah Son of Joseph, Rabbinic Calculations, and the Figure of Armilius," *Journal of the Association of Jewish Studies* 10 (1985): 141–64.

61 Raphael Patai, *The Messiah Texts* (Detroit: 1979), 123. Hefzivah in *b. San.* 94a.

62 Himmelfarb, 69.

63 The prophets also spoke out against the worship of the asheroth. "I will cut off your images and your pillars from among you, and you shall bow down no more to the work of your hands; and I will root out your Asherim from among you and destroy your cities" (Mic 5:13–14).

64 Shmuel (1954), 82. On the worship of the statue as reference to Christianity, see also Levi, "Apocalypse de Zorababel," *REJ* 70 (1920): 59. For other references to "idolatry" of Christians and blasphemy of those who eat swine and believe the end time has passed, see R. Edelmann, "Bestimmung, Heimat und Alter des Synagogalen Poesie," *Oriens Christianus* 29 (1932): 27.

65 Chrysippus of Jerusalem, *Oratio in Sanctam Mariam Deiparam* 1, ed. M. Jugie, *Homélies Mariales Byzantines* in *Patrologia Orientalis* 19, 3 (Turnhout: 1974): 219.

66 Targum to Song of Songs, last verse. See Marvin Pope, *Song of Songs: A New Translation with Introduction and Commentary* (Garden City, N.Y.: 1977), 93, and R. Loewe, "Apologetic Motifs in the Targum to the Songs of Songs," in *Biblical Motifs: Origins and Transformations,* ed. A. Altmann (Philip W. Lown Institute of Advanced Judaic Studies, Brandeis University); *Studies and Texts* (Cambridge, Mass.: 1966), 3:159–96.

67 On the expansion of Jerusalem to cover the entire land and beyond even to Damascus, see *Sifre Deuteronomy,* ch. 1 (ed. Finkelstein, 7–8). Also scroll 11Q Temple at Qumran, Cave 11, Sanders (1985), 86–87.

68 See *Midreshei Geulah,* 78, l. 69; on Sukkoth, see text of Jellinek, 56; on prayer at the gates of the city, Levi (1920), 135. On this point, see Baras (1982), 334.

69 *Midreshei Geulah,* 78.

70 Avi-Yonah (1976), 256.

71 Baras (1982), 334.

72 E. Fleischer, "An Early Jewish Tradition of the End of Byzantine Rule in Eretz Israel," *Tsiyon* 36 (1971): 110–15 (in Hebrew).

73 Text from Abraham Bar Hiyya, in *Sefer Megillat ha Megalleh* (ed. Z. Poznanski [Berlin: 1924]), 99, ll. 22–26; see Amnon Linder, "Jerusalem, Focus of Confrontation," in *Vision and Conflict in the Holy Land,* ed. Richard I. Cohen (Jerusalem: 1985), 12.

74 The *Disputation of Sergius the Stylite against a Jew* 20.8, ed. A. Hayman (*CSCO,* vol. 338; Louvain: 1973), 67, l. 13 in Syriac text, 65 in English translation. The mention of the blessing of Abraham and the Jew's question occurs at 20.9 Syriac, 67, ll. 20–21 and in English, 66, ll. 6–7. The text makes explicit mention of "kingdom" as one of the things that Christians have taken from the Jews. A Syriac Christian legend says that if after the crucifixion Christians were to find the true cross, then "the Hebrew people will no longer rule, instead the Kingdom and the glory will be turned over to the worshippers of the crucified." See J. Straubinger, *Die Kreuszauffindungslegende* (Paderborn: 1912), 327.

75 The embassy is no doubt apocryphal, but it is unlikely that the sentiment attributed to the Jews would have had to be invented by Sebeos. The text is from the Armenian historian Sebeos, ed. F. Macler (1904), 94–96. English translation and brief discussion of the context of the passage in Patricia Crone and Michael Cook, *Hagarism: The Making of the Islamic World* (Cambridge: 1977), 6–9. The setting is an encounter between Jews of Edessa and Muhammad. Muhammad is presented as defending Jewish claims to the land: "God has promised this land to Abraham and his posterity after him forever; he acted according to His promise while he loved Israel. Now you, you are the sons of Abraham and God fulfills in you the promise made to Abraham and his posterity. Only love the god of Abraham, go and take possession of your country which God gave to your father Abraham, and none will be able to resist you in the struggle, for God is with you."

Chapter 11
The Jerusalem Above Wept over the Jerusalem Below

1 Theodoret of Cyrus wrote, "Let them show us *their* Jerusalem delivered from tears. For that city [Jewish Jerusalem] was handed over to many misfortunes, whereas this city [the heavenly Jerusalem] alone enjoys life without grief and free of tears" (*Is.* 65:19 [Guinot, 3:324]).

2 *Life of John the Almsgiver,* Leontius bishop of Neapolis, chap. 9. Text edited by Hippolyte Delehaye, "Une Vie inédite de Saint Jean l'Aumonier" in *Analecta Bollandiana* 45 (1927): 23.

3 *Lam.* 1.1, *PG* 81, 780–81. According to Origen in the book of Lamentations Jerusalem symbolizes the perfect soul. Hence, in the text weeping refers to the soul falling from its proper country into confusion (*PG* 13, 612a).

4 Bibliographical information on the text in chap. 10, n. 28.

5 The Arabic versions fill out some of the historical details in the text. G. Garitte, "La sepulture de Modeste de Jerusalem," in *Le Museon* 73 (1960): 127–33.

6 The work has attracted the attention of historians, partly because the Byzantine historians give few details on the Persian conquest. Their works are "heartbreakingly laconic," remarks A. Couret: "It seems as though their works would be found wanting if they described the extent of that catastrophe which devastated the East." See his "La Prise de Jerusalem par les Perses, en 614," in *ROC* 2 (1897): 125–64. In this article Couret also gives the text of one of the Arabic versions with a French translation. For a partial English translation of the Georgian text, see Fredrick C. Conybeare, "Antiochus Strategos' Account of the Sack of Jerusalem in A.D. 614," *The English Historical Review* 25 (1910): 502–16.

7 This story of the clever virgin passed into Western literature as an independent tale and is narrated in detail and with religious feeling in the Renaissance poem *Orlando Furioso* by Ariosto. The story runs as follows: a virgin from a convent on the Mount of Olives had been given to a Persian soldier as his concubine. First she convinced the soldier that she possessed a magic ointment which could protect him from harm. Then she rubbed some of the ointment on her shoulders and asked him to strike her. Of course the blow killed her at once, but it preserved her chastity and frustrated the young soldier's amatory ambitions. On this story, see G. Levi Della Vida, "'Stratagème de la Vierge' et la Traduction Arabe du 'Patrum Spirituale' de Jean Moschus," in *Annuaire de l'Institut de Philologie et d'Histoire Orientales et Slaves* 7 (1939–44): 144–57; C. Bonner, "The Maiden's Stratagem," *Byzantion* 16 (1941–42): 142–61.

8 J. T. Milik, "Topographie de Jérusalem," Mélanges de l'Université de Josip de Beyrouth (Beirut: 1964).

9 Cf. 2 Baruch 80.2, hiding of the holy vessels lest they be polluted.

10 Part of the *Capture of Jerusalem* is a letter of the patriarch Zachariah that has also been preserved in Greek: *PG* 86, 2 col. 3227–34.

11 An interesting feature of this work is its use of typology: "I do not weep over the Temple of the Jews; I do not weep over the Temple about which Jeremiah the prophet wrote his lamentation; I do not weep over the ark in which was the staff and manna and the tables on which God wrote with his own finger. . . . I do not weep over gilded walls; I do not weep over sculpted stone; I do not weep over magnificent portals; I do not weep over high colonnades; I do not weep over columns and precious stones. . . . I do not weep over that which was in the 'law' . . . but I weep over a spiritual gift. I do not weep over those things that were in *types*, but over those which were in *truth*" (1.16).

In reading the Scriptures, Christians juxtaposed the "types" of the Old Testament (events, persons, and things from Israel's history) and the "truth" of the New Testament (the events, people, and things associated with Christ and the birth of the church). Earlier events were seen as figures or models that foreshadowed the spiritual events in the New Testament, the truth that had come with the revelation in Christ. The sacrifice of Isaac, for example, was seen as a type of the sacrifice of Christ. Like a plaster or clay model constructed by an artist in preparation for sculpting the statue itself, the type pointed to the greater thing that would one day appear. The type was perishable, the spiritual reality eternal. In the Exodus from Egypt through the Sea of Reeds, the Jews were delivered from *temporal* or *earthly* bondage; but those who were washed in waters of Baptism received *eternal* redemption. Similarly, the paschal lamb had to be offered *each year*; but the offering of Christ on the cross had taken place *once for all*.

In the traditional understanding, the truth that supplants the type was always a *spiritual* reality. With respect to Jerusalem this meant that the Jerusalem above displaced the Jerusalem below. In the words of the second-century bishop Melito of Sardis cited earlier, "The Jerusalem below was precious, but it is worthless now because of the Jerusalem above; the narrow inheritance was precious, but it is worthless now because of the widespread bounty. For it is not in one place nor in a little plot that the glory of God is established, but on all the ends of the inhabited earth his bounty overflows" (*pass.* 44–45).

Although Strategos, like Melito, employs the rhetorical strategy of contrasting the type with the truth, it is apparent that something is awry. He uses the refrain "I do not weep over" to set forth a series of historical examples designed to contrast the earthly city of ancient Israel with the new spiritual reality. But when Strategos reaches the end of his list of examples, and the reader anticipates a reference to the "spiritual gift" over which he *does* weep, Strategos is silent. He never mentions the new that is to be contrasted with the old. The reason of course is that he cannot, because the truth to which he refers is an earthly city like the Jerusalem of old.

Strategos's rhetoric overtakes his experience and his logic. His reiteration of the phrase "I do not weep over" falls flat rhetorically, for he is lamenting gilded walls, sculpted stone, magnificent portals, and, of course, the Temple of God in Christian Jerusalem. But to mention these things would make it plain that he is weeping over earthly Jerusalem, just as Jeremiah wept centuries ago over the fall of the earthly Jerusalem. Hence the passage concludes lamely with the restatement of a principle, "I do not weep over those things that were in types, but over those which were in truth." To be sure, he depicts the sack of Christian Jerusalem in great detail elsewhere in the work; but in this context, where he employs the typological scheme, he avoids mentioning the new, for the obvious reason that the new had all the features of the old. The author of Lamentations said, "The Lord has scorned *his altar,* disowned *his sanctuary*" (Lam 2:7); and Strategos wrote, "It is appropriate that we describe the sadness that has overcome us, the devastation of his *holy places*" (1.20).

Once Christians began to lament the destruction of the Jerusalem below as the Jews once lamented the captivity of Zion, the old Christian distinction between types and truth became anachronistic. For the truth had acquired the same earthbound quality that once marked the type. The historical and political fate of Jerusalem became a theological matter as much for Christians as it was for the Jews, and the language of the Scriptures about Jerusalem could now be interpreted "literally," not just spiritually. Strategos even applies Jesus' beatitude to those who weep over the fall of the earthly Jerusalem: "Blessed are those who mourn, for they will be comforted" (1.19). In his *Commentary on Lamentations* Origen cites this beatitude with respect to a mystical weeping over the fall of the soul (*PG* 13, 608).

12 He attributes the city's troubles to the factionalism of blues and greens, rival political and religious parties in the city (chap. 2) and the treachery of Bonosus, count of the East, against the patriarch Zacharias (chap. 4).

13 Strategos draws on a pastiche of texts from Ezekiel 36:12, 14, 16, 20, 26, 27.

14 Strategos draws a parallel between Zacharias and David, who feared the people when he opposed their wishes (5.12).

15 The two monks who had been captured by the Persians realized that the situation of the city, the "City of God," as it is called in this passage, was growing hopeless (5.26). "Because of the multitude of our sins, God has handed us into your hands." The inhabitants of Jerusalem asked why they had not been told from the beginning that the city would be destroyed. To which the monks replied, "We are not prophets!" When we were first taken out of our caves and came to the city we saw an angel standing on the wall of the city with a flaming spear, and at that moment we thought the city was safe. But then another angel came down and said, "Depart from here, because the Lord has handed over the Holy City into the hands of the enemy. And the company of angels departed, because they were not able to oppose the command of God." When the angels departed, "We knew then that our sins exceeded God's mercy. But take heart, brethren, because God does not do this out of hate, but that he might chasten us." As David had said, "Blessed is the one whom the Lord chastens (Ps 93:2)" (5.32).

At this point, the narrator includes a vision of another monk, a certain John from Mar Saba (the monastery established by Sabas on the brook Kidron) (6.1). This disciple asked John whether the city would be destroyed and its inhabitants taken captive. John said, "Who am I that you ask this thing of me, for I am a sinful man." The disciple beseeched him with tears and John said, "O my son, I see that you want to see this thing; I will tell you what God has communicated to me. I tell you that five days ago I was pondering this thing when I had a vision of someone taking hold of me. He stood me before Golgotha, and the entire community was crying out, 'O Lord, have mercy on us.' And I looked and saw Jesus Christ standing over the cross; and I saw the Virgin Mary beseeching him and interceding for the people. And Jesus Christ responded to her saying, 'I do not hear their prayer because they corrupted my temple.'

"The people cried out, 'O Lord, have mercy on us. With tears and groaning we go up to the temple of Mar Constantine [the great Martyrium] where the cross is kept.' Then I [the monk] ascended with them to the temple of Mar Constantine, and when I put my head inside that I might pray in that place where the cross is, I saw a great deal of sludge coming out of the place and filling the temple. There were two old men from the leaders standing there and I called out to them and said to them, 'Don't you fear God? We are not able to pray because of this mud.' And the two old men answered and said to me, 'All of this is because of the evil deeds and sins of the priests.'

"And I responded and said, 'And are you not able to cleanse it?' And the two old men said, 'This mud will not be cleaned up until a fire from heaven descends and burns it up.' As he finished the account of his vision the old monk knew he was going to die, and, as he spoke with his disciple, the Persians arrived and killed him."

16 In Jewish tradition God weeps over the destruction of the temple. Peter Kuhn, *Gottes Trauer und Klage in der rabbinischen Überlieferung* (Leiden: 1978), and Melvin Glatt, "God the Mourner—Israel's Companion in Tragedy," *Judaism* 28 (1979): 72–80.

17 Robert Markus, *Saeculum: History and Society in the Theology of St. Augustine* (Cambridge: 1970), 28.

18 *Symm.* 2. 635–41.

19 *Ezech.* prologue (*CC* 75, 3).

20 *Chronicon Anonymum Pseudo-Dionysianum,* ed. J.-B. Chabat, *CSCO,* Scriptores Syri (Paris: 1927), 3.1:193, ll. 4–5; trans. 3.1:143–44 (Louvain: 1949). *Life and Example of Our Holy Father Arsenius the Great,* ed. G. F. Tsereteli, *Zapiski,* istoriko-filogicheski fakultet, St. Petersburg University, 50 (1899): 22; Palladius, *Lausiac History,* 54.7. I owe these references to Walter Kaegi, *Byzantium and the Decline of Rome* (Princeton: 1968), 154–55.

21 Kaegi (1968), 155.

22 Augustine, *civ.* 1.2.1. Orosius, *hist.* 1, prol. 14. Again, see Kaegi (1968), 160. The sack of Constantinople by the Avars and Persians in 627 C.E. did generate religious feelings that were similar to those felt at the loss of Jerusalem in 614 C.E. See the homily on the siege attributed to Theodore Synkellos. See F. Makk, *Traduction et commentaire de l'homélie écrite probablement par Théodore le Syncelle sur le siège de Constantinople en 626* (Szeged: 1975), 298–99.

23 On the genre, "Anacréontique" in *DACL* 1, 2 (1907): 1863–72. Text of the poems, ed. M. Gigante, *Sophronii Anacreontica,* in *Opuscula,* Testi per esercitazioni academiche 10/12 (Rome: 1957).

24 Gigante (1957), 10.

25 On Sophronius, Christoph von Schönborn, *Sophrone de Jérusalem: Vie monastique et confession dogmatique,* Théologie Historique, 20 (Paris: 1972).

26 The book of Sophronius's friend John Moschus, *Spiritual Meadow,* is an important source for attitudes toward Jerusalem and the holy land in the early seventh century. Here is one of his stories about a sailor from the Dead Sea. The sailor helped a monk bury a friend in a mountain, and then stayed with him for a year, finding great peace. When the sailor knew he was to die, he asked the monk, "Take me to Jerusalem that I might adore the holy cross, and the holy Anastasis of Christ our God" (91). Moschus speaks of Jerusalem as the "city of God" (24, 100), "theopolis" (divine city; 33, 34, 37, 40, passim), and "the holy city of Christ our God" (92, 105). On occasion, however, he will use the same term for Antioch in Syria (92). He speaks of the "holy Jordan" (16) and the "holy mount of Olives" (24) and the "holy mountain" of Sinai (170).

27 Text of "On the Capture [of Jerusalem] by the Persians" in Gigante (1957), 102–07. See also Couret (1897), 133ff.

28 C. Clermont-Ganneau, "The Taking of Jerusalem by the Persians A.D. 614," *Palestine Exploration Fund Quarterly Statement* (1898): 36.

29 Couret (1987) points out that for Antiochos Jerusalem is a city of malefactors, whereas for Sophronius it is a community of saints (146).

30 Melito of Sardis, *frg. 1* (ed. S. Hall, 63).

31 Sophronius's two poems on Jerusalem, *Anacreontica* 19 and 20, in Gigante (1957), 118–27. Translation into English by John Wilkinson (1977), 91–92.
32 John of Damascus, *imag.* 3.33–34; also 1.16.

Chapter 12
The Desolate Amalek Rose Up to Smite Us

1 On Muslim conquest of Palestine, Fred McGraw Donner, *The Early Islamic Conquests* (Princeton: 1981), 91–156; Philip Mayerson, "The First Muslim Attacks on Southern Palestine (A.D. 633–634)," *Transactions and Proceedings of the American Philological Association* 95 (1964): 155–99; W. E. Kaegi, "Heraklios and the Arabs," *Greek Orthodox Theological Review* 27 (1982): 109–33; J. Moorhead, "The Monophysite Response to the Arab Invasions," *Byzantion* 51 (1981): 579–91; R. J. Lilie, *Die byzantinischen Reaktion auf die Ausbreitung der Araber* (Munich: 1976).
2 Theophanes, *Chronographia* 336. Text ed. C. de Boor (Leipzig: 1883).
3 Jacut, *Geographisches Wörterbuch,* ed. Ferdinand Wüstenfeld (Leipzig: 1869), 4:1015.
4 Theophanes, *Chronographia* 332.
5 Text in H. Usener, "Weihnachtspredigt des Sophronios," in *Rheinisches Museum für Philologie* 41 (1886): 506–07. See also his sermon "On Holy Baptism," in *Analekta Hierosolymitikes Staxyologias* (Brussels: 1963), 5:166–67; see W. Kaegi, "Initial Byzantine Reactions to the Arab Conquest," *CH* 38 (1969): 139–49.
6 Eutychius, *Chronicle, CSCO* 44:133 (ET, vol. 45:111). See J. Gildermeister, "Die arabischen Nachtrichten zur Geschichte der Harambauten," *ZDPV* 13 (1890): 1–24; Herbert Busse, "Tempel, Grabeskirche und Haram as-sarif. Drei Heiligtümer und ihrer gegenseitigen Beziehungen in Legende und Wirklichkeit," in Busse-Kretschmar, *Jerusalemer Heiligtumstraditionen* (1987): 1–28.
7 On the tradition that the temple was located at Bethel, see *Genesis Rabbah* 69.7, on the verse "This is none other than the house of God, and this is the gate of heaven" (Gen 28:17).
8 Schick (1977), 116. Also A. S. Tritton, *The Caliphs and Their Non-Muslim Subjects* (London: 1970).
9 See Schick (1977).
10 Quran, Sura 17:4–7; P. Soucek, "The Temple of Solomon in Islamic Legend and Art," in J. Gutmann, *The Temple of Solomon: Archaeological Fact and Medieval Tradition in Christian, Islamic and Jewish Art* (Missoula, Mont.: 1976), 77–78. On Muslim veneration of Jerusalem, see "The Sanctity of Jerusalem and Palestine in Early Islam," in *Studies in Early Islamic History and Institutions* (Leiden: 1966), 135–48.
11 *Al-Qiyama* (Resurrection) and *al-Qumamah* (dung).
12 This account comes from the fourteenth-century work *Muthir al-Ghiram* (Exciter of desire for visitors of the Holy City and Syria). It was written by Jamal ad-Din Ahmad in 1351. Translation by G. Le Strange, *Palestine under the Moslems* (1890), 139–42.

13 On Muhammad's night journey and ascent to heaven, see *The Life of Muhammad.* A translation of Ishaq's *Sirat Rasul Allah* with introduction and notes by A. Guillaume (Oxford: 1955), 181–87.

14 Sophronius, *Christmas Sermon* (Weihnachtspredigt, ed. Usener, 514).

15 Ibid., 515.

16 Theophanes, *Chronographia* 333–34.

17 In 634, as the Arab armies began the invasion of Palestine, some Christians thought the end of the world was at hand. See *Doctrina Jacobi nuper baptizati,* 63 (ed. N. Bonwetsch [*Abhandlungen der koeniglichen Gesellschaft der Wissenschaften zu Göttingen, phil-hist. Klasse,* n.f., vol. 12:, Nr. 3, 1910). "After only a short period, perhaps just a decade, of uncertainty, people became aware that a new, Arab empire had arrived on the scene, replacing the Sassanid entirely, and half the Byzantine. In such times the Christian population resorted to the book of Daniel to find divine backing for these major upheavals" (Sebastian Brock, "Syriac Views of Emergent Islam," in *Studies on the First Century of Islamic Society,* ed. G. H. A. Juynboll [Carbondale, Ill.: 1982], 20).

18 Edition of the Vatican MS Syr. 58 and English translation in Francisco Javier Martinez, "Eastern Christian Apocalyptic in the Early Muslim Period: Pseudo-Methodius and Pseudo-Athanasius" (Ph.D. diss., Catholic University of America, 1985).

19 Ibib., 25–33.

20 The interpretation of the text is disputed. Paul J. Alexander argued for Jewish antecedents, whereas G. J. Reinink and Martinez (and others) have argued that many of the ideas can be traced to Syriac Christian sources. P. J. Alexander, "The Medieval Legend of the Last Roman Emperor and Its Messianic Origin," *Journal of the Warburg and Courtauld Institute* 41 (1978): 1–15, and idem, *The Byzantine Apocalyptic Tradition,* ed. Dorothy de F. Abrahamse (Berkeley: 1985). For Reinink's views (and criticism of Alexander), see particularly "Die syrischen Wurzeln der mittelalterlichen Legende vom romischen Endkaiser," in *Non Nova, sed Nove. Mélanges de civilisation médiévale dédiés à W. Noomen* (Gröningen: 1984), 195–209; "Ismael, der Wildesel in der Wüste: Zur Typologie der Apokalypse des Pseudo-Methodius," *BZ* 75 (1982): 336–44; "Der Verfassername 'Modios' der syrischen Schatzhöhle und die Apokalypse des Pseudo-Methodius," *Oriens Christianus* 67 (1983): 46–64. For the chiliastic background of apocalyptic traditions in this period, see Klaus Berger, *Die griechische Daniel-Diegese. Eine altkirchliche Apokalypse* (Leiden: 1976), 80–87.

21 F. 118v (Martinez [1985], 122). Martinez writes, "The interest that PM shows in the Holy Land can easily be explained by the shock caused in the east by the loss of the holy places to the Arabs" (6).

22 "He has appeared once for all at the *end of the age* to put away sin by the sacrifice of himself" (Heb 9:26; cf. 1.1). See Origen, *princ.* 1, pref. 4, and Jerome on Micah 4:1, "It shall come to pass in the latter days that the mountain of the house of the Lord shall be established as the highest of the mountains." He says that this text, and its parallel in Isaiah 2:1–2, refers not to the "end of the ages," but to the "first coming" of Christ (*Comm. in Michaem* 4.1–7, *CC* 76, 472).

23 F. 129v. (Martinez [1985], 143).
24 F. 130v. (Martinez [1985], 144–45).
25 F. 131r. (Martinez [1985], 145).
26 F. 130r. (Martinez [1985], 144).
27 On the Antichrist, see W. Bousset, *The Antichrist Legend* (London: 1896); Bernard McGinn, *Visions of the End: Apocalyptic Traditions in the Middle Ages* (Columbia: 1979). For the Jews Armilius plays a role similar to that of the Antichrist in Christian tradition. He is the last enemy to be overcome. See Marc Philonenko, *Pseudepigraphes de l'Ancien Testament et Manuscrits de la Mer Morte* (1967), 1:45–61.
28 Cyril of Jerusalem, *catech.* 15.12.
29 F. 133r. (Martinez, 149).
30 F. 134r. (Martinez, 150).
31 F. 135v. (Martinez, 152–53).
32 F. 136v. (Martinez, 154).
33 *Book of Zerubbabel,* ll. 30ff.
34 Text published by L. Ginzberg, *Genizah Studies in Memory of Doctor Solomon Schechter* (*Texts and Studies of the Jewish Theological Seminary of America* [New York: 1928], 7:310–12). I cite the translation of Bernard Lewis, "On That Day: A Jewish Apocalyptic Poem on the Arab Conquests," *Mélanges d'Islamologie: Volume dédié à la memoire de Armand Abel,* ed. Pierre Salmon (Leiden: 1974), 197–201. For a longer version of the poem, see Joseph Yahalom, "On the Value of Literary Works as Sources to Elucidate Historical Questions," *Cathedra* 22 (1979): 125–33 (in Hebrew).
35 F. 124v. (Martinez [1985], 134).
36 F. 134v. (Martinez [1985], 153).
37 This passage is taken from the longer version of the poem published by Yahalon, ll. 72–74. Of course these lines from Isaiah 2:3 and Micah 4.2, like most of the lines in the poem, are citations from the prophets.
38 F. 135v. (Martinez [1985], 152–53). According to Pseudo-Methodius (f. 126r.; Martinez [1985], 136), the Holy Cross is located at the "center of the earth." The theme is traditional, as we have seen (Cyril of Jerusalem, *catech.* 13.28). For its place in Syriac-speaking Christianity, see Martinez (1985), 180–81.
39 Martinez (1985) contrasts Pseudo-Methodius with an apocalypse written in Egypt a few decades later: "Contrary to Pseudo-Methodius . . . Pseudo-Athanasius does not say a word about a possible Byzantine recovery nor a political deliverance from Muslim rule. Their coming is just the beginning of the labor pains of the end, the final judgment is at hand, and the only concern of the author is his call for religious and moral reform" (268). On the political hopes of Pseudo-Methodius, see also Brock (1982), 19.

Epilogue

1 *Expugnatio Hierosolymae* A.D. 614 (*Sin. Ar.* 428) 23, ed. Gerardo Garitte, *CSCO* 340 (Louvain: 1973), 53–54. See J. T. Milik, "Topographie de Jérusalem," *Mélanges de l'Université de Josip de Beyrouth* 37 (Beirut: 1960–61), 127–89. A ser-

mon preached by an eyewitness of the Persian conquest gives the number of dead as 65,000 (*PG* 86.2; 3236b).

2 Jonathan Z. Smith, *Map is Not Territory. Studies in the History of Religions* (Leiden: 1978) 110.

3 *Ep*. 14 (*PG* 91, 540).

4 *The Chronicle of John, Bishop of Nikiu,* chap. 118.10; translated by R. H. Charles (London: 1916), 188. For discussion of the changes wrought by the arrival of the Muslims, see Robert Schick, "The Fate of the Christians in Palestine during the Byzantine-Umayyad Transition, A.D. 600–750" (Ph.D. diss., University of Chicago, 1977), 278. Summary of his conclusions in "Christian Life in Palestine during the Early Islamic Period," *BA* 51 (1988): 118 ff.

5 For a summary discussion of the finds at Um er-Rasas, with spectacular photographs, see Michele Piccirillo, "The Mosaics at Um er-Rasas in Jordan," *BA* 51 (December 1988): 18ff. For fuller account, Michele Piccirillo, "Um er-Rasas Kastron Mefaa," Supplement to *La Terra Sancta* (November-December 1986).

6 Schick (1977), 278.

7 On the mosque in Damascus, see Al-Muqadassi, *Ahsan at-Taqasim fi Ma'rifat al-Aqalim,* 159, ed. Andre Miquel (Damascus: 1963), 174. On the building of the Dome of the Rock, see S. Goitein, "The Historical Background of the Erection of the Dome of the Rock," *JAOS* 70 (1950): 104–08. Goitein notes that the phrase "God has no companion" is repeated five times in inscriptions decorating the interior of the Qubbat as-Sakhra and that lines from Surah Maryam 19.34–37 which deny Jesus' divine sonship are cited along with the prayer: "Pray for your Prophet and Servant [not Son, of course] Jesus" (106). According to Oleg Grabar, the Dome of the Rock played a role in Islam's "symbolic appropriation of the land." See his discussion in *The Formation of Islamic Art* (New Haven: 1973), 48–67.

8 Al-Muqaddasi, 167.

9 Sidney Griffith, "Stephen of Ramlah and the Christian Kerygma in Arabic in Ninth-Century Palestine," *JEH* 36 (1985): 31.

10 J.-B. Chabot, *Chronique de Michel le syrien; patriarche jacobite d'Antioche (1166–1199)* (Paris: 1899–24), 3:32.

11 *PG* 97, 1504d.

12 B. Violet, "Ein zweisprachiges Psalmfragment aus Damaskus," *Orientalische Literatur-Zeitung,* 4 (1901), cols. 384–403; 425–88.

13 Griffith (1985), 39.

14 Ibid., 41.

15 Ibid., 45

16 The "treatise" on the "traces of Christ" is part of a much larger work, *The Book of Demonstration (Kitab al-Burhan) that goes under the name of Eutychius of Alexandria,* ed. Pierre Cachia, *CSCO,* vols. 192, 209 (text), vols. 193, 210. See paras. 310–65. On the continuation of pilgrimage to Jerusalem among Christians of the East, see J. M. Fiey, "Le pèlerinage des Nestoriens et Jacobites à Jérusalem," in *Cahiers de civilisation médiévale* 12 (1969): 113–26, and of the West, Wilkinson (1977).

17 *Book of Demonstration,* para. 310. The "traces of Christ" may have been written by Theodore Abu Qurra who lived for a time as a monk at Mar Saba. See Michel Breydy, *Études sur Sa'id Ibn Batriq et ses Sources* (*CSCO* 450; Louvain, 1983), 92.

18 The Shahadah is the central affirmation of Muslims: "There is no god but God and Muhammad is the apostle of God." It begins with the words, "I bear witness [*ashhadu*]." The treatise on the "traces of Christ" reads *tashhadu.*

19 *Book of Demonstration,* passim, beginning with para. 311.

20 John of Damascus, *imag.* 1.13; 3.33–34 (ed. B. Bonifatius Kotter, *Patristischen Texte und Studien* [Berlin: 1975], 17:86, 137–39).

21 *Book of Demonstration,* para. 310.

22 Ibid.

23 "Totum mysterium nostrum istius provinciae urbisque vernaculum est" (*ep.* 46.3).

Select Bibliography

Abel, F. M. *Histoire de la Palestine depuis la conquête d'Alexandre jusqu' à l'invasion arabe.* Paris, 1952.

Alobaidi, S. J., Y. Goldman, and M. Kuechler. "Le plus ancien guide juif de Jérusalem." In *Jerusalem. Texte-Bilder-Steine,* edited by Max Kuechler and Christoph Uehlinger, 37–82. Göttingen, 1987.

Alon, Gedaliah. *The Jews in Their Land in the Talmudic Age.* Jerusalem, 1980.

Amaru, Betsy Halpern. "Land Theology in Josephus' Jewish Antiquities." *JQR* 72 (1981): 201–29.

Amir, J. "Philo's Version of the Pilgrimage to Jerusalem." In *Jerusalem in the Second Temple Period. Abraham Schalit Memorial Volume,* edited by A. Oppenheimer et al., 154–65 (in Hebrew). Jerusalem, 1980.

Aptowitzer, A. "The Temple Above in the Agada." *Tarbiz* 2 (1931): 257–87 (in Hebrew).

Aptowitzer, V. "Les premier possesseurs de Canaan." *REJ* 82 (1926): 273–86.

Armstrong, Gregory. "Fifth and Sixth Century Church Buildings in the Holy Land." *Greek Orthodox Theological Review* 14 (1969): 17–30.

______. "Imperial Church Buildings in the Holy Land in the Fourth Century." *BA* 30 (1967): 90–102.

Avi-Yonah, Michael. *Encyclopedia of Archaeological Investigations in the Holy Land.* 4 vols. Englewood Cliffs, N.J., 1975–78.

______. *The Madaba Mosaic Map With Introduction and Commentary.* Jerusalem, 1954.

______. *The Holy Land. From the Persian to the Arab Conquests (586 B.C. to A.D. 640).* Grand Rapids, 1977.

______. "The Economics of Byzantine Palestine." *IEJ* 8 (1958): 39–51.

______. *Gazetteer of Roman Palestine.* Jerusalem, 1976.

Bagatti, B. "Eulogie Palestinesi." *Orientalia Christiana Periodica* 15 (1949): 126–66.

______. *Antichi Villaggi Cristiani della Guidea e del Neghev.* Jerusalem, 1983.

______. *The Church from the Gentiles in Palestine. History and Archaeology.* Jerusalem, 1971.

______. *Gli antichi edifici sacri di Betlemme.* Jerusalem, 1951.

Baldovin, John. *The Urban Character of Christian Worship. The Origins, Development, and Meaning of Stational Liturgy.* Rome, 1987.

Baras, Zvi, Shmuel Safrai, Yoram Tsafrir, and Menachem Satran. *Eretz Israel from the Destruction of the Second Temple to the Persian Conquest.* Vol. 1. Jerusalem, 1982 (in Hebrew).

Black, M. "The Festival of the Encenia in the Ancient Church with Reference to Palestine and Syria." *JEH* 5 (1954): 78–86

Bottini, G. C., L. DiSegni, E. Alliata, editors. *Christian Archaeology in the Holy Land. New Discoveries.* Essays in honour of Virigilio C. Corbo, OFM. Jerusalem, 1990.

Brock, Sebastian P. "The Rebuilding of the Temple under Julian: A New Source." *Palestine Exploration Quarterly* 108 (1976): 103–07.

______. "A Letter Attributed to Cyril of Jerusalem on the Rebuilding of the Temple." *Bulletin of the School of Oriental and African Studies* 40 (1977): 267–86.

______. "Syriac Views of Emergent Islam." In *Studies on the First Century of Islamic Society,* edited by G. H. A. Juynboll, 9–22. Carbondale, 1982.

Brox, Norbert."Das 'Irdische Jerusalem' in der altchristlichen Theologie." *Kairos* 28 (1986): 152–73.

Brueggeman, Walter. *The Land: Place as Gift, Promise, and Challenge in the Biblical Faith*. Philadelphia, 1977.
Burrell, David, and Yehezkel Landau. *Voices from Jerusalem: Jews and Christians Reflect on the Holy Land*. New York, 1992.
Busse, Herbert, and Georg Kretschmar. *Jerusalemer Heiligtumstraditionen in altkirchlicher und fruehislamischer Zeit*. Abhandlungen des deutschen Palaestinavereins. Wiesbaden, 1987.
______. "The Sanctity of Jerusalem in Islam." *Judaism* 17 (1968): 441–68.
Chiat, Marilyn Joyce Segal. *Handbook of Synagogue Architecture*. Chico, Calif., 1982.
______. "Synagogues and Churches in Byzantine Beit She'an." *Journal of Jewish Art* 8 (1980): 6–24.
Chitty, D. *The Desert a City*. Crestwood, N.Y., 1966.
Clermont-Ganneau. "The Taking of Jerusalem by the Persians A.D. 614." *Palestine Exploration Fund Quarterly* (1898): 36–54.
Conybeare, Fredrick C. "Antiochus Strategos' Account of the Sack of Jerusalem in 614 A.D." *The English Historical Review* 25 (1910): 502–17.
Corbo, V. C. *Il Santo Sepolcro di Gerusalemme. Aspetti archeologici dalle origini al periodo crociato*. Vol. 1 Testo (*Studium Biblicum Franciscanum*, coll. maior 29). Jerusalem, 1982.
Coüason, Charles. *The Church of the Holy Sepulchre in Jerusalem*. London, 1974.
Couret, A. "La Prise de Jerusalem par les Perses en 614." *Revue de l'Orient Chrétien* 2 (1897): 125–64.
Crowfoot, J. W. *Early Churches in Palestine*. College Park, 1971.
Cyril of Scythopolis: The Lives of the Monks of Palestine. Translated by R. M. Price. Annotated by John Binn. Kalamazoo, Mich., 1991.
Dauphine, Claudine. "Jewish and Christian Communities in the Roman and Byzantine Gaulanitis: A Study of Evidence from Archaeological Surveys." *PEQ* 114 (1982): 129–81.
Davies, W. D. *The Gospel and the Land*. Berkeley, 1974.
______. *The Territorial Dimension of Judaism*. Berkeley, 1982.
Delano Smith, Catherine. "Geography or Christianity? Maps of the Holy Land before A.D. 1000." *JThS* 42 (1991): 142–52.
Donner, Fred McGraw. *The Early Islamic Conquest*. Princeton, 1981.
Donner, H., and H. Cüppers. *Die Mosaikkarte von Madaba*. Vol. 1, Tafelband. Wiesbaden, 1977.
Drake, H. A. "Eusebius on the True Cross." *Journal of Ecclesiastical History* 36 (1985): 1–22.
______. "A Coptic Version of the Discovery of the Holy Sepulcher." *Greek, Roman and Byzantine Studies* 20 (1979): 381–92.

Dryvers, Jan Willem. *Helena Augusta* Leiden, 1992.

Eisen, Arnold M. *Galut. Modern Jewish Reflection on Homelessness and Homecoming*. Bloomington, 1986.

Fascher, E. "Jerusalems Untergang in der urchristlichen und altkirchlichen Ueberlieferung." *Theologische Literaturzeitung* 85 (1960): 81–98.

Feldman, Louis H. "Some Observations on the Name of Palestine." *HUCA* 61 (1990): 1–23.

Festugière, A. J. *Les moines d'Orient*. 3 vols. Paris, 1962–66.

Fiey, J. M. "Le pelerinage des Nestoriens et Jacobites à Jérusalem." *Cahiers de Civilisation médiévale* 12 (1969): 113–26.

Figueras, Pau. *Byzantine Inscriptions from Beer Sheva and the Negev.* Beersheva, 1985.

———. "Beersheva in the Roman-Byzantine Period." *Boletín de la Asociación Española de Orientalistas,* 135–62. Madrid, 1980.

Finney, Paul Crosby. "Topos Hieros und christlicher Sakralbau in vorkonstantinischer Überlieferung." *Boreas. Münsterische Beitraege zur Archaeologie* 7 (1984): 193–225.

———. "Orpheus-David: A Connection in Iconography between Greco-Roman Judaism and Early Christianity." *Journal of Jewish Art* 5 (1978): 6–15.

Fleischer, E. "An Early Jewish Tradition of the End of Byzantine Rule in Eretz Israel." *Tsiyon* 36 (1971): 110–15 (in Hebrew).

Flusin, Bernard. *Miracle et histoire dans l'oeuvre de Cyrille de Scythopolis.* Paris, 1983.

Forsyth, G. H., and K. Weitzmann with I. Sevcenko and F. Anderegg. *The Monastery of Saint Catherine at Mount Sinai—The Church and Fortress of Justinian I.* Ann Arbor, 1970.

Frolow, Anatole. *La Relique de la Vraie Croix. Recherches sur le Développement d'un culte.* Paris, 1961.

Fuks, Gideon. *Scythopolis—A Greek City in Eretz Israel* (in Hebrew). Jerusalem, 1983.

Gafni, Isaiah. "Reinterment in the Land of Israel: Notes on the Origin and Development of the Custom." *The Jerusalem Cathedra* 1: 96–104. Jerusalem, 1981.

———. *The Glory of the Holy Land.* Cambridge, 1982.

Gaston, Lloyd. *No Stone on Another.* Leiden, 1970.

Geiger, Joseph. "The Spread of Christianity in *Eretz Israel* from the Beginning until the Time of Julian," in Baras, Safrai, et al. (1982), 1: 218–35 (in Hebrew).

Gil, Moshe. *Palestine during the First Muslim Period (634–1099).* 3 vols. (in Hebrew). Tel Aviv, 1983.

Gildermeister, J. "Die arabischen Nachtrichten zur Geschichte der Harambauten." *ZDPV* 13 (1890): 1–14.

Goitein, S. "The Historical Background of the Erection of the Dome of the Rock." *JAOS* 70 (1950): 104–08.

______. "Jerusalem in the Arab Period." *Jerusalem Cathedra* 2 (1982): 168–96.

Graham, Stephen. *With the Russian Pilgrims to Jerusalem*. London, 1914.

Gretser, Jacob. *De sacris et religiosis peregrinationibus libri quattuor*. Ingolstadt, 1606.

Griffith, Sidney. "Stephen of Ramlah and the Christian Kerygma in Arabic in Ninth-Century Palestine." *JEH* 36 (1985): 23–45.

______. "Greek into Arabic: Life and Letters in the Monasteries of Palestine in the Ninth Century; The Example of the Summa Theologiae Arabica." *Byzantion* 56 (1986): 117–38.

Groh, Dennis. "The Onomastikon of Eusebius and the Rise of Christian Palestine." *Studia Patristica* 18: 23–31. Kalamazoo, Mich., 1983.

______. "Jews and Christians in Late Roman Palestine: Towards a New Chronology." *BA* 51 (1988): 80–98.

Gutmann, I. M. H. *Eretz Israel in Midrash and Talmud. Festschrift zum 75-jährigen Bestehen des jüdischen-theologischen Seminars*. Breslau, 1921.

Gutwein, Kenneth C. *Third Palestine. A Regional Study in Byzantine Urbanization*. Washington, 1981.

Halbwachs, Maurice. *La Topographie Légendaire des Évangiles en Terre Sainte*. Paris, 1971.

Hartmann, Richard. "Die Palästina-Route des Itinerarium Burdigalense." *ZDPV* 33 (1910): 169–88.

Heidegger, Johann Heinrich. *Dissertatio de peregrinationibus religiosis*. Schaufelbert, 1620.

Heinemann, Joseph. "The Blessing 'Who Rebuilds Jerusalem' and Its Metamorphoses." *Hayyim Schirmann Jubilee Volume*, 93–101 (in Hebrew). Jerusalem, 1970.

Heyer, Friedrich. *Kirchengeschichte des heiligen Landes*. Stuttgart, 1984.

Hill, Charles E. *Regnum Coelorum, Patterns of Future Hope in Early Christianity*. Oxford, 1992.

Himmelfarb, Martha. "Sefer Zerubbabel." In *Rabbinic Fantasies: Imaginative Literature from Classical Hebrew Literature*, edited by David Stern and Mark J. Mirsky, 69–90. Philadelphia, 1990.

Hirschfeld, Yizhar. *The Judean Desert Monasteries in the Byzantine Period*. New Haven, 1992.

______. "Gerasimus and His Laura in the Jordan Valley." *Revue Biblique* 98 (1991): 419–30.

______. "Masada in the Byzantine Period—The Marda Monastery." *Eretz Israel. Studies Investigating the Land and Its Antiquities. Festchrift for Yigael Yadi*, 262–74 (in Hebrew). Jerusalem, 1989.

———. "List of the Byzantine Monasteries in the Judean Desert." *Christian Archaelogy in the Holy Land,* ed. Bottini (1990): 1–90.

Hoffman, Lawrence A., ed. *The Land of Israel: Jewish Perspectives.* Center for the Study of Judaism and Christianity in Antiquity, No. 6, Notre Dame, 1986.

Honigmann, E. "Juvenal of Jerusalem." *DOP* 5 (1950): 207–79.

Hunt, E. D. *Holy Land Pilgrimage in the Later Roman Empire A.D. 312–460.* Oxford, 1982.

Ish-Shalom, Michael. *Christian Travels in the Holy Land.* Tel Aviv, 1965.

Jaeger, David M., ed. *Christianity in the Holy Land.* Studia Oecumenica Hierosolymitana, Vol. 1. Jerusalem, 1981.

Jones, A. H. M. "The Urbanization of Palestine." *JRS* 21 (1931): 77–85.

Jonge, Marianus de. "Josephus und die Zukunftserwartungen seiner Volkes." In *Josephus-Studien,* edited by Otto Betz, Klaus Hacker, and Martin Hergel, 205–19. Göttingen, 1974.

Jüdische Volk-Gelobtes Land. Die biblischen Landverheiszungen als Problem des juedischen Selbstverstaendnisses und der christlichen Theologie. Edited by W. P. Eckert, N. P. Levinson, and M. Stöhr. Munich, 1970.

Kaegi, Walter Emil, Jr. "Initial Byzantine Reactions to the Arab Conquest." *Church History* 38 (1969): 139–49.

Kashner, A. "Jerusalem as a 'Metropolis' in Philo's National Consciousness." *Cathedra* 11 (1979): 45–56.

Kimelman, Reuven. "Rabbi Yohanan and Origen on the Song of Songs: A Third Century Jewish-Christian Disputation." *HTR* 73 (1980): 567–95.

Klausner, Joseph. *The Messianic Idea in Israel.* New York, 1955.

Klein, S. "The Travelogue *Itinerarium Burdigalense* to the Land of Israel." *Tsiyon* 6 (1934): 12–38 (in Hebrew).

Klein, S. *Sefer Yishuv. Places of Settlement from the Time of the Destruction of the Second Temple to the Conquest of Eretz Israel by the Arabs* (in Hebrew). Jerusalem, 1978.

Kremer, Joseph. "Zur Geschichte des Begriffs 'Terra Sancta.'" In *Das heilige Land in Vergangenheit und Gegenwart,* vol. 3, edited by Valmar Cramer and Gustav Meinertz, 55–66. Köln, 1942.

LeQuien, Michael. *Oriens Christianus.* 3 Vols. Paris, 1740.

Levine, Lee I. *Ancient Synagogues Revealed.* Detroit, 1982.

Lewis, Bernard. "On That Day. A Jewish Apocalyptic Poem on the Arab Conquests." Mélanges d'Islamologie. Volume dédié à la memoire de Armand Abel, edited by Pierre Salmon, 197–201. Leiden, 1974.

Lewy, H. "Emperor Julian and the Building of the Temple." *Tsiyon* 6 (1940–41): 1–32 (in Hebrew).

Lifschitz, B. "Scythopolis. L'histoire, les institutions et les cultes de la ville à l'époque hellénistique et impériale." *ANRW* II.8 (Berlin, 1977): 262–94.

Lilie, R. J. *Die byzantinischen Reaktion auf die Ausbreitung der Araber.* Munich, 1976.

Linder, Amnon. *Jews in Roman Imperial Legislation.* Jerusalem, 1987.

———. "Jerusalem between Judaism and Christianity in the Byzantine Period." *Cathedra* 11 (1979): 109–40 (in Hebrew).

Mader, E. *Mambre.* Freiburg im Breisgau, 1957.

Ma'oz, Zvi U. "Comments on Jewish and Christian Communities in Byzantine Palestine." *PEQ* 117 (1985): 58–62.

Maraval, Pierre. *Lieux saints et pèlerinages d'Orient. Histoire et géographie. Des origines à l'conquête arabe.* Paris, 1985.

———. "Une Querelle sur les pelèrinages autour d'un texte patristique (Gregoire de Nysse, Lettre 2). *Revue d'histoire et de philosophie religieuses* 66 (1986): 131–46.

———. "Egerie et Grégoire de Nysse, pèlerins de Palestine." Atti del Convegno internazionale sulla Peregrinatio Egeria, 315–31. Arezzo, 1990.

Margolioth, M. *Halakhoth on the Land of Israel from the Genizah,* 139–41. Jerusalem, 1974.

Matsumoto, Shigeru. "The Meaning of Sacred Places as Phenomenologists of Religion Understand It." *Tenri Journal of Religion* 10 (October 1969): 45–56.

McGinn, Bernard. "Iter Sancti Sepulchri: The Piety of the First Crusaders." In *Essays on Medieval Civilization.* The Walter Prescott Lectures, edited by B. K. Lachner and K. R. Phelp, 33–71. Austin, 1978.

Meinardus, F. A. *The Holy Family in Egypt.* Cairo, 1986.

Melamed, E. Z. "The Onomasticon of Eusebius." *Tarbiz* 3 (1932): 314–27 (in Hebrew).

Mendels, Doran. *The Land of Israel as Political Concept in Hasmonean Literature.* Tübingen, 1987.

Meyers, Eric M., and James F. Strange. *Archaeology, the Rabbis and Early Christianity.* Nashville, 1981.

Meyers, Eric M. *Jewish Ossuaries—Reburial and Rebirth.* Rome, 1971.

———. "Early Judaism and Christianity in the Light of Archaelogy." *BA* 51 (1988): 69–79.

Milik, J. T. "Topographie de Jérusalem." *Mélanges de l'Université de Josip de Beyrouth* 37 (1961): 127–89.

Moorhead, J. "The Monophysite Response to the Arab Invasions." *BZ* 51 (1981): 579–91.

Moulin, Pierre du. *De euntibus Iersolyma.* Paris, 1551.

Murphy-O'Connor. *The Holy Land: An Archaeological Guide From Earliest Times to 1700.* New York, 1986.

Negev, Avraham. *Tempel, Kirchen und Zisternen.* Stuttgart, 1983.

———. ed. *Archaeological Encyclopedia of the Holy Land.* New York, 1972.

Neubauer, A. *La Géographie du Talmud.* Hildesheim, 1967.

Neusner, Jacob. *Judaism and Christianity in the Age of Constantine.* Chicago, 1987.

Neusner, Jacob, William Green, and Ernest Frerichs, ed. *Judaisms and Their Messiahs at the Turn of the Christian Era.* Cambridge, 1987.

Noonan, Thomas. "Political Thought in Greek Palestinian Hagiography (*ca. 526–ca. 630*)." Ph.D. dissertation, University of Chicago, 1975.

Notaras, Chrysanthus. *History and Description of the Holy Land* (in Greek). Vienna, 1728.

Ousterhout, Robert, ed. *The Blessings of Pilgrimage.* Urbana, 1990.

Ovadiah, Asher, and Carla Gomez de Silva. "Supplementum to the Corpus of the Byzantine Churches in the Holy Land (Part I)." *Levant* 13 (1981): 200–61.

______. "Supplementum to the Corpus of the Byzantine Churches in the Holy Land (Part II)." *Levant* 14 (1982): 122–70.

______. *Corpus of the Byzantine Churches in the Holy Land.* Bonn, 1970.

Patrich, Joseph. "The Monastic Institutions of Saint Sabas." Ph.D. dissertation, Hebrew University, 1989 (in Hebrew).

Pederson, Sister Kirsten. *The History of the Ethiopian Community in the Holy Land from the Time of Emperor Tewodios II till 1974.* Jerusalem, 1983.

People, Land and State of Israel in *Immanuel.* Published by the Ecumenical Research Fraternity, No. 22–23. Jerusalem, 1989.

Perrone, L. *La chiesa di Palestine e le controversie christologiche.* Brescia, 1980.

Peters, F. E. *Jerusalem: The Holy City in the Eyes of Chroniclers, Visitors, Pilgrims, and Prophets from the Days of Abraham to the Beginnings of Modern Times.* Princeton, 1985.

Peters, Joan. *From Time Immemorial: The Origins of the Arab-Jewish Conflict over Palestine.* New York, 1984.

Philonenko, M., and M. Simon. *Les Pèlerinage de l'antiquité biblique et classique à l'occident médiéval.* Université de Science Humaine de Strasbourg, Centre de Recherches d'Histoire des Religions. *Études d'histoire des Religions,* No. 1. Paris, 1973.

Piccirillo, Michele. *I Mosaici di Giordania.* Rome, 1986.

______. "The Mosaics at Um er-Rasas in Jordan." *BA* 51 (1988): 208–231

______. *Um er-Rasas Kastron Mefaa in Giordania.* La Terra Sancta. Jerusalem, 1986.

______. *Chiese et Mosaici della Giordania Settentrionale.* Studium Biblicum Franciscanum, Collectio Minor, No. 30. Jerusalem, 1981.

______. *Chiese e Mosaici di Madaba.* Studium Biblicum Franciscanum, Collectio Maior, No. 34. Jerusalem, 1989.

Pietrella, E. "I pellegrinaggi ai Luoghi Santi e il culto dei martiri in Gregorio di Nissa." *Augustinianum* 21 (1981): 135–51.

Piganiol, André. "L'hemisphairion et l'omphalos des lieux saints." *Cahiers archaéologigues* 1 (1945): 10–14.

Rabello, Alfredo M. *Giustiano, Ebrei e Samaritani.* Milan, 1987.

Rivers, T. "Pattern and Process in Early Christian Pilgrimage." Ph.D. dissertation, Duke University, 1983.

Rubin, Ze'ev. "The Church of the Holy Sepulchre and the Conflict between the Sees of Caesarea and Jerusalem." *The Jerusalem Cathedra* 2 (1982): 79–99.

Safrai, Shmuel. "Pilgrimage to Jerusalem after the Destruction of the Second Temple." In *Jerusalem in the Second Temple Period. Abraham Schalit Memorial Volume,* edited by A. Oppenheimer et al., 376–93 (in Hebrew). Jerusalem, 1980.

———. *Die Wallfahrt in Zeitalter des Zweiten Tempels.* Neukirchen, 1981.

Saller, Sylvester J., and Bellarmino Bagatti. *The Town of Nebo (Khirbet El-Mekhayyat) with a Brief Survey of Other Ancient Christian Monuments in Transjordan.* Jerusalem, 1949.

———. *The Town of Nebo.* Jerusalem, 1949.

Sanders, E. P. *Jesus and Judaism.* Philadelphia, 1985.

Scharf, Andrew. *Byzantine Jewry.* New York, 1971.

Schick, Robert. "The Fate of the Christians in Palestine during the Byzantine-Umayyad Transition, A.D. 600–750." Ph.D. dissertation, University of Chicago, 1987.

Schiwietz, Stephan. *Das morgenländische Mönchtum.* Vol. 2, *Das Mönchtum aus Sinai und in Palästina im vierten Jahrhundert.* Mainz, 1904.

Schmidt, K. L. "Jerusalem als Urbild und Abbild." *Eranos Jahrbuch* 18 (1950): 207–48.

Scholem, Gershom. *The Messianic Idea in Judaism.* New York, 1971.

Schönborn, Christoph von. *Sophrone de Jérusalem. Vie Monastique et Confession Dogmatique.* Théologie Historique, No. 20. Paris, 1972.

Schwartz, Joshua. "Aliya from Babylonia during the Amoraic Period 200–500 C.E." *The Jerusalem Cathedra,* edited by J. Levine. 3: (1983), 58–69.

Schweid, Elizer. *The Land of Israel. National Home or Land of Destiny?* New Jersey, 1985.

Schwerin, Ursula. "Die Aufrufe der Paepste zur Befreiung des heiligen Landes." Ph.D. dissertation, Berlin, 1936.

Shahid, Irfan. *Byzantium and the Arabs in the Fourth Century.* Washington, 1984.

———. *Byzantium and the Arabs in the Fifth Century.* Washington, 1989.

Sharon, Moshe, ed. *The Holy Land in History and Thought.* Leiden, 1988.

Sivan, Hagith. "Who was Egeria? Piety and Pilgrimage in the Age of Gratian." *HTR* 81 (1988): 57–72.

Smith, Jonathan Z. *To Take Place*. Chicago, 1987.

———. *Map Is Not Territory: Studies in the History of Religions*. Leiden, 1978.

Soucek, P. "The Temple of Solomon in Islamic Legend and Art." In *The Temple of Solomon: Archaeological Fact and Medieval Tradition in Christian, Islamic and Jewish Art,* edited by J. Gutmann, Missoula, 1976.

Starr, Joshua. "Byzantine Jewry on the Eve of the Arab Conquest (565–638)." *Journal of the Palestine Oriental Society* 15 (1935): 280–93.

Stemberger, Günther. "Die Bedeutung des 'Landes Israel' in der rabbinischen Tradition." *Kairos* 25 (1983): 176–99.

———. *Juden und Christen in Heiligen Land: Palästina unter Konstantin und Theodosius*. Munich, 1987.

Stone, Michael E. "Holy Land Pilgrimage of Armenians before the Arab Conquest." *Revue Biblique* 93 (1986): 93–110.

Strecker, Georg, ed. *Das Land Israel in biblishcher Zeit*. Göttingen, 1983.

Stroumsa, G. "'Vetus Israel': Les juifs dans la littérature hiérosolymitaine d'époque byzantine." *RHR* 205 (1988): 115–31.

Sukenik, E. L. *The Ancient Synagogue of Beth Alpha*. Oxford, 1932.

Suriano, Fra Francesco. *Treatise on the Holy Land*. Translated by Theophilus Bellorini and E. Hoade with preface by B. Bagatti. Jerusalem, 1949.

Thomsen, Peter. "Palästina nach dem Onomasticon of Eusebius." *ZDPV* 26 (1903): 97–188.

Trillingham, J. Spencer. *Christianity among the Arabs of Pre-Islamic Times*. London, 1979.

Tritton, A. S. *The Caliphs and Their Non-Muslim Subjects*. London, 1970.

Tsafrir, Yoram. *Eretz Israel from the Destruction of the Second Temple to the Muslim Conquest*. Vol. 2 (in Hebrew). Jerusalem, 1984.

———. "The Maps Used by Theodosius: On the Pilgrim Maps of the Holy Land and Jerusalem in the Sixth Century C.E." *DOP* 40 (1986): 129–145.

———. "The Byzantine Setting and Its Influence Ancient Synagogues." In *The Synagogue in Late Antiquity,* edited by Lee I. Levine, 147–58. Philadelphia, 1987.

———. "Jerusalem." *Reallexicon zur byzantinischen Kunst,* 3:525–615. Stuttgart, 1978.

Tsafrir, Y., and Y. Hirschfeld. "The Church and Mosaics at Horvat Berachot, Israel." *DOP* 33 (1979): 293–326.

Turner, Victor, and Edith Turner. *Image and Pilgrimage in Christian Culture*. Columbia, 1978.

Turner, Victor. "The Center Out There." *HR* 12 (1973): 191–230.

Tzaferis, Vasilios. *The Excavations of Kursi-Gergasa, Atiquot,* 16. English series. Jerusalem, 1983.

———. "The Ancient Synagogue at Ma'oz Hayyim." *IEJ* 32 (1982): 215–44.

———. *The Holy Land.* Athens, 1987.

Urbach, Ephrain, ed. *Jerusalem through the Ages* (in Hebrew). Jerusalem, 1968.

Urman, Dan. *The Golan: A Profile of a Region during the Roman and Byzantine Periods.* Oxford, 1985.

Vair, R. J. "The Old Testament Promise of the Land as Reinterpreted in First- and Second-Century Christianity." Ph.D. dissertation, Graduate Theological Union, Berkeley, 1979.

Vikan, Gary. *Byzantine Pilgrimage Art.* Washington, 1982.

Vincent, H., and F. M. Abel. *Jérusalem: Recherches de Topographie, d'archéologie et d'histoire.* 2 vols. Paris, 1912–26.

Voulgarakis, E. *The Theological Interpretation of Jerusalem by the Ancient Church* (in Greek). Athens, 1968.

Walker, P. W. L. *Holy City, Holy Places?* Oxford, 1990.

Weinfeld, Moshe. "Possession of the Land—Privilege or Obligation. The Conception of the Promised Land in the Sources from the Period of the First and Second Temple." *Tsiyon* 49 (1984): 129–35 (in Hebrew).

Weitzmann, K. "*Loca Sancta* and the Representational Arts of Palestine." *DOP* 28 (1974): 31–55.

Wilken, Robert L. "Early Christian Chiliasm, Jewish Messianism, and the Idea of the Holy Land." *HRT* 79 (1986): 298–307.

———. "Byzantine Palestine. A Christian Holy Land." *Biblical Archaeologist* 51 (1988): 214–37.

———. "Heiliges Land." In *Theologische Realenzyklopaedie* (Berlin, 1984), 14:684–94.

———. *John Chrysostom and the Jews.* Berkeley, 1983.

———. "The Restoration of Israel in Biblical Prophecy: Christian and Jewish Responses in the Early Byzantine Period." In *To See Ourselves as Others See Us: Christian, Jew, "Others" in Late Antiquity,* edited by Jacob Neusner, Ernest S. Frerichs, and Caroline McCracken-Fleshner, 443–72. Chico, Calif., 1985.

Wilkinson, John. *Jerusalem Pilgrims before the Crusades.* Jerusalem, 1977.

———. "Architectural Procedures in Byzantine Palestine." *Levant* 13 (1981): 156–72.

———. *Egeria's Travels.* London, 1971.

———. "The Beit Alpha Synagogue Mosaic: Towards an Interpretation." *Journal of Jewish Art* 5 (1978): 16–28.

———. "Architectural Procedures in Byzantine Palestine." *Levant* 13 (1981): 156–72.

Windisch, H. "Die ältesten christlichen Palaestinapilger." *ZDPV* 48 (1925): 145–58.

Index